The Jefferson Conspiracies

Also by David Leon Chandler:

The Binghams of Louisville (1988)
Henry Flagler (1986)
Dialing for Data (1984)
100 Tons of Gold (1978)
The Natural Superiority of Southern Politicians (1977)
The Criminal Brotherhoods (1976)
Brothers in Blood (1975)

The Jefferson Conspiracies

A President's Role in the Assassination of
Meriwether Lewis

•

David Leon Chandler

William Morrow and Company, Inc.
New York

Library of Congress Cataloging-in-Publication Data

Chandler, David Leon.
    The Jefferson conspiracies : a president's role in the
assassination of Meriwether Lewis / David Leon Chandler.
        p.   cm.
    Includes bibliographical references and index.
    ISBN 0-688-12225-6
    1. Lewis, Meriwether, 1774–1809—Death and burial.   2. Jefferson,
Thomas, 1743–1826.   I. Title.
F592.7.L68   1994
973.4′8′092—dc20
                                                                93-47264
                                                                CIP

Printed in the United States of America

First Edition

1   2   3   4   5   6   7   8   9   10

BOOK DESIGN BY LISA STOKES

To Batou and Mary

Acknowledgments

· · · · · · · · ·

The Jefferson Conspiracies began more than twenty years ago when David Leon Chandler began to investigate the seemingly impossible nature of Meriwether Lewis's death in 1809 at an inn in middle Tennessee. What David has written was complete at the time of his own death in January, save for a caption or two.

Lewis, the grand explorer and young politician, was a part of David's and my life together from the beginning. Our first trip included a visit to the memorial that marks Lewis's last night alive. On that brilliantly sunny June day in 1980, we stood in front of the truncated pillar that symbolized the abrupt ending of Lewis's life. Even though we were in the middle of green parkland, the air seemed gray; a swarm of bees came after us, and the camera malfunctioned. It all felt so terribly wrong.

That David was able to bring together what he called a "Founding Fathers whodunit" is a tribute to his skill and tenacity as a researcher and writer. He had help, of course, from research institutions and libraries around the country, earlier works on the players in this book, and from the occasional source who went above and beyond to assist. Such people include Jill Garrett, of Maury County, Tennessee, an expert on the local documentation of Lewis's death, and many more who deserve thanks.

Also to be acknowledged are David's agent, Jed Mattes, who provided continual encouragement, and David's editors at Morrow, Elisa Petrini and Bob Shuman, whose suggestions and ideas strengthened the work. Agent and editors have been models of grace under pressure during a difficult time.

As has been David's family, people who never tired of hearing him test theories and probe more and more deeply to find out what happened to Meriwether Lewis in the real world of early American politics.

—MARY VOELZ CHANDLER

Contents

• • • • • • • • •

The Jefferson Conspiracies

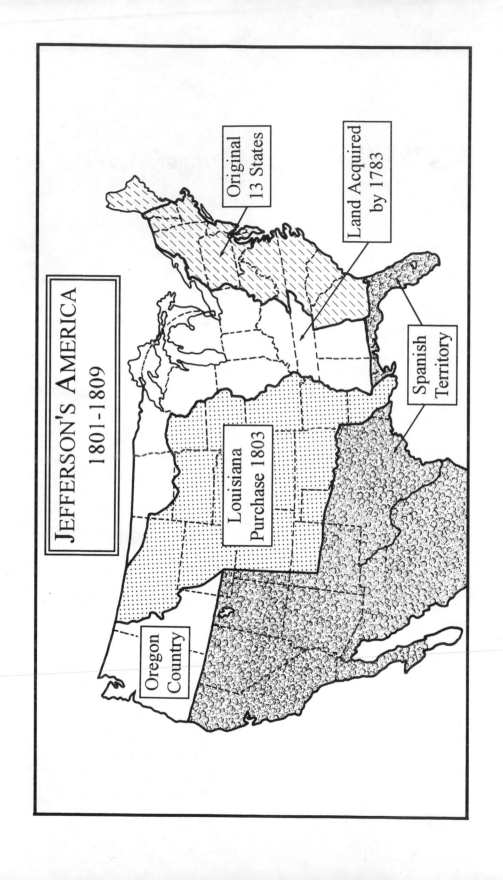

JEFFERSON'S AMERICA
1801-1809

Original
13 States

Land Acquired
by 1783

Spanish
Territory

Louisiana
Purchase 1803

Oregon
Country

The Killing, 1
· · · · · · · · ·

IN THE FALL OF 1809, Thomas Jefferson had been retired from the presidency for eight months, passing executive leadership to his chosen successor and fellow Virginian, James Madison. The sixty-six-year-old Jefferson had returned to Monticello, the Greco-Roman villa he had built on a hilltop overlooking the colonial town of Charlottesville, Virginia. The home was politically appropriate to Jefferson's changed posture on the national stage. Seventy miles west of Richmond and one hundred and twenty miles southwest of Washington, Monticello was isolated yet close to power.

The plantation's design and construction had spanned the entire Promethean career of the man who was the author of the Declaration of Independence; the governor of Virginia; the secretary of state under George Washington; the vice president under John Adams; founder of the University of Virginia; and the third president of the United States, from March 1801 to March 1809. In his spare time, he was also an architect of renown, a naturalist, an agriculturist, a scientist, an inventor, and the first superintendent of the U.S. patent system.

Monticello reflected Jefferson's mania for experiment and his delight in inventions. Its thirty-five rooms dazzled visitors with the owner's many creations, which included narrow hidden stairways, a door with circular windows, specially devised dumbwaiters and disappearing

beds. He had helped to develop a special writing machine which allowed the automatic copying of letters; he had devised and patented a
moldboard for plows, a swivel chair, a pedometer, and a camp stool.
Outside the house, there was a Jefferson-designed weathervane that
could be read from indoors. In the hallway, a Jefferson-designed clock
was perpetually wound by cannonball weights and displayed not only
the time but the days of the week. Upstairs, a Jefferson-designed bed
could be pushed to the ceiling, clearing the room for daytime work.
Throughout the house, rooms were separated by Jefferson-designed
sliding double doors which moved inward and outward with a single
push. The dining room, too, was designed by Jefferson and had a set
of rotating circular shelves in the wall so he could have intimate dinners
without the presence of servants. This because Thomas Jefferson—the
inventor of many things, launcher of the American Empire, and world-
class intriguer—distrusted the gossip of his household slaves.

Monticello and Jefferson's life-style were molded in the aesthetics
and classicism of Europe yet brilliant with American invention. There
were other ironies, too. It was a grand château sketched and crafted
by the world's most honored egalitarian—a man who argued for emancipation in his draft of the Declaration of Independence and many other
historical documents. But Monticello was built and staffed almost
exclusively by slaves, hundreds of slaves whom Jefferson would own
until the end of his or their lives.

On the night of November 26, Thomas Jefferson was alone in his
private quarters. It was after nine o'clock and beside his bed a house
slave had stocked a cabinet with a goblet of water, a decanter of wine,
a plate of light cakes, and a candle.

The centerpiece of the bedroom-study was a long table which held
a set of carpenter's tools and scientific instruments. On the walls were
shelves lined with a profusion of books, maps, globes, and charts. In
the windows were pots of roses and geraniums and tomatoes and other
plants with which Jefferson was experimenting. His pet mockingbird
was flying about the room, sometimes perching on the tall man's
shoulder as he sat at the long table and reviewed the papers sent to him
from the capital.

Five rooms at Monticello were set aside for his sole use. Except for
servants, no one entered except by invitation. Three of the rooms were

for books, one was his study, and the fifth was his bedroom. He kept a simple and comfortable schedule. Breakfast was at eight. Afterward, in the English manner, guests were invited to amuse themselves for the morning while Jefferson retired to his work. Dinner was at four in the afternoon, and when that was over, he walked and talked with guests. He had a light tea at eight. At nine he firmly withdrew to his private apartment. There he would read until about midnight and then sleep.

Now, on this dark night, the Virginia legend was in an ankle-length woolen robe. The bed was pulled down but he was not in it. There was no fire lighted in the room although the nights were becoming frosty—as was his temper.

Still athletic despite his age, tall and so awkwardly rangy that the English ambassador had said he looked like a gawky farmer, Jefferson rose from his desk and crossed to a mirror where he began brushing his reddish-gray hair back into a pompadour. He gathered it into a knot at the back, Indian style, and tied it. Then, with a soft whistle, he held out his hand. The mockingbird flew to him promptly. Giving it reassuring clucks and strokes, the aging Prometheus returned the bird to its cage and walked down the stairs.

What had agitated him so was that a guest had arrived with news of the death of his friend Meriwether Lewis—a boy Jefferson had helped raise to manhood and who had been like the son he never had. Thomas Jefferson would hear about this catastrophe firsthand from the man who had been at Meriwether's side.

At the time of the midnight visit, Jefferson's favorite, Meriwether Lewis, lay buried in the thickly wooded wilderness of middle Tennessee. The country looked then much as it does today—ridge-backed hills sliced by deep glens, deep hollows shadowed by woods, and the whole dark forest cleaved by clear-cold streams. In this fall of 1809, the daytime colors were in full explosion with red, gold, and yellow leaves blanketing the forest floor. But in this night had come an unforeseen horror. In the lean-to kitchen of a frontier farm, a woman was surprised by a pistol shot. A man cried out from her yard, "Oh, Lord!" Another shot. Silence. Minutes later the bleeding victim was clawing at her door. "Oh, Madam! Give me some water! Heal my wounds."

She remained frozen behind the cabin wall. Peering through a chink in the logs, she saw him stagger and fall.

His skull torn open, he rose to his knees, struggled about the yard seeking water, crying for help. This went on for hours before he fell quiet in a distant mound of leaves, stabbed and mangled with a knife or a razor. His throat was ripped and bullets had blown away his forehead and exposed his brains.

As Priscilla Griner watched, the man, who was a stranger to her, died in that land of oak, dogwood, cottonwood, and azalea.

The death marked the beginning of a historical mystery, a Founding Fathers' whodunit, the major players being not only Jefferson but Aaron Burr, John Randolph of Roanoke, and the powerful, Machiavellian commandant of the U.S. Army, General James Wilkinson.

The vibrant man who died in such undeserving pain and so alone in those early hours of October 11, 1809, was Meriwether Lewis, *the* Lewis of Lewis and Clark. Not only was he leader of the transcontinental exploration, he was also governor of the Louisiana Territory and a shining hero at the height of an illustrious career.

He was thirty-five years old.

Meriwether Lewis was sometimes called "the Red Stork" because of his carrot-color hair and birdlike look. He had been Jefferson's private secretary, a protégé and kinsman of the legendary leader. But Lewis had an identity in his own right. Not only was he acclaimed worldwide for his expedition to the Pacific, he was a pioneering scientist poised on the eve of publication of his journals. Among the most popular of national heroes, he was a future candidate for the presidency, being a member of the "Virginia junto," Jefferson's plan for a succession of Virginia presidents.

In the late summer of 1809, Lewis, lean and tough as a willow, had left St. Louis on a secret mission to see President James Madison. But halfway to the nation's new capital at Washington, D.C., the young governor died in that farmyard on the Natchez Trace.

In a famous obituary, Jefferson would claim that his secretary had a pathology of depression and that Lewis was a habitual drunkard.[1] It was an incredible verdict, seemingly unsupported, but one that scotched investigations before they could lead to answers. Jefferson's ruling was powerful not only because he was the immediate ex-president and a giant of world politics but because it was Jefferson who had lifted Lewis up to the halls of the mighty. And it was Jefferson who, presumably, knew Lewis best.

There were and are facts, fancies, and fantasies in the case. And they all surround Lewis and lead back to Thomas Jefferson.

The midnight visitor to Jefferson was Lewis's personal servant, John Pernier, a man dimly lit by history. Although Pernier would stay at Monticello for four days, nothing has come down to us of what he told Jefferson.

It is a very strange omission because Thomas Jefferson was a man who recorded virtually every detail of his life, from the births of colts to the number of nails and bricks manufactured at his plantation. And yet, not a detail about the death of his protégé, his Virginia neighbor who was a national hero and a high government official, one personally recruited and appointed by Jefferson.

Red-haired and freckled, Meriwether was Jefferson's lifelong neighbor. But more than that, he lived with Jefferson like a son for more than two years at the half-built, unpainted White House. Side by side, they had bachelored together in the huge, nearly vacant house "like two mice in a church," said Jefferson in a letter to his daughter.

But whatever passed between Pernier and Thomas Jefferson has not survived into history. There is not a single particular of Lewis's death or of what Pernier witnessed. Jefferson sent Pernier on to Washington to see President Madison, but only with a request that the government should pay Pernier's back wages because, as Meriwether's valet, Pernier was regarded by Jefferson as having been in official federal employment. Jefferson's accompanying letter made no mention of suicide or murder nor did Jefferson say that Pernier gave any details about Lewis's death. Jefferson told Madison only that a federal agent named James Neelly was "in possession of two trunks of the unfortunate Governor Lewis."

Jefferson's request for back wages amounted to an endorsement of Pernier, of whom little else is known. In other references, Pernier has been variously described as a French Creole, a Spaniard, a mulatto, and a former servant of Jefferson's who had accompanied Lewis to St. Louis, although Jefferson gave no such indication in his letter to Madison.[2]

So what to make of Lewis's death?

The sole direct witness to speak of Lewis's death was the innkeeper's wife, Priscilla Griner. Her words were first recorded eighteen months after Lewis's death, in the spring of 1811, when she was interviewed by the renowned ornithologist Alexander Wilson.

Priscilla Griner, who spelled her surname differently from the popular name for the inn, was about thirty-five years of age at the time.[3] Married to a moderately wealthy farmer and businessman, Robert Evans Griner, then forty-two, Priscilla had given birth to her eighth living child just four months prior to Lewis's arrival at the inn. Like that of many frontier families, the Griner homestead was virtually a community unto itself. The inn's population included Robert and Priscilla Griner, the baby boy nursing at his mother's breast, two Griner daughters and five sons—all in their teens or older—and two slaves.

Alexander Wilson was a friend of Lewis's who had been engaged by the explorer several years earlier to make drawings of new bird species found on the Pacific expedition. In the spring of 1811, while journeying from Philadelphia to New Orleans on another mission, Wilson made a detour to visit his friend's grave.

To his surprise and dismay, Wilson found the young governor's body had been tossed in a shallow pit and covered only with stones and trash lumber. Wilson learned there had been no government investigation of his friend's death nor even funeral services. The body had simply been "buried close by the common path with a few loose rails thrown over his grave."

Wilson's interview with Mrs. Griner is enhanced by his qualifications as a scientist, for he was no ordinary reporter. To this day, Alexander Wilson is considered the father of American ornithology and was among the world's leading scientists of his era. A skilled observer, he wrote Priscilla's story almost immediately after he heard it from her. It can be assumed to be a faithful transcript. But how strange a report it is—describing a frontier woman, accustomed to birth and death, who is so disturbed by her guest that she cannot sleep. She tells of a man who arrives in a state of extreme agitation, who checks his gunpowder supply, and who is so prepared to bolt that he takes his saddle to bed with him. She was apparently unaware that her guest was a governor and national hero because he did not identify himself and his clothing was concealed by a large flowing "duster," a riding robe in common use at the time.

In a crucial part of her narrative, she hears a pistol shot, then something heavy hits the floor. Then another shot, and then Meriwether Lewis was at the door of the lean-to kitchen, which was only a few paces away from his bedroom within the main house. But, hearing shots, a heavy fall, and a cry for help, she can do no better than peer out at him through cracks in the wall of her kitchen.[4] She made no mention of suicide.

Here is Wilson's diary entry dated May 6, 1811, as the ornithologist was headed south from Nashville:

I rode six miles to a man's of the name of Grinder, where our poor friend Lewis perished. In the same room where he expired, I took down from Mrs. Grinder the particulars of that melancholy event, which affected me extremely. This house or cabin is seventy-two miles from Nashville, and is the last white man's as you enter the Indian country. Governor Lewis, she said, came there about sunset, alone, and inquired if he could stay for the night; and, alighting, brought his saddle into the house. He was dressed in a loose gown, white, striped with blue. On being asked if he came alone, he replied that there were two servants behind, who would soon be up. He called for some spirits, and drank a very little. When the servants arrived, one of whom was a negro, he inquired for his powder, saying he was sure he had some powder in a canister.

The servant gave no distinct reply, and Lewis, in the meanwhile, walked backwards and forwards before the door, talking to himself. Sometimes, she said, he would seem as if he were walking up to her: and would suddenly wheel round, and walk back as fast as he could. Supper being ready he sat down, but had eaten only a few mouthfuls when he started up, speaking to himself in a violent manner. At these times, she says, she observed his face to flush as

*if it had come on him in a fit. He lighted his pipe, and drawing a
chair to the door sat down, saying to Mrs. Grinder, in a kind tone
of voice, "Madam this is a very pleasant evening." He smoked
for some time, but quitted his seat and traversed the yard as before.
He again sat down to his pipe, seemed again composed, and
casting his eyes wishfully towards the west, observed what a sweet
evening it was. Mrs. Grinder was preparing a bed for him; but he
said he would sleep on the floor, and desired the servant to bring
the bear skins and buffalo robe, which were immediately spread
out for him; and it being now dusk the woman went off to the
kitchen, and the two men to the barn, which stands about two
hundred yards off.*

*The kitchen is only a few paces from the room where Lewis was,
and the woman being considerably alarmed by the behavior of her
guest could not sleep, but listened to him walking backwards and
forwards, she thinks, for several hours, and talking aloud, as she
said, "like a lawyer." She then heard the report of a pistol, and
something fall heavily on the floor, and the words "O Lord!"
Immediately afterwards she heard another pistol, and in a few
minutes she heard him at her door calling out "O, Madam, give
me some water, and heal my wounds."*

*The logs being open, and unplastered, she saw him stagger back
and fall against a stump that stood between the kitchen and room.
He crawled for some distance, raised himself by the side of a tree,
where he sat about a minute. He once more got to the room;
afterwards he came to the kitchen door, but did not speak; she
then heard him scraping the bucket with a gourd for water; but it
appears that this cooling element was denied the dying man!*

*As soon as day broke and not before, the terror of the woman
having permitted him to remain for two hours in this most deplorable situation, she sent two of her children to the barn, her husband
not being at home, to bring the servants; and on going in they
found him lying on the bed.*

*He uncovered his side and showed them where the bullet had
entered; a piece of the forehead was blown off, and had exposed
the brains, without having bled much. He begged they would take
his gun and blow out his brains, and he would give them all the*

*money he had in his trunk. He often said "I am no coward; but I
am so strong, so hard to die." He begged the servant not to be
afraid of him, for that he would not hurt him. He expired in about
two hours, or just as the sun rose above the trees. He lies buried
close by the common path, with the few loose stones thrown over
his grave. I gave Grinder money to put a post fence round it, to
shelter it from the hogs, and from the wolves; and he gave me his
written promise he would do it.*

*I left this place in a very melancholy mood, which was not much
allayed by the prospect of the gloomy and savage wilderness which
I was just entering alone.*[5]

Wilson's interview with Mrs. Griner has disturbed historians ever
since it was published. For one thing, who were the "servants" who
found Lewis in the bed—the Griners' or Lewis's? Lewis was traveling
with James Neelly, a federal officer. But there is no hint of Neelly in
Priscilla's account. Why? Did Lewis neglect to mention him? Or did
Priscilla erase him? And what was there about Robert Griner that made
Wilson so wary that he demanded a *written* promise of proper burial?
And where are the voices of the several other witnesses? Were they
not present at the time of Wilson's visit? Robert Griner was there; why
don't we hear from him? Or his sons and daughters?

Nearly one hundred years passed before such basic questions were
raised in print, and they came not from any historian or government
investigator but from Elliott Coues, who, like Wilson, was a celebrated
naturalist and ornithologist.

While preparing an edition of the Lewis and Clark journals, Coues
addressed the mysteries surrounding Lewis's death, saying that while
"there is no room to doubt [Alexander] Wilson's painstaking correctness . . . the narrative of Mrs. Grinder is . . . not to be believed under
oath. The story is wildly improbable upon its face; it does not hang
together; there is every sign that it is a concoction on the part of an
accomplice in crime, either before or after the event."[6]

Coues believed that "Mrs. Grinder was privy to a plot to murder
Governor Lewis, and therefore had her own part to play in the tragedy.
even if that part were a passive one."

In Coues's view, Mrs. Griner may have stumbled onto a murder after the fact and "she told a story to shield the actual criminal or criminals. [Only] on either of these theories could we understand Mrs. Grinder; otherwise her story is simply incredible."

Lewis's more modern biographers, Richard Dillon and Vardis Fisher, likewise believed Lewis was murdered, although, like Coues, they failed to come up with the who or why of it. Other authors who have wrestled with the question of his death include Henry Adams, Paul R. Cutright, Jonathan Daniels, Donald Jackson, Dumas Malone, and Dawson Phelps. With the notable exception of Daniels, the majority of them have accepted Jefferson's verdict of suicide. But whether murder or suicide, all the arguments are ultimately based on the single tale of Lewis's death as told by Priscilla Griner.

Although Jefferson would ultimately declare Lewis's death to be suicide, that would not come until a letter written five months later, when the Monticello planter wrote to an army colleague of Lewis's. The ex-president's letter was to Captain Gilbert Russell, the Fort Pickering commandant who persuaded Lewis to cancel his trip down to New Orleans. Jefferson told Russell that Lewis's death

> *was an act of desperation. He was much afflicted & habitually so with hypochondria. This was probably increased by the habit into which he had fallen & the painful reflections that would necessarily produce in a mind like his.*[7]

It is unclear what Jefferson meant by Lewis's "habit." Most historians have assumed it was a reference to laudanum, an alcoholic solution of opium in common use at that time. Others think it was a reference to heavy drink.

Did Lewis commit suicide, unlikely as that seems, or was it murder? Was Lewis's death deliberate or accidental? Did he awaken to find someone rifling his trunks? Or was it a planned assassination, bungled because of stout resistance?

Could robbery have been a motive?

Lewis left Fort Pickering with about one hundred dollars cash. People have been murdered for less. But if it was robbery, why were Lewis's expensive watch, customized pistols, dirk, matchbox, and other valuables found in his cabin?

There are other questions: Why did Thomas Jefferson insist it was suicide? Why did Jefferson specify there was a strain of insanity, which no historian before or since has ever found? Why did Jefferson dwell on Lewis's "habit"? If Lewis had been a confirmed alcoholic or drug abuser Jefferson surely would have known of it. However, if such were the case, would Jefferson have solicited Meriwether to serve as his personal secretary or have selected him to lead the prized Pacific expedition? There was no "habit" mentioned by Lewis's partner, William Clark, nor by any of more than a dozen subordinates who accompanied them during that demanding two-and-a-half-year trek across the unexplored Rockies to the Pacific and back. In St. Louis, Lewis's most vicious enemy—his second in command, Territorial Secretary Frederick Bates—was ready to pounce on any sin, but never once did Bates mention alcoholism, drug abuse, or depression.[8]

In later chapters, we will see other descriptions of Lewis's death, including a later interview with Priscilla Griner in which she described two strange men who rode up to the inn and quarreled with Lewis that fatal evening. She also presents us with a puzzle concerning a bizarre exchange of clothes between Lewis and Pernier.

As in a detective story, some of these apparent contradictions conceal answers to what actually happened.

Now, come forward in time some two hundred years. Mystery is in the wind as one stands beside a pillar in a small national park about five hundred yards off the Natchez Trace Parkway in the woods of Tennessee. Bees buzz and the air is heavy with the smell of forest, of tupelo, persimmon, dogwood, and oak. In the center of a clearing is a tall headstone financed by the state of Tennessee and built in 1848 by Lemuel Kirby, a local sculptor, whose fee was five hundred dollars including materials. Looking up, we see the top of the column, some twenty feet high, truncated to denote Meriwether Lewis's violent and premature end—a ghostly marker, an eerie column, broken and almost forgotten in the middle of nowhere. Beneath it rests the skeleton of the young Virginian himself, the army officer chosen by Jefferson in 1801 to be his presidential secretary, and afterward Jefferson's personal choice to lead the historic expedition to the Pacific.[9]

What happened?

The answer will be found in the intrigues of Aaron Burr, Alexander Hamilton, John Randolph of Roanoke, and the now-forgotten master conspirator, General James Wilkinson, commandant of the U.S. Army from 1796 through 1812.[10] Wilkinson was an intimate of Aaron Burr and Benedict Arnold and a member of the notorious Conway Cabal, which attempted to discredit George Washington and elevate General Horatio Gates to the supreme command of the Continental armies. To fill out his varied and adventure-filled dossier, America's top general also was a paid secret agent of Spain for most of his military life.

Wilkinson could not have played his role of secret agent so long and so successfully without the help of his unlikely co-conspirator— Thomas Jefferson, a divinity in our history but a man of enormous contradictions.

In the day-by-day practice of politics, Jefferson could be vengeful and ruthless. As president, he personally engineered the impeachment of Supreme Court Justice Salmon Chase because Chase was ruling too regularly against Jefferson's political allies. Jefferson made shameful deals with Alexander Hamilton—hiding Hamilton's land manipulations in return for political considerations. Jefferson was a betrayer even in the seduction of his friends' wives. That's *wives*, in the plural. There were at least two such entanglements that he acknowledged and there may well have been others that went undetected. This does not include his alleged affair with his slave Sally Hemings, an accusation that, as we shall see, is popularly accepted, biographically doubtful, but probably irrelevant to any discussion of character.

But Jefferson could also be sacrificing and visionary. It is well known that—risking his lands, his Monticello, his very life—he was a leader of the American Revolution and author of those words that stirred first America, then France, and eventually many other nations into revolution for democracy. Words that spread over the centuries and continents:

We hold these truths to be self-evident, that all men are created equal. . . .

Architect, statesman, author, scientist, tinkerer, farmer, archaeologist, and vintner, he had not only "a happy talent of composition," but was a builder of empire. In the years of Lewis's travails, he will betray his principles and deceive Congress about the Louisiana Purchase, but to the nation's enduring advantage. He will stretch the United States from ocean to ocean at a time when he has no army worthy of the name and a pitifully meager navy. He will do this with skillful and manipulative politics, playing all factions against the others. Manipulating. Taking risks. Keeping secrets.

To unravel the intrigues and motives behind the mask of Thomas Jefferson and the death of Meriwether Lewis, we must begin in 1774, the year of Lewis's birth, of Jefferson's emergence on the national scene, and of the first shots of the American Revolution.

The Nation, 1774–1789

• • • • • • • • •

ALTHOUGH FIRST SETTLED IN 1607, the Virginia of Lewis and Jefferson's time was still a wilderness just beginning to fill with people. Wherever settlers landed on the Atlantic coast their feet trod rich loam and they were beneath or near the shade of trees. The eastern American forest reached almost without break from Quebec to Florida and westward to the Mississippi.

The frontiersmen were an amazement to the world. Their migration demographics were new to history. Unlike the German barbarians, the Mongols, or Vikings, these were neither raiders nor soldiers. They were settlers, barely armed and often helpless victims dying by the thousands to establish their families. They were farmers and carpenters, mechanics and small businessmen driven to free land by the need for space and opportunity.

Bernardo Gálvez, the Spanish governor of the Louisiana territory, feared them mightily:

> This prestigious and restless population, continually forcing the Indian nations backward and upon us, is attempting to get possession of all the continent. . . . Their method of spreading themselves and their policy are so much to be feared by Spain as are their arms. . . . A carbine and a little maize in a sack are enough for

an American to wander about in the forests alone for a whole
month.

A visiting French official, Pierre Clément de Laussat, also was awed
by the phenomenon:

> Wherever the Anglo-Americans go, the earth becomes fertile and
> progress is rapid. . . . They are the first to immigrate, clear the
> land, people it, and then push on again and again without any end
> or trade but to open the road for new colonists. . . . When twenty
> of these colonists collect together in one place, two printers arrive,
> one a Federalist, the other an anti-Federalist; then the doctors;
> then the lawyers; then the adventurers. They drink toasts; they
> elect a speaker. They lay out a city. They beget children at plea-
> sure. Finally they advertise vast territories for sale. They inveigle
> and fleece as many buyers as possible. They inflate the figures of
> population in order that they may appear to have 60,000 inhabi-
> tants as soon as possible, for that gives them the right to become
> an independent state and must be represented in Congress . . .
> and behold, one more star in the flag of the United States."

The American genius for mass communications was much in evidence. An English traveler, Charles Janson, expressed dismay at the
proliferation of newspapers:

> Printing and bookselling have been extended to the most remote
> parts of the country. Several newspapers are printed in Kentucky;
> and almost every town of more than a few score houses, in every
> state, has a printing office from which the news is disseminated.
> There is no tax whatever on the press, and consequently every
> owner of one can print a newspaper with little risk among a people
> who are all politicians.

Rough roads connected the towns and the few cities, but road transportation was too chancy for major commerce. Heavy wagons mired
themselves in mud or broke axles against rocks, ruts, and stumps. Only
boats could sustain heavy cargo. Thus the harbors of New England,

New York, and the South were the most quickly developed regions. Educational facilities, commercial centers, and capitals grew there. Towns were placed chiefly on the seacoast and at the heads of navigation of the rivers. Commerce was their only support, for the days of the manufacturing towns had not yet come.

As late as 1774, roads were still scarce. Only three crossed the Alleghenies, two of them in Pennsylvania and one in Virginia. Traveling charges were half a dollar for each meal. "These only differ in there being vegetables at the dinner table, and spirits and water, as an execrable beverage," complained the European guest. "At breakfast and supper there are also hot dishes, and generally very indifferent coffee."

The "execrable beverage" was a popular toddy of raw apple brandy and water. Whiskey and especially imported rum were pricier and less common.

Thomas Jefferson avoided such hard drink, preferring the natural wines of France. In this, as in many other habits, he was more elitist than populist.

Some clues to Jefferson's contradictory nature can be seen in an official presidential portrait done by Rembrandt Peale in 1805. It is an excellent head and shoulders view of Jefferson who has collar-length hair and is wearing a fur-collared robe. It is not a photograph, not a random accident of movement or emotion captured by the camera. It is an artist's interpretation of a man Peale came to know after months of sittings. The posing president stares skeptically at us. His look is cynical, suspicious. We recoil, put off by—what? Not by hostility. But rather by the sheer *absence* of friendliness. What Peale saw was a man who insisted on distance. Cold. Impenetrable. The Great Democrat was, to Peale's eye, cold and unapproachable.

Sixty-two years of age when the portrait was painted, Jefferson was tall and still rangy—six feet two and about a hundred and ninety pounds. His once-red hair had turned sandy gray. His eyes were light blue, impressive with intelligence.

Though the Peale portrait shows a handsome man, Daniel Webster, writing in the early years of Jefferson's presidency, found him homely, and many found him too easygoing and casual for the dignities of the era. Wrote Webster: "Limbs uncommonly long; his hands and feet very large, and his wrists of an extraordinary size. His walk is not precise and military, but easy and swinging. He stoops a little, not so much from age as from natural formation." The great diarist Senator William Maclay had a similar impression: "His clothes seem too small for him. He sits in a lounging manner, his whole figure has a loose, shackling air." Augustus Foster, secretary of the British Legation, said Jefferson had "grey neglected hair; his manners good-natured, frank and rather friendly, though he had somewhat of a cynical expression of countenance. He wore . . . slippers down at the heels—his appearance being very much like that of a tall, large-boned farmer."

His political career had begun at the age of twenty-six in Williamsburg, when that tiny village of two hundred houses was the capital of Virginia.

Jefferson was thirty-one years older than Meriwether Lewis, being born in Albemarle County on April 13, 1743.

Although Jefferson treated his pedigree lightly, his mother, Jane Randolph Jefferson, came from one of the first families of Virginia; his father, Peter Jefferson, was a well-to-do landowner, although not in the class of the wealthiest planters.

There was a tradition of the self-sufficient frontiersman in the Albemarle and young Tom Jefferson was one of his class, raised barefoot and hardy, taught to depend on his own resources to survive. As a horseman, he was "an uncommonly fine rider" and familiar with the habits of coons and possums.

There is a family story about his determination to be a huntsman.

When he was ten, he was handed a gun by his father and sent out into the woods alone in order to develop self-reliance. The inexperienced boy was wholly unsuccessful in bagging any game until he stumbled upon a wild turkey caught in another hunter's trap. Tom Jefferson tied the turkey to a tree with his garter, shot it, then brought the abducted trophy home in triumph. While attending the College of William and Mary (1760–1762), Jefferson studied law with the prestigious George Wythe, the first professor of law in the United States. In this period, Jefferson wrote cock-of-the-walk letters to friends about the great "comforts of the single state" and dwelt on the many sexual opportunities provided him by the women of Williamsburg—or so he hinted in his letters.

After completing his law studies with Wythe in 1769, Jefferson sought and won a seat in the Virginia House of Burgesses. In a series of reelections, he would serve there for the next six years. In 1770, while still a delegate, he began building Monticello on land inherited from his father.

The mansion, which he designed in every detail, took years to complete, but part of it was ready for occupancy when Jefferson, at age twenty-eight, married the twenty-three-year-old widow Martha Wayles Skelton on January 1, 1772.

At the House of Burgesses, Tom Jefferson was viewed by all sides as a man of exceptional intellect. Typical Virginia planter class in his angular, rawboned look and classical education, he became a power among political liberals, a group led by his elders—George Washington, Patrick Henry, George Mason, the Randolphs and the Lees.[1]

It is illuminating of young Jefferson's character that while he courted the influential Henry as a friend, his mind was not closed to the great orator's faults. In a letter, Jefferson dissected Henry like a laboratory specimen: "I have frequently shut my eyes while he spoke and when he was done asked myself what he said, without being able to recall a word of it. He was no logician but he was eloquent as Homer."

The Virginia liberals came into power in the spring of 1774 when news was received of the Boston Tea Party. From that moment, they and their Massachusetts counterparts led the cautious but sure movement by the colonies to a complete break with Great Britain.

When the first Continental Congress convened in the summer of 1774, Jefferson was in Virginia writing a draft for the legislature which would be published as *A Summary View of the Rights of British America*.

This pamphlet was to provide his first impact on the revolution. It argued that colonial allegiance to the king was voluntary on the basis of a theory of natural rights. He insisted the colonies could not be ruled by Parliament because colonials had no vote in that body. He asked: "Can any reason be assigned why 160,000 electors [the number of Englishmen eligible to vote] in the island of Great Britain should give law to four millions in the states of America . . . ?" As a solution, he proposed that the colonies and England enter a mutual trade pact making them "a commonwealth of nations." He thus became among the first to anticipate the British Commonwealth of self-governing nations.

Although Jefferson did not then propose separation from the Crown, it was noted that he referred to "states of America," not colonies. He further rankled conservative feelings by blaming Great Britain for introducing the African slave trade, "a lasting problem."

Jefferson wrote:

> *The abolition of domestic slavery is the great object of desire in these colonies, where it was unhappily introduced in their infant state. But previous to the enfranchisement of the slaves we have, it is necessary to exclude all further importations from Africa; yet our repeated efforts to effect this by prohibition, have been hitherto defeated by his majesty's negative; thus preferring the immediate advantages of a few African corsairs to the lasting interests of the American states, and to the rights of human nature.*

A Summary View marked Jefferson's emergence on the national scene. In it were the roots of independence.

The Virginia legislature rejected his advice as too radical, but the pamphlet would be published in Philadelphia during the Congress and reprinted in London, where it would gain Jefferson a place on the king's list of American traitors.

Although time has dimmed the memory of their passion, the American Revolution was fought by ordinary men who rose to exceptional bravery, being willing to lay down their lives for freedom in a family quarrel that began as a protest and grew into a war.

The Revolution was a seedbed for political careers, a dark forest where there sprouted not only strength and independence but conspiracy and intrigue. Sprung from the Revolution would be the careers and relationships of Burr, Jefferson, and Hamilton and of lesser names like James Wilkinson.

By 1774, the consensus complaint of the colonists was against a British system that demanded "taxation without representation." Among the loudest and earliest voices to demand not only representation but full independence was that of Samuel Adams, a forty-six-year-old brewer who was also clerk to the Massachusetts legislature. In 1768, he used the *Boston Gazette* and other newspapers to promote the patriot cause and to keep alive opposition to the Crown.

During the 1760s and into the early 1770s, rebellious incidents and British retaliations erupted throughout the colonies, but particularly in Massachusetts and Virginia. In 1773, the middle-aged Adams himself led a group of rebels dressed as Indians to board ships in Boston harbor and throw tea overboard—the Boston Tea Party. When King George III ordered reprisals, the call went out from Boston in May 1774 for rebel delegates from the thirteen colonies to meet in Philadelphia for the first Continental Congress.

The Massachusetts delegation included John Hancock, a Boston shipowner and smuggler, Sam Adams, and Sam's younger, more moderate cousin John Adams. Warrants had been issued for their arrest, and to elude capture they rode in a curtained coach through New York and New Jersey to meet at the town of Frankfort outside Philadelphia for a preconvention caucus with other northern delegates.

Out of the Frankfort meeting would arise a Yankee policy to put southerners, most especially Virginians, at the head of everything in order to take British military pressure off New England. Since Virginia was the most populous state, it would be wise to let ''Virginia take the lead,'' as John Adams described it. Virginians would be their shield, although it was not anticipated that Virginians would become their leaders.

According to Adams, Virginia's prominence in early American history was due almost entirely to that northern policy rather than southern political skills. Adams recorded that without the Frankfort plan, ''Mr. Washington would never have commanded our armies, nor Mr. Jefferson have been the author of the Declaration of Independence; nor Mr. Richard Henry Lee the mover of it.''

In that summer and fall of 1774, Jefferson was in Virginia, having failed in a hometown bid for election to the first Continental Congress.[2] He was still in Richmond in the spring of 1775 when news came that Great Britain had responded to the colonials' petition of grievances by occupying Boston and closing the port. From there a British brigade was marching to wipe out the rebels' munitions store at Concord, some twenty miles northwest of Boston. To get to Concord, the British planned to cross the Charles River and pass through the village of Lexington.

As it happened, they were met there by colonial militia, called Minutemen, an encounter that resulted in the "shot heard round the world." That British shot was fired at Lexington Green, the name for the town common or square, used for cattle grazing and occasional public events. There the Revolutionary War began, a mere skirmish fought by seven hundred British Redcoats against seventy-three embattled farmers led by John Parker, captain of the Minutemen.

What happened that brave day when a line of farmers stood to block British passage was recorded by George Bancroft, later to be the secretary of the navy and founder of the academy at Annapolis. His words still stir emotion:

There they now stood, side by side, under the provincial banner, with arms in their hands, silent and fearless, willing to shed their blood for their rights, scrupulous not to begin civil war. . . .

John Parker, the strongest and best wrestler in Lexington, had promised never to run from British troops; and he kept his vow. A wound brought him on his knees. Having discharged his gun, he was preparing to load it again, when he was stabbed by a bayonet, and lay on the post which he took at the morning's drum-beat. So fell Isaac Muzzey, and so died the aged Robert Munroe, who in 1758 had been an ensign at Louisburg. Jonathan Harrington was struck in front of his own house on the north of the common. His wife was at the window as he fell. With blood gushing from his breast, he rose in her sight, tottered, fell again, then crawled on hands and knees toward his dwelling; she ran to meet him, but only reached him as he expired on their threshold. Caleb Harrington, who had gone into the meeting house for powder, was shot as he came out. Samuel Hadley and John Brown were pursued, and killed after they had left the green. Ashahel Porter, of Woburn, who had been taken prisoner by the British on the march, endeavoring to escape, was shot within a few rods of the common. Seven men of Lexington were killed, nine wounded; a quarter part of all who stood in arms on the green.

The result was a British massacre of peaceful townsfolk who sought to block the troops' passage but not to fight them.

Militarily it was a disaster for the simple folk but an opportunity for their leaders. A few miles away at Concord, the rebel chief Sam Adams, heedless of his own danger and with the voice of a prophet, cried, "Oh, what a glorious morning is this!" for he saw his country's independence hastening on.

Immediately after the skirmish at Lexington, the British were met at Concord's North Bridge by a larger force of American militia, and this time the rebels were intent on killing, not stopping. Pressing against their gunfire into the town, the British were unable to find the munitions. As they retreated to Boston, the colonists pursued, harrying and harassing their oppressors all the way to the city where they began their siege on April 19, 1775.

Down in Virginia, the British governor, Lord Dunmore, was removing from the magazines in Williamsburg all the powder belonging to the colony and placing it on a British schooner in the James River. Dunmore's timing was coincidental because the news of Lexington and Concord had not reached Virginia and wouldn't for two weeks.

The governor's action so incensed the Virginians that thirty-eight-year-old Patrick Henry led a company of freedom fighters in a raid on the capital. Dunmore wisely removed himself and his family to another British ship in the harbor, the man-of-war *Fowey*.

Moving in an opposite direction was thirty-two-year-old Thomas Jefferson who, to protect his family from the British, removed them from their Elk Hill home on the James back to Monticello. Reluctant to accept the fact of war, Jefferson wrote a friend that Lexington and Concord was an "accident" between the king's troops and the "brethren" of Massachusetts Bay Colony.

The siege of Boston only encouraged England to send more armies. In response, the second Continental Congress convened on May 10, 1775, in Independence Hall in Philadelphia to form its own "continental" army.

Boston's John Hancock sat as president and among the new members was Thomas Jefferson, who had now joined the delegation from Virginia. It was the first trip outside of Virginia for the thirty-two-year-old planter, except for a brief medical trip in his youth to Philadelphia. Now he hauled north again, crossing his Rubicon.

"It marked his entrance on the continental stage as a public man," according to his modern biographer, Dumas Malone. "But for the challenge of political crisis he would have continued to be a prosperous planter, a responsible local leader, a humane and enlightened Virginian who operated of necessity within a restricted sphere and spent most of his time at home."

Jefferson arrived in Philadelphia to find that northern prejudice favored Hancock to lead the proposed army. But John Adams, pursuing the Frankfort advice to place the Virginians at the head of everything, nominated Colonel George Washington, who even then sat in Congress in his uniform. Hancock was bitterly chagrined to lose the office despite general agreement that Washington's selection would bind the South to the North.

Adams said Hancock was beside himself:

> Mr. Washington, who happened to sit near the door, as soon as he heard me allude to him, from his usual modesty, darted into the library room. Mr. Hancock, who was our President, which gave me an opportunity to observe his countenance while I was speaking on the state of the colonies, heard me with visible plea sure. But when I came to describe Washington for the commander, I never remarked a more sudden and striking change of countenance. Mortification and resentment were expressed as forcibly as his face could exhibit them.

Although we think of Washington as the man in the Gilbert Stuart portraits, white-haired and grim, the new general of the army was then an athletic forty-three years old, a large executive type, over six feet tall with reddish hair and blue-gray eyes, who walked with an authoritative air. A surveyor by training, he and his wife, Martha, were the heirs of a prosperous Virginia gentry of English descent. Washington already had a formidable military reputation as a young colonel in the French and Indian Wars (1754–1763) where, among other achievements, he had rescued British regulars under General Edward Braddock near present-day Pittsburgh.[3]

On June 16, 1775, Washington became Congress's unanimous choice as commander in chief of the Continental forces. In accepting the appointment, Washington insisted that he serve without pay, to receive only reimbursement of expenses.

For the next seven years, George Washington would fight a three-front war—against the British, against a feckless Congress, and against his own backstabbing generals.

Charles Lee, a self-congratulatory English defector, thought he should be in total command of the Continental army. The Adjutant General, Horatio Gates, was another intriguing English hero who conspired to replace Washington. The Inspector General was Thomas Conway, an Irishman who also would cause much grief. Nearly all of the eight brigadier generals were openly scornful of their rank. Even the minor officers competed in their jealousies.

Washington took command of the "army" surrounding Boston on July 3, 1775. Eight months later the British gave in to the siege and withdrew by sea. It was an enormous victory, not only of arms but for American morale. The British could be and were beaten.

In the meantime, the Congress had continued to meet. At Philadelphia on June 7, 1776, a declaration of independence was offered by Virginia's senior delegate, Richard Henry Lee.

Lee asked the Congress to resolve that "these United Colonies are, and of right ought to be, free and independent States, that they are absolved from all allegiance to the British Crown and that all political connection between them and the State of Great Britain is, and ought to be, totally dissolved."[4]

The boldness of it put Congress on the spot. Although the war was a year old and battles had been fought—Lexington, Concord, the British driven out of Boston—this was the first time that the colonies were asked to officially declare themselves free of Great Britain.

A year earlier, the colonies had been seeking a commonwealth. Now they wanted full independence.

So treasonable were Lee's resolutions that the prudent Congress did not enter them even in its secret journals. Nothing but a slip of paper now preserves the original form.

John Adams, "The Atlas of Independence," promptly seconded the motion. But only four of the thirteen colonies were ready to immediately abolish their ties to the Crown. The remainder hung back for various reasons. To gain time, the independence faction agreed to wait three weeks. In the meantime, Congress appointed a five-man committee of John Adams, Benjamin Franklin, Robert Livingston, Roger Sherman, and Thomas Jefferson to "prepare a declaration to the effect of the said first resolution."

During the three-week hiatus, news arrived that King George III had hired twenty thousand German troops to subdue the rebellion. His action poured gasoline on the fire and brought the remaining colonies into full agreement for independence.

Meanwhile, the committee had appointed the actual writing of Lee's resolution to Jefferson, who had come to Philadelphia with a literary reputation derived in large part from his *Summary* pamphlet.

John Adams, future president, would note that Jefferson "brought with him a reputation for literature, science, and a happy talent of composition. Writings of his were handed about, remarkable for the peculiar felicity of expression. Though a silent member in Congress, he was so prompt, frank, explicit, and decisive upon committees and in conversation . . . that he engaged my heart."

To the British loyalist Tories, however, young Jefferson was a "lean and grinning Cassius" typical of the rebel politicians, "a man of sinew and bone."

Cassius came back with his draft seventeen days later, on June 28. The core of it was captured in these immortal lines:

> *We hold these truths to be self-evident, that all men are created equal, that they are endowed by their Creator with certain unalienable Rights, that among these are Life, Liberty and the pursuit of Happiness. That, to secure these rights, governments are instituted among men, deriving their just powers from the consent of the governed; that, whenever any form of government becomes destructive of these ends, it is the right of the people to alter or*

*abolish it, and to institute a new government, laying its foundations
on such principles, and organizing its powers in such form, as to
them shall seem most likely to effect their safety and happiness.*

It was the birth announcement of a new social order not only for
America but for the world.

"Into the monumental act of independence, Jefferson poured the
soul of the continent," said his contemporary, Ezra Stiles, the president
of Yale University. "As a common man, he would have been a crank,
but he raised idiosyncrasy to the dignity of genius," said another
historian, C. H. Van Tyne.

Despite the passion and glory of the words, the Congress tabled the
draft until it had decided on whether to even seek independence. That
decision came on July 2, 1776, when Lee's resolution was adopted.
Independence was officially declared on that day—not July 4—with
the colonies, now become independent "states," voting 12–0. New
York abstained because much of its population remained loyal to King
George.

Thrilled with the boldness of the event, John Adams wrote to his
wife on July 3 that the nation henceforth would be celebrating a new
national holiday—Independence Day, the Second of July:

*A resolution was passed without one dissenting colony, "that
these United Colonies are, and of right ought to be, free and
independent States. . . ."*

*The second day of July, 1776, will be the most memorable epoch
in the history of America. I am apt to believe that it will be
celebrated by succeeding generations as the great anniversary
festival. . . . Solemnized with pomp and parades, with shows,
games, sports, guns, bells, bonfires and illuminations from one end
of this continent to the other, from this time forward, forevermore.*

On July 4, the edited Jefferson draft of Lee's resolution was approved
by Congress—after several clauses were excised, including a condemnation of the British monarchy for imposing slavery upon America.

The Declaration made Jefferson internationally famous, although

John Adams thought the best of it had been edited out by the Congress and much of the remainder was "hackneyed."

Adams would say that he had persuaded Jefferson to write the Declaration on the argument "You are a Virginian and a Virginian ought to appear at the head of this business." After the Declaration was drawn, Adams said, he and the Virginian "conned the paper over. I was delighted with its high tone and the flights of oratory with which it abounded, especially that concerning negro slavery which, though I knew his Southern brethren would never suffer to pass in Congress, I certainly would never oppose. . . .

"Congress was impatient and the instrument was reported, as I believe, in Jefferson's handwriting, as he first drew it. Congress cut off about a quarter of it, as I expected they would."

The result, said Adams, contained "not an idea but what had been hackneyed in Congress for two years before. The substance of it is contained in the declaration of rights and the violation of those rights in the Journals of Congress in 1774. Indeed, the essence of it is contained in a pamphlet voted and printed by the town of Boston before the first Congress met, composed by James Otis," a Boston lawyer and writer who had been instrumental in forming the first Continental Congress.

Neither Adams nor Jefferson liked the congressional editing. "They obliterated some of the best of it" and left what was commonplace, said Adams. "I have long wondered that the original draft has not been published. I suppose the reason is the vehement philippic against negro slavery.

Characteristically, Jefferson hid his pride of achievement and said his work was "neither aiming at originality of principle or sentiment, nor yet copied from any particular and previous writing, it was intended to be an expression of the American mind."

He was annoyed by the excisions which he said were caused "by the pusillanimous idea that we had friends in England worth keeping terms with." Unlike Adams, Jefferson thought the censorship on the slavery issue came from the North as well as the South:

The clause reprobating the enslaving the inhabitants of Africa was struck out in complaisance to South Carolina and Georgia, who had never attempted to restrain the importation of slaves and who, on the contrary, still wished to continue it. Our northern brethren also, I believe, felt a little tender under those censures; for though their people had very few slaves themselves, yet they had been pretty considerable carriers of them to others.

The Declaration as we know it today appeared July 6 in the *Pennsylvania Evening Post*, but Congress did not order a final written version until July 19. It was not signed by the members until August 2. John Hancock was the first to put his name on the document but for more than six months Congress hid the identities of Hancock and his fifty-five co-signers because the Declaration was an act of treason which could send them all to the gallows.

Meanwhile, up and down the American coast George Washington's army was striking and retreating, striking and retreating. In these early years of the war, Washington was often outmaneuvered by the British. Ignorant of many of the basics of generalship, he neglected routines such as reconnaissance, seldom had accurate intelligence of the enemy's whereabouts, and regularly split his forces unwisely. But he had two magnificent qualities that carried him through his painful early period—aggressiveness and perseverance. Time after time—at New York and Brandywine, at Oriskany and Philadelphia—the British generals won battles and declared the war was won. The Americans and Washington were subdued. But then Washington would come back like the phoenix.

He *would not* be kept down.

In the last months of 1776, desperately short of men and supplies, Washington despaired. After capturing Boston, he had lost New York City to the British; enlistment was almost up for a number of the troops, and others were deserting in droves; civilian morale was falling rapidly; and Congress, faced with the possibility of a British attack on Philadelphia, had withdrawn from the city to a temporary capital in Baltimore.

Then, on Christmas night, 1776, Washington led his troops across the iced-up Delaware. Surprising and routing the hated Hessian garrison, he advanced to Princeton, where he drove out the British main force, forcing them into a retreat that carried them all the way back to New York. He had begun the New Year by recovering all of New Jersey. Morale and honor were restored.

In the meanwhile, Jefferson—never militarily inclined—was alternating between his building program at Monticello and his duties in the Virginia House of Delegates at Williamsburg.[5]

The tides of war ebbed and flowed over the next nine months. The turning point came in the fall of 1777 while Washington was harassing British forces who by now were occupying Philadelphia. The pendulum swung permanently in the American direction in what began as a small series of battles in the northern woods of New York, near the village of Saratoga.

Saratoga commanded the Hudson Valley and the northern approaches to the thirteen colonies. Descending upon this crucial junction from Canada was the flamboyant British commander, "Gentleman Johnny" Burgoyne.

In the First Battle of Saratoga, on September 19, 1777, the Americans were defeated as a result of the hesitancy and bungling of their commander, Horatio Gates, and despite fierce and courageous initiatives by Generals Benedict Arnold and Daniel Morgan.

"Gentleman Johnny" settled in victoriously on the battlefield at Saratoga to await reinforcements and to write letters home. King George received the news of Burgoyne's triumph by bursting into his wife's sitting room and shouting, "I have beaten them! I have beaten all the Americans!"

However, even at that moment of monarchical glee, Burgoyne's reinforcements were being sidetracked by Washington's attack on Germantown, near Philadelphia. In the meanwhile, circling like a pack of wolves in winter, waiting for the moment to strike, the remaining American forces at Saratoga were being reinforced daily by the arrival of new militia. By the beginning of October, some eleven thousand colonials had surrounded Burgoyne's six thousand British regulars, Indians, and German mercenaries.

On October 7, Burgoyne sent out a reconnaissance in force—nearly half his command—in an effort to break through the American lines and find a way out of the trap. They were hit and hit hard by Arnold and Morgan. A series of furious fire fights ensued over the next several days, ending in the capture of the British army and the surrender of "Gentleman Johnny."

We have no record of what the king had to say about that.

In the aftermath of the battle, Horatio Gates lobbied Congress successfully to have himself officially declared "the Hero of Saratoga." Adding insult, wanting to spite the true hero, Benedict Arnold, Gates then gave the honor of receiving Burgoyne's sword to his aide-de-camp, a young Marylander named James Wilkinson. It was a distinction that would later lead directly to Wilkinson's promotion to brigadier. The true champions of the battle, the common soldiers and their fighting officers led by Arnold and Morgan, were less than pleased with this turn of events because Gates's basic contribution had been to stay out of the way while Arnold and Morgan did the work. Arnold, who was severely wounded in the late stages of the campaign, was so alienated that he would later betray the Americans at West Point and defect to the British.[6]

While Saratoga was an enormous victory in its own right, its bigger payoff came when the news reached Paris. Frenchmen hauled American ambassador Ben Franklin onto their shoulders and marched him through the cheering streets. When they put him down, French women sat in his lap and tousled his thin gray hair. On February 6, 1778, the French government, ever eager to jump on the British when they thought they had a chance, brought France into the war on America's side. The British responded by declaring war against Louis XVI.

In the spring of 1779, the Spanish joined France as allies against the hated British, although refusing to diplomatically recognize the new American states. With their own vast colonial empire in the New World, the Spanish did not want to set a precedent for independence.

Saratoga had turned the American Revolution into a world war. No longer could the British concentrate their forces on America. The entry of the French and Spanish forced England to protect the farthest reaches of trade and empire—from the Channel to the European Atlantic coast, to the Mediterranean, to India and the Pacific. America was no longer the top priority, slipping to fourth or fifth behind concerns for the

Channel, the Atlantic ports and sea-lanes, and the sugar-rich West Indies.

As spring broke in Spanish New Orleans, Governor Bernardo Gálvez assembled seven hundred men and brilliantly conquered English settlements at Manchac, Baton Rouge, and Natchez, thus solidifying Spanish control of the Mississippi. Gálvez followed that up by leading a march on Mobile, compelling surrender of that fort and thus wresting from the British control of east and west Florida.

The British struck back in the spring of 1780. They still held New York and they began a giant pincer movement to outflank the Continental Army with an amphibious invasion in the southern states. Sir Henry Clinton and Sir Charles Cornwallis landed with 7,600 men near Charleston, South Carolina, and overwhelmed 2,500 Continental soldiers, who were taken prisoner. Soon afterward, the whole state was overrun and brought under British military control.

In England, newspapers once again said the American revolt was beaten.

And, indeed, it looked as if the pincers were closing on Washington, who had British in front of him at the gates of New York and other hostile English troops climbing up his backside from the Carolinas.

In South Carolina, the few Americans who were left were being chased and harried by a rampaging British cavalry commander, Lieutenant Colonel Banastre Tarleton, a warrior so rapacious and daring, so fierce and swift in the field, that his commandant, Lord Cornwallis, proudly called him his "Hunting Leopard." It was the Hunting Leopard who would burn the Lewis plantation and nearly capture Thomas Jefferson.

From Charleston, the British pressed west toward the mountains with Tarleton in the fore, overrunning American brigades and reveling in the humiliation of the rebels. Receiving the battle reports in New York, Washington wrote that he had "almost ceased to hope." His army was without bread or meat, "half-starved, imperfectly clothed, riotous, and robbing the country people from sheer necessity," he wrote. Desertion was continual.

To buy time and prevent encirclement, Washington moved to halt the British at Cowpens in western South Carolina. On January 17, 1781, against Tarleton, he sent his best: a force led by the Saratoga hero Daniel Morgan and supported by the steady infantry of Nathanael Greene and the daredevil cavalry of Henry "Light-Horse Harry" Lee. At the Broad River, Morgan formed his lines to await Tarleton's inevitable attack. Though the Americans were outnumbered, their ambush was perfect. The brief, violent engagement resulted in such a trouncing for the British that fewer than two hundred of Tarleton's force of eleven hundred men escaped. The Americans lost twelve dead and sixty wounded.

It was a repeat of Saratoga. Morgan had done it again. The stunning victory against Cornwallis's elite bought the time Washington needed to swing his main force down from New York and south to face Cornwallis.

Rendezvousing with a French army outside of Princeton, New Jersey, Washington led a combined force of sixteen thousand French and Americans on a fast march south to a peninsula in eastern Virginia. There, above Norfolk, he met Cornwallis in the Battle of Yorktown.

Supported by guns and supplies from the French fleet, the allied armies caught the British in a trap. After a desperate resistance, unable to escape across the York River because of bad weather, Cornwallis surrendered on October 19, 1781, and seven thousand British regulars became prisoners of war.

It was almost four years to the day since Saratoga.

Despite the crushing victory, peace wasn't settled in Paris until two years later. But the Americans had won the war at Yorktown.[7] And almost instantly the first map of the United States was published and sold by Connecticut silversmith and printing innovator Abel Buell.

Writing in the same year of Yorktown, Yale University president Ezra Stiles looked into his crystal ball. With amazing prescience, he saw a turning point in world history:

We shall have a communication with all nations in commerce, manners and science beyond anything heretofore known in the world. Manufacturers and artisans and men of every description may come and settle among us. [The English language] will probably become the vernacular tongue of more numerous millions than ever yet spoke one language on earth.

As men looked back from the year of Yorktown, they would see clearly, and perhaps for the first time, that the personal leadership of George Washington was the chief reason why America had not fallen apart before France came to its aid.

In the meantime, the man who had done as much as anyone to start the war, certainly the man who became the symbol of it, saw no military action. In the crucial summer of 1776, Thomas Jefferson sped away from the Continental Congress immediately following adoption of the Declaration of Independence to return home to Virginia.

Although regularly harried by British troops, he would not leave Virginia until the war was over. Jefferson had declared himself "not a military man" and he stuck to that posture throughout his life.

The war advanced into prominence and opportunity such men as George Washington, Benjamin Franklin, John Adams, and Jefferson. With them went their protégés—Alexander Hamilton, Aaron Burr, John Paul Jones, John Marshall, and James Monroe. The war also advanced the careers of lesser names, famous then, mostly forgotten now, like James Robertson, George Rogers Clark, Henry Knox, Elbridge Gerry, William Blount, and the young Maryland doctor-turned-general James Wilkinson.

The war made Princeton aristocrat and scholar Aaron Burr a colonel at age twenty-one, and a good one who distinguished himself at the battles of Monmouth and Bunker Hill.

Jefferson's Albemarle neighbor James Monroe was eighteen years of age when he left the College of William and Mary in March 1776 to enlist as a lieutenant in a Virginia regiment. His unit then marched north to join Washington's army. Monroe fought in the battles around New York that summer and was one of the conspicuous heroes of the icy Battle of Trenton in December 1776. He served for two more years, earning Washington's praise as "a brave, active, and sensible officer"—qualities that would become the hallmarks of his long public career.

A young immigrant from the West Indies, Alexander Hamilton, enlisted in the militia and fought in the battles around New York City in 1775 and 1776. His energy and intelligence brought him to

Washington's attention and for four years he was invaluable as the commander's personal aide-de-camp. Hamilton proved to be a talented field officer, leading a battalion that fought with conspicuous bravery at Yorktown.

As we shall see, for the next twenty-five years those men who came of age in the Revolution—Hamilton, Burr, and Jefferson—would be at one another's throats and backs, locked in a fierce rivalry, out of which would arise a permanent philosophy of American government and politics for two centuries to come.

Caught in the fallout would be an innocent bystander, Meriwether Lewis, who would become a victim to the ambition of all three men, but primarily to the schemes of his prince and mentor, Thomas Jefferson.

Thomas Jefferson's war years began in peace. They would end in personal tragedy. He went shopping on the afternoon of July 4, 1776, even as the Congress was adopting his draft of the Declaration of Independence. Finally finished with his work, he prowled the shops of Philadelphia to buy his wife six pairs of shoes, seven pairs of gloves, and an armful of "sundries." He also found toys for his daughter, Martha, then four years old.

He was impatient to leave the Congress because he feared his wife, Martha, whom he called "Patsy," was ill. He wrote to his friend Richard Henry Lee in Virginia, "I receive by every post such accounts of the state of Mrs. Jefferson's health that it will be impossible for me to disappoint her expectations of seeing me."

Upon arriving at Monticello, he found that the illness was not as serious as he had thought. He decided not to return to Philadelphia, however, and following adjournment of the second Congress a few months later, he joined the newly formed Virginia House of Delegates where he would serve through 1779.[8] Joined by James Madison, George Mason, and his old law teacher, George Wythe, Jefferson sought to liberalize Virginia's institutions by introducing a number of bills involving finance and the manumission of slaves. But these were all defeated, being resisted fiercely by the conservative planter class. The times were not ready for his reforms.

Jefferson nevertheless retained his popularity, both among his political colleagues and the masses, and in June 1779 he was elected governor of Virginia. The dark events that followed would almost drive him out of politics. His enemies would criticize his performance as war governor mercilessly. Most seriously, he would be accused of incompetence and failure to provide for the adequate defense of his Richmond capital in 1780 despite an imminent British invasion. His ensuing flight from the British in 1781 would bring accusations of ineptitude, cowardice, and "pusillanimous conduct."

He would fare no better in his own legislature, where conservatives defeated his bill to create a system of tax-supported elementary education for all except slaves. The planters also beat back Jefferson's measures to create a public library and to modernize the curriculum of the College of William and Mary. There was a war going on and—try as he might—Jefferson lacked the strength to drag Virginia kicking and screaming into social reform.

His bill on religious liberty touched off a quarrel that would stir turmoil in the commonwealth for the next eight years. The legislation was significant because no other state—indeed, no other nation—provided for complete religious liberty at that time. Jefferson's bill stated "that all men shall be free to profess, and by argument to maintain, their opinions on matters of religion, and that the same shall in no wise diminish, enlarge, or affect their civil capacities." Many Virginians regarded the bill as an attack upon Christianity. It did not pass until 1786, and then mainly through the perseverance of James Madison.

Jefferson left the governorship in June 1781. But even as he was writing his last official letters, word came of a surprise raid into the Albemarle by the swaggering British cavalry commander Banastre Tarleton.

The Hunting Leopard had ridden into Virginia hot for revenge after taking his drubbing in South Carolina, where he lost part of a hand.

Now, in the summer of 1781, driven and harried north, Cornwallis and Tarleton were moving into Virginia, the largest of the colonies and the financial base for the military leaders of the Revolution. It was the Britishers' earnest intention to capture the Virginia legislature and perhaps end the war by breaking rebel morale. If they moved fast enough, they hoped to bag the hated author of the Declaration of Independence himself, Thomas Jefferson.

The colonel and two hundred and fifty mounted troops swept through the eastern Piedmont in a rage of burning and pillaging. Ahead of Tarleton, like so many foxes fleeing the hounds, went Jefferson and the Virginia legislators, abandoning Richmond for the presumed safety of Charlottesville some seventy miles to the northwest.

Riding captured blooded Virginia racehorses, the terrifying and terrorizing Tarleton cremated the American army supplies outside Charlottesville, then split his force. One party was sent to bag Jefferson at Monticello while the other descended on the legislators in Charlottesville itself. But before Tarleton could close the trap, the legislators fled farther west to Staunton while Jefferson vanished entirely.

"The attempt to secure Mr. Jefferson was ineffectual," a depressed Tarleton would write in his battle report. "Watching from his home, he discovered my British dragoons from his house [and] before we could approach him, he had provided for his personal safety with a precipitate retreat."

In fact, Jefferson's retreat wasn't all that precipitate. Warned by a rider shortly before sunrise of the British approach, Jefferson had deliberately downed a glass of old Madeira, then sent off his guests and family by carriage. He did not himself leave Monticello until nearly everyone else was gone and the enemy was in telescope view at Charlottesville. Only then did Jefferson ride off, leaving two slaves, Martin Hemings and Caesar, as sole custodians of the house.[9]

Tarleton captured a handful of dilatory legislators at Charlottesville but spared Monticello from the torch. General Cornwallis's other officers were not so gentle. Making bivouac for ten days at Jefferson's Elk Hill plantation on the June River, Cornwallis let his soldiers run wild. Barns were burned and crops destroyed. Cornwallis's dragoons slaughtered stock and horses and departed with thirty slaves—an act that Jefferson never forgot nor forgave.

Throughout the Piedmont, the British occupied and looted other plantations including those of the Lewises and the Randolphs. All useful cattle and horses were driven off and slaves rounded up and taken along.

Much of Virginia was reduced to ashes.

The pillaging and terror left permanent scars. John Randolph, a year older than Meriwether Lewis, would later tell friends: "I well remember flying with my mother and her newborn child from Benedict Arnold; and we were driven by Tarleton and other British Pandours from pillar to post. The impression is indelible.''

In June 1781 Jefferson retired from office, leaving under a cloud and writing his young friend and neighbor James Monroe that he had ''stood arraigned for treason of the heart and not merely the weakness of the head.'' Of political ambition, he declared, ''every fibre of that passion [is] thoroughly eliminated.'' He wanted nothing other than to plant grapes at Monticello.

Less than four months after Jefferson's retirement, Washington and his French allies defeated the British in the final military campaign of the war.

Despite ultimate victory, the war years had not been good for Jefferson. His wife, Martha, who had borne him six children in ten years, fell ill at age thirty-three and died in September 1782. The blow was so shattering that some historians believe he felt forever afterward responsible and held himself to blame.

There may have been cause for that.

Although Martha was a frail woman who experienced difficult pregnancies, the robust Jefferson had been unwilling to deny himself the pleasures of the marital bed. During their entire marriage, Martha never went longer than two years without conceiving a child.

Martha died on September 6, 1782, a bare four months after giving birth to her and Thomas's sixth child, a daughter named Lucy Elizabeth.

In Martha's final months, knowing she was dying, Jefferson rarely left her bedside. Shortly before her death, he read to her some lines of his own:

> —And every time
> I kiss thy hand to bid adieu, every absence which
> follows it, are preludes to the eternal separation
> which we are shortly to make!

In her last hours, he brought to her bedroom their only two children who would survive into adulthood—Martha and Maria. He also gathered up to the bedroom the slave family of Betty Hemings, and the two senior house slaves on the plantation—Great George and his wife, Ursula.

The presence of Great George and Ursula was to be expected. It was common for slaves in their position to be regarded as quasi members of the family.

The Hemings, however, were a special case. Although they were slaves, they were Thomas Jefferson's in-laws, four of them being half sisters to Martha Jefferson.

The Hemings family had come to Monticello as part of Martha's inheritance from her father, the planter John Wayles. The matriarch, Betty Hemings, was an attractive, light-skinned mulatto, the daughter of a white English sea captain and a black African mother. According to well-documented sources, six of her ten children were sired by Martha's father, John Wayles.[10] Martha, therefore, was half sister to four Hemings present at the bedside—Betty, Nance, Critta, and Sally.

The deathbed scene itself was actually recorded by Edmund Bacon, one of Jefferson's overseers. Bacon, who received his account from the servants present, said Martha was holding her husband's hand when Jefferson vowed never to marry again:

> . . . when Mrs. Jefferson died they stood around the bed. Mr. Jefferson sat by her, and she gave him directions about a good many things that she wanted done. When she came to the children she wept and could not speak for some time. Finally she held up her hand [and] she told him she could not die happy if she thought her children were to have a stepmother brought in over them. Holding her other hand in his, Mr. Jefferson promised her solemnly that he would never marry again. And he never did.[11]

When Martha died, her body had to be lowered from a window because the servants were unable to move her through the house of narrow, winding stairways.

Her suddenly widowed husband became despondent and went into retreat, riding heedlessly day after day over the hills. He, a man who saved masses of papers in his lifetime, destroyed all correspondence with Martha. He hid his heart. All he kept was a lock of her hair and that note in which he bade her adieu.

Martha's death came about the time Jefferson was elected to the feeble national Congress formed under the Articles of Confederation. There he made more contributions of enduring importance to the nation. In April 1784 he submitted *Notes on the Establishment of a Money Unit and of a Coinage* for the United States in which he advised the use of a decimal system. This report led to the adoption of the dollar, rather than the pound, as the basic monetary unit in the United States.

As a congressman, Jefferson again returned to the subject of slavery, proposing to exclude it from all of the American western territories after 1800. Although a slave owner himself, he believed that slavery was an evil that should not be permitted to spread.

Slavery existed everywhere in the colonies, not widely regarded by the white or red inhabitants of the continent as an evil until the Quakers began to teach a higher morality.

The first abolition society was the Society for the Relief of Free Negroes Unlawfully Held in Bondage, organized in Philadelphia by Benjamin Franklin and physician-scientist Benjamin Rush.

The antislavery movement manifested itself in two strategies, both of which were favored by Jefferson. One strategy sought to prohibit the importation of slaves and the other the extinction of the institution. Economics dictated that first must come the ban on importation, then the full prohibition.

Following the Revolution, the northern states began phasing out slavery in a manner designed to compensate the owners. The strategy was called "gradual emancipation," defined as "the extinction of slavery by depriving it of its hereditary quality." Slaves freed in this generation would bear free children in the next, thus phasing out the practice.

The first absolute prohibition of all slavery, present or future, came in 1777 from Vermont, the territory in which slavery economics were weakest. New Hampshire followed in 1784.

In many northern states, however, slavery remained economically

desirable. A New York history published just eighteen years before
Jefferson's *Summary* had noted:

> *. . . the province being so poorly inhabited, the price of labor
> became so enormously enhanced, that we have been combined to
> import Negroes from Africa, who are employed in all kinds of
> servitude and trades.*

As late as 1788, the New Yorker John Jay was defending the slavery
compromise in the Constitution, which in effect sanctioned slavery by
allowing the famous three-fifths rule. (For the purpose of congressional
representation, each male slave counted as three fifths of a free male.)
Rationalizing such a position, Jay wrote to an English abolition society
that slavery was so entrenched in America it would take much time to
change it: "Prior to the late revolution, the great majority, or rather
the great body, of our people had been so long accustomed to the
practice and convenience of having slaves, that very few among them
even doubted the propriety and rectitude of it."

Nevertheless, in 1781, New York abolished the *sale* of slaves *within
its own borders* and eight years later it decreed that children born to
slave parents after July 4, 1799, were free. Most northern slaveholders,
including the New Yorkers, got rid of their slaves not by freeing them
but by selling them in the South, thus transferring the problem at a
profit.

It was such economic considerations that caused Jefferson's 1784
congressional legislation banning slavery throughout the United States
to be narrowly defeated. The vote would have carried for abolition had
one congressman been present—John Beatty of New Jersey, who was
sick and confined to his lodging. "Thus," Jefferson correctly prophe-
sied, "we see the fate of millions unborn hanging on the tongue of one
man, and heaven was silent in that awful moment."

Emancipation would not come to the bulk of America's slave population for another eighty years. Until then, the process moved slowly.
By the first census of 1790, only Massachusetts was without slaves.
Virginia, the largest state in the nation, with a total population of
692,000, had 300,000 slaves, 43 percent of its people. Pennsylvania
had 434,000 people, including 4,900 slaves; New York's 340,000

population included 22,000 slaves. Even the abolitionist stronghold of Vermont, formerly the Republic of New Connecticut, had 20 slaves despite its law prohibiting bondage. In sum, by the 1790 census there were an estimated 750,000 slaves in the United States—20 percent of the national population.

Jefferson's personal record on the matter of slaves is fogged with contradiction. In public, he was among the most ardent opponents of the institution, repeatedly risking not only his political career but his own fortunes. But the private Jefferson was another matter.

At any given year, he owned between two hundred and three hundred slaves. He would die in 1826 owning two hundred and sixty. By virtually all accounts Jefferson treated his slaves humanely, if one overlooks the practice of enslavement itself. But he was sometimes stern. Although he is never known to have personally flogged a slave, he himself recorded standing by while a hardened slavebreaker tied up one of his runaways and had the man "severely flogged in the presence of his old companions" as an example to the plantation.

The biggest scandal of his lifetime involved a slave relationship. Although historically doubtful, it was never directly rebutted by him. The rumor alleged a years-long affair between Jefferson and Sally Hemings, one of Martha Jefferson's half sisters and thus Jefferson's sister-in-law (although certainly never recognized as such in any of their lifetimes).

Furthermore, according to the legend, the offspring of the Jefferson-Hemings union were themselves kept in slavery. This is an enormous stretch of belief because there is no proof that Jefferson and Hemings had sexual relations, let alone children.[12]

Another dark suggestion of warped doings was an anonymous note found in Jefferson's correspondence after his death. The note was apparently written to Jefferson concerning a visit to Monticello by Kentucky senator John Brown, a longtime friend of Jefferson's and a staunch political ally. The note seems to have been sent as a friendly warning but no historian has been able to establish its truth or falsity. The note reads:

> *. . . you will excuse the liberty when you look at my intention.*
> *I should think it a crime to listen to the base falsehoods utter'd*

*against you without informing you of them. Mr. Brown says he
slept at Monticello one night and was wakened in the morning by
the most lamentable cries. He looked out and to his utter astonishment saw you flogging in the most brutal manner a negro woman.*

One can suppose that Thomas Jefferson's posture toward slavery was
that of an addict toward drugs. He saw the corruption in it, but could
not cure himself of it.

At the close of the Congress in 1784, Jefferson, Benjamin Franklin,
and John Adams were named to a committee assigned to pursue commercial treaties in France. That same year the planter-politician published *Notes on Virginia*, which established his reputation as a scientist
and philosopher. In 1785 he succeeded Benjamin Franklin as minister
to France, where he witnessed the beginning of the French Revolution.
The resulting bloodshed gave him grave doubts as to whether the
French people could duplicate the American example of republican
government. His advice, more conservative than might be anticipated,
was that France should instead imitate the British system of constitutional monarchy.

As for his own mission, he found that the European countries were
indifferent to American economic overtures. "They seemed, in fact,"
Jefferson wrote, "to know little about us. . . . They were ignorant of
our commerce, and of the exchange of articles it might offer advanta-
geously to both parties." Only one country, Prussia, signed a pact
based on his negotiations.

While he was in France, a new constitution was proposed, debated,
and ratified in the United States.

To a large degree, these debates concerned the merits of a strong,
urban-based central government versus a weaker, rural-based confederacy. Had Jefferson been present, it is likely that his arguments would
have shifted the scales toward the rural view. As it was, the centralist
ideas of Alexander Hamilton carried the day.

Throughout much of his life, Jefferson's career was ensnared with
that of Alexander Hamilton. It is not too much of a stretch to say that

the two men were *the* Founding Fathers, because their views have shaped the course of American political philosophy unto this day.

Their repeated collisions were very much a matter of historical permutations. Had twenty-eight-year-old Alexander Hamilton not emerged from the war as George Washington's protégé and closest confidant, he wouldn't have become secretary of the treasury, a post that allowed him to shape modern America. Had Hamilton not become secretary, he wouldn't have distressed Jefferson nor instigated political parties. Nor would Hamilton have become leader of the New York Federalists, a course that led him to a fatal encounter with Aaron Burr on the dueling fields of New Jersey. Had the duel not occurred, then Burr would not have fled to the west—a movement that led Jefferson to charge Burr with treason, for reasons we shall review. From the charge of treason, there followed other entanglements. At the end of the chain comes the doom of Meriwether Lewis, an innocent who had little to do with any of the events that killed him.

Alexander Hamilton was born on the West Indian island of Nevis, probably in 1755. His exact birth date and the circumstances of his early life are difficult to determine because he was the illegitimate son of Rachel Fawcett Lavien and James Hamilton, both of West Indian trading families.

Modern research has established that young Hamilton spent his youth mostly on the island of Saint Croix, where he was apprenticed as a clerk. In 1772 he was sent to New York City by his guardian. Soon afterward, he enrolled at King's College and, at age nineteen, entered the growing dispute between the American colonies and the British government by writing fervent tracts filled with doctrines of rebellion and natural rights derived from the philosopher John Locke.

Hamilton's personal life and social position took a decisive turn in December 1780, when he married Elizabeth Schuyler, daughter of the wealthy and influential General Philip Schuyler. The marriage put Hamilton in the center of New York society and by age thirty he had built a distinguished military career, knew intimately most of the leaders of the American Revolution, and had achieved high social standing, being recognized as one of the leading lawyers in the country.

Like Jefferson, he was elected to the Continental Congress in 1782, where he became a leading advocate of a highly centralized government—stronger than that provided for by the then-operative Articles of Confederation. As aide to Washington, he had been well acquainted with how the rivalry among the states had almost killed the Revolution. He now called for a strengthened Congress and more efficient executive departments.

In 1787 the Continental Congress was about to go bankrupt, and Hamilton was among the first delegates to call for a Constitutional Convention to amend the Articles. The delegates, however, immediately set about not to amend the old document but to write a new one— the Constitution that exists today, as amended and clarified by such additions as the Bill of Rights.

The convention opened in Philadelphia on May 25, 1787, and was composed mostly of young lawyers like Hamilton who were in their twenties and thirties. There were a few oldsters. Pennsylvania's John Dickinson was fifty-four. The dean of the assembly was the still active Benjamin Franklin, then eighty-one.

There is a consensus among historians that the delegates' knowledge concerning government, both theoretical and practical, made it perhaps the most brilliant such gathering ever assembled. During the early sessions Hamilton advocated a national government that would have virtually abolished the states and even called for a president-for-life. Even as that was being debated, the delegates knew whom they wanted as the nation's first leader.

During the second half of the convention (July 27 to September 17) the members fought over conflicting interests such as those between commerce and agriculture and between slaveholders and others. The most controversial issue was none of those, however, but the composition of the executive branch and the means of electing the executive; this was settled on September 6 with the adoption of the Electoral College system suggested by Franklin. On September 17 the Constitution was signed by the delegates.

There followed a period of national debate to ratify the new document. Although the proposed Constitution was not as strong as he wished it to be, Hamilton was among its strongest supporters, co-authoring the "Federalist" essays along with John Jay and James Madison. Those brilliant essays stressed the need for a stronger union, the utility of a national taxing power, and the importance of the executive and judicial branches of the federal government.

After the Constitution was ratified by the states in 1789, fifty-five-year-old George Washington was called away from retirement at Mount Vernon and elected president, with John Adams as vice president. Washington named John Jay as the first Chief Justice. In the same year the Bill of Rights was adopted as the first ten amendments to the Constitution and New York City became the first national capital. The number-one job in Washington's Cabinet went to Hamilton, who would be secretary of the treasury from 1789 until 1795. The number-two job went to Jefferson as secretary of state.

Although Jefferson always claimed to be an uneasy politician, he readily accepted this elevation to the most public political arena. As a popular leader, he seemed singularly out of place. He never showed himself in crowds. By all accounts, including his own, he was a mediocre public speaker, as historian Henry Adams would later note:

> During the last thirty years of his life, he was not seen in a Northern city, even during his Presidency; nor indeed was he seen at all except on horseback, or by his friends and visitors in his own house. With manners apparently popular and informal, he led a life of his own, and allowed few persons to share it. His tastes were for that day excessively refined. His instincts were those of a liberal European nobleman, like the Duc de Liancourt, and he built for himself at Monticello a chateau above contact with man. The rawness of political life was an incessant torture to him, and personal attacks made him keenly unhappy. His true delight was in an intellectual life of science and art.

While there is no doubt that science and art were Jefferson's "true delight," it is equally true that he had dark obsessions. Their names were Alexander Hamilton and Aaron Burr.

Hamilton and Burr

• • • • • • • • •

DESPITE THE STRESSES and pulls between rebels and loyalists, farmers and manufacturers, slaveholders and abolitionists, northerners and southerners, there were no political parties when the American Revolution began, nor when it ended. The factions were united in a bigger cause, that of independence from England. It was only afterward, to meet the challenge of guiding the new nation, that U.S. political parties were created. Even then, partisan disputes did not become crucial until the opening of the First Congress at Federal Hall on New York City's Wall Street in March 1789.

The First Congress was a festive occasion with street parties everywhere and hundreds of houses in lower Manhattan open for one and all to take part. Buffet boards were piled with venison, bear, and fish of every kind, with birds and fruit, wines, ales, strong beers, ciders, and punch.

The festivities were to legitimize the new United States of America. The old Confederation of American States had foundered, the former colonies being unable to function under such a loose government. The war was won but prosperity had not arrived. The new Constitution, providing a two-house legislature, a chief executive, and a Supreme Court, promised a new era. Such was the feeling of the day.

New York City had been designated as the capital for the next seventeen months, a venue chosen because it was the repository of the records of the Continental Congress and because it was the nation's biggest port. The new Congress was anxious to get its hands on some money and figured to pass a quick customs tax when the first ships arrived from Europe and the Indies for the spring season.

The New York of 1790 began at the Battery and extended north roughly to present-day Fourteenth Street. New York was small potatoes by European standards, dwarfed by such cities as Paris or Istanbul with their palaces and half-million populations. Nevertheless, for America, New York was a major center. The first national census, taken that summer, showed the city with a population of just above 33,000. This was more than in Philadelphia city, although suburbs made Philadelphia the largest metropolitan area in the country.

Washington's arrival as president was stunning, arousing the admiration of New Yorkers, who already had a century-old reputation for dissipation, lawlessness, and a fast social life. One young Wall Streeter found Washington's equipage "the most splendid looking carriage ever exhibited among us, befitting the character of that chief of men. It was very large . . . drawn by six horses, Virginia bays. It was cream-colored, globular in its shape, ornamented with cupids supporting festoons, and with wreaths of flowers emblematically arranged along the panel work; the whole neatly covered with the best coach glass."

Philosophically, George Washington was a democrat, but both by training and taste he was devoted more to the patrician proprieties of life. Shortly after taking up quarters at the renovated Macomb mansion on "the Broadway," the new president announced that he would have one public audience a week to which all might come with petitions, as if to a king. At 2:00 P.M. the door of a great room at the mansion was thrown open and the petitioners would enter. The president would be standing erect, invariably clad in a plain black-velvet coat and breeches, a white or pearl-colored vest, yellow gloves, silver buckles at the knees and on the shoes, and his hair in a powdered wig. In his hands was a cocked hat, and at his side a steel-hilted sword with a white scabbard. As the visitors filed past they were introduced by name, and then they took their places at one side of the room. At a quarter past three the doors were closed and the president would then go along the sides of the room speaking some words to everyone. He had a good memory for names, and it was seldom that he was not able to say something appropriate to each caller. When this was done he returned to his first position. The guests approached and made their bows, and departed.[1]

Presidential dinners also were strictly regulated. Washington's guest list was restricted mostly to chief officers of the government and distinguished foreigners. The president sat at the middle of a long table opposite his wife, Martha. At one end would be one of his private secretaries and at the other end, another. After the soup came roasted and boiled fish, then meat, salmon, and fowl. Dessert began with apple pies and puddings, and ended with ice creams, jellies, watermelons, muskmelons, apples, peaches, and nuts. The middle of the table was decorated with artificial flowers made of silk.

"It was the most solemn dinner I ever sat at," sneered visiting Senator William Maclay of Pennsylvania. "Not a health drank, scarce a word said until the cloth was taken away. Then the president filling his glass of wine with great formality, drank to the health of every individual by name around the table. Everybody imitating him charged glasses, and such a buzz of 'health, sir,' and 'health, madam,' and 'thank you, sir,' and 'thank you, madam,' and so on I never had heard."

Other visitors also complained of the pomp and formality of the sessions. A Virginia congressman, accustomed to the ways of relaxed society, said Washington's receptions were too distant and stiff and required more bows than those of the Court of St. James's.

On the up side, the quality of the president's kitchen was judged by all to be excellent, with a good chef and having the best Madeira and claret, the fashionable wines of the day, which Washington imported from France.

The president's salary was fixed at $25,000 a year, a fair sum for the era, but out of it he had to pay his entertainment and living expenses. He usually had spent it all and more by the end of each year. He complained that another family could live on $2,500 a year in as good style as he lived for his $25,000.

The expenses, the life-style, and the levees continued when the capital moved to Philadelphia in 1790. Social life was insular and many members of Congress married into prominent local families, thus closing a circle of wealth and political power.

This nascent aristocracy, and the laws it would enact, irritated much of America, a rise of anger that would bring Thomas Jefferson to power.

Despite the vast acreage and millions of population, the American experiment in popular democracy was ruled by an amazingly small elite of propertied white males.

The symbol and even epitome of this oligarchy was not George Washington but Alexander Hamilton.

Hamilton's philosophy of government by an aristocratic elite was given in a speech he made to the 1787 Constitutional Convention:

All committees divide themselves into the few and the many. The first are the rich and well born, the other the mass of the people. The voice of the people has been said to be the voice of God; and however generally this maxim has been quoted and believed, it is not true in fact. The people are turbulent and changing; they seldom judge or determine right. Give therefore to the first class a distinct, permanent share in the government. They will check the unsteadiness of the second, and as they cannot receive any advantage by a change, they therefore will ever maintain good government. Can a democratic assembly who annually revolve in the mass of the people, be supposed steadily to pursue the public good? Nothing but a permanent body can check the imprudence of democracy.

In large part, political parties arose because of Hamilton's policies as treasury secretary. He argued that if the nation was to grow and prosper, its credit would have to be sound to encourage both foreign and domestic investment. He proposed, therefore, to create a national bank which would loan money to those businesses and industries favored by the administration. And he would seek commercial ties with Great Britain.

There was an immediate opposition from Jefferson and others who believed that such a bank would diminish agriculture and subvert the republican ideals of the American Revolution. Hamilton dismissed the objections, saying Jefferson's ideas were timid and backward-looking. With Washington's steadfast support, Hamilton began organizing a congressional majority for his policies.

Thus was born America's first political party, the Federalists—the name referring to Hamilton, John Jay, and James Madison, all of whom in the beginning backed Hamilton's economic strategy.

The First Congress was dominated by "federalists" with a small "f," so called because their leaders had written a series of highly successful essays urging passage of the new Constitution which was ratified in 1788. Those who preferred the old Articles or otherwise opposed ratification were called "anti-federalists."

At the time, neither group was considered a political party. They were not organized on any common political ground other than their position on the Constitution, and individuals did not cooperate to help one another achieve political office. More to the point, they did not *view* themselves as political parties. The drafters and signers of the Constitution were in near unanimous agreement that permanent political parties were anathema and that the "spirit of faction" encouraged competition adverse to the public interest.

It was noble philosophy but bad sociology. Even as the opening gavel banged down to begin the First Congress, splits were developing.[2]

Hamilton's fiscal policies were not entirely altruistic. Buried in his credit package was a call for the central government to pay off the states' debts. These debts were largely in the form of paper currencies (pounds, shillings, and dollars) and issued to pay for goods and services. But where the rub came was that the currencies had largely been used to buy farmland given to war veterans as bonuses—called bounties—for their military service.[3]

Once word of Hamilton's plan began to leak, speculators began to buy up the worthless "continentals" for a few cents, hoping for huge profits when Hamilton's Assumption Plan paid off.

Thus, through selective "leaking" of information, the Assumption Plan became a sweeping scheme to enrich the propertied and commercial classes in return for their support of the administration.

Although the uphill flow of money from the poor to the rich is at least older than the pyramids, Hamilton's scheme was the first, but certainly not the last, to be written into law by the American republic.

As Hamilton's plan neared completion, his friends began dispatching relays of fast riders and pilot ships at full sail to buy up the paper from remote wilderness families who were ignorant of the impending debt assumption and thought their paper money was worthless. The secretary's beneficiaries included a whole bevy of insiders such as Federalist congressmen and Hamilton's own father-in-law, General Philip Schuyler, who invested sixty thousand dollars in buying up the remote folks' land and currencies.

When news of the bounty frauds finally broke, however, it polarized the nation along economic lines, rich against poor. Old allies now became enemies. John Jay held tight with Hamilton during the assumption scandal of 1790 but James Madison denounced it as an unconscionable looting and split away from his fellow Federalists to form an opposition party.

As rumors of corruption built, Madison persuaded Jefferson to step into the fray. The nation now saw President Washington's two most powerful Cabinet members pitted against one another, each with powerful allies. And out of that Jefferson-Hamilton collision would come the first under-the-table political deal. The result would be the creation of a new national capital—Washington, D.C.

It worked this way:

As the vote neared for the Assumption Plan in the summer of 1790, Hamilton accidentally encountered Jefferson at the door of Washington's mansion in New York.

According to Jefferson's account, the two Cabinet members walked up and down the street. Hamilton pleaded his case for assumption and asked Jefferson's support. Jefferson withheld that, but did agree to host a small dinner where Hamilton could lobby the Virginia votes he needed for assumption. At the dinner, Hamilton presented his plan and sweetened the offer by agreeing to a Jefferson plan to continue use of Philadelphia as the national capital for ten more years, then move it permanently south to a new city, which would be called the District of Columbia.

With that compromise, the deal was made. The Assumption Plan and its payoff to speculators passed with no opposition from Jefferson.

Later Jefferson would concede in his memoir that as a result of assumption, "immense sums were filched from the poor and ignorant, and fortunes accumulated by those who had been [rich] enough before."

Opponents of assumption complained loudly that they'd been sold out by their leadership, which was a reasonably accurate way of looking at it.[4]

The national bank and its corollary Assumption Plan had exposed an imbalance of wealth and power which Madison and Jefferson hoped to correct. But their fight for reform was impeded by the economic tilt of the Founding Fathers. The 1787 Convention that framed the Constitution had been composed almost wholly of delegates chosen by legislatures that represented the planters of the South, and the mercantile, professional, and other wealthy groups of the eastern seacoast. Not one member represented in his immediate personal economic interest the small farming or mechanic classes, let alone enfranchisement for women, immigrants, or slaves. There were a few, notably James Madison, who would have allowed unpropertied white males to vote for the president and the Congress, but they were in the small minority and unsuccessful. All in all, it was a convention of elitist temperament.[5]

The nation itself, franchised and unfranchised, was split along ideological lines—those like Hamilton who favored an urban-oriented Big Government, and those like Madison and Jefferson who demanded a farm-focused Small Government.

The two factions had joined in the Revolution against the British but now they were locked almost as intensely in combat for political mastery of the new government.

The big-government Federalists, loyal to Washington, Adams, and Hamilton, would rule the country for the first decade. They were led by a handful of prominent and wealthy families largely made up of the old colonial aristocracy—the Jays, Cabots, Randolphs, Quincys, Livingstons, Adamses, Hancocks, Clintons, and Schuylers. Although as revolutionaries they had damned every form that suggested the habits of European courts, it was not very long before they themselves began to form something very like a court around President Washington.

Dismayed by the "royal court" and seeing the advantages of more democratic politics, Jefferson attacked Washington's administration

and Hamilton's conduct of the Treasury by using a ghostwriter—
one John Beckley, clerk of the House of Representatives and a man
sensitively placed to be Jefferson's spy. The ghostwritten broadsides
enraged Hamilton, who was more incensed by the deviousness of the
attack than by the words themselves.

Hamilton had his surrogates, too, among them South Carolina congressman William L. Smith, whose newspaper columns ripped Jefferson's ''pretenses,'' saying the Virginian had ''long ago excited the
derision of the many, who know that under the assumed cloak of
humility lurks the most ambitious spirit, the most overweening pride
and hauteur, and that the *externals* of pure Democracy afford but a
flimsy veil to the *internal* evidences of aristocratic splendor, sensuality
and Epicureanism.''

The split between Jefferson and Hamilton went ballistic in 1791 with
a brilliant Hamilton stratagem that gave the Federalists a monopoly of
the nation's raw supply of money.

The gambit was called the Bank of the United States.

Designed to imitate the Bank of England, the national bank had
headquarters in Philadelphia and branches in eight other cities. It had
the power to issue currency and was the fiscal agent for all government
income and disbursements. It also handled general commercial business, including the loan of money in return for interest.

Thus, with a single stroke, the Federalists could dole out cash in
the form of loans to those favored by the administration. Persons or
businesses in disfavor would be denied. Hamilton, indeed, saw such
patronage as the major political advantage for the new nation. The
powerful fortunes of the country would be forced to support the policies
of government out of self-interest, he said. And so they were.

The national bank was clearly designed to favor not only Federalists
but mercantile over agricultural interests, and Jefferson attacked it
immediately as unconstitutional. There was no authority anywhere in
the Constitution, he said, to charter such a bank.

Nevertheless, with President Washington's backing, Hamilton prevailed, and by doing so established an enduring, nation-defining doctrine of ''implied'' powers. In reply to Jefferson, Hamilton said the
Constitution gave Congress authority to pass any laws ''necessary and
proper'' to carry out designated powers. One of the designated powers

was to levy taxes and coin money. This implied, Hamilton argued, the power to create a national bank to safeguard and disburse the money.

The bank proved quite successful, not only at making money but at meeting Hamilton's political goals. However, its big-business, pro-administration bias so antagonized the Jeffersonians that they formed the nation's second political party, the Democratic-Republicans.[6]

Jefferson did not immediately take the helm of his party. As was his nature, he preferred to work from the wings, avoiding direct conflict while others bore the risks. In this case the *other* was James Madison, now a Virginia congressman, who officially began the Democratic party in 1791 on a local scale in Virginia. The earliest adherents were, in fact, called "Madisonians." A third member of the party's founders was James Monroe, who would become the junior partner of "the Virginia Dynasty." Following the Revolutionary War, Monroe had become a law student of Jefferson's and by 1790 under Jefferson's patronage had advanced to become U.S. senator from Virginia.

It was at this time, too, that Jefferson reached out for an alliance with Aaron Burr, another young man on the rise, just old enough to qualify as a Democratic-Republican nominee for senator. Born in February 1756, Burr was the son of a president of the College of New Jersey (now Princeton University) and the grandson of another. He could trace his ancestry back to the earliest Puritans. He had entered Princeton at the age of thirteen, graduated at sixteen, and gone on to become a Revolutionary War hero, rising to the rank of lieutenant colonel at the age of twenty-one. In 1782 he married Theodosia Bartow Prevost, the widow of a former British officer. They moved to New York City, where, like his contemporary Hamilton, Burr built a reputation as an excellent attorney and made important political connections.

In 1789 Burr was appointed attorney general of New York by Governor George Clinton, who described him as "the most rising young man in the state."

In 1791 the New York state assembly, which was controlled by partisans of Clinton, elected Burr to the U.S. Senate, where his brilliance, eloquence, and industry were immediately praised by colleagues.

Burr was a small, handsome man known for his sarcastic and cynical wit. He was not only an abolitionist but among the earliest political figures to argue for the full equality of "female intellectual powers," being a strong advocate of Mary Wollstonecraft's feminist *Vindication of the Rights of Woman*.[7]

Burr put his ideals into practice, unlike Jefferson, who preached abolition but kept his slaves and had no notions of the equality of women. Burr refused to own slaves and gave his own daughters classical educations equal to the best that could be obtained by men. He wrote his daughter Theodosia a series of letters in 1793 about the social and political equality of women, and throughout her brief life he urged her to hone and use her intellectual powers to the utmost.[8]

In May of 1791, Jefferson and Madison went to New York saying they were looking for rare plants and butterflies. In fact, they were looking for political allies against Hamilton's growing power over the nation. They met with Burr and soon thereafter the three formed a coalition which, with the support of Burr's Tammany Society, became the foundation of their new Democratic party.[9]

Burr was not only popular with Democrats in the strategic state of New York, but because of his stylish ways he had become a favorite of Federalists throughout the states. Indeed, the patrician Burr was in the odd position of being a Democrat in direct challenge to the Federalist leadership of Hamilton—comparable to the position of Dwight Eisenhower in the early 1950s when both national parties were courting him.

Hamilton saw Burr as a danger second only to Jefferson. In some ways, Burr's rivalry was felt even more acutely, a peculiarly sharp stick in the eye, because of Hamilton's low birth. Brilliant and attractive, Burr had been born to a position which the bastard Hamilton had had to force for himself by merit and marriage.

By the time of George Washington's unopposed reelection in 1792, the political parties were clearly defined. One evidence of it was the election itself, which had a close vote for vice president between Washington's Federalist running mate, John Adams, and Thomas Jefferson, who represented the Democratic-Republican party.

Adams, a former leader of the Massachusetts rebels, had become a virtual monarchist upon his return from France in the late 1780s. He was scolded by his closest friends, including Mercy Warren, a dramatist and historian of the period:

"From my own judgement and observation soon after your return from Europe in the year 1788, there was an observable alteration in your whole deportment and conversation. Many of your best friends saw, felt and regretted it. . . . Your ideas appeared to be favorable to monarchy and to an order of nobility in your own country."

She reminded Adams of a dinner conversation at his house where, "you insisted the people must have a master, and then added by a stamp of your foot, 'By God, they shall have a master.' In the course of the same evening you observed that you 'wished to see a monarchy in this country and an hereditary one, too.' You added with a considerable degree of emotion that you hated frequent elections, that they were the ruin of the morals of the people. . . ."

Jefferson likewise saw Adams as corrupted by European nobility, saying that Adams had returned from France "in the belief that the general disposition of our citizens was favorable to monarchy."

Despite the prominence and popularity of Washington and Adams, it was Hamilton who more and more was recognized as the true leader of the Federalists. In many respects, Hamilton ran the country during George Washington's two terms. Hamilton's power derived not only from Washington's favor but from his appointment as Washington's preeminent Cabinet officer—secretary of the treasury. This position put Hamilton in alliance with the monied interests of the young nation and through such interests gave him de facto control of the Senate. Opposing him were the Democrats, whom Hamilton called a "Mobocracy . . . hypocritical and violent bawlers for liberty in the very midst of slavery."

In the opinion of John Marshall, the disagreement between Hamilton and Jefferson was "in some measure, a difference of the situations in which they had been placed."

Marshall theorized that Hamilton's experience, being almost exclusively federal, had biased him in that direction, while Jefferson had been so influenced by the French Revolution that he disdained all "monarchal" government:

Until near the close of the war, Mr. Hamilton had served his country in the field, and just before its termination had passed from the camp into congress, where he remained for some time after peace had been established. . . . Mr. Hamilton, therefore, was the friend of a government which should possess in itself, sufficient powers and resources to maintain the character, and defend the integrity of the nation. . . .

Mr. Jefferson had retired from congress after the close of the war and was soon afterwards employed on a mission to the court of Versailles, where he remained [during the French Revolution]. In common with all his countrymen, he felt a strong interest in favor of the reformers; and it is not unreasonable to suppose that while residing at that court and associating with those who meditated some of the great events which have since taken place, his mind might be warmed with the abuses of the monarchy which were perpetually in his view, and he might be led to the opinion that liberty could sustain no danger but from the executive power.

It will be recalled that Jefferson had developed a "secret agent" against Hamilton in the House of Representatives. He was the ghost-writer, Clerk of the House John Beckley. Now in 1792, the third year of Washington's presidency, Beckley learned of a peculiar arrangement between Secretary Hamilton and Mr. and Mrs. James Reynolds, a social-climbing couple described at the time as people who "supported grandeur without apparently having friends, money or industry."

At the time of Beckley's interest, Treasury employee James Reynolds was in prison, charged with suborning perjury in an attempt at some petty swindle in the Treasury Department. On the surface it seemed to be a small matter. But Beckley was quick to check out any irregularity connected to Hamilton's department and he went to the jail to interview Reynolds. From that interview, Beckley unraveled a far more important story.

The clerk learned that Hamilton had been having an affair with Reynolds's wife, Maria, and either as compensation, blackmail, or a loan, Hamilton had paid more than one thousand dollars to the imprisoned Reynolds. This was a large sum. It is impossible to translate exactly into modern dollars, but Hamilton and the other Cabinet secretaries were earning five thousand dollars per annum, so it represented one fifth of his yearly income. (It was also double the salary of an army general of the period, who would have been earning five hundred dollars per annum.)

Beckley carried this information to Jefferson. It is unclear how involved Jefferson was in subsequent events, but just a few days later, Maria Reynolds was visited by a veritable committee of Jefferson henchmen—James Monroe, House Speaker John Muhlenberg, and Congressman Abraham Venable.

The unexpected majesty of their visit may have frightened her because, to their astonishment, Mrs. Reynolds confirmed that, yes, she and Hamilton were having an affair. Did they want proof? Well, she didn't have it because at the urging of her "Alex" she had burned his letters. She told them, however, that Alex had offered her husband "something clever" to leave the capital of Philadelphia and not return. She also said Alex had been a frequent visitor at the Reynolds house. "In the course of the conversation," Monroe recorded in his notes, "Mrs. Reynolds said that Colonel Hamilton had helped her husband from time to time, once giving him $1,100."

Armed with this information, the Jefferson committee next made a "grim and formal" call on Hamilton at his offices on December 15, 1792. Hamilton perceived his interrogators as the "Jacobin Scandal Club."

Other than that description, we have no report of Hamilton's reaction to their visit, but he must have felt the world had collapsed beneath his feet. He played for time, asking to meet again at his house that night so he could prove his innocence. The committee agreed. Hamilton then sent his wife and children out of the city so that he and the "scandal club" would be alone.

The committee arrived that night to find the treasury secretary had been joined by Oliver Wolcott, Hamilton's devoted aide and friend who would act as witness. As the committee listened under furrowed brows, Hamilton proceeded to lay out a full confession:

"Some time in the summer of 1791," he grimly told his accusers, "a woman called at my house in the city of Philadelphia, and asked to speak with me in private. She requested help in getting back to her home in New York to escape a cruel husband.'' Hamilton said he was impressed with her ''seeming air of affliction.'' He had no money with him at the time but promised some later in the day. That evening he took some cash to her address.

''I enquired for Mrs. Reynolds, and was shown upstairs, at the head of which she met me and conducted me into a bedroom. I took the bill out of my pocket and gave it to her. Some conversation ensued from which it was quickly apparent that other than pecuniary consolation would be acceptable.''

Frequent meetings followed, said Hamilton, ''most of them at my own house; Mrs. Hamilton with her children being absent on a visit to her father.'' After some time, he told the astonished committee, he wearied of the affair but could not escape it. He presented the visitors with pleading letters from Maria such as follows:

''I have kept my bed these two days,'' she wrote, ''and now rise from my pillow which your neglect has filled with the sharpest thorns.'' And again, ''I have woes to relate which I never expected to know except by the name. . . . Come therefore tomorrow sometime or else in the evening do I beg you. . . . God had I the world I would lay it at your feet.''

According to historian Jonathan Daniels, Hamilton's interrogators were embarrassed at such full disclosure. But the tale was not done.

''Now,'' said Hamilton, ''there came the blackmail.''

Hamilton presented the astonished visitors another letter from Mrs. Reynolds which warned that her husband needed to be appeased because he had learned of the affair and ''swore he will write Mrs. Hamilton.'' The secretary then produced a letter to him from an ''outraged'' and vengeful James Reynolds:

I am very sorry to find out, Sir, that I have been so cruelly treated by a person that I took to be my best friend instead of that my greatest enemy. You have deprived me of every thing that's near and dear to me. . . . Sir, you took advantage of a poor broken hearted woman. . . . I am now determined to have satisfaction. It shan't be only one family that's miserable.

Hamilton now met with Reynolds, who was by turns friendly and threatening. Finally, just before Christmas, 1791, Reynolds got specific: "I have this proposal to make to you: give me the sum of one thousand dollars and I will leave the town and take my daughter with me and go where my friend shan't hear from me and leave her to yourself to do to her as you think proper."

Hamilton said he paid the blackmail. On December 22, he gave Reynolds $600. On January 3, another $400. In dribbles, Hamilton put out another $415 during the month.

Hamilton looked up at his interrogators, then presented them with all the letters—the evidence which could destroy him.

They took pity. Monroe, Muhlenberg, and Venable "severally acknowledged their entire satisfaction, that the affair had no relation to Official Duties," according to Hamilton's witness Wolcott.

Although Wolcott wrote that the matter was done, Monroe was not so emphatic. In his report of the interview, he said: "We left Mister Hamilton under the impression our suspicions were removed. He acknowledged our conduct toward him had been fair and liberal. He could not complain of it. We brought back all the papers even his own notes, nor did he ask their destruction."

Monroe gave Beckley a report of the meeting and asked that Beckley keep the matter secret because it did not involve Hamilton's official duties. But the secret was not kept. Two days after Hamilton's amazing confession, Jefferson wrote in his notes that "the affair of Reynolds and his wife" was "known to James Monroe, Muhlenberg, Venable, Wolcott, Edmund Randolph, Beckley and Webb." And, of course, to Jefferson himself.

The scandal would remain dormant for four more years, although in the meantime Jefferson and Hamilton continued their war against each other, using the newspapers and the halls of Congress as their battlefields.

A further wedge between the men came in 1793, impelled by events in France where the Revolution was in full fury.

The news from Paris portrayed a world that was topsy-turvy. Up was down and black was white. Nature itself seemed in disorder. The Reign of Terror was directly threatening annihilation of the upper classes.

Louis XVI had been beheaded and France had declared war on Great Britain.

On the floor of Congress, John Randolph warned that such wayward democracy could lead to a national slave rebellion in the United States:

The French Revolution has polluted them, armed [the slaves']
nature against the hand that has fed. . . . I speak from facts when
I say that the night bell never tolls for fire in Richmond that the
mother does not hug her infant more closely to her bosom. I have
been witness of some of the alarms in the capital of Virginia.

We now come to the extraordinary election of 1796 where both party leaders—Hamilton and Jefferson—tried to rig the results *against* their own parties' chosen tickets. Both men's schemes centered around the peculiarities of the Electoral College system, which in those days did not designate who was running for president and who for vice president. Instead, the person receiving the most electoral votes, state by state, became president and the runner-up became vice president. Both Hamilton and Jefferson saw the opportunities for mischief and tampered with it.

The groundwork for their schemes was laid immediately following the Reynolds affair when President Washington approached Jefferson to make political peace, saying Hamilton was ready for such a truce. "The president expressed his wish that Hamilton and myself could coalesce in the measures of government," wrote Jefferson.

But Jefferson was leery of the offer, knowing Washington favored Hamilton not only because of their comradeship during the war but because the president disliked Jefferson's freethinking views on religion.

Jefferson backed away from the truce and instead resigned from the Cabinet, correctly convinced that Washington had come under the complete influence of Hamilton.

With that resignation, the war between the factions became fully engaged. In 1794, the new Democrats won a majority in the House. Two years later, the Democrats gained further momentum when Washington refused to run for a third term. Hamilton, unpopular with the masses, did not offer himself as a political candidate but instead conspired to deny the nomination to the anointed Federalist candidate, Adams. Hamilton favored Thomas Pinckney of South Carolina, whom he felt he could control.

There were no nominating conventions at that time and, except for the press and a little stump speaking, very little of today's contests of lies and other entertainments. In those days, they literally met in smoke-filled rooms, where the party chose Adams, who had been vice president during Washington's two terms.

On his side, Jefferson was named the Democratic candidate with Aaron Burr as the vice presidential nominee, a move dictated by the geography of the Electoral College, which needed Burr's northern votes. Jefferson and his fellow Virginians, however, were not so keen on the idea. They now viewed the popular Burr as the threat to a "Virginia Dynasty," an ambitious strategy whereby Jefferson, Madison, and James Monroe would succeed each other in the White House. Nevertheless, the Virginians agreed to back Burr because of the electoral arithmetic. The Democrats entered the election expecting to lose but hoping to make a good showing and pave the way for victory in 1800. So far, so good, except that Jefferson, too, had a conspiracy to turn. He figured to slow Burr down so that he would not be a threat to the dynasty.

As it turned out, the results would be better than they expected, thanks to their archenemy, Hamilton.

Hamilton and Adams thoroughly disliked one another, largely because they were two bulls in the same pen. Determined to sink Adams, Hamilton secretly lobbied Federalist electors in the South to vote for South Carolina's Pinckney and Jefferson, an all-South ticket which Hamilton supposed would deny votes for the official party candidate, Adams, and just might put his man Pinckney in the White House.

Not to be outdone in chicanery, Jefferson was pursuing his own plan against *his* party's choice by denying Burr electoral votes in Virginia.

Thus, by the time the electoral vote was due to be taken in the various state capitals the situation was this: The Federalists had nominated Adams and Pinckney, but the party leader, Hamilton, was secretly working to upset the ticket. The Democrats had nominated Jefferson and Burr, but their party leader, Jefferson, was working to embarrass Burr.

In Virginia, where the Democrats were strongest, Jefferson-controlled delegates gave one vote to Burr and fifteen votes to seventy-four-year-old Samuel Adams of Massachusetts, the Revolutionary War hero. Sam Adams, however, was *not* a candidate for any political office in 1796. The Virginia votes were simply an unexpected bouquet thrown toward him to take them away from Burr.

Historian Jonathan Daniels sarcastically notes, "Jefferson's great admiration for this early Revolutionary agitator strongly suggests that it was he who chose this Adams as one to whom votes could be thrown. . . ."

Hamilton's ploy misfired in a completely unexpected way. When results were in, John Adams prevailed with seventy-one votes. But to everyone's surprise, Hamilton's machinations had placed Jefferson a very strong second with sixty-eight votes. These votes were sufficient to elect Jefferson vice president—that office then going to the candidate with the second-highest vote, regardless of party affiliation.

In the fallout, the two *official* vice presidential candidates, Pinckney and Burr, ran third and fourth respectively, having been swindled out of the game.

Although the betrayal was obvious, Burr made no public protest. Instead, he proceeded to strengthen his power base in New York so that next time he might withstand the Virginians on more equal terms. It was an early example of "Don't get mad, get even."

In the aftermath of the election, Jefferson's provocateur, House clerk John Beckley, resurrected the James and Maria Reynolds scandal. It was done with Jefferson's knowledge and probable encouragement. But this maneuver carried a kicker, sort of a delayed time bomb which would explode in Jefferson's face years later. The bomb came in the person of an immigrant Scottish journalist named James Callender. Jefferson's alliance with Callender would come back to haunt the tall Virginian far beyond his lifetime.

For his debut, Callender authored a provocative pamphlet titled *The History of the United States for 1796.*

The broadsheet had little to do with 1796 or the United States, but it had very much to do with the history of Alexander Hamilton and Maria Reynolds. Reproduced were all the documents presented "in secret" to the Monroe committee some four and a half years earlier.

Although Jefferson's fingerprints were everywhere, there was no intimation in the preface or in the book of his complicity, except for a gratuitous introduction saying Jefferson's writings were "information without parade, and eloquence without effort." Callender also wrote that the government had "sagged" when Jefferson left Washington's Cabinet. As for Hamilton, he was "a threadbare lawyer."

The *History* landed in Philadelphia in June 1797 and was an instant sensation.

Hamilton was understandably furious, feeling he had been betrayed. The gentleman's code of silence in such matters had been violated. But who had done it? Monroe? Beckley? Jefferson? In reply to Hamilton's enraged inquiries, Monroe swore that he knew nothing about it and insisted that his copy of the documents "remained sealed, deposited in the hands of a respectable character in Virginia."

Who might that be? Hamilton was sure it was Thomas Jefferson. But thinking Monroe was lying, convinced that the little Virginian had violated a trust, Hamilton challenged him to a duel. Having little choice but to accept, a reluctant Monroe chose as his second his Senate friend Aaron Burr, a move that further outraged Hamilton because Burr was his foremost enemy. But, in fact, Burr may have saved one duelist's life. Prior to the duel, Burr met with Hamilton and deftly arranged a statement which Monroe could in honor sign and Hamilton could in honor accept.

The duel was canceled.

In the meantime, Hamilton continued to spin out of control.

After all his efforts to keep the Reynolds affair secret, he now published—over his own name and with his wife's agreement—an amazing confession. It included fifty pages detailing his trysts with Maria Reynolds, supported by another fifty pages of related letters and documents.

This extraordinary confession seems to have stemmed from Hamilton's belief that Jefferson's true design was to show that the money paid to Reynolds was not simple sexual blackmail but was part of an embezzlement scheme at the Treasury. Wrote Hamilton:

> *The charge against me is a connection with one James Reynolds*
> *for purposes of improper pecuniary speculation. My* real *crime is*

an amorous connection with his wife for a considerable time,
with his privy and connivance, if not originally brought on by a
combination between the husband and wife with the design to extort
money from me.

Jefferson must have fainted with delight at this turn of events. He
gleefully bought fifteen copies as gifts for friends, writing them that
Hamilton's ''willingness to plead guilty to adultery seems rather to
have strengthened than weakened the suspicions that he was in truth
guilty of speculations.''

During the next two years, as Jefferson moved toward the presidency,
the eighteenth century was drawing to a close. It was more than a
century, however, that was ending. It was an epoch. The wigged and
powdered men of the Enlightenment had done their jobs. Their world
had finally been pulled together into one piece, circumnavigated by
thought as well as by sailing ships. The era of kingdoms was giving
way to acts of empire.

The Age of Enlightenment had been exemplified by the American
Revolution, bringing much of the world to a secular philosophy. Feudal
structures and the great religions had been knocked down and people
encouraged to perceive value in their individual lives. The individual
was pressured to believe only what he or she could see, hear, smell,
taste, touch, or measure. Enlightenment, as exemplified in America,
raised the individual to the position of ultimate importance, adopted a
new faith in the progress of mankind, with the state as the natural
agent.

Although the century had begun with witch trials and a belief that
Indians were allied to the Evil One, it was ending with studies of
psychology, texts on hypnosis, and discussion of exotic phenomena
such as ''multiple personality.'' It was agreed that possession and
witchcraft did not exist, and superstition was being cast aside.[10]

Napoleon was conquering much of Europe. Haydn was composing
operas. Awakening from an opium-induced dream, Coleridge wrote
Kubla Khan and followed with *The Rime of the Ancient Mariner*. Goya
completed *Naked Maja*.

In America, Fulton had invented the *Nautilus*, a hand-operated, four-man submarine. Charles Brockden Brown published *Alcuin*, the first feminist novel. Defying reports that iron would poison the soil, the American Charles Newbold patented the first cast-iron plow, an invention that would change the world. Eli Whitney's cotton gin (1793), coupled with the first successful American sugar refinery, in New Orleans (1791), fueled the economics of slavery in the American South. Those technologies—the iron plow, the gin, and sugar refinement— spurred large-scale cultivation and geometrically multiplied the demand for field labor. Meanwhile, in the North, Whitney had also invented a musket-making machine which was hailed as the origin of mass production.

On March 3, 1797, Thomas Jefferson was installed in Philadelphia as president of the American Philosophical Society, sort of a Yankee equivalent of the French Academy. He was inaugurated the following day as vice president of the United States. Jefferson considered the philosophical appointment to be the greater of the two honors.

His new president, Adams, sent a delegation to Paris to mend relations with Napoleon's regime. But, emboldened by military success, the French ministers wanted bribes and asked for a loan from the United States before negotiations could begin. An outraged Adams identified the officials to Congress as X, Y, and Z, and the XYZ Affair of 1798 led to an undeclared naval war between France and the United States. It also led directly to the establishment by the Congress of a standing U.S. Navy.

In another foreign incident, a twenty-gun American warship, the *Baltimore*, was intercepted by a British squadron, boarded, and forced to surrender fifty-five of its crew whom the British claimed were deserters from the British Navy. Although all but five of the U.S. sailors were promptly returned, the affair caused great outrage in America and the *Baltimore*'s captain was dismissed from the service because he had not resisted.[11] Tempers were cooled when the British government disavowed the action of its captains and gave orders that henceforward American ships would be respected. They wanted no retaliatory raids on English coasts by American seamen such as John Paul Jones.

In the meanwhile, Hamilton and Adams had about had their fill of the wild-swinging assaults from Callender and other members of the Jeffersonian press. Claiming that a national emergency existed because of the undeclared French naval war, Hamilton persuaded Adams and Congress to pass the Alien and Sedition Acts in the summer of 1798. Ostensibly enacted on grounds of "national security," the four acts were in fact aimed at crippling Jefferson's Democratic party. (The Naturalization Act raised the residency requirement for citizenship from five years to fourteen years, thus disenfranchising and intimidating thousands of immigrants, mostly Irish, who had enrolled in the Democratic party. The Sedition Act was supposed to silence the administration's enemies by banning spoken or written criticism against (1) the government, (2) the Congress, or (3) the president.)

Although the acts nullified the guarantees of free speech and free press, both were upheld by the Supreme Court. The legislation was fiercely resisted by the Democrats. At the urging of Jefferson and Madison, the states of Kentucky and Virginia passed resolutions nullifying the acts on grounds that they were unconstitutional. Jefferson predicted the Alien and Sedition Laws could lead to a second revolution. But even as he waged war against the new acts, ten people were convicted. All of them were Democrats. All of them were journalists. And all went to prison.

The debates swept the country, involving the famous and the unknown, pro and con. In Virginia, two to three thousand people were on hand to hear Patrick Henry, grown conservative in his old age, caution against resistance.

Henry did not defend the correctness of the laws but instead concentrated on the hopeless consequences of challenging them. "Defy the President and the Congress," bellowed Henry, "and George Washington will roll over the dissenting states at the head of a federal army, and who will go against him?"

For perhaps two minutes there was silence in that Virginia square. No individuals among the thousands present dared answer Henry. Finally, a tall, slender young man stepped forward and took the speaker's stage. He bowed his compliments to Henry, to the crowd, and in a tenor's voice, so high it was almost feminine, asked all federal officers present to pay close attention. "For I herewith *damn* John Adams as a tyrant. I *damn* his Congress as the tool of tyranny and I stand here in defiance of the Sedition Act and *dare* arrest." He spent the next two hours lashing away with invective, in full challenge of the penalties. When he finished, none dared arrest him. They would have been lynched by the crowd.

The orator's name, the successor and conqueror of the great Patrick Henry, was John Randolph of Roanoke, and it was his first political speech.

Meanwhile, in this dark period for America, when the fear and reality of tyranny were at their height, Jefferson reassured a young college student, William Green Munford, that human intelligence would prevail:

> *I am one of those who think well of the human character generally. I consider man as formed for society, and endowed by nature with those dispositions which fit him for society. . . . To preserve the freedom of the human mind and freedom of the press, every spirit should be ready to devote itself to martyrdom, for as long as we may think as we will, and speak as we think, the condition of man will proceed in improvement.*

Jefferson's biographer Dumas Malone believes that in this letter Jefferson was showing that his ultimate hopes for humanity rested "not on any particular form of political organization or government, but on the freedom of intelligence."

Ultimately, the Democrats prevailed as the debate over the acts carried into the election of 1800 and was a major factor in the Democrats' victory.[12]

But the paths of Burr, Jefferson, and Hamilton were converging with increasing speed. The three men were locked in ruinous and deadly entanglements, and over the years their alliances and rivalries would shift like muds in the tide. Hamilton would be killed. Burr would be ruined. Only Jefferson would survive.

Meriwether Lewis

• • • • • • • • •

Even as the careers of Jefferson, Hamilton, and Burr headed to collision, there arrived on the national scene a new actor of promise. Meriwether Lewis was born on August 18, 1774. It was less than a year before Lexington and Concord, and Meriwether was the eldest of the five children of Robert Lewis and Lucy Meriwether.

Like his kinsman Jefferson, Lewis was raised in the Albemarle district of Virginia, red-clay country lush with bluegrass, catalpas, oaks, maples, and mimosa. Lewis's forebears, Nicholas Meriwether and Abraham Lewis, had pioneered the Albemarle, clearing the land and plowing the soil in a beautiful broad valley at the foot of the Blue Ridge Mountains beside the Fluvanna River.[1]

The Lewis family was very much part of the Virginia establishment, being among the earliest settlers of the area that is now the city of Charlottesville, close friends of the Masons, the Henrys, the Jeffersons, Randolphs, and Clarks. Meriwether's great uncle was married to a sister of George Washington. The boy himself grew up in a land of cavaliers—of aristocratic estates, fox hunts, and the lavish balls required by Virginia hospitality. But it was a world the British would soon put to flames.

Meriwether's father, Robert Lewis, was a lieutenant at Yorktown but died of pneumonia in the month following the battle.

Most of what we know about Meriwether's early days comes from Thomas Jefferson, who recorded that following the father's death, the boy

> continued some years under the fostering care of a tender mother
> . . . and was remarkable even in infancy for enterprise, boldness
> and discretion. When only eight years of age, he habitually went
> out in the dead of night alone with his dogs into the forest to hunt
> the raccoon and opossum. . . . No season or circumstance could
> obstruct his purpose, plunging through the winter's snows and
> frozen streams in pursuit of his object.

Shortly after the war, Meriwether's widowed mother, Lucy Lewis, married Captain John Marks, a wealthy landowner who carried Lucy and Meriwether to a new plantation in Oglethorpe County, Georgia, allowing the growing Meriwether to alternate between his homes in Virginia and Georgia.

As the boy grew into adolescence, he developed a reputation for coolheadedness. His biographer Richard Dillon describes young Lewis returning from a hunt and encountering a ferocious bull in a field. "The snorting beast lowered its head and charged the boy. Instead of running for cover, Lewis stood his ground, cocked the heavy hammer of his flintlock rifle and shot the animal dead in its tracks."

While the twelve-year-old Lewis was in Georgia:

> The Cherokees were on the warpath. He was with a body of
> settlers hiding in the woods. One of the men stupidly kindled a
> fire, giving away their location to the Indians. A shot was heard;
> the men panicked. Here and there they ran, grabbing up rifles
> while silhouetted by the dancing flames of the bright cookfire. Only
> young Meriwether Lewis had the presence of mind to dash a bucket
> of water on the fire to prevent his elders from becoming sitting-
> duck targets for the hostiles.[2]

Following his stepfather's death in 1792, Meriwether became head of the family and brought his mother and brothers back to Albemarle County, where he continued his education under private tutors. Here he also began to manage his father's thousand-acre estate with the help of his uncles. He became a successful farmer, "assiduous and attentive," Jefferson would note, "observing with minute attention all plants and insects he met with."

In 1794, President Washington called for troops to suppress the Whiskey Rebellion, a revolt by isolated farmers in western Pennsylvania who refused to pay a federal tax for the manufacture of whiskey. The making of whiskey was about the only way farmers could sell surplus grain because the nation's roads were virtually nonexistent and New Orleans was sealed by the Spanish. Nevertheless, Alexander Hamilton insisted on the tax to finance his Assumption Plan, and George Washington felt obliged to back his treasury secretary, right or wrong, thus proving the axiom that when authority is threatened, justice is the victim.

Ignoring the moral details, Meriwether was among the first to volunteer his services, joining the militia, where he served under Alexander Hamilton. By the time Lewis's Virginia volunteers reached Pennsylvania, however, the farmers were fleeing down the Ohio and Mississippi to safety in Spanish Louisiana. (Only a handful of rebels were captured and they were later pardoned by Washington.)

The failure to engage rebels was a disappointment to Meriwether, who wrote his mother: "I can see no honour or profit to be gained by living at the expense of the public without rendering her any service." But he was otherwise playful in his letters home, asking his mother to send his regards to "all the girls in Albemarle" and warning that he might be bringing "an Insurgent girl to see [you] next fall, bearing the title of Mrs. Lewis."

It was not to happen.

He loved solitary life. On October 4, 1794, he wrote to his mother, "We have mountains of beef and oceans of whiskey, and I feel myself able to share it with the heartiest fellow in camp." He was loath to return home to the farming routines of Locust Hill and decided instead to visit Kentucky to look over lands held by his mother there. Returning to his unit, he joined the regular army in May 1795 to become an ensign and soon was being swept down the Ohio to join the force of General "Mad Anthony" Wayne, victor over the Indians at Fallen Timbers. Lewis was present at Wayne's headquarters when the chiefs of the Wyandottes, Delawares, Ottawas, Shawnees, Chippewas, Miamis, Kickapoos, and other tribes filed in to set their hands to the Treaty of Greenville, August 3, 1795—a treaty that was "to put an end to a destructive war, to settle all controversies, and to restore harmony and friendly intercourse between the United States and Indian tribes."

It was Lewis's first direct contact with Indians and would spark a lifelong interest in them.

On November 6, 1795, he got into a scrap with a fellow officer, New York Lieutenant John Elliott, who claimed that a drunken Lewis had burst into Elliott's quarters and challenged him to a duel. A court-martial was held and the court decided resoundingly in Ensign Lewis's favor, the verdict being that he should "be acquitted with Honor."

To prevent further friction, however, Lewis was reassigned to the Chosen Rifle Company of elite riflemen-sharpshooters commanded by William Clark, a fellow Albemarlean. Meriwether's brief, eight-month association with Clark would begin an enduring friendship that several years later would prompt Lewis to enlist Clark as co-leader of the famous Pacific expedition, honoring a "long and uninterrupted friendship and confidence which has subsisted between us," Lewis would write.

Among Lewis's other friends in the unit was one Tarleton Bates of Pittsburgh, brother of a man who would become a major enemy when Lewis was governor of the Louisiana Territory.

Throwing himself into the military life, Meriwether wrote his mother, "[T]he general idea is that the Army is the school of debauchery but, believe me, it has ever proven the school of experience and prudence to your affectionate son."

In 1796, Meriwether was admitted to the Masonic Order.[3]

In this period, he was somewhat of a dandy, complaining to a friend of an inadequate tailor: "It would take up three sheets of paper, written in shorthand, to point out its deficiencies or, I may even say, deformities . . . the lace is deficient . . . the cape is deficient . . ." and so on.

Despite his later accomplishments, Meriwether was not a born trailblazer. During a march in 1796 from Detroit to Pittsburgh he got lost twice, running out of rations and *really* hungry for maybe the first time in his life, but not the last.

In the fall of 1797, he took command of Fort Pickering, a small post being built on the banks of the Mississippi at Chickasaw Bluffs, the site of modern Memphis. This is the same Fort Pickering that would play a key role in the final days of his life.

Located on the borders of several nations including the Chickasaws, Choctaws, and Cherokees, the new post was a university in the ways of Indians, and Meriwether submerged himself in the study of Indian customs and languages. In early 1799, Lewis was given a respite to do recruiting duty at Charlottesville, a short hop from his Locust Hill home. On March 3, he was promoted to lieutenant and afterward assigned to the Indian frontier at Detroit. In December 1800, he was promoted to captain, and while he was on temporary assignment in Pittsburgh, there would come a letter from the president.

Thomas Jefferson wanted Captain Lewis to come live at the White House as his personal secretary.

James Wilkinson

• • • • • • • • • •

IN LATE 1796, Surveyor-General Andrew Ellicott was in the Mississippi Territory to map western borders when outgoing president George Washington asked him to look into rumors that the Army's commanding general, James Wilkinson, was in the hire of Spain. It wasn't until after Washington left office, however, that Ellicott found his proof. On November 14, 1798, Ellicott sent to Philadelphia a copy of a letter written by Don Manuel Gayoso, governor of Spanish Louisiana. In the letter, Gayoso referred to Wilkinson's receiving payments from Spain, noting that certain incriminating documents "are all safe and never will be used against" Wilkinson if the general "will conduct himself with propriety—[because] the originals are at the court" in Madrid.

Ellicott's copy of the sensational evidence was given to President Adams's secretary of state, Timothy Pickering.

Government men were as loath then as now to investigate scandal in their own ranks. A horrified Pickering ordered Ellicott to drop the matter instantly. The secretary then informed President Adams that Ellicott had submitted certain rumors of Wilkinson's treason which were in fact unsubstantiated. Because of Pickering's endorsement, Adams felt compelled by honor to inform Wilkinson that there had been an investigation and to assure the general, "I respect your services and feel an attachment to your person, as I do every man whose name and character I have so long known in the service of our country, whose behavior has been consistent."

Who was this Wilkinson who stirred such dark suspicions and hasty apologies? The Marylander James Wilkinson first surfaces as a young officer in the Revolutionary War, where he was a colleague and contemporary of Alexander Hamilton and Aaron Burr. By the age of twenty, Wilkinson had become a hero at Saratoga and was promoted to brigadier general. From there he rose to commandant of the U.S. Army—to be honored, promoted, and reconfirmed by four successive presidents, Washington, Adams, Jefferson, and Madison. As commandant, he would be Jefferson's chief witness in the 1807 treason trial of Aaron Burr, and during all that time, from George Washington through Madison, he was secretly on the payroll of the king of Spain as "Number 13."

Fourteen years younger than Jefferson but a contemporary of Hamilton and Burr, Jamey Wilkinson was born in 1757 in Calvert County, Maryland, the Tidewater region of the peninsula formed by the Patuxent and Potomac rivers. Jamey's family was of the lesser landed gentry, and like many of his class, the boy received private tutoring until the age of fifteen when he was sent away to Philadelphia to study medicine. He arrived there in 1772, an impressionable teenaged boy, shorter than average but well-built and handsome. Almost immediately he became a hanger-on and mascot to the King's Royal Irish Regiment, which was then quartered in the city.

"I arrived in the evening," he tells us in his *Memoirs*, "and understanding a detachment of soldiers were quartered in the northern quarters, I, the next day, visited the barracks where four companies of the 18th or Royal Irish Regiment of infantry and a company of Royal artillery were stationed."

Fascinated, he gazed at their drill: "It appeared like enchantment, and my bosom throbbed with delight and that day inspired in me that love of things military ever after the guiding star of my life."

While at Philadelphia, he witnessed the opening of the first Continental Congress. A short time afterward, he graduated from medical school and returned to Maryland, where he began a practice. Then came the "shot heard round the world" at Lexington Green on April 19, 1775.

When the news filtered down to the Maryland bogs, young Jamey gave up his practice and went north to join the army then being organized by George Washington at Cambridge. On his way through Philadelphia, the boy was impressed with how much the city had changed in just two years:

> . . . the deepest gloom overcast the whole population; the blows of war were sudden and unexpected; the sword had been drawn; blood had been spilt, and lives had been lost. The citizens were seen assembled in crowds at the corners of the streets; alarm and terror were excited, but the bitter animosities of civil contest still slumbered; the whole city exhibited a scene of funereal gloom and stillness; men spoke in whispers, as if afraid of being overheard, and the solemn peal which issued from the bells of Christ Church gave to the conjuncture an air of mournful solemnity and oppressed with sorrow the unoffending loyal subjects of the largest city in British America. But this submission was short-lived; it soon gave way to indignation, resentment and denunciations.

He enlisted as a medical officer in a militia rifle company and served in several of the early campaigns, being quartered beside and friendly with Benedict Arnold, Aaron Burr, Alexander Hamilton, Charles Lee, and Horatio Gates.

Benefiting from his youthful exposure to the Royal Irish, Wilkinson soon established himself as a forceful disciplinarian in the young army. After the British evacuated Boston in the spring of 1776, Washington's troops marched away to besiege New York. Wilkinson, now a captain in that army, gave an order to an elderly New England lieutenant to form a marching column. The Yankee lieutenant was old enough to be Jamey's father and declined to obey such a stripling from the South. As Wilkinson tells it in his *Memoirs*, he immediately put the older officer under arrest, only to be confronted by the Yankee enlisted men who likewise refused Wilkinson's orders. At that juncture, wrote

Wilkinson, "I pulled my sword and announced that I would proceed from left to right, running every man through until they obeyed my orders or my strength failed longer to support me."

The men got the message. The aged lieutenant was arrested. And Jamey's conduct was brought to the attention of General Washington himself, a man who was particularly concerned about the lack of discipline in his army. Jamey quickly added to his reputation a few months later at Montreal when he saved a trapped brigade from capture by the British. General Benedict Arnold promoted the lad to major.

About that time the Congress gave a major general's commission to Horatio Gates, the former English officer who had defected to the Americans. Gates had come to the American army with great expectations. Of humble origins (his father was undistinguished and his mother an upstairs servant), Gates had left England and the British Army to escape a rigid social system that blocked advancement. Although General Washington had expressed doubts about Gates's loyalty and competence, to his dismay Congress appointed Gates to be the new commanding officer of the "army in Canada," an army that barely existed.

Needing a drillmaster, Gates offered Jamey the job of brigade-major on his staff and Wilkinson accepted. The why of the promotion is unclear. Part of it had to do with Wilkinson's reputation as a disciplinarian. But a contemporary historian hazarded the guess that Wilkinson "pandered to the vanity" of the pompous general. There is probably truth in that, too, because we know from other sources that Gates was peculiarly susceptible to flattery.

Gates and Wilkinson were men of ambition, a middle-aged Englishman with an inferiority complex but powerful connections and a young American with bounding confidence and exceptional energy. They became perhaps not like father and son but more like a rich uncle and a favored nephew.

No sooner were they joined up than Wilkinson became involved in the curious capture of another of Washington's senior generals, an ex–British officer named Charles Lee, whose loyalty was also suspect by Washington.

Two weeks before Christmas, 1776, Wilkinson was riding hard to carry a message from Gates to Washington. Arriving at Basking Ridge, New Jersey, Wilkinson stumbled into the divisional headquarters of General Lee to be told that the general was asleep. Wilkinson wrapped himself in a cloak and took his own rest for the remainder of the night in a corner of the main room of the tavern.

The next morning, a hungry and cold Jamey awoke to find General Lee hogging the fire and cursing their mutual commander in chief, George Washington:

> *General Lee observed that [Washington's] siege of Boston had led us into great errors; that the attempt to defend islands against a superior land and naval force was madness; that Sir William Howe could have given us checkmate at his discretion; and that we owed our salvation to Howe's indolence, or disinclination to terminate the war.*

According to Wilkinson, Lee then proceeded to "waste the rest of the morning in altercation with certain militia corps who were of his command, arguing about uniforms. . . ." To the hungry Jamey's annoyance, the general didn't cease his scoldings and pause for breakfast until ten. No sooner were the two trenchermen digging into their steaks and potatoes than a British cavalry troop made a surprise appearance. Wilkinson reported the incident in his *Memoirs*:

> *Having dined, I had risen from the table and was looking out of an end window down a lane about a hundred yards in length. It was then I discovered a party of British dragoons turn a corner of the avenue at a full charge. Startled at this unexpected spectacle, I exclaimed, "Here, sir, are the British cavalry." Where? replied the general. "Around the house," for they had encompassed the building.*

Wilkinson drew his pistols and looked for the general's guards. They were gone. "Accordingly, I sought a position where I could not be approached by more than one person at a time and with a pistol in each hand I awaited the expected search, resolved to shoot the first and the second person who might appear and then to appeal to my sword.''

The next thing Wilkinson heard, however, was a British voice declaring, "If the general does not surrender in five minutes, I will set fire to the house." A few seconds later, he heard the same British voice saying in a more relaxed tone, "Here is the general, he has surrendered."

There were hurrahs from the British troops and the sound of a bugle. Wilkinson peered out to see General Lee ignominiously being mounted on a horse—even worse luck!—*Wilkinson's* horse, "which stood ready at the door. The general was then hurried off by the British in triumph, bareheaded, in his slippers and blanket coat, his collar open and his shirt very much soiled from several days' use.''

The third-ranking officer in the American army had been hauled in like a tub of fish, even as his commanding general, Washington, was routing the Hessians and chasing the British to Princeton.

In his *Memoirs*, Wilkinson did not miss the chance to observe that had Lee obeyed Washington's order to cross the Delaware, there would have been no capture; had Lee not dawdled over breakfast to abuse his commander in chief, there would have been no disgrace.

The capture of such a high-ranking commander was an exhilarating albeit temporary victory for the British and a demoralizing disaster for the Americans. (A few months later, the British exchanged Lee for some of their officers, recognizing perhaps that the disputatious Lee was of more value to them in the American army than in a British prison camp. In 1780, Lee was finally dismissed from the army because of his unsoldierly slanders against Washington.)

As for Jamey, the British were so exultant over the capture of Lee that they stopped further search and overlooked the young man in the closet. Wilkinson carried his message, and very bad news, on to Washington, then rejoined Gates, who was on the march to Fort Ticonderoga in northeastern New York State.

There, at Ticonderoga, Wilkinson's toadying would lead to new advancement.

Strategically located near Lake Champlain on a main water route between Canada and New York City, Ticonderoga controlled the Hudson Valley, the northern doorway to the colonies. Known as ''The

Gibraltar of America,'' it had been captured from the British by Ethan Allen and his "Green Mountain Boys" in 1775. Now, Gates wanted to use it as his base for a Canadian invasion, hoping to add Quebec and Montreal to the American flag. In June 1777, however, Gates decided to move his command. As he prepared to leave, he failed to heed Wilkinson's advice to fortify a strategic ridge that overlooked the fort. Occupation of the ridge, Wilkinson noted, would protect a small American garrison Gates had left there to guard his flanks.

Wilkinson was right. Not three weeks later that same ridge was occupied by General "Gentleman Johnny" Burgoyne, who used it to recapture Ticonderoga, an event that Burgoyne happily proclaimed as one victory "that even American newspapers could not explain away."

Desperate to avoid blame for the disaster, Gates called on his political supporters in Congress for protection. At the same time, Gates asked his aide Wilkinson to maintain silence about his abandonment of the strategic ridge.

The cover-up worked. Gates's reputation survived and three months later Gates redeemed himself when he found Burgoyne at Saratoga. It was in that pivotal battle that Gates, grateful to Wilkinson for keeping his silence about the Ticonderoga blunder, bypassed Morgan and Arnold, promoted Wilkinson, a lad of twenty, to colonel, and delegated him to receive Burgoyne's sword in surrender. Wilkinson would rise to higher rank in his lifetime, but never again would his world be so wonderful.

The victory over Burgoyne gave confidence to a group of generals who wanted to oust General Washington and replace him with Gates, the new "Hero of Saratoga." The conspiracy would become infamous as the "Conway Cabal," named after General Thomas Conway, an Irish-born officer, previously in the French army, who had become Inspector General of Washington's army. Conway and Gates were backed by a faction in the Continental Congress plus a number of distinguished revolutionaries who included Washington's own disgruntled supply general, Thomas Mifflin, and the famed Philadelphia physician, scientist, and signer of the Declaration of Independence Benjamin Rush.[1] Their plan was to build a publicity campaign against

Washington and then have Congress vote the Virginian out of command.

Wilkinson, initially a bit player in the cabal, became the inadvertent cause of its exposure. Furthermore, with his uncanny knack for survival, he would not only avoid blame in the attempted putsch but emerge from the scandal with honors.

The scheme began to unravel in November 1777 at Gates's headquarters outside Philadelphia, where the general had been receiving letters from Conway about the coup. In the midst of the planning there came alarming news: Washington had somehow received copies of the Gates-Conway correspondence. The warning was soon confirmed by Conway himself, warning Gates that the plot had been uncovered by Washington.

Immediately, the conspirators began covering their tracks while Gates turned his attention to finding the traitor among them. There was a spy, certainly, but was he a soldier or a member of Congress?

As Gates pondered his problem, Wilkinson suggested the tipster must be Washington's young and ambitious aide, Colonel Alexander Hamilton. Hamilton had visited the Gates camp about the time the plot was unraveling. Hamilton had free run of Gates's headquarters and he was famously loyal to his chief. These were peculiarities enough to condemn him in Wilkinson's mind.

Acting on Wilkinson's suspicions, Gates tried a ploy. He informed General Washington that the advice of a cabal was false. The truth was, said Gates, that the rumor had been planted by a provocateur— perhaps in Congress, or maybe in Washington's own camp. Gates asked for an investigation so that ''your Excellency obtain as soon as possible a discovery, which so deeply affects the safety of the States. Crimes of this magnitude ought not to remain unpunished.''

Washington immediately saw through the gambit and riposted deftly, sending his reply to Gates via the President of Congress so that it would get wide distribution. Washington advised Gates that the ''provocateur'' was in fact ''your Colonel Wilkinson, [who] on his way to Congress October last fell in with Lord Stirling at Reading and, not in confidence, informed his aide de camp, Major McWilliams, that General Conway had written thus to you.''

It turned out that Wilkinson had gotten drunk with Stirling at a Reading tavern and spilled the entire story. Stirling had then informed George Washington.

Gates was apoplectic. He stood not only accused as a traitor but made to look a fool in the bargain. To save his reputation, Gates confronted Wilkinson and publicly accused *him* of being the provocateur, saying Wilkinson had made up the plot in order to ruin Gates.

General Washington must have hurt his sides laughing at such developments. But it got better. The next day saw Wilkinson challenging the elderly Gates to a duel. It was an act of utmost cheek because not only was Gates some thirty years older than Wilkinson, he was also his commanding officer.

Nevertheless, brushing aside threats of a court-martial, the cocky Wilkinson and his second showed up on the dueling field with loaded pistols at eight o'clock on the appropriate morning. They were met by Gates, unarmed, who asked for a private talk with his subaltern.

The old man took his former protégé for a short walk. Then, according to Wilkinson's account, Gates "burst into tears; took me by the hand, asked, did I injure you? I should as soon think of injuring my child."

Wilkinson, feeling "flattered, pleased," backed off from the duel. Gates next went to General Washington, pleading innocence and saying that he had "no personal connection nor previous correspondence" with Conway. As far as Gates knew, there was no cabal.

Gates was lying and Washington and Congress both knew he was lying. But inasmuch as the coup was crushed, and in the interest of national unity, Washington let the matter lie.

One ironical twist of the affair was that Wilkinson emerged a winner. Washington forever afterward thought Jamey, in the national interest, had deliberately betrayed Gates.[2]

Swollen with confidence, Wilkinson now began courting the Philadelphia heiress Anne Biddle, a member of the Biddle family whose male members had gained prominence as heroes in the war and would go on to become successful merchants.

James Wilkinson and Anne Biddle were married in Christ Church, Philadelphia, on the twelfth of November, 1778—eight months after the final act of the cabal. For the remainder of the war, Wilkinson remained close to Philadelphia while steadily moving up in the ranks. By war's end, he was a brigadier general, personally appointed by General Washington, who continued to credit Jamey with rescuing him from the Conway Cabal.

With the end of the war in 1783, Wilkinson used his wife's connections to find a job with a Philadelphia fur-trading concern and the couple moved to Kentucky, the new frontier.

Kentucky and Spain
• • • • • • • • •

AT THE CLOSE of the war, the American West was considered to be those lands between the Alleghenies and the Mississippi, a region first mapped by Europeans in the late 1600s when French trappers and missionaries explored from Canada down through the entire Mississippi Valley. For much of the century that followed, the area was closed to Americans by the barrier of the Alleghenies.

Although there had been some Virginian exploration west of the Alleghenies as early as 1670, the man who opened the region to settlement was a North Carolina farmer named Finlay, believed by some to be a wandering lunatic, who found a pass across the Blue Ridge and returned to his family after a long absence "with accounts of the marvellous beauty and riches of the country beyond the mountains."[1]

That same year, Finlay led a return party to this new land of Kentucky. Among his group was a Pennsylvania frontiersman by the name of Daniel Boone.

This land across the mountains was a paradise, the likes of which had never been seen in the Old World. North of the Ohio River was a forest home for numerous Indian tribes. South of the river was Kentucky, a wide tract of country unclaimed even by Indians, stretching across some 240,000 square miles, five times the size of England, larger than the nation of France. Watered by many streams, Kentucky was the Indians' legendary "happy hunting ground" in which there were vast herds of elk and deer disturbed only occasionally by a hunting party of braves. Here white families saw their first buffalo, buffalo that roamed in herds of thousands, buffalo that within sixty years would no longer exist east of the Mississippi. Here, in a land of moderate climate, were hardwood forests unencumbered by brushwood, stretching like a vast park from horizon to horizon across the entire territory. Poplars, oaks, and sycamores grew two hundred feet high. Abundant springs and streams, vast meadows and numerous salt licks. Pheasant, grouse, and passenger pigeons, delectable to eat, made the sky dark with their flight, putting the sun into eclipse.

News of this Eden spread among the frontier settlements of Virginia and the Carolinas and into Pennsylvania and the Northeast.

The first permanent Kentucky settlement was established by Finlay's agent, Daniel Boone, at some mineral springs, now Harrodsburg, in 1778, and thereafter a steady stream of immigration poured in from the east to settle present-day Kentucky and Tennessee. From there, the settlers filtered south into Mississippi and Alabama.

Soon, more numerous parties traversed the ridges, seeking out new gaps. The lands west of Pennsylvania and south of Lakes Erie and Huron became populated and were organized as the Northwest Territory to eventually form much of the states of Ohio and Michigan. To the west of that and extending to the Mississippi was the Indiana Territory, which would become parts of the states of Michigan, Indiana, Illinois, and Minnesota.

On maps and in history books, it all looks rather orderly and peaceful. But the living fact was a nightmare of death and danger, a firestorm of burning lodges, disemboweled children, raped women, massacred tribes, and scalped whites. It was the frightening tensions between red man and white that dictated the politics of the region.

One of the consequences of the Kentucky invasion had been to drive a wedge between the Indian tribes east of the Mississippi, essentially splitting their hunting grounds in half. North of the Ohio River were Wyandottes, Shawnees, Miamis, Kickapoos, and other tribes. South and east of the Tennessee River were powerful confederacies of Creeks, Cherokees, Chickasaws, and Choctaws. In between the two were the lands of Kentucky and Tennessee rapidly being occupied by whites.

The Indians were being driven back but they remained so terrible and ferocious that had they concentrated in attacks, they would almost surely have driven the whites back across the Appalachians. The whites, of course, were well aware of this danger and pursued a consistent and successful policy to pit the tribes against one another.

Into this land of unimaginable tension came the young Wilkinsons. Everywhere they looked there was the fear of Indians. Everywhere they went there was increasing talk of separation from the eastern states for better defense.

The situation was such a tinderbox that President Washington devoted a considerable portion to the subject in his Farewell Address of 1796, warning against separation, saying that politicians raised fears "to acquire influence within particular districts . . . agitating the community with ill-founded jealousies and false alarms; kindling the animosity of one part against another; formenting riot and insurrection."

Demagoguery was the same then as now. Fear and suspicions were seized upon by the unscrupulous and exploited and magnified so that the cynical might gain fortune and power.

Twenty years prior to the Wilkinsons' arrival, the whole territory had contained less than a few thousand people, almost all of them Indians. By the end of 1783, when the Wilkinsons arrived, there were an estimated twenty thousand whites there and they were arriving at the rate of eight to ten thousand more each year.

Following the Revolution, the biggest social ferment and hottest political issue was not Alien and Sedition Laws, or Hamilton's Assumption Plan, the Whiskey Rebellion, or even foreign affairs. It was the restlessness of the West, and James Wilkinson would be at the very center.

The twenty-seven-year-old Wilkinson opened a general goods store in the trading post of Louisville. The settlement had been founded as portage around the so-called "Falls of the Ohio," actually a lengthy, rock-strewn series of rapids which were the only impediment to navigation on the entire thousand-mile length of the Ohio from western

Pennsylvania to its meeting with the Mississippi. Louisville was an ideal site for a town or store because when the river was high boats had to slow down to navigate the stream. When the water was low, boats had to stop until the river rose.

At the time of Wilkinson's arrival, Louisville consisted of a courthouse, a jail, seven wooden huts, and a small fort. But the region was rich. "The lands are amazingly well adapted for tobacco, Indian corn, wheat, hemp, flax and for raising stock," wrote an observer. It held excellent opportunities for "a trade up and down the [nearby] Mississippi."

Even at that early date, the Blue Grass was already well supplied with militia-type "Kentucky Colonels," but a full-blown, *authentic* general was a rarity which immediately propelled young Jamey to prominence.

Backed by money from his relatives in Philadelphia, Wilkinson soon was able to add to his Louisville store by buying 12,550 acres of land near the present site of Frankfort. Here he opened a second store where he traded manufactured goods from the East for furs and agricultural products of the West. In addition, he now owned a lot of land—twenty square miles of it.

After acquainting himself with the territory, Jamey found even more land and made himself a new location on the Licking River near the present site of Lexington, which was then a village of a few scattered log cabins, a fort, and one main street. In 1784, the Wilkinsons opened the town's first general store.

From that launching pad the young general became entangled in Kentucky politics and commenced his great conspiracy—that of spy for the Spanish. He would become a key figure in a plan to separate Kentucky from the southwestern United States and join it to Spain as a new vassal republic.

When Wilkinson's role as a Spanish spy was about to be exposed, he would sacrifice his friend Aaron Burr. Later, Meriwether Lewis would be a victim of that same extended conspiracy.

By 1784, the Ohio River was dotted with trading posts or towns. From Pittsburgh, floating downriver and west, one came to Wheeling, Limestone, Newport, Cincinnati, and Louisville. Farther down, on the

Mississippi, were the Spanish settlements at New Madrid and Natchez.[2] But all traffic stopped at New Orleans. Possessed by the Spanish, New Orleans controlled all heartland commerce and the Spaniards were shutting it on and off like a water faucet. When the port was open, half the West's produce passed through. When it was closed, there was none.

Spain opened and closed New Orleans at whim and just before the Wilkinsons arrived in Kentucky, Spain had again closed all navigation on the lower Mississippi. The American government, weak from its recent war, did nothing, thus providing westerners with a strong reason for separation. Kentuckians felt that the national government wanted to protect eastern interests by allowing the Spanish to cut off western trade. With the river closed, Kentuckians would be forced to haul their goods over the Appalachians to eastern ports. However, if Kentucky was on its own, went the argument, it could settle the dispute with Spain quickly, either by negotiation or by seizing New Orleans with a citizens' army. As Kentucky thinking had it, if easterners could whip the British, then a few sharpshooting Kentuckians could damn sure scatter the Spanish.

The political and commercial situation was thus ripe for exploitation and into it stepped former brigadier general Jamey Wilkinson. He now got himself up as Kentucky's savior, the West's Man on a White Horse—quite literally, because he played himself up grand. He was now thirty years of age, already pompous. He had become a florid boaster, his boyish charms giving way to Falstaffian braggadocio, turning portly, given to public drunkenness and display. He rode a white stallion while regularly sporting a self-designed uniform complete with sword, long blue coat, golden epaulets, and tricornered hat, outfitted himself with a gilded carriage pulled by white horses attired in golden harness.

In late 1786, he began putting together a secession conspiracy, enlisting partners in a daring plan to exploit the indifference of eastern states to the welfare of the western settlements. It was Wilkinson's scheme to open the gates of the West by securing his own monopoly at New Orleans. To do this he was prepared to renounce his U.S. citizenship and become a citizen of Spain.[3]

Although Wilkinson's treason would be rumored in Kentucky as early as 1788 and such reports were even more widely circulated during the 1796 to 1800 administration of John Adams, he would manage to convince two courts-martial and three successive U.S. presidents of his innocence. Absolute proof of his betrayal would not come until nearly one hundred years later when the historian I. J. Cox discovered secret reports in Spanish archives.[4]

In April 1787, Wilkinson set sail from his landing on the Kentucky River near Frankfort. His two boats were loaded with flour, tobacco, bacon, hams, and butter, which he hoped to sell at a profit in New Orleans.

He was risking all with one throw of the dice. He had no authority either from Spain or the United States to enter Spanish territory. At any point past Spanish-held St. Louis, he not only risked seizure of his boats and cargo but also imprisonment. It was a gamble, but one he had done his best to tilt in his favor.

Having no passport, Jamey had prepared his passage by writing a friendly letter to the Spanish commandant at St. Louis. Just prior to the letter, the American war hero George Rogers Clark had seized Spanish subjects at Vincennes in Indiana Territory. Wilkinson now deplored that seizure on his own behalf and on that of all law-abiding Kentuckians. He wrote the Spanish commandant urging that Clark be hanged. The commandant replied in cheerful agreement and said that, should he ever get the chance, he would be glad to hang General Clark personally and invite Wilkinson to the happy event.

In May 1787, as Wilkinson neared the junction of the Ohio and Mississippi, he wrote again to the commandant. This time he directly requested a passport and permission to head downriver with his cargo to the Gulf and thence across to the Atlantic and up to Philadelphia. He implied there would be a small gratuity available for such favors.

It worked.

When Jamey reached St. Louis, he was given permission to continue through to New Orleans, which was as far as the commandant's authority extended. The commandant gave Jamey a dinner, signed his passport, and allowed him to proceed downriver.

Wilkinson arrived at New Orleans on July 2, 1787, tying up at the docks half a mile upriver from the city center, the Place d'Armes, later to be called Jackson Square.

New Orleans was situated on the east bank of the Mississippi, one hundred miles upriver from the Gulf of Mexico, an island surrounded on the east and west by water, on the north and south by swamp.

Founded in 1718 by the French and already having a worldwide reputation for wickedness, the city was a pestilential sinkhole which nevertheless was viewed by its inhabitants as a subtropical Paris. In keeping with such airs, its citizens had built one of the more improbable cities on the continent, a sweltering metropolis complete with an opera house, three theaters, several hotels, a college, two libraries, a cathedral, a number of smaller churches, half a dozen banks, perhaps two hundred bars and saloons, five lower schools for younger children, a firehouse with a modern pump engine, a jail, and at least a dozen of the finest brothels west of Paris.

Being royally French in culture and aristocratically Spanish in administration, the city had no newspapers to rouse up the populace. Those would come later with American democracy.

The city was nearly as populous as New York, and its sole land connection to the rest of Louisiana, and the world, was a "Metairie Road" built atop a ridge which ran through the swamp. The road was seasonal, however. Six months of the year it was submerged by rains and flood and the city was entirely an island accessible only by boat, barge, or ship.

Into this space, living in wet, humid heat, were crowded more than twenty-five thousand permanent residents, mostly Frenchmen under Spanish control, plus several thousand slaves, and another five thousand or so commercial visitors including Spaniards, Indians, Haitians, Cubans, Mexicans, and Jamey and his scattering of Kentucky boatmen.

New Orleans was an island metaphorically as well, insofar as it was a multilingual, multinational, multicultural Old World enclave surrounded by a wilderness of Indians, including the dreaded, cannibalistic Attakapas to the west.

New Orleans architecture, music, food, customs, and population were a mixture of French, Spanish, Indian, and African with very little

Anglo-American influence. The main aspect of New Orleans, its bones and body, was derived from the white Creoles. From them came the largest houses and public buildings, the design of parks and streets, the operas, the dominant customs, and, always, the law.

But the Caucasian body contained an African soul and moved to an African tempo. It was black Creole carpenters who had built the houses and subtly influenced the architecture. It was black rhythms one heard played in the homes and on the streets; black cooks tended the kitchens and black women the nurseries.

Beyond the docks and buildings of the city proper, later to be known as the "French Quarter," there was a softer New Orleans, a tropical paradise characterized by full moons and the tender looks of romance. On the northern edge of the city, running four miles between the city's ramparts and a large blue lake called Pontchartrain, there were clear waters, transparent as purest crystal, running over sand as fine and white as sugar. Appearing and disappearing through thick groves of magnolia trees, the trilling brooks appeared in a variety of forms and converged in a short stream called Bayou St. John. Even into the twentieth century, Choctaw pirogues used the bayou as an avenue from the lake to the Place d'Armes where they could set up a market and watch the doings on the Mississippi. It was here on the bayou that Wilkinson took quarters.

We now know from the captured Spanish documents that due to his communications in St. Louis, Wilkinson's military and political reputation had preceded him downriver. His arrival suited the purpose of the Spanish colonial government, represented in the person of Governor Esteban Miró and his administrative chief, Martín Navarro, whose title was *intendant* of Louisiana. These two Spaniards needed help to resist American pressures on their colony and in Jamey Wilkinson they saw their man.

Although the closure of the port required them to seize Wilkinson's boats as contraband, they instead allowed him to land and sent an honor guard to escort him to Government House, called the Cabildo.[5]

The first day of meeting was solely introductory. The Spanish chiefs found Wilkinson likable and their reception of the disaffected general was courteous and encouraging. "He is a young man of about thirty-three years of age although he looks older," said Miró's report. "His bearing and manners also indicate that he has had an excellent education.''

At Miró's encouragement on the second day, Wilkinson gave an ''extensive account'' of the conditions in Kentucky and explained his purpose in coming to New Orleans. He agreed to set down that purpose in a written report which the Spanish called ''a memorial.''

Wilkinson retired to his lodgings on Bayou St. John and began the memorial. As he wrote, it occurred to him that the surest way to secure his ties with Miró and Navarro was to renounce his American citizenship. Accordingly, he set down an oath of allegiance to the king of Spain, wrapping it in his characteristic bombast.

He began by justifying his defection:

> *Being born and educated in America, I embraced her cause in the recent revolution, and steadfastly I adhered to her interests until she triumphed over her enemy. This event, having rendered my services no longer needful, released me from my engagements, dissolved all the obligations, even those of nature and left me at liberty, after having fought for her welfare, to seek my own. . . .*

He next took an oath of loyalty to Spain, ''transferring my allegiance from the United States to his Catholic Majesty.'' The defection, he said, did not impair his integrity because ''no one can say of me with justice that I break any law of nature or of nations or of conscience of honor. . . . My conduct will be directed by principles of loyalty to my sovereign. . . .''

His price for treason was personal and exclusive rights to American trade on the Mississippi. In return, he promised to cause a revolt and secession in Kentucky, making it a ''vassal state'' to Spain. This arrangement would be accompanied by exclusive navigation of the Mississippi by the two parties. To aid and ignite Kentucky's secession, the Spanish government would continue to keep the port of New Orleans closed to the U.S. government:

> *. . . Spain will without hesitation peremptorily and absolutely refuse to Congress the navigation of the Mississippi, for should [the Spanish] form a treaty by which the Americans may become*

*entitled to the independent enjoyment of this navigation, there will
be destroyed the power which Spain now enjoys over the American
settlements.*

As a barrier against intrusion into Spanish Louisiana by other Americans, Wilkinson proposed the immediate "establishment of a fortified post at a trading station [New Madrid] some miles below the junction of the Ohio and the Mississippi."

He promised not only to return to Kentucky on Spain's behalf but to act as the king's "confidential agent near the seat of Congress who shall transmit regularly every act of that body which can in any shape affect the subject before us." Wilkinson bragged that he had the highest connections in the American capital and would pass on presidential confidences to his Spanish masters.

To further ensure the success of an independent Kentucky in vassalage to Spain, he asked Spanish guarantees of "the most inviolable secrecy."

He thought it "not out of reason to conclude that a man of great popularity and political talents will be able to alienate the western Americans from the United States, destroy the insidious designs of Great Britain and throw [the Kentuckians] into the arms of Spain." He, of course, was the man who would do that.

He knew full well that he was committing treason because in this memorial he cautioned Miró and Navarro: "I have committed secrets of an important nature such as would, were they divulged, destroy my fame and fortune forever."

As a binder for betrayal, the Spanish gave Wilkinson a license to trade some $75,000 worth of Kentucky goods through the port of New Orleans. This was an immense fortune in a time when the first presidential Cabinet members would make only $5,000 annually and the president himself $25,000.

Miró was so pleased with Wilkinson's defection that he wrote his superiors that the former general had promised "the delivering up of Kentucky into his majesty's hands, which is the main object to which Wilkinson has promised to devote himself entirely, [and] would forever constitute this province a rampart for the protection of New Spain."[6]

After selling his Kentucky cargo, Wilkinson left New Orleans by sailing ship and headed to the Gulf with a boatload of Spanish cargo taken on consignment for trade or sale in Kentucky. After a stop in the Carolinas, he left the ship in Alexandria, Virginia, and sent his goods ahead for unloading in Philadelphia where it would be shipped on to his trading posts in Kentucky.

With business taken care of, Spain's newest and most secret agent next called on no less an icon than George Washington at Mount Vernon, where the retired general was waiting for ratification of the new 1789 Constitution.

Since the years of the Conway Cabal, Washington had continued to hold his Jamey in regard although the Founding Father was not completely blind to Wilkinson's faults, describing Wilkinson about this time as "lively, sensible, pompous and ambitious."

Nevertheless, Washington had enough respect for his visitor to write about him to James Madison: "I am informed by General Wilkinson, who is just arrived here from New Orleans, that North Carolina is almost unanimous for adopting" the new Constitution, drafts of which were then in circulation. (Characteristically, Wilkinson's information was wrong. North Carolina would be among the slowest to ratify the Constitution.)

Wilkinson returned to Kentucky in splendor, arriving in a fine carriage with new "Negro servants" and clothes cut by the "best Philadelphia tailors." Quickly it was noised throughout the Blue Grass that the general had pulled off a dazzling commercial coup in New Orleans; he had succeeded where the state of Virginia and Congress had failed; he had secured a lifting of the oppressive embargo, a concession to send down the river each year fifteen hundred casks of tobacco. His whole enterprise was backed by Daniel Clark, a dashing young Irish merchant he had met in New Orleans. A cozy relationship would exist among Clark, Wilkinson, and the Spanish for nearly the next twenty years.

The spring of 1789 found Wilkinson in Kentucky, where he was up to his conspiratorial neck giving attention to his new business ventures. Due to his arrangements with the Spanish and Daniel Clark, he was prosperously loading goods at his Frankfort trading post for shipment downriver. He was also building a mansion on Wilkinson Street in

Frankfort and was busily engaged in land-claim speculations connected to the bounty-warrants scheme described earlier.

His expansive hospitality attracted a coterie drawn mostly from those who "danced and swore and played at cards," he wrote in his journal, men who drank deeply of Kentucky's already famous Bourbon whiskey. There were "convivial hours" at the general's table, during which "minds may have become relaxed and hearts unguarded."

His generosity and assiduous gathering of information soon led to rumors that his negotiations at New Orleans had covered subjects other than trade.

That fall another shipment of tobacco was sent downriver to New Orleans and Wilkinson went with it. He again met with Navarro and Miró to amend the part of his plan that would make Kentucky a vassal state to Spain. He had tested the political waters, he said, and while there was much popular support for independence, there was no way Kentuckians would subject themselves to a foreign power, most especially the hated Spaniards. Shifting his rudder accordingly, Wilkinson now proposed to his paymasters that they help make Kentucky not a vassal state but fully independent. In a new memorial, he advised them:

> *It will be more useful to the court of Spain to lay aside the idea of receiving the people of Kentucky under the dominion of His Majesty, and to employ all indirect means to cause the separation of this section of the country from the United States, which would likely be followed by a connection with Spain to the exclusion of any other power.*

He said he had enlisted confederates in the Kentucky movement to independence and they should be rewarded "in proportion to their influence, ability, or services rendered." He asked for a secret commission in the Spanish military service and a "pension," adding that in the case of his death "the allowance made to me should go to my wife and children."

He also asked for arms to complete the rebellion:

> *As soon as we shall have determined to withdraw from the government of the United States, we ought to have arms to defend*

*ourselves against the Indians or any other enemy that might pur-
pose to interfere with our measures, and we do not know where to
find these supplies except in New Orleans or at the Strait. [Detroit.
In effect, Wilkinson was threatening an alliance with the British.]*

*. . . I should recommend that the arms and ammunition destined
for this purpose should be sent secretly to L'Ance à la Graisse
[New Madrid, in what is now Missouri], from which in case of
necessity they could be taken to Kentucky in a few days.*

He enclosed a list of some twenty Kentucky officials by name and
position who, he said, the Spanish should pay yearly bribes of between
five hundred and one thousand dollars.

Wilkinson also renewed his loyalty oath to King Charles IV of Spain.

At this time, according to the Spanish archives, Wilkinson went on
the regular espionage payroll at two thousand dollars a year. A July
1792 report to the court from Gayoso, the Spanish commander at
Natchez, later referred to the arrangement:

*In Kentucky we have had Don Jaime Wilkinson well affected to
our side. He is a person of great talent and independence who has
twice come down to this province and presented several memorials.
In his own country he has performed several important services to
this province. Yet, although he was recommended by Don Esteban
Miró for a pension and other help, the resolution was delayed
because of bureaucracy.*

The Gayoso report indicated that in his 1787 dealings Wilkinson had
received a gold payment worth several thousand dollars, although no
record to that effect has yet been found in the Spanish archives.

By his perfidy, Wilkinson had accomplished what neither the states
nor federal government had been able to do. He had squeezed out of
the Spanish a concession that permitted him to navigate the Mississippi
and sell tobacco and beeswax, apples and butter, liquor and other
western products, all duty free, at New Orleans.

For the westerners wanting the use of the river, the long-desired
millennium had arrived, provided it went through Jamey's hands. In
Kentucky, General Wilkinson was seen as a hero.

Kentucky at this time was still part of Virginia. Faithful to his arrangement, Wilkinson returned to Lexington, where he lobbied the Virginia legislature for Kentucky to form its own republic and create an alliance with Spain.

He was also active in other services to the king of Spain. In one of these, he helped sink the plans of a Kentucky friend who had organized a company of Americans to invade Spanish Louisiana. Wilkinson sent a full disclosure of the invasion plans not to his own government but to Miró in New Orleans.

A year later, in 1790, Wilkinson learned that one James O'Fallon was putting together an army of Mississippi colonists to seize other Spanish lands. Wilkinson again informed Miró, but not his own government.

By 1791, Wilkinson's extravagances had somehow exceeded his newfound fortunes and he went bankrupt. A further blow came that year when Kentucky joined the union as a full-fledged state. This calmed the Kentucky fever for separation and killed Wilkinson's plan to make it an independent nation and ally of Spain.

More than ever Wilkinson now needed Spanish gold. He continued to send reports and in 1793 came up with another intelligence coup.

At the instigation of a trouble-making French ambassador, Citizen Edmond Charles Genêt, the same George Rogers Clark whom Wilkinson had once nominated for hanging now formed a "French Legion" with plans to sweep the Mississippi River clean of Spaniards. First Clark would clear St. Louis, then move on to New Madrid, Baton Rouge, and New Orleans. Learning of those plans, Wilkinson again informed the Spanish in New Orleans and advised just how to form defenses against Clark's legions. As a further precaution, Wilkinson said he had already bribed the leaders of the legion to betray Clark. Wilkinson told Governor Miró that there soon would be news that the legion was disbanded.

It is unclear what actual efforts, if any, were made by Wilkinson against Clark's battalion. But not long after Wilkinson's communication, the legion was in fact disbanded. Wilkinson subsequently informed the Spanish that he had incurred expenses for the bribes and asked that $4,500 be sent to him by the bearer of the letter, which it was.

In the meantime, the United States of America, barely two years old, was about to launch a campaign against the Miami Indians on the shores of Lake Erie. President Washington put out the call for a national army. The bankrupted Wilkinson reenlisted, seizing the opportunity to bail himself out—not only out of debt but out of Kentucky.

His old commander, Washington, received him gladly, commissioning him a lieutenant colonel, the only rank open at the time. Just a few months later a vacancy occurred and Wilkinson was promoted to brigadier general. Concurrent with the promotion, Spanish dispatches began to identify Wilkinson as "Number Thirteen" to disguise the fact they had an American general on their payroll.

Down in New Orleans, Miró had been replaced as governor by the Baron de Carondelet. Wilkinson wasted no time inviting Carondelet to "use the opportunity offered by an incompetent secretary of war, an ignorant commander-in-chief, and a contemptible union" to secure control of the entire Mississippi by force of arms.

Wilkinson's reference to the "ignorant commander-in-chief" wasn't to his benefactor George Washington but to Army Commandant Anthony Wayne. (Four years later, Wayne would die and be succeeded as ranking officer by Wilkinson.)

According to the archives, during the period from 1790 to 1794 the Spanish paid their American general $32,000 in gold. This while the U.S. Army was paying him fifty dollars a month plus a rations allowance.

By 1795, rumors of Wilkinson's Spanish connections had spread to Philadelphia. To guard against any possible arrest, he asked Carondelet to draw up a fake bill showing that the Spanish payments he had received were part of a business partnership with Miró. In his letter to Carondelet he advised: "If I am questioned by President Washington on my arrival at Philadelphia, I will avow a mercantile arrangement with New Orleans in which I still remain interested and on this ground I will account for the money. . . ."

Carondelet responded quickly, sending Wilkinson an official ledger sheet saying the money was the proceeds from a cargo of sugar that Wilkinson had traded in New Orleans. It proved unnecessary, however, because President Washington never questioned him directly, although

Washington did secretly assign the aforementioned surveyor Andrew Ellicott to look into the rumors of Spanish pay.

After Washington left office in 1797, diplomatic pressures from revolutionary France, primarily from the XYZ Affair, impelled President John Adams to prepare for war. Congress authorized the enlistment of ten thousand men as a provisional army and George Washington was once again called out of retirement and appointed Commander in Chief. A reluctant Adams acceded to Washington's request to appoint Alexander Hamilton as Inspector General, second in command to Washington. Their main field general was to be Wilkinson and a memo from Hamilton dated June 15, 1799, indicated that both he and Washington were wary about Wilkinson's integrity. Nevertheless, the ever pragmatic and cynical Hamilton encouraged Washington to *purchase* Wilkinson's loyalty:

It strikes me forcibly, that it will be both right and expedient to advance this gentleman [Wilkinson] to the grade of Major General. He has been long steadily in service and long a Brigadier. . . . I am aware that some doubts have been entertained of him, and that his character, on certain sides, gives room for doubts. Yet he is at present in the service; is a man of more than ordinary talent, courage and enterprise; an ambitious man . . . he will be apt to become disgusted if neglected, and through disgust may be rendered really what he is now only suspected to be. Under such circumstances, it seems to me good policy to avoid all just ground of discontent, and to make it the interest of the individual to practice his duty. If you should be also of this opinion, I submit to your consideration whether it would not be advisable to express it in a private letter to the Secretary of War.

Washington agreed with the strategy, replying:

I think, with you, that policy dictates the expediency of promoting Brigadier Wilkinson to the rank of Major General, and will suggest the measure to the Secretary of War as a private communication.

*It would feed his ambition, soothe his vanity and, by arresting
discontent, produce the good effect you contemplate.*

While Wilkinson was betraying his country, Washington and Hamilton continued to buy his services. It was a cynical time, as will be seen when Jefferson, too, brushes aside the warnings against Wilkinson in the interest of political expediency. An alarmed John Randolph of Roanoke will tell Jefferson that in embracing Wilkinson he has embarked "his reputation in the same bottom" with "the most finished scoundrel that ever lived."

Nevertheless, all three presidents—Washington, Adams, and Jefferson—would remain supportive of Wilkinson, a fidelity that is central to the mystery of Meriwether Lewis's death.

What caused Jefferson to "embark his reputation" alongside Wilkinson was the lure of a great treasure to the west—the unexplored and mysterious Louisiana Territory.

Louisiana, 1

•••••••••

THE LOUISIANA TERRITORY, first claimed by France, then Spain, and finally by the United States, is basically the watershed of the Mississippi River. First shown on a map of 1502, the river is among the earliest geographical features noted in the Americas. Its first known European exploration was in 1519 when Álvarez de Pineda sailed up the river which he named Río del Espíritu Santo to about present-day Baton Rouge and reported forty villages of Indians along the route.

The first documented crossing of the river was on May 8, 1541, by Hernando de Soto. Fleeing westward from the Chickasaws near present-day Memphis, he recorded crossing a great "river almost half a league broad. If a man stood still on the other side, it could not be discerned whether he were a man or no. The river was of great depth and of a strong current; the water was always muddie; there came downe the River continually many trees and timber."

After de Soto, the entire Mississippi Valley was neglected by Europeans for more than a century, the Spaniards failing to find gold and already having too much American land. Colonization fell to French Canadians, who began creeping down the river and in 1673 the Frenchmen Jacques Marquette and Louis Jolliet navigated the length of it. Nine years later, the sieur La Salle also came down from the north and at the present site of New Orleans planted a cross, naming the land Louisiana in honor of Louis XIV.

The river was so prone to floods that the first permanent European settlement was not on the river itself but on a western tributary, the Red River. This settlement was the village of Natchitoches, pronounced Nak'-ah-tosh, in 1691.

Canary Islanders from Mexico had moved upstream on the Mississippi to the mouth of the Red River, and thence up the Red to the foot of a "Great Raft" of trees—a huge logjam some hundred and sixty miles in length which blocked further ascent.[1] There the Islanders established the only "civilization" between Santa Fe and St. Augustine, Florida, a distance of some sixteen hundred miles. They were reinforced about ten years later by members of La Salle's colony from Old Biloxi.[2] Other French settlements soon followed, including Kaskaskia near modern St. Louis, Missouri, in 1699; Fort Toulouse in Alabama in 1714; and New Orleans in 1718.

The site of New Orleans was crucial because it controlled the two main entrances to the river—one from the mouth some hundred and twenty miles downstream, and the much shorter but shallower east-west route via the brackish Lake Pontchartrain which connected through a series of short, shallow passages to the Gulf.

The city of New Orleans, platted in 1718, was for its first thirty years "a mere assemblage of a few poor cabins . . . made of planks and mud . . ." surrounded by "wild beasts and savages equally barbarous," said the Abbé Antoine-François Prévost. But the village sat astride the entrance to the entire Mississippi Valley, a strategic post which the French continued to hold until 1762 when Louis XV signed Louisiana over to his cousin Charles III of Spain in order to keep it out of English hands. (The Louisiana deed, part of the Treaty of Fontainebleau, ceded "the island of New Orleans" and all land lying west of the Mississippi.)

Although Spain accepted "the gift" of maintaining a costly colony with reluctance, the little city of New Orleans and its people prospered. By the time of Jefferson's inauguration it had become one of the most important trading ports in North America, still controlling the Mississippi Valley.

Americans were not only looking to uncork New Orleans. They were also eyeing settlement in the lands beyond the Mississippi. What little was known of those western lands came from French trappers and Spanish missionaries who had explored to the foot of massive snow-capped mountains.

Despite nearly three hundred years of European presence in North America, the region west of the Mississippi was almost as unknown as the moon. Tales were told. Strange Indians had been seen here and there. There were great bears, taller than a man. And mountains so high that they were eternally blanketed with snow. But facts were few and they were held secret by the French and Spanish.

Since 1609, the Spanish had maintained a colonial capital at Santa Fe and had been intrigued by the high, eternally snowcapped peaks immediately to the north, in what is today's New Mexico, Utah, and Colorado.

Using impressed Indian labor, Spaniards began operating profitable gold, lead, and silver mines out of Santa Fe from about 1680. They also instituted a gainful fur trade.[3] During the early 1700s, Spanish patrols had reached into southern Colorado, Kansas, and on occasion as far as Nebraska. By 1739, French traders from Canada had reached Santa Fe by coming down a succession of rivers, then by land across Nebraska, Kansas, and the eastern plains of Colorado. A few years later, friars from Santa Fe reached Pike's Peak in Colorado, some ninety miles south of present Denver. Moving north and west across the Rockies in the vicinity of present-day Grand Junction, they traversed nearly the length of Utah, where they received reports from Indians of "a lake to the north which covers many leagues and its waters are noxious and extremely salty"—the Great Salt Lake. The friars recognized the importance of the Rockies, noting on their map that "this mountain range is the backbone of North America, since the many rivers that are born of it empty into the two seas, the South Sea [Pacific Ocean] and the Gulf of Mexico."[4]

By 1777, there was a trail linking Santa Fe and Los Angeles. In the next few years, trails were opened from Santa Fe to San Antonio and New Orleans.

Nevertheless, despite these individual commercial ventures, the Spanish showed little interest in a formal exploration or mapping of the mountains and rivers until American pressures were felt.

Much of that pressure came from Thomas Jefferson, whose abiding interest was not only in New Orleans but in all the western lands. As early as the 1780s, when Americans looked to borders no farther away than the Mississippi, Jefferson's vision extended to the Pacific.

His desire to explore those regions was first documented while he was minister to France in 1786. During his frolics in Paris Jefferson had met an American adventurer named John Ledyard, described by the Virginian as a "man of genius, of some science, of fearless courage and enterprise . . . and of roaming disposition." Ledyard had been a British Royal Marine with Captain Cook in Hawaii, having witnessed Cook's murder by the Hawaiians. After a successful escape from Hawaii, Ledyard showed up in Paris seeking funds to start a fur-trading business in the unexplored American Northwest.

That's where he met Jefferson, who proposed to Ledyard that he explore the American continent from west to east; that Ledyard "go by land to Kamchatka, cross in some of the Russian vessels to Nootka Sound, fall down into the latitude of the Missouri, and penetrate to and through that to the United States. He eagerly seized the idea," wrote Jefferson.

Ledyard was a confident fellow who thought he could walk across America with no more equipment than two dogs, an Indian pipe, and a winning personality. To get to Alaska, and then America, he proceeded to cross all of Russia and Siberia, reaching Kamchatka in 1789, where he was stopped and arrested on orders of Empress Catherine the Great.

"He was preparing in the spring," Jefferson tells us, "to resume in his journey when he was arrested by an officer of the Empress who by this time had changed her mind and forbidden his proceeding. He was put into a closed carriage and conveyed day and night, without ever stopping, till they reached Poland; where he was set down and left to himself."

The now penniless Ledyard eventually made his way to London, where he wrote Jefferson a new proposal—that he would come back to America and penetrate east to west from Kentucky to the Pacific. In the meantime, while awaiting Jefferson's reply, he took a side trip to Egypt and never emerged, dying mysteriously in Cairo.

Jefferson had already begun looking for someone else.

In 1792, startling news arrived in Philadelphia—a Captain Robert Gray had discovered the mouth of a great river on the Pacific coast. Gray was already a known hero, having a year earlier become the first American to circumnavigate the globe.

Now Gray was in the northern Pacific looking for a mythical Northwest Passage, a sea route connecting the Mississippi River to the Pacific via an east-west river suggested by earlier Spanish explorations and vaguely marked on maps as "Río de San Roque."

Arriving in the approximate vicinity of Río de San Roque, Gray and his trading ship *Columbia*, out of Boston, caught an offshore wind and made way over submerged sandbars to "a large river of fresh water, up which we steered."

He named it "Columbia's River," and when the news reached the Atlantic coast a few months later, America went wild. It was assumed that the eastward-flowing Missouri must connect somewhere in the mysterious mountains of the west with this new great river. If so, it meant there was indeed a Northwest Passage for trade with the fabled Orient. Christopher Columbus's dream was finally at hand.

Secretary of State Thomas Jefferson was immediately informed of Gray's momentous discovery and proposed to the American Philosophical Society in Philadelphia that a subscription be taken to explore the continent from east to west. Among the first to donate money to the enterprise were George Washington and Alexander Hamilton.

Apparently the first man to solicit the honor of exploring this western passage was Jefferson's eighteen-year-old Virginia neighbor Meriwether Lewis, even then itching to get off the farm and into action. "Captain Lewis," Jefferson wrote, "was then stationed at Charlottesville [and] warmly solicited me to obtain for him the execution of that object."

Gently, Meriwether's elder Virginia cousin and neighbor rejected Lewis because of his age. "I told him," said Jefferson, "it was proposed that the person engaged should be attended by a single companion only, to avoid exciting alarm among the Indians. This did not deter him."

Secretary Jefferson was still making general inquiries for an explorer and in June 1792 investigated the possibility of American botanist Moses Marshall going "up the Missouri" and thence to the Pacific. Nothing came of it and Jefferson settled on a Frenchman, André Michaux, a botanist then studying in the United States. Michaux himself had been promoting the idea of exploring the West along the bed of the Missouri. Thinking he had found his man, Secretary of State Jefferson drew up a commission with specific instructions for Michaux:

> The chief objects of your journey are to find the shortest and most convenient route of communication between the United States and the Pacific Ocean . . . and to learn such particulars as can be obtained of the country through which it pass, its productions, inhabitants and other interesting circumstances. As a channel of communication between these States and the Pacific Ocean, the Missouri, so far as it extends, presents itself under circumstances of unquestioned preference. It has, therefore, been declared as a fundamental object. . . .[5]

Michaux started from Philadelphia in July 1793. He was in Kentucky when word reached the now private citizen Jefferson that his French botanist was in fact the secret agent of the French ambassador to the United States, the troublemaking revolutionary Citizen Edmond Charles Genêt. Genêt, the intriguer who had sponsored George Rogers Clark's French Legion, was now using Michaux as his agent to subvert Spanish Louisiana. When James Wilkinson caused news of the Clark plot to hit the papers, it had the unforeseen result of revealing Michaux's connections to Genêt. Jefferson found Michaux too much of an embarrassment and canceled the commission. Michaux returned to Philadelphia.

Still, the Missouri beckoned as the American path to the Pacific as the Mississippi was the route to the Gulf.

In 1792, the Spanish hired a French frontiersman named Pierre Vidal to open a route through eleven hundred miles of Indian territory between St. Louis and Santa Fe. Later this would become famous as the Santa Fe Trail.

To fill in the blank spaces on the North American map, New Orleans Governor Carondelet recruited another Frenchman—engineer Nicolas de Finiels—to explore the region watered by the Missouri. Under international law, whoever held the source of a navigable stream could claim free passage over the full route of that stream. It was thought that the Missouri headwaters might connect to other streams leading either south to Santa Fe or west to the Pacific, and the Spanish wanted to ensure that no one claimed those headwaters other than themselves— a right that could be gained only by discovery.

As it happened, Finiels himself did not venture much farther west than St. Louis. Instead he relied on Indians and trappers for information.

They told him that the Missouri emanated from a huge waterfall coming out of the western mountains. Finiels reported: "Tradition has it that there is a long chain of very high rocky mountains that run northwest to southeast in the northern part of New Mexico. The mountains are covered with trees, and it is assumed that ancient forests extend from there all the way to the shores of the Pacific Ocean."

Exploration would be dangerous. Finiels warned his Spanish employers that there were tales of new and fierce Indian tribes along the Missouri, Indians known as Cheyenne, Crow, and Sioux. "The last are a large and ferocious tribe. . . . They may be considered the Tartars of this part of the world [who] interdict communications with the Mandans by harassing traders; they pillage, ransom and sometimes massacre them if a means is not found to avoid their surveillance."

As Jefferson neared the presidential election of 1800, he was of the firm belief that free navigation of the Mississippi was absolutely necessary to preserve American commerce.

The lack of roads had created two separate nations held apart by terrain. Eastern and western Americans were divided at every point by at least one hundred miles of forest and mountain. Although the entire population, free and slave, west of the mountains was fewer than four hundred thousand, they tended to think of themselves as the foundation of a new empire, as isolated as "the Jutes or Angles in the fifth century," wrote Henry Adams. The westerners' link to the world was not the broad Atlantic but the Mississippi and the Gulf—a life-and-death gate that was controlled by Spanish arms.

There were many conspiracies spurred by the desperation of Kentuckians and Tennesseans to break the Spanish choke point at New Orleans. Although James Wilkinson was the most insidious of these conspirators, the best known at the time was Tennessee senator William Blount.

Blount's case illustrates Thomas Jefferson's rather liquid value system, one that seemed to ebb and swell depending on the direction of Jefferson's needs. In the space of ten years—between 1797 and 1807—Jefferson would (1) rescue William Blount for attempting to separate the western states; (2) persecute and prosecute Aaron Burr for a similar but much lesser plot; and (3) pardon James Wilkinson for acts far more treasonable than either Burr's or Blount's.

Born in 1749, William Blount was a brawny six-footer with orange-colored hair and the pugnacious nature of his fellow North Carolinians, a people who already bore a reputation for dangerousness. "Familiar with the horse and rifle and unaccustomed to restraint," said General Light-Horse Harry Lee, "they are a race of wild and ardent temper, less capable of labor and less willing to endure it than most."

Like so many of the founding politicians, Blount was a Revolutionary War hero. When Congress organized the Tennessee Territory in 1790, Blount became its governor, naming young Andrew Jackson as his attorney general. Blount held that position until 1796 when Tennessee became a state and he rejoined Congress as a Tennessee senator.

Like so many westerners, Blount found his interests were being deliberately stymied by the Federalist administration, which had little interest in confronting the Spanish for control of the Mississippi. In the first place, the Federalists wanted Spain's goodwill because they were negotiating for control of Spanish Florida. In the second, the Federalist commercial interests were satisfied to have their western products flow to and through eastern ports and cities.

Blount was unwilling to accept the status quo and after returning from the new Congress in early 1797, he entered into secret negotiations with the British government to mount an attack on Spanish possessions, including New Orleans. He would send an army of Tennessee volunteers and Indian allies to attack by land while the British fleet struck by sea. New Orleans would be opened as a port and the Mississippi would be guaranteed to American trade.

Unfortunately for Blount, he put all of this in writing. His letter was intercepted by opponents in the Federalist party and taken to the Senate where Blount's chief supporter, Vice President Jefferson, was the presiding officer. In a move to embarrass Jefferson and the Democrats, the Federalist Secretary of State Timothy Pickering announced that Jefferson was a conspirator in the plot—daring him to bring Blount to account. Times were hot. The first of the activist first ladies, Abigail Adams, lamented *in print* the absence of a guillotine, not only for Blount but for Jefferson, too.

Pickering, who later would do nothing against his administration's own General Wilkinson, now moved to imprison Democrat Blount even before there was a trial. Jefferson resisted, saying Blount had done nothing wrong and, anyway, it was all a Federalist plot to embarrass a Democratic senator.

Nevertheless, an official Senate inquiry was forced. As presiding officer, Jefferson had to ask his friend Blount if the incriminating letter was his. Pale and shaking, Blount said he could not identify it without reference to his papers. He asked for and got a three-day delay to locate said documents. In the meantime, the Senate seized Blount's clothes, trunks, and private papers. When the three days were up, the House impeached Blount and so anxious was the Federalist-dominated Senate to get in its punches early that they expelled Blount and then ordered him to face trial. No fool he. Before the night was out Blount was spurring his horse back home to Tennessee, where he would remain for the rest of his life to avoid federal arrest.[6]

In the meantime, his benefactor was preparing to assume the presidency of the United States. There was, however, a hitch: votes in the Electoral College indicated Thomas Jefferson was tied with his own vice president, Aaron Burr.

Jefferson

• • • • • • • • • •

THE NEW CENTURY was welcomed with the ascent of balloons and the booming of cannon. Ballooning had been the rage since Jean-Pierre Blanchard made the first American air voyage in Philadelphia in 1793. The forty-year-old Frenchman took off from the yard of the Walnut Street jail before a crowd of thousands. Thomas Jefferson and his daughter Maria, then aged fourteen, were there—craning their necks up to watch. Wearing a cocked hat with white feathers, Blanchard had made a grand spectacle as he waved the tricolor of France with one hand and the American flag with the other. For forty-six minutes the French aeronaut floated in the air, suspended beneath an enormous yellow silk balloon in a spangled blue boat. Noting Blanchard's descent fifteen miles away into New Jersey, the ever-practical Jefferson immediately saw the advantages of flight. That night he wrote home to Monticello that "the security of the thing appeared so great, that everybody is wishing for a balloon to travel in. I wish for one sincerely, as instead of ten days I should be within five hours of home."

Democracy and freedom were taking wing and the future seemed full of promise. The Americans were being offered a paradise. In the national elections held throughout the summer, Jeffersonia had put down Hamiltonia. Democracy had defeated autocracy. The proletariat was at last getting its seat at the table. Jefferson mockingly boasted to a friend, "The arrogance of the proud hath ceased, and the patient and meek look up."

And now, on November 27, 1800, Thomas Jefferson, incumbent vice president, had arrived in Washington to claim his prize as president. Jefferson was the popular nominee of the Democratic-Republican party. His verification by the Electoral College was to be but a formality, a coronation.

There had been no electioneering in the modern sense of parades, conventions, stump speeches, or town hall appearances. The election basically had been decided by state legislatures and party caucuses which had been meeting throughout the summer and into the fall. The electors themselves were chosen by a variety of means, but mostly by the legislatures. "Election day," December 3, was a formality. The electors would meet in their respective state capitals and cast their votes for president and vice president. Their sealed ballots would then be sent to the new federal city of Washington, where they would be presented and opened by the presiding officer of the Senate, in this case, Vice President Thomas Jefferson.

It was a lock.

The man and the brand-new capital were not new to each other.[1] Next to George Washington, Jefferson was the man most responsible for the federal city's creation, instrumental in its move from Philadelphia, which had been the capital for the previous ten years. "If Washington was its father, Jefferson might perhaps be called its uncle," his biographer Dumas Malone would write.

The District of Columbia site was the land along the Potomac that had been donated by Virginia and Maryland in 1790, following recommendation by George Washington, who, not seeking a monument to himself, had proposed that the place be called "Federal City."

The scratchily built national capital was much more like a Potemkin village than a city, dotted with empty storefronts and facades put up by speculators. Gallatin sneered that the federal city was "far from being pleasant or even convenient. Around the capital are seven or eight boarding houses, one tailor, one shoemaker, one printer, one washing woman, a grocery shop, a pamphlet and stationery shop, a small dry goods shop and an oyster house. This makes the whole of the federal city.''

The new district incorporated two existing towns—Georgetown on the Maryland side, with a population of about three thousand, and Alexandria on the Virginia side, with a population of about five thousand. The ''city'' of Washington was smaller than both.

Capitol Hill was located on the Eastern Branch of the Potomac at the center of the district, situated on a rise called Jenkins Hill, one side of which stepped down into a broad meadow.

By the time of Jefferson's arrival, Congress had been in session ten days. As the outgoing vice president, Jefferson would normally have been on hand the first day to attend to his duties, but he had carefully delayed his coming until after President John Adams's farewell speech to Congress. Jefferson wished to avoid an embarrassment to the defeated outgoing president.

The Adamses were not so generous. Attributing Jefferson's delay to more epicurean motives, Abigail Adams wrote her daughter: ''It is said [Mister Jefferson] is on his way, but travels with so many delicacies in his· rear that he cannot get on fast, lest some of them should suffer.''

Jefferson had taken rooms within easy reach of the Capitol at Conrad and McMunn's boardinghouse, located on the south side of Capitol Hill at the newly platted corner of New Jersey Avenue and C Street. Commonly referred to as Conrad's, the boardinghouse was one of seven or eight such hostels clustered around the Hill.

The vice president shared a community dining table with some thirty other executives and congressmen. However, unlike the others, including his Swiss friend Albert Gallatin, Jefferson was not obliged to share a bedroom. In deference to his present office and his impending presidency, Jefferson was given a suite which included a parlor and a bedroom all to himself. Once settled in, he began daily walks to the Capitol to preside over the Senate.

He was a fastidious diner, leaning toward vegetarian menus, ''eating little animal food,'' he would write, ''and that not as an aliment so much as a condiment for the vegetables which constitute my principal diet.'' He believed in the medicinal and nutritional value of wine, having daily ''the doctor's glass and a half of wine and even treble it with a friend.'' He avoided hard liquor, preferring ''malt liquors and cider as my table drinks and my breakfast is of tea and coffee.'' Each morning he would bathe his feet in cold water.

In this year of 1800, the Congress was meeting in the north wing of the Capitol, which was still under construction. The south wing was still in the design stage, stalled by lack of financing, and would not be occupied as the House of Representatives until 1803. The Supreme Court was in an even worse fix. Not only was it unbuilt, it didn't even exist on paper. Space for it had been inadvertently left out of the architects' plans. To compensate, the court was allowed to hold sessions in the thirty-foot-long Senate Clerk's Office in the north wing of the Capitol. The Supreme Court would meet there for the next seven years.

At the time, the House of Representatives was considered the more important branch of the Congress. The important early debates on the Constitution, states' rights, nullification, and secession had all taken place in the House. It had sessions open to the public and the press, and its members were directly elected by the people. In contrast, the Senate sessions were closed and its members were selected by state legislatures.[2] The openness of the House was sought by politicians ambitious to broadcast their causes or themselves. Senate members were regarded with suspicion because of their secret sessions, their wealth, and their autocratic ways. But the difference between the two bodies was designed as a necessity. The House, because of its two-year election spans, had a propensity to inflame and be inflamed, to be demagogic. Percolating with the dangers of tyranny, it might react too immediately to the public. The Senate was seen as the saucer that cooled the coffee. Members there, shielded from public clamor by six-year elections, could consider measures coolly and decide on them with detachment.

Below Capitol Hill was a sluggish stream called Goose Creek by Marylanders and the Tyber by Virginians. Its banks were being leveled to make way for the still-unborn Pennsylvania Avenue, now little more than a cowpath connecting the unfinished Capitol to the unfinished executive mansion. Down this proposed avenue, a mile and a half away and separated from the Capitol by swamp, was an incomplete, gray-stone building which was officially known as the President's House, but was already being referred to as the White House because of whitewash sealer applied by Scottish stonecutters during its construction in the 1790s. It was the center of a small complex where office buildings were being erected for administrative staff. Scattered between the White House and the Congress were some six hundred other structures—shops, stables, boardinghouses, printers, and the like, many half-finished, built on private land to accommodate a population of some three thousand people. Prices were very dear.

After George Washington died at the age of sixty-seven on December 14, 1799, the federal city took his name and became his monument— situating itself on a plateau below his Mount Vernon burial place.

For legislators and their families, moving from the previous capital in Philadelphia down to Washington was like moving from heaven to hell. Washington, D.C., was at the end of a wilderness. Even getting there was a tough ride, said a stagecoach traveler:

In the winter season, during the sitting of Congress, every turn of your wagon wheel is for many miles attended with danger. The roads are never repaired; deep ruts, rocks and stumps of trees, every minute impede your progress, and often threaten your limbs with dislocation.

Arrived at the city, you are struck with its grotesque appearance. In one view from the capitol hill, the eye fixes upon a row of uniform houses, ten or twelve in number, while it faintly discovers the adjacent tenements to be miserable wooden structures. . . . In some parts speculators have cleared the wood from their grounds, and erected temporary wooden buildings; others have fenced in their lots and attempted to cultivate them but the sterility of the land laid out for the city is such that this plan has also failed. The country adjoining consists of woods in a state of nature and in some places of mere swamps, which give the scene a curious patchwork appearance. . . . Neither park nor mall, neither churches, theatres, nor colleges could I discover. . . .

Strangers after viewing the [public] offices of the new nation are apt to inquire for the city, while they are in its very center.

There were, in fact, three churches. Christ Church Episcopal occupied one of those small frame buildings in 1800. St. Patrick's Catholic church on F Street and St. Andrew's Presbyterian, also frame structures, opened their doors in 1799. And there was one theater, the National, which opened August 22, 1800.

But our visitor found that even the White House, though built of good stone, was in a shambles: "The ground around it, instead of being laid out in a suitable style, remains in its ancient rude state so that, in a dark night, instead of finding your way to the house, you may, perchance, fall into a pit or stumble over a heap of rubbish."

The keeper of that house, Abigail Adams, had mixed feelings about it. In a letter to her daughter dated November 1800, she began with a complaint about its isolation but ended with an appreciation of the site's beauty:

"Woods are all you see from Baltimore until you reach *the city*, which is so only in name. Here and there is a small cottage, without a glass window, interspersed among the forests, through which you travel miles without seeing any human being."

The first lady found the view pleasant enough but the nights were cold. "If they would let me have wood enough to keep fires, I would be pleased . . . but surrounded with forests, can you believe that wood is not to be had because people cannot be found to cut and cart it!"

As for the White House itself, "we have not the least fence, yard or other conveniences." Her servants were hanging laundry to dry in an unfinished audience hall named "The East Room." Nevertheless, she concluded that it was "a beautiful spot, capable of every improvement and the more I view it, the more I am delighted with it."

The 1800 election victory by the Democrats had inflamed the nation, with certain quarters even contemplating the extreme of civil war. The prospect of Jefferson's presidency was regarded, even proclaimed by Jefferson himself, as a Second American Revolution.

It was the intention of Jefferson, Madison, and their political party to turn the United States away from privilege, class, and oligarchy and toward democracy. Jefferson's Democrats very consciously intended to set a political example for the world and even for history.

The nation was polarized primarily between the haves and have-nots because money, then as now, was what made the wheels go round. Money not only created barriers between classes, it caused differences among men. Jefferson and his army chief, James Wilkinson, were always short of it. Alexander Hamilton was corrupted by it. Aaron Burr, while generous, was so careless with it that it would send him on a fateful expedition. And Meriwether Lewis was heedless of it.

The opulence of the ruling class was in sharp contrast to the poverty of the average family, which in ninety-five cases out of a hundred were farming families. They lived as their forebears had lived a thousand years earlier in the days of King Arthur and Charlemagne. They made their own clothes, forged their own tools, butchered their meat, harvested their wheat, and cobbled their own shoes. A study of Delaware farms in the period shows that while Americans had land they had little else. The average farm was of about one hundred acres, the most a single family could plow. The typical family had a one-room log cabin or house, measuring about eighteen feet by twenty feet; no barns or sheds; no livestock other than a milk cow; no draft animals, ox or horse; and no machinery. Farm equipment consisted of a hoe, a reaping hook, a hand sifter for grain, and a plow. The farmer, his wife and children usually pulled the plow.[3]

The poverty extended everywhere in the nation. Although New England was on the verge of an industrial explosion, in 1801 that region was still struggling. Henry Adams tells us Boston was falling apart, its crooked, narrow streets bulging with filth, its population dwindling, its harbor somnolent. Puritan morals still ruled social intercourse. Life was plain and recreation was simple. Sleighing, riding, dancing, skeet and target shooting, and other innocent pastimes were considered acceptable entertainment.

In the South, with its Cavalier tradition transported from royalist England, things got wilder. Horseracing and cockfighting had long been favorites. Parties were rowdier than in the North, dancing more spirited and bodices lower. In all areas of the country, men and women drank alcohol and used tobacco with such enthusiasm that foreigners regarded it as a national disease.

Church life, almost always Protestant Christian in one form or another, was a central factor in communities north and south. In the villages of New England the Congregational minister was often the most influential man in town. He ruled the conduct of the citizenry, censored their manners, and did not hesitate to interfere in their politics.

Thomas Jefferson, whom the orthodox freely denounced as an infidel and—even worse—a freethinker, had good reason to complain of the New England ministry's interference in politics. Jefferson's religious skepticism was not unique among the southern planters, who can best be described as favoring a Unitarian outlook, preferring to be viewed as "liberal Christians" to distinguish their ways from those of intolerant Yankee Christians.

The year 1800—Jefferson's nineteenth century—arrived in America to find formal education moribund. The faculty of Harvard University consisted of the president, three professors, and four tutors. Bishop Madison was teaching a group of barefoot boys at William and Mary College in the deserted colonial capital of Williamsburg.

Agricultural products, particularly tobacco and lumber, were the chief articles marketed by rural communities. Wheat was raised everywhere except in the coastal regions. Fishing was important in the Northeast. The South was only at the beginning of its great cotton and sugar cultivation.

Despite the oligarchic nature of the ruling government, the country was in relatively good shape when George Washington left office in March of 1797, to be succeeded by John Adams. The financial system was well established. The Indian threat east of the Mississippi had been largely eliminated. And Jay's Treaty (1794) with England and Pinckney's Treaty (1795) with Spain had enlarged U.S. territory and reduced diplomatic difficulties—although at the cost of angering revolutionary France.

By this November of 1800, the thirteen original states had grown to sixteen and been joined by three territories—Mississippi, Indiana, and the Northwest (Ohio). Only twenty-five years earlier, the states had been a narrow ribbon of territory extending from the shores of the Atlantic to the eastern slope of the Appalachians. Now the nation of 1800 reached to the Mississippi and measured 850,000 square miles, comparable in size to Europe, the source of most of North America's population, which had nearly doubled since the census of 1790.

The United States of 1800 was roughly trapezoidal in shape, bounded on the corners by what would become the states of Maine, Georgia, Mississippi, and Minnesota. The Atlantic coastline marked the border on one side and the east bank of the Mississippi River on the other. This vast territory was flanked by British Canada on the north, the Atlantic Ocean to the east, Spanish Louisiana on the west, and the Spanish Florida peninsula to the south.

Population density was sparse, fewer than five people per square mile, the vast majority of them still residing on the Atlantic seaboard. In 1790, when the first census was taken, the population of the United States had been 3.9 million. By 1800, it had increased to 5.3 million, an increase due almost entirely to births. Immigration had been cut off by the Revolution and was further impaired by the outbreak of general war in Europe in 1793. Although many efforts had been made to attract immigrants, by 1800 the estimated annual immigration was not more than four thousand people.

Most of the several million Indians who originally inhabited the eastern United States had been absorbed, eradicated, encircled, or pushed into Canada or across the Mississippi by the great European migration.

In the South, there were no true cities other than Charleston. The Virginia capital of Richmond counted only 7,000 people. Norfolk and Petersburg had populations of fewer than 3,000. The largest city in the nation was greater Philadelphia with 75,000. New York was a city of some 61,000 souls at the southern end of Manhattan Island. It would not experience the explosion of growth that would make it one of the world's great cities until construction of the Erie Canal in the 1820s.

Baltimore had 26,800. Boston, once the most remarkable of colonial cities, had slipped to fourth with 25,000.

If viewed from a distance, these cities of the Enlightenment would be quite recognizable to a modern visitor. There were multistoried buildings made of wood, brick, or stone and with glass windows. Streets were often paved, usually with brick or cobblestone. There were shops, markets, street merchants, theaters, taverns and coffee shops, many with their own advertising signs. Horse-drawn trolleys provided public transportation. Bands played in the parks. Church spires dotted the landscape. Newspapers were everywhere.

Up close, however, one encountered a life closer to the Middle Ages. Street crime was uncommon but disease and fire were rampant. There was no plumbing, no petroleum, no heating stoves or electricity. There were public baths but otherwise bathing was minimal.

There was definitely an upstairs-downstairs division among the classes. The richer citizens were generally well-laundered in person and dress, well-groomed, properly tailored and shod. They slept in clean beds, were cared for by servants, and had a vigorous nightlife.

Everyone ate well, but the poor tended to live from dawn to dusk. Artificial light was confined to whale-oil lamps and tallow candles, both of which were expensive. The poor, most of whom were northern European immigrants, often had head lice, and their mattresses and houses were infested with bedbugs, pinhead-sized parasites that sucked the blood and left red stains on pillows and sheets. There was little pest control. Rats and mice abounded, as did flies and mosquitoes. Food smells were pervasive for all classes, cooked in fireplaces that were kept going even in summer. Not until the invention of the coal stove fifty years later would the fireplace be replaced as the main cooking agency.

There was little sewerage. Rich and poor alike used chamber pots and outhouses. When privies were filled, slaves or convicts dug out the sludge and loaded it on carts called "honey wagons" to move it to a dumping site, which was often the nearest river or creek. Disease and odors were bred not only from human waste but from the cows, chickens, pigs, and horses that inhabited virtually every block.

In 1800, slavery was just beginning to be phased out.

By the time Jefferson arrived to claim his presidency, the economic feasibility of slavery was being fueled in the South by operation of the first successful sugar refinery in Spanish-controlled New Orleans (1791) and the invention of the cotton gin (1793). Those technologies spurred large-scale cultivation and geometrically multiplied the demand for field labor.

The election of 1800 began in Philadelphia in the congressional sessions during the spring of that year. Each party held a caucus of its congressmen and senators and selected its candidates for president and vice president. The Federalists decided on Adams and Charles Cotesworth Pinckney of South Carolina, the latter being the brother of

Alexander Hamilton's choice in 1796 and now a sectional choice designed to deprive Jefferson of southern votes. As in 1796, the Democrats declared for Jefferson and Burr, which was another ticket based partly on sectional considerations. There would be no popular election either in the form of primaries or a general election. Despite their private nature, or maybe because of it, elections were a lot rougher in those days than now.

For Federalists, it was somewhat a replay of the 1796 election in that Hamilton, pursuing his own agenda, would again attempt to sabotage the party's nominee—President John Adams. But the historical surprise would come at the end of the year when the electoral votes were counted by Jefferson's Democrats.

Hamilton, desperate to regain control of his party from John Adams, spent the summer writing pamphlets and otherwise engaging in intrigues against Adams, all to no avail. Hamilton also tried to steal the Democrats' electoral votes by fixing two key states—Pennsylvania and New York.

In the Pennsylvania scheme, Hamilton got the Senate to refuse to accept the Democrats' electoral victory on the basis of a technicality. The Democrats raised such an uproar, however, that a compromise was reached whereby seven votes went to the Federalists and eight to the Democrats.

In New York, Hamilton wanted the passionately anti-Burr governor, John Jay, to call the outgoing Federalist legislature back into session and nullify the Democratic victory there, too, by changing the method of choice of the presidential electors. However, Hamilton's proposal was leaked to a Democratic newspaper and Governor Jay backed away from the scheme.

By mid-November 1800, all of Hamilton's machinations had failed. Although no official electoral vote had been counted, sufficient results had been leaked to the press to show that the Democrats had won the national election.

It was then that Jefferson rode to Washington to claim his long-awaited prize. He arrived, however, to find rumors circulating that because of Hamilton's various manipulations, particularly in Pennsylvania, there was a strong possibility of a tie between him and Burr in the electoral votes. Other rumors began to float that if this proved true, then the Federalists had a plan to prevent either Democrat from gaining the presidency by tying the House into knots, denying a majority to either Jefferson or Burr. Thus the presidency would go to the next man in line—the incumbent *Federalist* secretary of state, John Marshall.

Uncertain of what schemes might be afoot, Jefferson attempted to sound out Burr in a letter dated December 15:

> *I understand several of the high-flying Federalists have expressed the hope that the two [Democratic] tickets may be equal, and their determination in that case to prevent a choice by the House of Representatives, which they are strong enough to do. . . .*

The thought of being cheated out of the presidency so unsettled Jefferson that he endorsed a plan to surround Washington City with troops in order to prevent a Federalist coup. He would hold the government in a military grip until a new constitutional convention could meet and repair the confusions of the Electoral College.

On December 28, when an unofficial tally of electors reached Washington, it became certain that Jefferson and Burr were tied. The election was to be decided in the House of Representatives. And the Congress that had jurisdiction to decide was not the incoming Democratic House but the outgoing, lame-duck Federalist-majority House. It was, therefore, the Federalists who would decide which Democrat they wanted as president. The Democrats, however, had an ace in the hole. While the Federalists constituted a majority in the House, they did not control a majority of the states, because of the makeup of the various delegations. The state edge actually went to the Democrats, and fortunately for Jefferson, the tie was to be resolved by one vote per state, the representatives of each state caucusing to cast their single vote.

Jefferson would need a majority of nine states to win.

In the meanwhile, Jefferson's suspicions about Burr were proving unfounded. The New Yorker was making no move to exploit the confusion. To the contrary, he wrote Jefferson to reconfirm their respective status: "My personal friends are perfectly informed of my wishes on the subject and can never think of diverting a single vote from you." Burr said he had no doubt that Jefferson would win the presidential vote and, "As far forth as my knowledge extends, it is the unanimous determination of the Republicans of every grade to support your administration with unremitted zeal."

These reassurances seemed to relax Jefferson and he wrote his daughter Maria that Burr's "conduct has been honorable and decisive. . . ."

Nevertheless, suspicions were being bandied about in the newspapers that the Federalists and Burr were conniving a way to steal the election before the secret certificates of the electors were opened on the second Wednesday in February 1801. According to biographer Dumas Malone, the uncertainties "must have been exceedingly trying for Jefferson, though it would not have been like him to say so." The would-be president spent New Year's Day, 1801, with George Washington's widow at Mount Vernon. He spent the remainder of January attending to Senate duties.

During that January, the opposition Federalist majority in the Congress confirmed John Marshall as Chief Justice and agreed as a group to support Burr, whom they regarded as the lesser of the two evils. Meanwhile, their titular party leader, outgoing president John Adams, remained aloof from the intrigues.

Not so Alexander Hamilton. Jealous of both Adams and Jefferson, he was even more averse to Burr. He did not want to see his power base in New York eroded by Burr's elevation to the presidency. Hamilton lobbied hard to swing the Federalist vote back to Jefferson, writing friends that "Jefferson is to be preferred. He is by far not so dangerous a man" as Burr.

Hamilton argued cynically that Jefferson's "pretensions to character" would make him easier to handle. Hamilton felt that Jefferson's integrity—whether real or feigned—ensured a certain and predictable path. There was "no fair reason to suppose [Jefferson] capable of being corrupted," said Hamilton. As for Burr, Hamilton insisted he was absolutely lacking in character—in modern terms, a sociopath. Therefore, Burr was "unpredictable and impossible to handle."

Despite such lobbying, Hamilton was unable to sway the main body of Federalists. They continued to feel they had less to fear from Burr and more to gain.

To Burr's credit, there is not the least evidence that he contrived to displace Jefferson, or to take advantage of the Federalist favor. Even

Jefferson faulted Burr only for failing to issue any new disavowals. This may have been an act of deception on Burr's part, as some later historians have theorized. But it is more likely that Burr felt that his December utterances on the subject were sufficient. That disclaimer was certainly well known, having been distributed by Jefferson's friends to several newspapers for republication and never retracted by Burr.

As the voting deadline neared, a survey prior to the opening of the certificates made Jefferson confident of seven states and hopeful for an eighth. But the crucial ninth proved elusive.

Finally there arrived the second Wednesday, the eleventh of February, 1801, and the two houses met in joint session to count the ballots state by state as the Constitution prescribed. The certificates of the electors of the sixteen states were opened by Jefferson in his capacity as presiding officer of the Senate. He himself declared the result, which showed the expected tied electoral vote, 73–73. The Senate then declared that the election would be decided by the House, whereupon that body retired to its own small chamber and began deliberations.

The first ballot showed four New England states, South Carolina, and Delaware for Burr, for a total of six votes. Eight states went for Jefferson. Vermont and Maryland abstained—undecided because their delegations couldn't agree. The House balloted thirty-five times during the next five days with no change in result. Throughout, the vote remained six states to eight for a total of 73 electors each.

The thirty-sixth ballot was the breakthrough. The Federalists within the divided Vermont and Maryland delegations suddenly abstained, throwing those states into Jefferson's column and giving him a majority of ten.

He was now elected president. There would be no militia stranglehold on Washington, and no constitutional coup. The process had prevailed.

There also would never be a repeat of such confusion. Just prior to the election of 1804, Jefferson shepherded through a Twelfth Amendment, which provided that presidential electors vote separately for president and vice president.

Although it has become a commonplace that Burr maneuvered to steal the election from Jefferson, there is no proof of such a scheme.

There is proof, however, that Jefferson justly contrived to secure his own election.

The official House history tells us that after the thirty-fifth ballot, the deadlock was broken by Congressman James Bayard of Delaware, who successfully lobbied his fellow Federalists in the Vermont and Maryland delegations to abstain and thus throw their states to Jefferson.

Bayard convinced his fellow delegates that Burr's chances for election were impossible. With Jefferson's militia in mind, Bayard argued that failure to appoint Jefferson would result in civil war "at the expense of the Constitution."

Bayard's assessment was realistic but it seems to have been in some part self-serving.

We now know that on the night of February 16, just after the deadlocked thirty-fifth ballot, Bayard went to Conrad's boardinghouse and met secretly with members of Jefferson's inner circle. In return for switching his influence, Bayard wanted certain guarantees, which included his naming the federal tax collectors in Philadelphia and Wilmington. One of Jefferson's top aides, General Samuel Smith, gave Bayard the guarantees. The following morning, Bayard delivered the votes as promised.

Dumas Malone and other biographers assert that there was no evidence that Jefferson was directly involved in the deal. And in a memorandum written some five years later for his personal files, dated April 15, 1806, Jefferson himself somewhat warily denied involvement:

> *I do not recollect that I even had any particular conversation with General Samuel Smith on this subject. Very possibly I had however, as the general subject & all its parts were the constant themes of conversation in the private* tête à têtes *with our friends. But certain I am that neither he, nor any other republican ever uttered the most distant hint to me about submitting to any conditions or giving any assurances to anybody; and still more certainly was neither he nor any other person ever authorized by me to say what I would or would not do.*

In that same year of 1806, indeed, in an act that prompted Jefferson's memorandum above, Bayard insisted there was a deal. He said he and certain other House members tried to get the best "terms of capitulation" they could, although he did not claim to have met directly with Jefferson.

As for Jefferson's aide, Smith, he admitted giving Bayard the guarantees, but said he had not been specifically authorized to do so by Jefferson.

Deal or no deal, Burr, just turned forty-five, was now not only certain to be vice president, but if tradition followed its course he would follow Jefferson as president. But that was not the way Jefferson saw it. To him, Burr was still the main threat to the Virginia Dynasty—a succession of two-term presidencies in which his own would be followed by those of Madison and Monroe.

On the morning of March 4, 1801, Thomas Jefferson was preparing to be sworn in as the third president of the United States, the first to be installed at the new capital of Washington, D.C.

He had reformed his image since his ambassadorial days when, upon returning from France, he arrived in Philadelphia with a "suit of silk, ruffles and an elegant topaz ring . . . conspicuous in red waistcoat and red breeches, the fashion of Versailles," according to Senator William Maclay. The back-country Pennsylvanian grumbled that Jefferson "had been long enough abroad to catch the tone of European folly."

In these later years, Jefferson was spurning such peacock adornments, having adopted the clothing of a simple Virginia farmer more fitting to his populist style. It is unclear whether his fashion statement was a matter of evolved preference or a calculated pose, but even those small matters of costume gave grounds for complaints about his character.

The renowned pastor Nathaniel Emmons warned his New England congregation that the president-elect was a manipulative fraud:

> *He possesses, in a high degree, the art of captivating and corrupting all sorts of people with whom he converses. And when he is clothed with the ensigns of royalty, his power and opportunity of corrupting his subjects will greatly increase. His sentiments and manners are a living law to his subjects. In his familiar intercourse with all around him, he undoubtedly seizes those soft moments*

which are the most favorable to his malignant design of seduction.
He esteems nothing too low, nor too mean to be done, that would
serve to eradicate every moral and religious principle from the
minds of the people . . . the nation will rue the day, and detest
the folly, delusion and intrigue, which raised him to the head of
the United States.

The opinion of New England clergymen notwithstanding, Jefferson
had won the presidency and was now prepared to officially take the
prize. Once installed, he would do away with the trappings of White
House ceremony and the Federalist royal court. Believing that the
national government should concern itself mostly with foreign affairs
and leave local matters to the states, he planned budget cuts in all
branches of government.

Whether men loved him or hated him, they agreed he had an original
cast of mind, a freethinker on all subjects. Charles Jared Ingersoll—
author, historian, and congressman—found Jefferson's ''manners were
easy, though not elegant, his address unassuming and agreeable.'' But
like Pastor Emmons, Ingersoll also found Jefferson manipulative, even
deceitful:

His colloquial talents are considerable and he understands per-
fectly the art of managing an unwieldy majority of the representa-
tives. . . . He lives in one corner of a half-finished, half-furnished
palace, plain even to peculiarity in his appearance and establish-
ment, accessible to everybody at all times, affecting the most repub-
lican simplicity, and as carefully subversive of common forms, as
most men in his situation would have been carefully observant of
them. . . .

In the view of men like Emmons and Ingersoll, Jefferson was not to
be trusted. Ingersoll found Jefferson to be a pragmatic idealist, ''well
read in books, but better in mankind,'' but his ''idealism is often put
aside when it becomes impractical. Though geography and natural
history are beholden to his researches and patronage, politics has swallowed up all his ideas.'' He is disdainful of the trappings of power,
''but his conduct toward individuals is too often marked by vindic-

tiveness and duplicity, and the statesman frequently sinks in the politician. As sagacity is his strongest talent, insincerity is his most
prominent defect.''

Shortly before noon on the day of inauguration, Jefferson left his
lodgings at Conrad's boardinghouse and, accompanied by a few
friends, walked across the muddy square to the Senate wing of the
partly built Capitol. Trailing behind him were two lone representatives
of the outgoing Adams administration—Benjamin Stoddert and Samuel
Dexter, respectively the secretaries of the navy and treasury. A militia
from the neighborhood provided escort but there was no parade, no
sidelines full of cheering well-wishers. Indeed, much of the country
did not wish him well. For their inaugural story, a Boston newspaper
ran a black-bordered obituary reading:

YESTERDAY EXPIRED

Deeply Regretted by Millions of grateful Americans,
And by *all* GOOD MEN,
The FEDERAL ADMINISTRATION
of the
GOVERNMENT of the *United States*:
Animated by

A WASHINGTON, an ADAMS: - a HAMILTON, KNOX,
PICKERING, WOLCOTT, McHENRY, MARSHALL,
STODDERT and DEXTER

Outgoing President Adams chose to ignore the inaugural, grouching
that a ''group of foreign liars, encouraged by a few ambitious native
gentlemen, have discomfited the education, the talents, the virtues
and the property of the country.'' His reference was primarily to the
reappearance of writings of Jefferson's pet journalist, the Scotsman
James Thompson Callender.

Adams himself had packed and scooted from town by 4:00 A.M.,
leaving empty the boxlike, unfinished White House that had so daunted
his wife, Abigail.[4] Also leaving before dawn to avoid the inaugural

was the bitterly hostile Speaker of the House, Thomas Sedgwick of Massachusetts.

Jefferson's inaugural was to be the most austere and humble, even the loneliest, in the history of such events.

As the fifty-seven-year-old president-elect ascended the steps of the Capitol with his tiny retinue behind him, there was a small crash of artillery. Entering the Senate chamber, Jefferson took his old seat in the vice president's chair. At his right was Aaron Burr, the new vice president. At his left was the man who would give him the oath of office, John Marshall. It was Marshall's first appearance as Chief Justice of the United States. In the whole country, it would have been difficult at that moment to find three men who more thoroughly disliked one another than Thomas Jefferson, John Marshall, and Aaron Burr.

John Marshall was a Federalist who held Jefferson's theories in despise and Jefferson himself in antipathy.[5] More austere and simple in manner than even the great Democrat, Marshall believed Jefferson to be an immoral opportunist. In Marshall's eyes, Jefferson had undermined George Washington by resigning from the Cabinet, weakened the office of the presidency, and now, at the moment of oath, Marshall predicted Jefferson's demagoguery would "increase his personal power, [because] the morals of the [man] cannot be pure."

Jefferson had no kinder regard for the Chief Justice, whom he dolefully described as "a gloomy malignant." But they stood dutifully side by side, with Burr behind them, as Marshall held out the Bible on which Jefferson swore to "preserve, protect and defend the Constitution of the United States."

The organization of the new government had already been made. Madison was the designated secretary of state. The Swiss immigrant Albert Gallatin was designated as secretary of the treasury. And Jefferson was content to retain Adams secretaries, Dexter and Stoddert, in the government for a few more months until he could find suitable replacements.

Prior to his inauguration, Jefferson had written to the commandant of the army, James Wilkinson, then in Pittsburgh, requesting that Captain Meriwether Lewis be transferred to Washington in "utmost haste" so that "he might sometimes aid us with informations of interest, which we may not otherwise possess. A personal acquaintance with him, owing from his being of my neighborhood, has induced me to select him, if his presence can be dispensed with without injury to the service.''[6]

Accompanying the Wilkinson instruction was a letter to Meriwether Lewis. It put a mysterious emphasis on a western connection:

The appointment to the Presidency of the U.S. has rendered it necessary for me to have a private secretary, and in selecting one I have thought it important to respect not only his capacity to aid in the private concerns of the household, but also to contribute to the mass of information which it is interesting for the administration to acquire. Your knowledge of the Western country, of the army and of all its interests and relations has rendered it desirable for public as well as private purposes that you should be engaged in that office.

The salary of the president's secretary was small, five hundred dollars per year. But Thomas Jefferson knew his protégé well and he played to Lewis's ambition: ''It would be an easy office, would make you know and be known to characters of influence in the affairs of our country, and give you the advantage of their wisdom. You would of course save also the expense of subsistence and lodging as you would be one of my family.''[7]

This warm invitation was written a bare six days after Jefferson had eked out his narrow victory over Aaron Burr in the Electoral College.

It was a grand time for young Lewis, the dawn of a new world, full of opportunity. Dull, gray winter was gone. Spring was in the air. The change of seasons and of administrations brightened all of his horizons.

The young, freckle-faced Virginian was full of confidence, invited to the center ring of ''the second American Revolution.'' Bursting with pride, stunned by the unsolicited, personal summons from the president, he could not help immediately boasting to a friend:

I cannot withhold from you the agreeable intelligence I received on my arrival [at Pittsburgh] by way of a very polite note from Thomas Jefferson, the newly elected President of the United States, signifying his wish that I should accept the office of his private secretary. This unbounded, as well as unexpected confidence, conferred on me by a man whose virtue and talents I have ever adored, and always conceived second to none, I must confess did not fail to raise me somewhat in my own estimation. . . . I deem the prospect too flattering to be neglected by a man of my standing and prospects in life.[8]

Upon receipt of his travel orders, the lanky, twenty-six-year-old infantry captain drew three horses from the army quartermaster at Pittsburgh and packed his belongings aboard.

Although the distance was less than two hundred and fifty miles, it was not an easy ride. The road between Pittsburgh and Philadelphia was not much better than a deer path. South of Philadelphia, wrote Henry Adams, ''the road was tolerable as far as Baltimore, but between Baltimore and the new city of Washington it meandered through forests; the driver chose the track which seemed least dangerous and rejoiced if in wet seasons he reached Washington without miring or upsetting his wagon.'' Beyond the Potomac, the roads became steadily worse, until south of Petersburg, Virginia, even the mails were carried on horseback. Except for a stagecoach link between Charleston and Savannah, there were no other roads worthy of the name in the southern states.

Riding over highways turned into wallows by spring rains, it took Meriwether twenty-two days to ride to Washington, arriving only to find that the president had left the capital one day earlier. However, there was a message from Jefferson inviting Lewis to join him ''for a few days of relaxation'' at Monticello.

Not wanting to put even more hard riding under his rear, Lewis declined and instead stayed in Washington.

Despite its primitive state, the city held certain attractions for Lewis. He was supposed to have been in love with one of the famous belles of the day, Theodosia Burr, daughter of Aaron Burr. Legend has it that when Meriwether arrived in Washington to take up his assignment, he intended to propose marriage to her. Instead, he learned that two months earlier she had wed the enormously wealthy young South

Carolinian Joseph Alston and they had left the city. Disappointed, Lewis turned to his new career with even fiercer energy.

Another dark cloud was that Meriwether's elevation was not universally admired. Thomas Bates, father of Lewis's friend Tarleton, suggested to his other son, Frederick, in May 1801, that the appointment should have gone to one of the brothers, the father saying: "Capt. Lewis has received and accepted the appointment of private secretary to the President, so that my golden dreams have been delusive."[9]

Jefferson's half-finished, half-furnished White House had a small household. The president's $25,000 salary quintupled his vice-presidential income, but he was still in debt. To help maintain the cavernous White House, he invited James and Dolley Madison to move in with him. Dolley became the de facto first lady. Jefferson found a chef who could do French cuisine and brought eleven servants, all slaves, from Monticello. The Virginian Meriwether Lewis fit nicely into the ensemble.

Soon, however, in this era of easy slander, rumors began that Jefferson's interest in boarding the Madisons was based on an undue familiarity with Dolley.

Dorothea Payne Todd Madison, known to contemporaries and history as "Dolley" or "Dolly," was a woman of personality and expression and a certain experience. She had been married at the age of twenty-two to Philadelphia lawyer John Todd, a Quaker of good standing. They had two sons, but in the yellow fever epidemic of 1793 the family was stricken. Only Dolley and her oldest son, John Payne Todd, survived.

Dolley and her widowed mother, Mrs. John Payne, operated a very select boardinghouse in Philadelphia, which catered to the elite of the then national capital. Among the boarders was Aaron Burr and regular visitors included President Washington and Secretaries Hamilton and Jefferson.

Another constant caller was little Jimmy Madison. In a note to a friend, Dolley confided, "Aaron Burr says that the great little Madison has asked to be brought to see me this evening."

The great little Madison was forty-three at the time, nearly twenty years older than Dolley and a couple of inches shorter. He was not only small but prim, especially in comparison to the flashy but graceful object of his heart.

Burr, also small, but known to be a womanizer, was anything but prim, and many in Philadelphia wondered about Dolley's relationship with him. But it seems to have been more a trusted friendship than an affair, and on May 13, 1794, Dolley named Burr as the one by whom she wished her child to be raised if she should die.

Four months later, Dolley and James Madison were married at the home of her sister Lucy at Harewood in what is now West Virginia.

Dolley arrived in Washington on the arm of her husband, the new secretary of state. Unable to find immediate quarters, they accepted Jefferson's invitation to stay with him at the White House.

She was now thirty-three, in the full bloom of womanhood. She was lithe and graceful as a palmetto, with skin the color of rich cream and eyes of bright violet. Her hair was long and the color of dark mink. She pinned it up loosely behind her, and except for formal occasions, when she wore gowns of low décolletage, her dress was simple, so as not to detract from her startling beauty, according to Washington Irving. She often wore boots, a beige cotton skirt of ankle length, and a white linen shirt with the upper buttons undone. She was just too devastating to be running around loose in a house of bachelors, a circumstance that inspired much vicious comment. For example, observers such as Margaret Bayard Smith, a close friend of Jefferson's, sniffed that she wished Dolley Madison's "virtue matched her grace."

Many rumors centered on the possibilities between Dolley and Jefferson, who had just turned fifty-eight years old on April 23. He was amused, writing disingenuously to his then ally John Randolph: "I thought my age and ordinary demeanor would have prevented any suggestions in that form, from the improbability of their obtaining belief. . . ."

But by the end of May, the gossip had proved too much even for the hardened Madisons, who took another house. The president wrote his daughter Martha: "Mrs. Madison left us two days ago to commence housekeeping, so that Captain Lewis and myself are left like two mice in a church." Jefferson's married daughters were unable to leave their families in Virginia to take Dolley's place.

It was about this time that Jefferson sent Lewis to see an old friend, a visit that would haunt Jefferson for the remainder of his life.

The man Lewis was sent to see was James Thompson Callender, the Scottish journalist who had so skillfully carved up Alexander Hamilton in the Reynolds affair.

Since that time, Callender had become a regular borrower of money and other favors from the Democratic leader, almost a pensioner of Jefferson's. He referred to himself as Jefferson's "assistant writer." But as rewarding as his services to Jefferson might be, they also carried great risks. Because of Callender's anti-Federalist writings, Adams and Hamilton had made him a target of the Alien and Sedition Laws and sent orders for his arrest. Harried by federal marshals from job to job, the quasi-fugitive found protection under Virginia Democrats and eventually wound up writing for the *Examiner*, one of four newspapers in the small Virginia capital of Richmond (population 5,735).

In Richmond, Callender commenced writing against Hamilton and the Federalists "such a Tornado as no government ever got before." He published a new book, *The Prospect Before Us*, which in his words damned "Adams in particular and Federalists in general." When he complained he was "in danger of being murdered," Jefferson reassured him that although "the violence which was meditated against you lately has excited a very general indignation in this part of the country, our state [of Virginia] has been remarkable for its order and submission to the laws."

The Adams administration, however, gave as good as it got, and in June of 1800, Callender was arrested and tried before Federalist Judge Samuel Chase, who, on rigged evidence, found the journalist guilty of sedition. Callender was sent to prison and from there he wrote Jefferson a series of famous "letters from Richmond jail."

When Jefferson became president, he pardoned and freed Callender, but the journalist wanted more—demanding that his fine of two hundred dollars also be returned. When it wasn't, the furious Callender turned on his benefactor and wrote to Secretary of State Madison that "Mr. Jefferson has not returned one shilling of my fine. I now begin to know what ingratitude is." Callender told Madison he was in love and to win his bride he needed a permanent job—like that of postmaster in Richmond, a job paying about fifteen hundred per year, a handsome sum for the period. Madison was wary, keeping Callender at arm's length while telling Monroe, who was then governor of Virginia, that it was difficult to deal with a man "whose imaginations and passions have been so fermented."

Jefferson, too, was writing Monroe, saying that he, like Madison, should remain distanced from Callender in the matter. But Jefferson also wanted "to take from Callender all room for complaint" and enclosed a check for fifty dollars to help defray the fine.

The check was still in the mail when the angry Callender showed up in Washington and took quarters in a cheap boardinghouse. Before he could make a scene at the White House, Jefferson sent Meriwether Lewis with another fifty dollars to appease the writer.

The visit was not a success. Callender took the money but sent back a threat, causing Jefferson to write Monroe:

> *His language to Captain Lewis was very high toned. He intimated that he was in possession of things which he could and would make use of in a certain case; that he received the fifty dollars not as a charity but as a due, in fact as hush money; that I knew what he expected, viz. a certain office, and more to this effect. Such a misconstruction of my charities puts an end to them forever. . . . He knows nothing of me which I am not willing to declare to the world myself. . . . I gave to him from time to time such aids as I could afford, merely as a man of genius suffering under persecution, and not as a writer in our politics. It is long since I wished he would cease writing on them, as doing more harm than good."*

Not long afterward, Callender became editor of another Richmond newspaper—*The Recorder*—where he began a war of slanders against Jefferson that hasn't really quieted to this day. In his opening broadside, Callender confessed that Jefferson had co-authored or commissioned all the "seditious" articles against Adams and the Federalists. Striking a second time, the embittered Scot resurrected old charges against Jefferson, such as his alleged cowardice in the Revolutionary War.

Callender followed with just about every story he could gather from overseers and scandalmongers about Jefferson's past life—charging him with having a family of Negro children by the slave Sally Hemings; saying that Jefferson had been ordered out of the house of a certain Major Walker for pursuing Walker's wife; accusing Jefferson of having swindled his creditors by paying debts in worthless currency; and with having privately subsidized Callender himself to write the violently anti-Federalist *The Prospect Before Us*, even to furnishing material about the Hamilton-Reynolds affair for the same book.

Jefferson winced under the barrage, which was picked up and distributed nationally by the Federalist press and printed even in sometimes friendly journals such as the *New York Evening Post*.

The accusations were given credibility because Jefferson, among others, partially confirmed some of them.

Major John Walker, an old and trusting friend of Jefferson, said that Jefferson pursued Mrs. Walker before their marriage and even afterward had "renewed his caresses and placed in Mrs. Walker's gown a paper tending to convince her of the innocence of promiscuous love." Jefferson stole into "the room where my wife was undressing or in bed." He "attempted to seize her on her way from her chamber—indecent in manner." Walker said he had not taken immediate action because he had only learned of these things after Jefferson had gone to France.

Jefferson partially confirmed the Walker indiscretions, writing to his secretary of the navy, Robert Smith: "I plead guilty to one of their charges, that when young and single I offered love to a handsome lady. I acknowledge this incorrectness. It is the only one founded in truth among all [Callender's] allegations against me."

Jefferson also had carried on an affair, or attempted an affair, in Paris with Maria Cosway, the talented and beautiful wife of Richard Cosway, the most eminent English miniaturist of his time. Jefferson was forty-three and a recent widower; Maria was twenty-seven and enchanting, with golden hair and violet eyes, a gifted artist and musician. Their relationship was torrid and brief, ending when Jefferson returned to America in 1789.

As for the Sally Hemings charge, Jefferson remained silent, except for an indirect denial in a letter to Hamilton's surrogate editor, South Carolina congressman William L. Smith.

Callender specifically accused Jefferson of taking the slave Hemings to Paris as his mistress, but under guise of being maid to his daughter

Martha. Callender claimed that the widowed Jefferson kept a willing Hemings as his concubine upon his return from France in 1789 and that Hemings bore him five children.

There was sufficient fact in the story to sustain it for nearly two centuries. There indeed *were* blue-eyed, blond-haired mulatto slaves at Monticello, and Jefferson *did* show partiality to the Hemings children, all of whom he emancipated. But mainstream historians explain that this was due to the connections between the Hemings family and Jefferson's late wife.

Furthermore, modern investigators such as Dumas Malone, Jonathan Daniels, and Virginius Dabney have shown that Sally's lover was another member of the Jefferson clan, probably a nephew named Peter Carr or his brother Samuel, or both.

The scandal might have died out except that in the post–Civil War year of 1873, one of Sally Hemings's sons, Madison Hemings, gave a famous account to the Pike County, Ohio, *Republican* in which he claimed Thomas Jefferson sired him and four other of Sally's children. He said that during his mother's stay in Paris, she became pregnant by Jefferson:

> *He desired to bring my mother back to Virginia with him but she demurred. She was just beginning to understand the French language well, and in France she was free, while if she returned to Virginia she would be re-enslaved. So she refused to return with him. To induce her to do so he promised her extraordinary privileges, and made a solemn pledge that her children would be freed at the age of twenty-one years. In consequence of his promises, on which she implicitly relied, she returned with him to Virginia. Soon after their arrival she gave birth to a child, of whom Thomas Jefferson was the father. It lived but a short time. She gave birth to four others, and Jefferson was the father of all of them.*

Madison's story, however, was ridiculed at the time by those who knew him best. A bare five days later, the *Waverly Watchman*, of the same county, said such stories were common:

We have no doubt that there are at least fifty Negroes in this county who lay claim to illustrious parentage. . . . The children of Jefferson and Madison, Calhoun and Clay far outnumber Washington's body servants when Barnum was in the height of his prosperity. They are not to be blamed for making these assertions. It sounds much better for the mother to tell her offspring that "master" is their father than to acknowledge to them that some field hand, without a name, had raised her to the dignity of a mother. . . .

Nevertheless, the story was sustained during the era of Reconstruction and was revived by modern historians such as Fawn Brodie. No one, however, has offered any proof, documentary or otherwise, to counter the arguments of historians such as Daniels, Malone, and Dabney.

In the matter of Sally Hemings, the verdict would at the least be "unproven." But true or false, the whole accusation is irrelevant as it applies to Jefferson's character.

What would it say about character if Jefferson had had an affair with Hemings? That he was an adulterer? Yes. That he had sexual and perhaps emotional longings? Yes. And, possibly, that he exploited a person over whom he had enormous power? Again, yes. But all those matters of character are already established. Jefferson himself admitted to adultery, at least once during his marriage and once again after his wife died. Because of letters to his wife and to Maria Cosway, his capacity for both lust and emotion are known. And as for exploitation of others, he owned hundreds of slaves during his lifetime, at the very time he himself was denouncing slavery as immoral.

The most horrifying aspect of the Hemings accusation is that Jefferson would have allowed his own children to remain in slavery. But even there we have something of a precedent because the slave children of the Carrs would also have been his kin.

The case for character, or lack of it, is therefore established whether weighed against the social codes of Jefferson's time or our own. In the limited area of sex and romance, Jefferson was no more—or no less— than human; on the more important scale of exploitation and hypocrisy, the tall Virginian comes up guilty of both. The Hemings question in itself is extraneous except, were it proven true, to confirm what is already established.

One curious footnote to the tale is the death of Callender himself, and the similar death of one of the slaves, James Hemings, Sally's older brother.

Freed by Jefferson in 1796, James Hemings went to Paris, then returned to Monticello, alcoholic and rootless, as a free-lance cook. Leaving Monticello shortly afterward, he apparently killed himself in Baltimore in 1801. President Jefferson was not satisfied that it was a suicide and ordered an extensive investigation, which confirmed the fact.[10]

But Jefferson evidenced no such concern shortly afterward, in July 1803, when James Thompson Callender's body was found in the James River, drowned in three feet of water. The coroner's jury said accidental death while drunk. Callender's former paper, the *Richmond Examiner*, however, suggested suicide or murder. There was no further investigation, as there would be no investigation eight years later in the alleged suicide of Meriwether Lewis.

But those curious deaths lay ahead. In the summer of 1801 came news that the French First Consul and head of state, Napoleon Bonaparte, had signed a peace with England and had sent out a military expedition to strengthen his hold on France's North American colonies. It posed an enormous threat to the western borders of the United States.

Now began a chain of events which at the time seemed relatively minor to the kings and rulers of the world, but which would prove to be historically momentous.

In 1800, Spain announced the Treaty of San Ildefonso, which gave back the Louisiana Territory and the Caribbean island of Santo Domingo to France. This carried ominous implications for the young United States because its western borders would no longer be buffered by weak, conciliatory Spain but by the rapacious revolutionaries of France—led by a regime already well on its way to conquering Europe and the Mediterranean countries. The fear of French expansion in the Americas was confirmed in October 1801 when Napoleon Bonaparte signed his peace with England and immediately sent an expedition to

Haiti, the western half of the island of Santo Domingo and the richest sugar-producing colony in the Caribbean.

Bonaparte was outspoken about his intentions. From the twin French colonial bases of New Orleans and Santo Domingo, he would reestablish the French empire in North America. He instructed his agents in New Orleans to tamper with every adventurer from Pittsburgh to Natchez; to buy up every Indian tribe in the Georgia and Northwestern territories; to fortify every bluff on the west bank of the Mississippi from St. Louis south; and to create a series of French settlements which in a few years would discourage the Americans from crossing that river.

Jefferson's initial reaction was despondency. "From this moment, we must—for our protection—*marry* ourselves to the British fleet and nation."

History, however, is very much a case of "for lack of a shoe, a horse was lost . . ." and events are sometimes sent tumbling by small, unpredictable details.

The unpredictable in this case was a black revolutionary named François Toussaint. Inspired by the French Revolution, Toussaint had led a slave revolt in 1791 which gained control of Haiti but did not declare independence. Now, eleven years later, Napoleon belatedly sent an army headed by his best general, Charles Leclerc, to Port au Prince to subdue the rebels. Leclerc captured Toussaint, but Haitians led by two other revolutionaries, Jean-Jacques Dessalines and Henri Christophe, remained at large. The war went on.

By the end of 1802, France had lost thousands of soldiers, not to rebels but to yellow fever. Leclerc was dead, his army annihilated by disease. Plantations were destroyed, labor was paralyzed, and the population reduced to barbarism. While Toussaint lay dying in a French prison, the guerrillas of Dessalines and Christophe committed themselves to a racist frenzy of genocide, determined to massacre every white and mulatto they could find. Horror followed horror until all but the blackest of Haitians were dead or had fled the island. Dessalines took the title of Emperor Jacques I and upon his assassination was succeeded by Christophe.

Haiti was no longer available as Napoleon's base. Without that island there was no springboard to the continent. Furthermore, Napoleon faced a renewed war with Great Britain and needed his available funds for that enterprise. Napoleon's plans for a French North America were shelved.

Watching all this from Washington, Jefferson set in motion a scheme to remove the last French fingerhold on the continent, their base at New Orleans. Such a removal, Jefferson calculated, would open the way for American expansion to the Pacific.

Jefferson's expansion strategy involved two grand strokes, each coordinated to the other, a two-flank attack to checkmate the First Consul. The keystone to his plan was to buy the city of New Orleans. Coupled with that, he wanted to send his secretary, Meriwether Lewis, up the Missouri to find the link to the Columbia River and thence to the Pacific.

Accordingly, Jefferson sent instructions to his ambassador in France, Robert Livingston, to meet with French foreign minister Talleyrand to sound out Napoleon about buying New Orleans and Spanish Florida. Simultaneous with that, the president and Lewis began working out the details for the expedition to the Pacific.

In January of 1803 Jefferson sent a secret message to Congress requesting authority to send an expedition across twenty-two hundred miles of territory controlled by Spain, legally owned by France, and claimed by Great Britain whose traders and explorers had been active in the territory for the previous ten years. Beginning at the American bank of the Mississippi, opposite St. Louis, Lewis's expedition would enter French territory and journey up the Missouri, across the Rockies, and thence along the Columbia to the Pacific. There Lewis would plant an American flag and stake a solid claim to the Oregon country.

Apart from the physical dangers involved in crossing half a continent of unexplored territory, there were two legal problems facing the President: (1) The expedition violated French and Spanish sovereignty, and (2) the Oregon claim was probably illegal because the U.S. Constitution did not specifically allow such territorial expansions.

Jefferson decided he would deal with those complications when it became necessary.

As for Livingston's mission, Jefferson had no idea of buying all of Louisiana; he just wanted New Orleans. As late as March 1803, it wasn't for sale. A month later, it was. In mid-April 1803, as Livingston dickered for the port of New Orleans, Napoleon's minister Talleyrand surprised him by asking, "What will you give for the whole?" On an overnight whim, Napoleon had decided to abandon his North American holdings and offer the largest garage sale in history.

Having no time to contact Washington, Livingston moved ahead on his own.

By his authorization, on April 30 the United States purchased for the equivalent of about fifteen million dollars the island of New Orleans plus the Louisiana Territory. The latter encompassed nearly one million square miles of land extending up the entire bed of the Mississippi River and westward to the Rocky Mountains and beyond. Perhaps more important, it filled the gap between the great river and the newly claimed Oregon territory. If Lewis's expedition to the Columbia were to prove successful, the United States would stretch from sea to sea.

Thus did the desires for freedom on an impoverished Caribbean island provide Thomas Jefferson with the opportunity to remove France as a threat and make the United States a continental power—an accident of historical timing which Jefferson recognized and seized.

Immediately, the Federalists realized that the Purchase meant a shift of political gravity away from eastern cities and toward the agrarian West, the bastion of Democratic power. Already fading as a national power, the Federalists saw Louisiana as their death warrant. Senator Samuel White of Delaware warned, "As to the Louisiana, this new, immense unbounded world, if it should ever be incorporated into the Union, which I have no idea can be done but by altering the Constitution, I believe it will be the greatest curse that could at present befall us."

The Federalist congressman Roger Griswold of Connecticut insisted that the expedition and purchase "threatens, at no very distant day, the subversion of our Union."

Lewis and Clark

•••••••••

WHEN NEWS of the Louisiana Purchase reached Jefferson, his most immediate concern was the constitutional aspect. He and his party were strict constructionists, meaning that the Constitution allowed *only* what it specifically allowed. And *nowhere* did the Constitution provide for the addition of territory or states. How was the president to legalize what his ministers had just done? Thinking of ratification by the Senate, Jefferson chose to view himself as a wayward guardian for his nation: "I did this for your good; I pretend to no right to bind you; you may disavow me, and I must get out of the scrape as I can; I thought it my duty to risk myself for you."

Nevertheless, he was convinced that the purchase was illegal, writing Kentucky senator John Breckinridge, "The Executive, in seizing the fugitive occurrence which so much advances the good of their country, have done an act beyond the Constitution." But, while recognizing the illegality, the president wanted to avoid any public discussion, warning: ". . . nothing must be said on that subject which may give a pretext for retracting, but that we should do *sub silentio* what shall be found necessary."

Jefferson was also prepared to lie to Congress about the matter—a practice adhered to by virtually all American presidents over some two hundred years of history until Democratic congressmen of the 1980s decided to prosecute it as a crime. Jefferson may not have been the first president to lie to Congress,[1] but he was among the most explicit, putting the watchword of the day, *sub silentio*, in an instruction to his Cabinet:

> *I infer that the less we say about constitutional difficulties the better; and that what is necessary for surmounting them must be done* sub silentio.

Even as Jefferson worked to keep the whole thing quiet, letters arrived from Robert Livingston in Paris urging quick ratification because Napoleon might change his mind at any instant. As Jefferson was writing intimates that the less said about the constitutional matter, the better, one of his steadiest supporters, Wilson Cary Nicholas, advised that there was no problem. The Constitution did not prohibit *acquiring* new land or states; it said only that new states could not be formed out of old ones without the consent of the state to be dismembered.

That was good enough for Thomas Jefferson. And it would prove good enough for the Senate.

In the meanwhile, the president had gained enormous political capital. "The acquisition of Louisiana and the peaceful manner of possession have raised Jefferson and his friends to a high point of popularity and regard," observed the French chargé, L. A. Pichon. His counterpart, the British chargé, sniffed that the Louisiana business "has elevated the President beyond imagination in his own Opinion."

Pressing forward to develop the new empire, the president instructed his army commander, General Wilkinson, to explore the Mississippi between St. Louis and the upper falls of St. Anthony (present-day Minneapolis). It was already known that the Mississippi was basically two rivers. Above St. Louis, the Mississippi is a comparatively calm and transparent stream, flowing with a silvery surface between varied shores and among islands and sylvan sandbanks. At St. Louis, however, the mighty Missouri tumbles in and the Mississippi becomes a dark, turbid, and boiling torrent. It "sweeps with an irresistible force covered with large swells and whirlpools like a boiling cauldron. Shores become wreck heaps of vast deposits of mud and rubbish. Landslips cause the banks to be cut perpendicular.'' One year there is created an island five thousand acres in lush extent. The next year it is gone. The river is so swift and its thrust so powerful that it actually digs into the earth in its rush to the sea, plowing its channel narrower and deeper as it flows south receiving the waters of three more of the world's largest rivers—the Ohio, the Arkansas, and the Red. All those rivers pour in their floods and are swallowed.

Jefferson also arranged with Wilkinson to develop a fifteen-day express mail service from Washington to New Orleans by way of Nashville and Natchez. The president next began developing a plan to move all Indians from the east side of the Mississippi to the west; and he informed Tennessee officials that they could consider the Tombigbee their river all the way down to Mobile Bay and the Gulf because America would soon own West Florida, which the Spanish had deeded to the French and which the president—but not the Spanish—assumed came as part of the Purchase. Simultaneously, Jefferson ordered Meriwether Lewis to explore to the Pacific and establish an American claim on Oregon.

The Lewis and Clark project was encrusted with politics. As early as December 1802 the Spanish minister to the United States, Don Carlos Martínez de Yrujo, had written the Spanish court warning of Jefferson's plan to penetrate to the ''Southern Ocean.'' Yrujo also had told Jefferson himself that the Spanish court could not look favorably upon the enterprise. The Spaniards feared that the Americans not only would encroach on their mines in New Mexico, but would establish a port on the Pacific where they could exert influence on the core of Spanish fortune—Peru.

But Jefferson was not to be put off. He was already instructing Lewis to be aggressive in his push to the headwaters of the Columbia and thence to the Pacific: ''Without waiting for permission, we shall enter into the exercise of the natural right we have always insisted on with Spain, to wit, that of a nation holding the upper parts of a stream having a right to innocent passage through them to the ocean. We shall prepare her to see us practice on this and she will not oppose it by force.''

In January 1803 a treaty establishing trading posts with the Indian tribes was about to expire and Jefferson used that as his excuse to send Congress a confidential message asking for funds for the Lewis expedition. The president recorded a ringing endorsement for Lewis, who, he said, would carry the project to success:

I have had opportunities of knowing him intimately. Of courage undaunted, possessing a firmness and perseverance of purpose which nothing but impossibilities could divert from its direction; careful as a father of those committed to his charge, yet steady in the maintenance of order and discipline; intimate with the Indian character, customs and principles; habituated to the hunting life; guarded, by exact observation of the vegetables and animals of his own country, against losing time in the description of objects already possessed; honest, disinterested, liberal, of sound under- standing, and a fidelity to truth so scrupulous that whatever he should report would be as certain as if seen by ourselves—with all these qualifications, as if selected and implanted by nature in one body for this express purpose, I have no hesitation in confiding the enterprise to him.

Lewis wanted a co-captain in the expedition and he wrote to his friend William Clark, who was then at a frontier farm in the Indiana territory across the Ohio River from Louisville. Lewis informed Clark that the Congress had secretly authorized an expedition to explore the Missouri-Columbia route and asked Clark to be co- captain—to recruit the "good hunters, stout, healthy, unmarried men accustomed to the woods and capable of bearing bodily fatigue" needed in the expedition.

In the meantime, Jefferson invoked strict secrecy, making his mes- sage to Congress "confidential" and giving evasive hints to the public that the explorers would be going *up the Mississippi*, not the Missouri. In a letter of April 27, 1803, Jefferson advised Lewis that "the idea that you are going to explore the Mississippi has been generally given out; it satisfies public curiosity and masks sufficiently the real destina- tion."

But who was the secret to be kept from? Not the British, French, or

Spanish. All of them had been advised by Jefferson of the true destination in order to obtain passports of safe conduct for the expedition.

The secret was to be kept from other Americans.

Jefferson and his Cabinet were afraid the Federalists would scotch the project. For example, Attorney General Levi Lincoln warned the president of "the perverse, hostile and malignant state of the opposition," which had the capacity to arouse public sentiment against the project.

The Democrats' fears were not misplaced. The Hamilton and Adams factions suspected the worst, and their suspicions were reinforced when Napoleon decided to sell Louisiana.

But Democratic support was immense and a gleeful Jefferson wrote Lewis that the Federalist "bitterness increases with the diminution of their numbers and despair of a resurrection."[2]

Indeed, the Spanish ambassador thought Federalists in the Senate would be able to kill the expedition before it began:

> *I have learned that [the President] has already taken a step towards the execution. Nevertheless, I have understood that the good judgement of the Senate does not see the advantages that the President proposes in this expedition, and that on the contrary, they feared it might offend one of the European nations, and consequently it is very probable that the project will not proceed.*

However, the more accurately informed British minister seemed to be privy to the most secret sessions of Congress, noting:

> *The President has for some years past had it in view to set on foot an expedition entirely of a scientific nature for exploring the Western Continent of America by the route of the Great River Missouri. . . . The gentleman he has selected for the journey is his secretary, Captain Meriwether Lewis, a person in the vigour of his age, of a hardy constitution and already acquainted with the manners of the Indians by his residence in the western settlements. He is to be accompanied by a small party of eight or ten boatmen of his own selection, and such Indian hunters as he can prevail upon to accompany him. . . ."*

Jefferson, now sixty years old, was vicariously enjoying the planning and outfitting of the expedition with Lewis but he also worried over his young friend's fate. Despite Jefferson's efforts at secrecy, word had inevitably leaked. When Lewis asked Clark to accompany him and cautioned him to keep secret the destination, Clark replied that word of the project and its destination had been abroad in Louisville for several weeks.

Jefferson made Lewis the sole commander, but gave him authority to appoint a successor—"to name the person . . . who shall succeed to the command on your decease." Accordingly, Lewis chose Clark, technically second in command although Lewis would consistently refer to Clark as co-leader of the Corps of Discovery.

As the day for departure to the Mississippi neared, Lewis wrote several letters to reassure his mother that all would be well, gentle lies that promised, "My route will be altogether through tribes of Indians who are perfectly friendly to the United States." How did he know that? The area was unexplored. And as it happened, the Indians weren't "perfectly friendly." Indeed, several of them would try to kill him.

At Jefferson's request, the famed Philadelphia physician-scientist Benjamin Rush sent Lewis eleven rules to optimize health on the journey.[3] These included advice to always wear flannel next to the skin; to maintain good bowel habits; "to drink moderate amounts of whiskey, no more than three tablespoons straight per day; to take molasses and vitriol with every meal; to wear shoes without heels so as to afford equal action to all the muscles of the legs"; and to wash the feet every morning in cold water. The last suggestion was one Jefferson had followed all his life and to which he credited his good health in his advanced years.

By June 1803, Lewis was already in Philadelphia, on his first pro-longed stay in the city. Knowing that he'd need to shoot the stars in order to precisely map half of an unexplored continent, he began training in celestial navigation with Andrew Ellicott, the astronomer and government surveyor who had earlier turned up the Spanish evidence against James Wilkinson.

The City of Brotherly Love was then the premier metropolis. More than New York, it was the commercial, cultural, and industrial center of the land. Said the English traveler Charles Janson:

*The houses are well built, chiefly of red brick, and in general
three stories high. In some of the new streets uniformity is observed, particularly in Sansom street which may vie with those of
the fashionable parts of London. A great number of private houses
have marble steps to the street door, and in other respects are
finished in a style of elegance. The streets are paved with large
pebble-stones in the carriage road and the foot pavements, which
are raised ten or twelve inches higher, with brick. They are tolera-
bly well lighted and guarded in the night.*[4]

The streets were planted with rows of poplars to shade the avenues
and the large downtown public market was "well supplied and its
regularity and cleanliness indicate good living and wholesome regulations. No article can be offered for sale here without first being submitted to the inspection of one of the clerks of the market, who seizes
unwholesome articles, and a fine is inflicted upon the owner." There
were fresh fish packed in ice, turkeys, quail, good beef, excellent butter
and poultry, and "a profusion of vegetables." There were possum,
ham, "squirrels, which are by many preferred to the rabbit, and sometimes raccoons." Prices in general were less than half those in London.

Founded by William Penn in 1681 as a haven of religious and racial
freedom, Philadelphia was not only the political center of the Revolutionary War but also renowned for its intellectual attainments. It was
there that Benjamin Franklin established the University of Pennsylvania
(1740), Pennsylvania Hospital (1751), and the colonial postal system,
making it self-supporting (1753). In his spare time, Franklin opened
the nation's first daily newspaper (1784).

The city had its dark side, too, much of its waterfront being condemned by contemporary visitors for its uncleanliness, narrow alleys,
and filth.

The technological wonder of Philadelphia, even the nation, was a
giant steam engine which pumped the drinking water from the Schuyl-
kill.[5] "Water is thus raised upwards of thirty feet above the highest
ground in the city, and is conveyed by subterraneous pipes to what
they call hydrants; which are placed in the streets at equal distances.
The water is not suffered to flow constantly, but upon the slightest
touch of the small handle of the hydrants, it rushes with impetuosity."

Another marvel was the public library, open to all, and with more than twenty thousand books.

Foreigners were struck by the gusto of the populace. ''The streets in the evening are crowded,'' wrote one. ''The ladies emerge from their confinement, and pay visits by moonlight; while the girls sport and play without hats or cloaks, uninterrupted often till near midnight.''

The Europeans, expecting to find crudeness in a new country, were caught unprepared by their hosts' great fortunes. Hear the Duke of Rochefoucauld-Liancourt:

> *The profusion and luxury of Philadelphia on great days, at the tables of the wealthy, in their equipages, and the dresses of their wives and daughters are, as I have observed, extreme. I have seen balls on the president's birthday where the splendor of the rooms, and the variety and richness of the dresses did not suffer in comparison with Europe; and it must be acknowledged that the beauty of the American ladies has the advantage in the comparison. The young women of Philadelphia are accomplished in different degrees, but beauty is general with them. They want the ease and fashion of Frenchwomen; but the brilliancy of their complexion is infinitely superior. Even when they grow old they are still handsome; and it would be no exaggeration to say, in the numerous assemblies of Philadelphia it is impossible to meet with what is called a plain woman.*

The men, too, gleamed and glittered when the mood was upon them. One dandy boasted to his diary that he had dressed himself ''in a light French blue coat, with a high collar, broad lapels, and large gilt buttons, a double-breasted Marseille vest, Nankeen-colored cashmere breeches, with white silk stockings, shining pumps, and full ruffles on my breast and at my wrists, together with a ponderous white cravat, with a pudding in it, as we then called it; and I was considered the best dressed gentleman in the room.[6]

By July 15, 1803, Lewis was in Pittsburgh building boats when he received news from Jefferson advising that the treaty from Paris ceding Louisiana had arrived in Washington. The vast West was now owned by America. It would be Meriwether's job to start mapping the new property. He now sent another letter to Clark asking him to look about Kentucky for unmarried young men to make up the party.

Two days later, the journalist Callender was found drowned in a shallow pool of the James River.

By July 26, Lewis still had not received a reply from Clark and in those days of uncertain communication he feared further delay. Accordingly, he wrote to Jefferson to propose a substitute—one Lieutenant Moses Hooke, a twenty-six-year-old commissary agent at Pittsburgh whom Lewis considered fit for the job. Jefferson's secretary of war, Henry Dearborn, acceded to the suggestion for what would have become the Lewis and Hooke Expedition and was cutting orders for Hooke when Lewis received the acceptance from Clark. And a joyous one it was.

"I will cheerfully join you," wrote Clark, "and partake of the dangers, difficulties and fatigues and I anticipate the honors and rewards of the result of such an enterprise, should we be successful in accomplishing it."

Back in Washington, Jefferson received the news with much satisfaction. "William Clark accepts with great glee the office of going with Captain Lewis up the Missouri."

Both captains were unabashed Jeffersonians and anxious to make their president look good. This air of politics would sustain throughout the journey, from the east coast to the west and back. The success or failure was identified directly with Jefferson and the Democratic party.

Jefferson's written instructions to Lewis were to ascend the Missouri, find its source, and proceed thence to the Pacific:

> *Your situation as secretary of the President has made you acquainted with the objects of my confidential message to the Congress. . . . You are appointed to carry them into execution. . . . The object of your mission is to explore the Missouri river and such principal streams of it as, by its course and communication with the waters of the Pacific ocean, whether the Columbia, Oregon, Colorado or any other river, may offer the most direct and practicable water communication across this continent.*

By this time the boats were assembled at Louisville. Clark had recruited seven young men and taken along his slave named York. Clark noted that ''the young men that I have engaged or rather promised to take on this expedition are the best woodsmen and hunters of young men in this part of the country.''

On his way downriver to meet Clark at the Falls of the Ohio, Lewis picked up two more men at Maysville, Kentucky. They were Joseph and Reubin Field, brothers described by Lewis as ''active and enterprising.'' The expedition now included George Shannon, the youngest member of the party; Charles Floyd, who would be made a sergeant of the Corps; Nathaniel Pryor, a Kentucky-born orphan who was named the Corps's other sergeant; John Shields, a blacksmith, gunsmith, mechanic, and at age thirty-four the oldest man in the party and by Lewis's estimate the most useful; John Colter, who following the expedition would discover the geysers of Yellowstone and become a legendary mountain man; William Bratton, a large, muscular giant over six feet tall and the official Corps blacksmith as well as an excellent hunter; George Gibson, a native Pennsylvanian and a competent fiddler, who was used as an Indian interpreter; and York, first name unknown, a black slave owned by Clark, who was not technically enlisted into the Corps although he was among its most valuable members.

By October 1803, Lewis and Clark were in Illinois. The Congress had ratified the Purchase, but the Spanish commandant in St. Louis had not received official word from his own government of the transfer. He politely rebuffed Lewis's request to enter St. Louis and proceed up the Missouri. Neither surprised nor displeased by the rejection, Lewis began setting up winter quarters on the east bank while he waited for the communication gap to close. He was comfortable with the delay, figuring it would provide time for the ice floes to melt on the waterways up the Missouri.

On December 12, 1803, the fully prepared Lewis and Clark Expedition made camp on the east bank of the Mississippi opposite its confluence with the Missouri. Across the river and slightly downstream was St. Louis, then a little city of about two hundred stone structures which stretched along the river for about a mile.

Seen from the east side of the Mississippi, St. Louis was a beautiful site, rising gradually from the shore to the rim of a bluff, like an amphitheater. The northern capital of French and Spanish Louisiana, the city was situated hundreds of miles from the civilization of the East and South and surrounded by actively hostile Indians. The city's inhabitants were hardy, adventurous, and quarrelsome. The main business was furs. Furs were gold, and St. Louis was the jumping-off place where mountain men went looking for fortune. Two fifths of them never returned. Some drowned, others were killed by bears and panthers, but most were done in by Indians. Yet each year more men headed in canoes up the Missouri, across the plains, and to the foothills of the Rockies. For many, their last sight of civilization was the brawling gateway town of St. Louis, notorious for bear fights and gambling houses, for duels and street brawls.

Despite the forty years of Spanish occupation, French was the main language spoken. The farmers and boatmen were Frenchmen, and agriculture and navigation were carried on according to French systems. For food, the inhabitants cultivated a large commonly held field to the west of the city, which supplied them with wheat and corn.

Merchants and the wealthy class dressed well, in the Parisian fashion, and deported themselves like gentry. But the dress of the common people was foreign to Americans. The voyageurs, "couriers du bois," and the farriers scarcely ever wore hats but instead tied cotton handkerchiefs around their heads. A white blanket-coat was the general wear in winter and in summer a white cotton shirt. Whether of man or woman, legs were covered by buckskin pants in the winter and colored cotton in the summer.

The dwellings, too, were built after French models and the town was protected by small round towers constructed of sod. St. Louis in 1804 was as much a French village as though it were located in France.

The main fortification and lookout point was a bluff of perpendicular rock, thirty feet high, which extended from the foot of Chestnut street up the riverbank. In the distance, a few miles to the north, was the meeting place of two of the world's greatest rivers—the Missouri and the Mississippi.

The country around the city was open and rolling prairie which was bare of trees. Just beyond the outskirts of the town was an old white stone fort, San Carlos, built in 1780. The beginnings of an oak forest could be seen about five miles northwest of the town. A bit to the northeast were conical mounds, called by the inhabitants *La Grange de Terre*, relics of the ancient Indian mound-building civilization.[7]

On the east bank, at the mouth of the small Wood River, Lewis and Clark named their bivouac Camp DuBois, "Camp of the Woods." With time on his hands, Lewis proposed to Jefferson that they enlarge the mission by moving up the "Canceze [Kansas?] River and towards Santa Fe," which Lewis believed to be much closer than it actually was.

Wanting no problems with Spain, Jefferson gave him a quick negative and told his ward to stick to the job at hand.

Such an excursion would be more dangerous than the main expedition up the Missouri and would, by an accident to you, hazard our main object which, since the acquisition of Louisiana, interests everybody in the highest degree. The object of your mission is single—the direct water communication from sea to sea formed by the bed of the Missouri and perhaps the Oregon. . . . Neither you nor Mister Clark should be exposed to risks by going off your line.

Jefferson's priorities were plain. He wanted to nail down America's claim to the Oregon coast. All other matters were secondary. As for expanded mapping, Jefferson explained that he intended to send separate expeditions up the Red and the Arkansas to further explore the new country now owned by the United States. As a bonus to Lewis, he enclosed information from a French trapper concerning Indians whom the Corps might encounter up the Missouri:

The Crow nation inhabit near the Rocky mountains.
The Sioux inhabit the northern part of the Mississippi and are hostile to the Ricararas, Mandans, Big-Bellies and others. Others of them live on the river St. Pierre. They have from 30,000 to 60,000 men and abound in firearms. They are the greatest beaver hunters and could furnish more beavers than all the nations besides. . . . The Cayoguas [Kiowas], Caminabiches [Commun-

ches], and Pitapahatos are to the south and southwest of the Ricararas on a branch of the Missouri. They have had no communication with whites.

The president closed with a personal note, saying he was arranging for Washington newspapers to be forwarded to Lewis on a regular basis while "your friends and acquaintances here and in Albemarle are all well as far as I have heard."

In another communication, the president gave specific instructions to Lewis on how to treat with Indians he might meet.

You should inform those whose country you will pass that their late fathers the Spaniards have agreed to withdraw all their troops from all the waters and country of the Mississippi and Missouri, that they have surrendered to us all their subjects Spanish and French settled there, and all their posts and lands; that henceforward we become their fathers and friends, and that we shall endeavor that they shall have no cause to lament the change. . . . Although you will pass through no settlements of the Sioux, yet you will probably meet with parties of them. On that nation we wish most particularly to make a friendly impression because of their immense power. . . .

However, one of Jefferson's goals concerning the Indians was about to be frustrated. To reduce tensions, the president had planned to remove the thousand or so Frenchmen, Spaniards, and Americans living west of the Mississippi and turn the new Louisiana country over to the Indians as a permanent reservation where they could "retire with unmolested prosperity." After interviewing a number of settlers, however, Lewis advised that it would be difficult if not impossible to remove them. As it happened, the trans-Mississippi region was so quickly engulfed with population that Jefferson's plan never had a chance.

By winter's end, the Corps consisted of the two young officers (Lewis was twenty-nine and Clark was thirty-three); the nine young men from Kentucky; fourteen soldiers of the U.S. Army who had volunteered their services; two French boatmen; Clark's personal servant, York; and the official interpreter and hunter, George Drouillard. All except York were enlisted to serve as privates during the duration of the expedition, and three sergeants (Floyd, Ordway, and Pryor) had been appointed by the captains. In addition to the main party, another seven soldiers and nine boatmen were to accompany the Corps up the Missouri as far as the Mandan nation in order to assist in carrying stores, or in repelling an attack, which was believed to be most likely in that area rather than any other.

In a nicely toned letter, Jefferson asked for cooperation from a personal friend of his, Henri Peyroux, the former French commandant in St. Louis:

> *Since coming to the administration of the U.S., I have taken the earliest opportunity in my power to have [the Missouri-Pacific] route explored, and Captain Lewis with a party of twelve or fifteen men is authorized to do it. His journey being merely literary, to inform us of the geography and natural history of the country, I have procured a passport for him and his party, from the Minister of France here, it being agreed between him and the Spanish minister, that the country having been ceded to France, her minister may most properly give authority for the journey. This was the state of things when the passport was given, which was some time since. But before Captain Lewis's actual departure we learn through a channel of unquestionable information that France has ceded the whole country of Louisiana to the U.S. by a treaty concluded in the first days of May. I am sure you will not be scrupulous as to the authorities on which this journey is undertaken, and that you will give all the protection you can to Captain Lewis and his party in going and returning. . . .*

Even as Jefferson was writing his letter, some fifteen hundred miles to the southwest, in the Cabildo of New Orleans, the Spanish were plotting the doom of Meriwether Lewis and his Corps. "I am intent," wrote the Marquis de Casa Calvo to his superiors, "on destroying the hasty and gigantic steps which our neighbors are taking towards the

South Sea, entering by way of the Missouri and other rivers of the west bank of the Mississippi.''[8]

From Chihuahua, Mexico, the commandant of the Spanish Interior Provinces, Nemesio Salcedo y Salcedo was enraged by the expedition to the Pacific and was taking steps to kill or capture "Captain Merry Weather Lewis":

> *I am informed of all . . . regarding the penetrating of the Missouri River. . . . This step on the part of the United States at the same time that it took possession of the province of Louisiana; its haste to instruct itself and to explore the course of the Missouri whose origin they claim belongs to them, extending their designs as far as the South Seas, forces us necessarily to become active and to hasten our steps in order to cut off their gigantic steps. . . . I sent a party of Comanche Indians [and] others of those who are affected to us to reconnoiter the country as far as the banks of the Missouri River in order to examine if the expedition of Merry has penetrated into these territories to acquire all possible knowledge of its progress and even to stop them, making efforts to apprehend it. . . . The only means which presents itself is to arrest Captain Merry Weather and his party, which cannot help but pass through the nations neighboring New Mexico, its presidios or rancherias. A decisive and vigorous blow will prevent immense expenditures and even countless disagreeable replies which must originate between the respective governments. . . .*

Salcedo asked the governor of New Mexico, Joaquín del Real Alencaster, to dispatch "Otos, Loups, Pawnees" and other tribes to a council in Santa Fe where they could be incited against Lewis and the Americans. To tell the Indians to beware the Americans, to warn them that "the ideas of the Americans can be nothing other than to destroy them in a few years" by taking possession of the Missouri and Arkansas.

The reason Salcedo was so alarmed, not to mention well informed, was that he was receiving detailed reports on Lewis's movements and mission from none other than the commander in chief of the American army, James Wilkinson.

*   *   *

Although word of Napoleon's sale of Louisiana had reached New Orleans by June 6, 1803, the ceremonies of transfer didn't begin until November 30, when the Spanish met the French in the Place d'Armes, the city's central parade ground and plaza which lay between the river's levee and the Cabildo, or the Maison de Ville, as it was briefly known under the French.

The lower end of the square abutted the docks and the river. The upper end was bounded by the city's two most important buildings— the St. Louis Cathedral, seat of religious power, and the Cabildo, the two-storied, stuccoed-brick building of Moorish design which was the seat of secular power.[9] On the side of the square between the Cabildo and the river were apartment houses and shops. On the side between the Cathedral and the river was the governor's residence.

The actual hand-over of documents took place on a balcony of the Cabildo so that all the city could see from the plaza. Accepting on behalf of France was Pierre Clément Laussat, an arrogant, old-style revolutionary who had come to Louisiana in late 1802 as prefect on orders of Napoleon. Laussat's Spanish counterpart was the Marquis de Casa Calvo, the boundary commissioner who had been sent by the captain-general of Cuba to act with Governor Salcedo in turning over the colony to France.

The Spanish flag came down and the French tricolor went up, but there was no cheering. The American consul, Daniel Clark, reported to Jefferson, "Except for the cannon not a sound was heard. The most gloomy silence prevailed and nothing could induce the crowd to express the least joy or give any sign of satisfaction on the occasion." By nightfall, however, the two governments had primed the pump by opening their treasure chests—royalist Spain seeking to outdo Republican France in a dazzling rivalry of balls, concerts, dinners, theater, and other entertainments.

Seventeen days later, the American delegation arrived, being led by General Wilkinson and the young governor of Mississippi, William C. C. Claiborne. They and their military escorts camped two miles outside the city walls.

The day of December 20 dawned clear and bright with a faultless sky overhead, a good omen. At nine o'clock the French militia mustered and marched into the Place d'Armes and the crowd began to mass in the streets. A cannon shot from Fort St. Charles signaled that the American troops had left their camp and were marching toward the city. As they reached the gate, a salute of twenty guns boomed from the fort.

Passing down Tchoupitoulas Street, the Americans marched into the plaza. General Wilkinson and Governor Claiborne were on horseback, Wilkinson riding a handsome white stallion with leather and gold harness. They were followed by a mounted detachment of dragoons in red uniform, four pieces of artillery, cannoneers, two companies of infantry and one of carabineers. To further enhance the ceremony, Daniel Clark had arranged for a noisy claque of Americans to lead cheering for the event.

No fewer than five thousand people had gathered for the event. Some were serious, some sorrowful; others boisterous and merry. On the banquettes beside the Place d'Armes, courtesans flaunted their charms from open carriages; families had come from all over the city to picnic on the lawn; hawkers sold apples and sweets and roasted nuts. There was cider and wine aplenty. Rocking chairs were loaded off wagons so elderly grandmothers could see and sew and gossip. Children romped and screamed; boys wrestled and girls played tag and jump-the-rope. It was a festive event and men and women of all descriptions turned out to see it. There were the righteous and the wicked, the young and the old; people of all nationalities, all colors, and all conditions of freedom.

Lining up in front of the French and Spanish soldiery, the American commissioners dismounted and proceeded to the Cabildo, where they were received by the Prefect Laussat and officers and citizens of the city. When the legal formalities were done, Laussat led Wilkinson and Claiborne onto a balcony. Below them was the plaza and beyond that the Mississippi, where a long line of decorated sailing ships and barges lay along the broad, tree-shaded levee.

Two thousand men and women were in the square, a crowd of people of all shapes, sizes, and colors. Their costumes ranged the globe, from the tall boots and broad hats of the Spanish to the flowing robes and curled swords of Turkestan. There were Americans, French, Spanish,

Italians, quadroons, Jamaicans, Haitians, Orientals, and even a few
Hindus in saris and with jewels on their foreheads. Above them at the
far end of the plaza was the balcony of the official party. From that
vantage point, Wilkinson regarded the throng sourly and was overheard
commenting to Claiborne that the mob couldn't have been bigger had
it been "drawn by an announcement of the Second Coming."

Even the slave markets had closed for the event. The primary auction
mart was located just a few blocks away, at Maspero's Exchange,
where the big main room had two trading blocks. But on this day, the
slave-trading Maspero and Lafitte brothers were in attendance at the
Place d'Armes.

Servants circulated on the balcony with trays of champagne and carts
of coffee for the master class while the masses below elbowed and
shoved each other, necks craned up—a pecking order, which was and
is the way things were and are.

There was no cheering, no celebratory balls or parties following the
American transfer. The French inhabitants had prospered for forty
years under the light hand of Spanish rule.[10] They had regarded their
Spanish cousins as sympathetic—fellow members of a Roman Catholic
culture. The Americans were seen as barbarians, who walked the streets
with the air of personal purchasers. They had come in with a small
army led by two commissioners who spoke neither Spanish nor French.
Friction was constant. Every day produced a duel. Claiborne's private
secretary and brother-in-law was killed trying to refute a slander by a
Frenchman.

The French prefect Laussat wrote his government:

*It was hardly possible that the Government of the United States
should have made a worse beginning, and that it should have sent
two men (Messrs. Claiborne, Governor, and Wilkinson, General)
less fit to attract affection. The first, with estimable private qualities, has little capacity and much awkwardness, and is extremely
beneath his place; the second, already long known here in a bad
way, is a flighty, rattle-headed fellow, often drunk, who has committed a hundred impertinent follies. Neither the one nor the other*

understands a word of French or Spanish. They have on all occasions, and without delicacy, shocked the habits, the prejudices, the character of the population.

The Spanish government was deeply disturbed by the sudden turn of events that had put their colonial borders cheek by jowl with the aggressive Americans. Looking for a buffer, they still hoped that Jefferson would implement his plan to establish an exclusive Indian reservation in the new Louisiana lands. By such a move, wrote the Spanish ambassador, not only would the United States be free of Indians in the eastern lands, but it would provide a shield between the Americans and Spain, ''stopping the motives of war,'' wrote Don Carlos Martínez de Yrujo.

Hoping to facilitate some easement of tensions, Casa Calvo lingered in New Orleans with his Spanish guard for months following the ceremonies. The major reason was his duty as boundary commissioner, trying to decide on a demarcation line between Spanish lands and what was now American territory. At the time, Spain controlled Texas and much of what is now southwestern Louisiana. Spain also held the Florida peninsula plus a thin strip of the Mississippi Gulf Coast running from Pensacola to the gates of New Orleans.

Due to ambiguities in treaties between Spain and France, and then between France and the United States, it was unclear whether Spanish Florida was included in the Louisiana Purchase. Spain, of course, insisted that it was not included. Napoleon, who had not yet received any significant portion of the fifteen million dollars purchase money, had no enthusiasm for pressuring Spain and declared that France was uninvolved. In the meantime, Jefferson was pursuing several avenues to acquire Florida, including direct negotiations with Spain, outright purchase, and the threat of war. Casa Calvo was gathering information on all these matters for his government.

A secondary reason for Casa Calvo's delay was a series of secret meetings he was holding with Spain's top spy, General Wilkinson.

No sooner had the ink dried on the New Orleans transfer treaty than Wilkinson began negotiating with Casa Calvo and Don Vicente Folch, the visiting governor of West Florida. As in his previous intrigues, Wilkinson exacted a pledge of secrecy, then relayed detailed plans of the Lewis and Clark expedition. Wilkinson said the enterprise was designed to establish an American invasion route to Santa Fe and the gold and silver mines of New Mexico. During these meetings, Wilkinson insisted the Spaniards never mention him by name in their dispatches but instead refer to him as Number Thirteen.

Wilkinson's meetings with the Spaniards began in early February 1804. In March, as Lewis and Clark waited on the east bank of the Mississippi opposite St. Louis, Wilkinson submitted a memorandum to Folch recommending that Lewis and Clark should be stopped or arrested as soon as they crossed the river:

> *An express ought immediately to be sent to the governor of Santa Fe and another to the Captain-General of Chihuahua, in order that they may detach a sufficient body of chasseurs to intercept Captain Lewis and his party, who are on the Missouri River, and force them to retire or take them prisoners.*

Wilkinson was due to return to Washington and he promised to send more reports because he knew "what was concealed in the heart of the President." To facilitate his cooperation, the general suggested the Spanish might want to settle an old debt now.

Wilkinson told the new Spanish representatives that some fifteen years earlier he had been promised an annual pension of $2,000 but that for the past ten years he had received nothing. He said he was owed $20,000 for past accounts plus another $7,000 for expenses. After some further negotiation, Casa Calvo paid $12,000 on account and said he would remit the remainder once he had received funds from Havana.[11]

This was an enormous sum, coming at a time when Wilkinson earned a mere $225 a month from the Army.

In May, Casa Calvo wrote the governor in Chihuahua that President Jefferson intended the expedition to open a route to the Pacific, thereby threatening Mexico and Peru. The only means to prevent such a threat, said Casa Calvo, was "to arrest Captain Merry Weather and his party":

> *A decisive and vigorous blow will prevent immense expenditures and even countless disagreeable replies. . . . I do not doubt that*

Your Excellency will give orders that the most efficacious steps be taken to arrest the referred to Captain Merry and his followers, who, according to notices, number twenty-five men, and to seize their papers and instruments that may be found on them.

The recommendations by Casa Calvo, and Wilkinson, were endorsed by the king of Spain, who authorized Spanish forces to stop "the expedition of the American Captain Merry Weather" and said that an official complaint against the expedition was being lodged with President Jefferson.

There is no doubt where Casa Calvo's information was coming from. In another communication, that of September 24, 1804, he advised Cevallos, commandant-general of the Interior Provinces, that he had "just received a letter from the subject known by Number Thirteen . . . information that Captain Lewis Merry Weather is at a distance of more than ninety-one leagues [about two hundred and fifty miles] from the Mississippi" and that "Number Thirteen . . . asks for money."[12]

No fewer than three Spanish attempts were made to capture Lewis and Clark. One of these, led by Lieutenant Acundo Melgares ranged north to the Pawnee villages of Nebraska and ultimately arrested not Lewis and Clark but the leader of another Jefferson expedition to the west—Captain Zebulon Pike.

In his dealings with Casa Calvo and Folch, Wilkinson had urged them not to give up Florida unless they could exchange it for all the American lands west of the Mississippi. It was Wilkinson's feeling that Jefferson would take that deal rather than go to war. According to documents recovered from Spanish archives, Wilkinson told Folch that "the population of the United States would not be tempted to scatter itself beyond the Mississippi and thus Mexico and Peru would be safe from an army of adventurers similar to the ancient Goths and Vandals."

Pursuing this line of reasoning, Wilkinson advised that Spain should strongly fortify both the Texas and Florida frontiers. And they should continue efforts to "arrest the exploring party under Captain Lewis" and break up any settlement along the Missouri because that would be the American "road to Santa Fe."

These were the suggestions being made by the commander in chief of the American army just after he had accepted the transfer of Louisiana to his government.

Meanwhile, seven hundred miles to the north, Spanish officials in St. Louis had transferred Upper Louisiana to Captain Amos Stoddard, who accepted on behalf of the French. Stoddard allowed the flag of the French Republic to fly over the fort of San Carlos for the next twenty-four hours, then replaced it on March 4, 1804, with the flag of the United States.

Five days later, Stoddard was joined by Meriwether Lewis, who was acting as representative of the president.

When Lewis and Stoddard entered the St. Louis Cabildo, Spanish soldiers set off a six-cannon salute, the most they could muster at the small fort. On the low bluff overlooking the wide, gray river, a cheerful crowd of about four hundred fur traders and farmers in buckskin stood beside Indians in breechclouts, with wives and children of both milling about. Among them was fifty-three-year-old Auguste Chouteau, who had helped found St. Louis some forty years earlier.[13]

After reading a statement of transfer, the Spanish commandant placed Stoddard in formal possession. Stoddard signed the document of transfer, which was witnessed by Lewis. Upper and Lower Louisiana were now part of the United States.

Residents were not visibly unhappy about the transfer, but there was some apprehension about new American laws. Perhaps uppermost in their concerns was the matter of slavery. There were about a thousand slaves in the new territory and they had become unruly in the expectation they would be freed, as had been done in the states of the American Northeast. St. Louis's leading citizen, Auguste Chouteau, warned Stoddard that there was "amongst the blacks a fermentation—which may become dangerous" and urged a "watchful policy." Later in the year, Governor William Henry Harrison of the Indiana Territory and three Indiana judges arrived in St. Louis, heard the several sides of the issue and caused a slave code to be included in the district's laws. The code outlawed importation of slaves from foreign lands but allowed domestic slavery to continue. Slaves could not assemble in large gatherings, buy or sell guns or real property, strike a white person, or testify in court against a white person. Whipping was an acceptable punishment, but mutilation was forbidden.

For the next several months, Lewis and Clark continued their preparations for the ascent of the Missouri. The expedition departed on May 21, as Stoddard informed Secretary of War Dearborn:

> *[Lewis] began the expedition with a barge of eighteen oars, attended by two large pirogues; all of which were deeply laden and well manned. I have heard from him about sixty miles on his route, and it appears, that he proceeds about fifteen miles per day—a velocity seldom witnessed on the Missouri; and this is the more extraordinary as the time required to ascertain the course of the river and to make the other necessary observations must considerably retard his progress.*

The "pirogues" actually were keelboats propelled by oars. Lewis's "barge" was a flatboat, fifty-five feet in length and the flagship, as it were, of the little fleet.

The Americans were bucking against a muddy, swift-flowing stream, flowing with a silvery surface between varied shores and among islands and sandbanks. The land beyond the river's banks was incredible. For a breadth of three miles beside the river, the fields were rich and well wooded. Beyond that there was an immense rolling prairie and through the plains could be seen occasional streams containing flour mills.

For the greater part of the journey upstream, Indians were conspicuous by their absence. When Indians did appear, they were friendly or, at all events, not hostile. In the whole of the upward trip, the expedition's only unpleasant brushes were with the Sioux, although no open attack was made.

The Sioux, Clark reported, were impudent because of their trade connections to Canada:

> *These Indians are distributed in parties under indifferent names; they wander from one part to another from the banks of the river to the plains following the game and the opportunities to plunder without having a fixed place of residence, and are in a continual*

state of war. They are the Indians who have most inconvenienced us, showing jealousy that the Indians farther up trade, receive arms and other goods. They have a trade or commerce more regular with the Northwest [Canadian] Company from which they receive merchandise via Lake Winnepeg, and are thus independent of our good will.

Higher up the river, near present-day Bismarck, North Dakota, Lewis and Clark came to the Mandans, finding many with fair hair and blue eyes. The Mandans dwelt in villages of permanent wigwams, and near the site of the main Mandan town, Lewis and Clark made winter camp.[14]

"The Mandans," Clark wrote in his journals, "cultivate maize of small grain, with which we maintain ourselves in abundance. Buffalo are found in numerous herds and are of great corpulence. Elk and mountain goats are very numerous. . . .

"From the information we receive concerning the upper country, it is yet about six hundred miles to the great cataract or falls which are formed by the chain of mountains named Rocky, in which it is presumed the Missouri ends or begins."

It was at Fort Mandan that the Americans met a pregnant prisoner of the Mandans, one Sacajawea, a native of the Shoshone tribe to the west.[15] Sacajawea, whose name meant "Bird Woman," was a Shoshone who had been kidnapped by a fur-trading relative of her Canadian "husband," Toussaint Charbonneau, and given to him. She had borne Charbonneau's son in the spring of 1805. When Lewis and Clark moved upriver shortly afterward, Charbonneau was hired as an interpreter. Sacajawea came with him and proved much more helpful than her cowardly and incompetent husband. Her contributions would include rescue of the party's boats, and the saving of Meriwether Lewis's life. Her presence during a chance meeting with her long-lost Shoshone band would not only again save the Americans' lives but provide the horses that carried the party across the Continental Divide.[16]

Going west from the Mandan country in present-day North Dakota, there was one vast plain inhabited by numerous herds of buffalo, "attended by their constant shepherds, the wolves," antelopes nursing their young, and herds of elk. He saw

*plains covered with a leek green grass, well calculated for the
sweetest and most nourishing hay—interspersed with copses of
trees, spreading their lofty branches over pools, springs and
brooks of fine water. Croups of shrubs covered with the most
delicious fruit is to be seen in every direction and nature appears
to have exerted herself to beautify the scenery by the variety of
flowers . . . a country of magnificent scenery enjoyed by nothing
but the buffalo, the elk, the deer, the bear, and the savage Indians.*

Behind Lewis, however, there were events afoot far more dangerous
to him than Indians. In the spring of 1805, about the time Lewis and
Clark left Fort Mandan, James Wilkinson was sent to St. Louis to
assume the governorship of Upper Louisiana. Among Wilkinson's first
official acts was a letter to Secretary of War Dearborn complaining
that ''Captain Lewis'' had exceeded his authority by causing the appointment of Auguste Chouteau as Indian agent—an act that Wilkinson
saw as a dilution of his own authority at St. Louis, gratuitously described by the general as a ''mongrel community.''

Even more dangerous to Lewis's future was a secret meeting between
Wilkinson and Aaron Burr at Fort Massac, a lonely military outpost
on the northern shores of the Ohio about forty miles north of where
that river meets the Mississippi.[17]

Burr and Wilkinson were exploring a scheme to invade Mexico and
seize it from the Spanish, sort of a rebirth of the old Blount scheme to
mount an attack on Spanish possessions with an army of western
volunteers.

Rivers Are Crossed
• • • • • • • • • •

Тне ривснаѕе of Louisiana had nearly killed off the Federalist
party. Jefferson's balloon was soaring so high that none could shoot it
down. Nevertheless, they kept trying. In Washington, no less a penman
than William Cullen Bryant was taunting the president with lines about
Sally Hemings:

> *Go, Wretch, resign the presidential chair,*
> *Disclose thy secret measures, foul or fair . . .*
> *Go, scan, Philophist, thy Sally's charms,*
> *And sink supinely in her sable arms.*

In the same month of December 1803, there appeared a political
pamphlet titled *An Examination of the Various Charges Exhibited
Against Aaron Burr*, written by one "Aristides." Aristides denounced
the scattered accusations that Burr had been willing to steal the 1801
presidency and offered, instead, proof of the actual deal made to assure
Jefferson's election.

This hit Jefferson in his most tender spot. And while Aristides was
not Burr himself—the writing was far too direct to come from that
master of subtlety—the attack was perceived as having Burr's endorsement.[1] Jefferson pretended indifference, snubbing it thus:

*I began to read it but the dullness of the first page made me give
up the reading for a dip into here and there a passage, till I came
to what respected myself. The falsehood of that gave me a test for
the rest of the work, and considering it always useless to read lies,
I threw it aside.*

Despite his affected nonchalance, the president was furious. On
January 26, 1804, nearly three years after taking office, Burr went to
the White House for a fateful discussion of a second term. The only
version of what transpired comes from Jefferson and it can be suspected
of a self-serving bias. But according to Jefferson, Burr offered to
withdraw from the vice-presidential nomination in ''the interest of the
[Democratic] cause.'' In declining office, Burr did suggest, however,
that Jefferson and his friends had falsely maligned him on charges of
scheming. The president claimed noninvolvement, telling Burr: ''That
as to the attacks excited against him in the newspapers, I had noticed
it but as the passing wind. . . .''

Three weeks after the White House meeting, Burr officially withdrew
from the Democratic ticket and announced his nomination as candidate
for governor of New York. And with that, his fate was sealed. He was
now out there alone, no longer protected by the interests of the national
party. Burr did not know it at the time, but in that winter of 1803–1804,
commencing with the pamphlet and ending with his White House tête
à tête, he had come to the beginning of his political end.

About this time, Jefferson set in motion his constitutional reform to
require electors to vote specifically for president and vice president,
correcting accidents like the one that nearly made Burr the chief executive.

Having disposed of Burr and the Electoral College problems, Jefferson now turned to Samuel Chase of Maryland, an associate justice of
the U.S. Supreme Court. Chase was a mouth-frothing Federalist given
to damning the Democrats in his court and throwing journalists into
prison for violation of the Sedition Act. For example, with one appre-
hensive eye cocked on revolutionary France, Chase had told a Baltimore grand jury in May 1803 that Jefferson's ideas that all men ''are
entitled to enjoy equal liberty, and equal rights, have brought a mighty

mischief upon us; and I fear that it will rapidly progress until peace and order, freedom and property, shall be destroyed.''

Chase's remarks were reported widely by newspapers and only served to further enrage a president who was already peeved at rulings made by Chief Justice John Marshall, also a Federalist.[2] Now, with Chase, Jefferson began to brood on the bias of the federal courts. In 1804, Jefferson suggested that his congressional leaders impeach Chase for making political speeches during the trials of two Jeffersonian journalists.

Chase was being run up the flagpole to see if he could be removed on grounds of misconduct. It was felt by the Democrats that if Chase could be so removed, other justices could likewise be unseated—up to and including the particular stone in the presidential shoe, John Marshall.

Accordingly, in March 1804, Chase was impeached by the House. But as preparations were made for trial in the Senate, there came one of the most astonishing scandals in American history—a meeting between Burr and Wilkinson that would lead to the trial of the vice president of the United States on charges of treason.

Aaron Burr had just turned forty-eight years of age in February 1804 when he announced he would not accept nomination or reelection to a second term. Burr seems to have set his eye on the presidency and to do that he needed to sever his connections to Jefferson and run for governor of New York. To Burr's surprise, however, his state-house run was defeated handily through the efforts of Alexander Hamilton. All at once, it seemed that Burr had turned his political career into a dead-end street. But there was even worse to come.

On May 23, 1804, while brooding at Richmond Hill, Burr's opulent country home on the northern fringes of New York City, he received a note from General James Wilkinson saying he was in the vicinity and "to save time, of which I need much and have little, I propose to take a bed with you this night, if it may be done without observation or intrusion. . . .''

The general arrived shortly before 9:00 P.M., splendidly turned out in a braided uniform of his own design. The details of what transpired at the meeting are unknown except for a note to Burr from Wilkinson the following day which referred to a Louisiana "rum barrel." The second note invited Burr to meet with eight "particular friends and see my maps," a reference to a collection of manuscript maps of Texas, New Mexico, and other northern colonies of Spain which Wilkinson had brought from New Orleans.

From these bits of surviving notes and references, it is reasonable for historians to infer that the meeting bore the seeds of what would later be called the Burr Conspiracy.

The ties between Burr and Wilkinson dated back to the Revolutionary War when both were among the first to join George Washington's command. The bond had been strengthened with Wilkinson's marriage into the family of the Philadelphia Biddles—intimate friends and strong supporters of Burr. A further tie was that Burr had arranged for Wilkinson's sons, James and Joseph, to be accepted as students at the colonel's alma mater, the College of New Jersey, later Princeton.

From what can be deduced from a variety of documents, the initial Burr-Wilkinson plan seems to have involved a partnership to develop an agricultural colony near Natchez, Mississippi. The colony was to have been only a springboard to a larger design, namely a new nation encompassing the discontented western and southern states. With the help of Britain and Spain, those states would sever themselves from the Union and form a new nation centered around New Orleans.

At the New York meeting, Wilkinson persuaded Burr that the first step toward establishing a Natchez colony was for Burr to get Wilkinson appointed as governor of the Louisiana Territory. From that vantage point, they would have a base from which to carve a new republic out of the Spanish lands in the west.

Despite his lame-duck status as vice president, Burr was in a position to secure such a favor because Jefferson sorely needed his goodwill and offices in the prosecution of the aforementioned Justice Chase.

Even as the Burr conspiracy and the Chase trial moved along their converging tracks, a third calamity hove into view. The vice president of the United States, Aaron Burr, was preparing to shoot and kill his political enemy, the former treasurer of the United States, Alexander Hamilton.

Hamilton had taken little overt part in the New York gubernatorial

Charles Willson Peale's famous portrait of Thomas Jefferson dates from
1791, when the inventor-statesman was in his late forties and before his
first term of office as president. Peale (1741–1827) was a preeminent
painter of his time in the United States, and left portraits of many
presidents and military leaders.

James Madison, here seen in an engraving taken from the portrait by Gilbert Stuart, served as secretary of state during both Jefferson administrations, later as president.

Political intrigue swirled around Aaron Burr, as it did so many high-profile personalities of the time. Pictured here in 1802, Burr became vice president under Thomas Jefferson in 1800 on the thirty-sixth ballot but may be remembered more for his duel with Alexander Hamilton.

"The President's House," seen in an engraving circa 1800, eventually became known as the White House, site of many additions and renovations over the decades.

William Clark, painted by Charles Willson Peale, year unknown, was Meriwether Lewis's partner on the trek west to find a navigable path to the Pacific Ocean.

James Wilkinson, military profiteer and the man branded a "finished scoundrel," as captured by Charles Willson Peale

Meriwether Lewis survived an expedition across half of what is today known as the United States, only to be murdered in 1809. Seen here in a drawing by Saint-Memin, in the collection of the Missouri Historical Society in St. Louis, where Lewis governed the northern portion of the Louisiana Purchase.

Alexander Hamilton saw the governing of the new United States as a
business enterprise. After the painting by Daniel Huntington

The duel between Alexander Hamilton and Aaron Burr in 1804
came about when Burr felt challenged politically and, in turn,
challenged Hamilton to a showdown in a field in New Jersey.
Hamilton was mortally wounded in the incident.

Dolley Madison as painted
by Gilbert Stuart. She was
married to James Madison
but became White House
hostess during part of
Thomas Jefferson's presi-
dency.

A young, statuesque George Washington, as captured by Charles
Willson Peale in a mix of military and bucolic grandeur

At his beautiful Virginia home, Monticello, gentleman farmer Thomas
Jefferson experimented with agriculture, architecture, and inventions,
although the house was often in disrepair.

election and his *Evening Post* had behaved with unaccustomed decorum. But in the privacy of his library, Hamilton had secretly written articles and letters calculated to destroy Burr. Finally Hamilton did so once too often. On the eve of the election, there appeared three letters in the Albany *Register* accurately naming Hamilton as the author of slanders against Aaron Burr. The most inflammatory of the letters had Hamilton describing Burr as "a dangerous man and ought not to be trusted with the reins of government." But there was more, said the letter writer: "I could detail to you a still more despicable opinion which General Hamilton has expressed of Mr. Burr."

On the eighteenth of June, Burr sent a friend, William Peter Van Ness, to Hamilton seeking either a repudiation of the letter, an explanation, or an apology.[3]

Hamilton argued, quibbled, and evaded, but offered no explanation, denial, or apology to Van Ness. Caught in his own web, Hamilton defiantly sent word to Burr that he could "not without manifest impropriety make the avowal or disavowal which you seem to think necessary."

There were further exchanges of letters between the two, with the level of animosity and affront escalating step-by-step.

On June 27, still unsatisfied, thinking he was being toyed with, Burr sent his challenge.

It was not the first time that either Burr or Hamilton had been involved in a duel. It will be recalled that after publication of the Reynolds documents, Hamilton had called out James Monroe and it was Burr who acted as peacemaker. Even earlier, in 1778, Hamilton had called out General Charles Lee because of Lee's disrespect toward General Washington at the Battle of Monmouth.

And now Hamilton, a somewhat eager duelist, accepted Burr's challenge.

By mutual agreement, the duel was postponed for ten days while Hamilton cleared cases he was trying in the circuit court. In the meantime, both men tried to lead normal lives. On July 4 they even sat side by side at a banquet, but did not speak to one another. Burr was reserved, Hamilton animated, according to those present.

Although unknown at the time and little reported since by historians, during this period the stressed Burr fought another duel. His opponent was one Samuel Bradhurst, married to a cousin of Burr. The marriage had become strained, and when Burr approached Bradhurst to effect a reconciliation, the meeting degenerated into insult. A duel was then fought with swords, ending with Bradhurst being slightly wounded in the arm.[4]

Now, on the eve of July 11, both Burr and Hamilton wrote personal letters. Hamilton left his for posterity, claiming that his duel was done in the interests of justice and that he had "strong reasons" for censuring Burr.

Burr's letters were more private, addressed to his daughter Theodosia and her husband, Joseph Alston. He advised Theodosia to burn his correspondence from women and left instructions concerning a particular lady to whom he considered himself beholden. Her father told Theodosia she was the cause "of a very great portion of the happiness which I have enjoyed in this life."

On the eve of the duel, Burr was told that Hamilton had written a statement for posterity expressing an intention to withhold his fire. Burr's only recorded comment was: "Contemptible, if true."

Both men arrived promptly on the morning of July 11, 1804, the parties gathering on a narrow wood on Weehawken Heights overlooking the New Jersey side of the Hudson River.

They faced each other at ten paces, pistols in hand. If Hamilton intended to hold his first shot, his nerve failed him. To the contrary, he fired the first shot in such a rush that it went wild. An instant later, Burr's ball hit Hamilton in the stomach with a fatal wound.

That sequence of events was reported by the seconds on both sides, who published the only document that represents an agreement as to the facts:

> . . . The fire of Colonel Burr took effect, and General Hamilton almost instantly fell. Colonel Burr then advanced towards General Hamilton, with a manner and gesture that appeared to General Hamilton's friend to be expressive of regret, but without speaking turned about and withdrew, being urged from the field by his friend . . . with a view to prevent his being recognized by the surgeon and bargemen who were then approaching. No further communication took place between the principals, and the barge that carried

Colonel Burr immediately returned to the city. We conceive it
proper to add that the conduct of the parties in this interview was
perfectly proper as suited the occasion.

The ball had hit Hamilton in the lower ribs, lodging in the center of
his body, paralyzing his spine. The former treasurer and author of the
Federalist doctrine died twenty-eight hours later, leaving his wife and
seven children heavily in debt.[5]
For Hamilton, as a friend wrote, "It was a moment in which his
great wisdom forsook him. A moment in which Hamilton was not
himself. He yielded to the force of an imperious custom."

Previous duels, including two involving the district attorney and
mayor of New York respectively, had not excited the legal interests.
But Hamilton's political friends went after Burr like hounds after a
fox. So irregular was their vengeance that Burr was first indicted on a
charge of murder in New York, where no shot had been fired. In the
clamor, New Jersey followed suit. Warrants were issued for Burr's
arrest. The second officer of the United States became a fugitive.
Burr took refuge with his friend Charles Biddle in Philadelphia,
arriving there July 24. A local newspaper was dismayed: "Colonel
Burr, the man who has covered our country with mourning, was seen
walking with a friend in the streets of this city in open day."
Burr wrote his son-in-law, Alston, "In New York I am to be disfran-
chised, and in New Jersey hanged. Having substantial objections to
both, I shall not, for the present, hazard either, but shall seek another
country."
As it happened, the British ambassador to the United States, Anthony
Merry, passed through Philadelphia a few days after Burr's arrival.
Burr sent a message to Merry via one of Burr's friends—Charles
Williamson, a land developer and former British intelligence agent.
Merry was an interested audience. The British minister, competent
and even expert in many matters, was biased against America. He
disliked the new nation and he disliked Jefferson. Acerbating the matter
was Merry's wife, who felt she and her husband had been deliberately
snubbed by Jefferson when, upon their arrival in Washington in 1803,
the president had invited them to the same White House dinner as the

minister of France. The two countries were then at war and Jefferson's casual treatment of the two nations' sensitivities smacked of either bland indifference to diplomatic protocol, or worse; perhaps he was making a point of his neutrality at the Merrys' expense. In either case, Mrs. Merry deeply resented it and vowed to make Jefferson pay and pay.

Now, after receiving news from the fugitive Burr, Merry advised his government that the vice president was offering to betray his country:

> *I have just received an offer from Mr. Burr, the actual Vice President of the United States (which situation he is about to resign) to lend his assistance to His Majesty's Government in any manner in which they may think fit to employ him, particularly in endeavoring to effect a separation of the western part of the United States from that which lies between the Atlantic and the mountains, in its whole extent. His proposition on this and other subjects will be fully detailed to your Lordship by Colonel Williamson, who has been the bearer of them to me, [author's emphasis] and who will embark for England in a few days. It is therefore only necessary for me to add that if, after what is generally known of the profligacy of Mr. Burr's character, His Majesty's Minister should think proper to listen to his offer, his present situation in this country, where he is now cast off as much by the Democratic as by the Federal Party, and where he still preserves connections with some people of influence, added to his great ambition and spirit of revenge against the present Administration, may possibly induce him to exert the talents and activity which he possesses with fidelity to his employers.*

As damning as Merry's report might appear, it seems to be based more on inference than on specific statements from either Williamson or Burr. Over the next few years, Williamson himself would write no fewer than fourteen letters to British government figures urging cooperation. However, in none of those surviving letters did Williamson mention the severance of part of the United States. Those interpretations seem to have been made by Merry, who would later acknowledge that he lacked specific information on Burr's plans.

Williamson also went to England to lobby with the government to finance Burr in various scenarios of western doings, but those concentrated on a plan to invade Mexico. Williamson said that through Burr, the United States and Great Britain would combine "in the Conquest of Mexico" and in annexing the Spanish-owned Floridas, East and West. If Britain would provide some two hundred thousand pounds in financing, said Williamson, "I would expect before next August to see 50,000 North Americans, with Colonel Burr at their head, far on their march to the City of Mexico."

Nothing came of Williamson's offers, not because the British lacked interest but because Napoleon's expanding grab on the Continent was absorbing all British resources.

Burr, still vice president, returned to Washington in October 1804 to preside over the Senate for the final time. Perhaps the most important item on his agenda was to oversee the trial of Justice Chase. Although still an outcast and fugitive in New York, New Jersey, and New England, Burr was temporarily immune from arrest.

The prosecution of the impeachment had fallen upon John Randolph, then Jefferson's leader in the House. Randolph and his House team of prosecutors would present the case to the Senate, which was judge and jury and headed by Vice President Burr.

Recognizing Burr's ability to influence the trial, Jefferson suddenly did his best to woo his former running mate. Offices were given to Burr's in-laws and friends and, significantly, laid out along the precise lines suggested by Wilkinson at his earlier New York meeting with Burr.

Apparently at Burr's suggestion, Wilkinson was appointed to a three-year term as governor of the Louisiana Territory. Burr's brother-in-law, Dr. Joseph Browne, was named secretary. Their combined powers were immense. As governor-general, Wilkinson controlled the courts and land offices. The latter power was virtually a license to print money. The territory was public land, up for sale, and control of the titles was a potentially inexhaustible gold mine. Wilkinson commanded the militia, collected the taxes, supervised all relations with the Indians, and appointed a business partner of his, Pierre Chouteau, as Indian agent.

If there was a plot to sever western lands, and by this time there was certainly a scheme to *develop* them, Jefferson had set the stage by firmly placing Louisiana in the administrative hands of General Wilkinson and, by extension, Aaron Burr.

To further conciliate the vice president, Jefferson invited Burr to dinner at the White House and encouraged Madison and Gallatin to renew their old friendships with him. At the same time, Jefferson's Democratic senators unsuccessfully petitioned the governor of New Jersey to drop the murder charges. Everything was done to bring Burr back into the fold of the administration.

Such was the price Jefferson paid for seemingly nothing more than the ouster of Justice Chase.

Burr played his end of the bargain to the hilt, accepting all the appointments and blandishments with the smoothest of pleasure. He prepared the Senate chambers in celebratory colors for the trial with banners of red, white, and blue. The Senate benches were covered with crimson cloth and the galleries, reserved for congressmen, ladies, and special guests, were decked with green velvet. Special boxes were done in blue muslin and set aside for prosecution and defense.

In February 1805, just after Jefferson was officially elected to his second term, the trial began.

Burr's role as presiding officer excited much comment, much of it sarcastic. The Federalist senator William Plumer wrote, "This is the first time, God grant it may be the last, that ever a man indicted for murder presided in the American Senate. We are indeed fallen upon evil times. The high office of President is filled by an infidel; that of Vice President by a murderer."

Justice Chase's chief defense counsel was Luther Martin, an often besotted but brilliant Baltimore attorney. Martin tore the prosecution's case to shreds, rather quickly securing the acquittal of Chase on grounds that a federal judge could not be impeached for something that was not subject to criminal indictment. For Jefferson's benefit, Martin made the point that holding opposing political views was not criminal.

Following the trial, Jefferson was sworn in as president and George Clinton, sixty-five-year-old former governor of New York, was sworn in as vice president.[6] Among those present at the inauguration was

Aaron Burr, witness to himself being put out of office and apparently out of prospects.

Burr, perhaps the most liberal and cerebral American politician of his era, now began his final slide to disaster. But even at that moment the French ambassador, Louis Turreau, was writing to his foreign minister, Talleyrand, that the immediate ex-vice president would not go quietly into retirement:[7]

> *Mr. Burr's career is generally looked upon as finished; but he is far from sharing that opinion, and I believe he would rather sacrifice the interests of his country than renounce celebrity and fortune. Although Louisiana is still only a Territory, it has obtained the right of sending a delegate to Congress. Louisiana is therefore to become the theater of Mr. Burr's new intrigues; he is going there under the aegis of General Wilkinson.*

It had become common knowledge that Burr and Wilkinson were engaged in some sort of western adventure. But the precise nature of those plans was a matter of much speculation—even to the principals themselves.

Among those speculating about the enterprise was Ambassador Turreau, who had the French gift for personal detail and precisely accurate invective. Fixing a daggerlike eye on America's senior general, he informed Talleyrand:

> *General Wilkinson is forty-eight years of age. He has an amiable exterior. Though said to be well informed in civil and political matters, his military capacity is small. Ambitious and easily dazzled, fond of show and appearances, he complains rather indiscreetly, and especially after dinner, of the form of his government, which leaves officers few chances of fortune, advancement, and glory, and which does not pay its military chiefs enough to support a proper style. He listened with pleasure, or rather with enthusiasm, to the details which I gave him in regard to the organization, the dress, and the force of the French army. My uniform, the order with which I am decorated, are objects of envy to him; and he*

seems to hold to the American service only because he can do no better. General Wilkinson is the most intimate friend, or rather the most devoted creature, of Colonel Burr.

Meanwhile, the governor of New Mexico, Joaquín del Réal Alencaster had indeed invited to Santa Fe the chiefs of several Indian tribes to confer on capturing or killing the Americans. Alencaster also dispatched a Spanish cavalry troop under Don Pedro Vial to find and capture Lewis.

Traveling by night to avoid hostile Indians, Vial reached the Arkansas River on November 5, 1805, but was attacked by Indians. After a stiff, three-hour battle, the Spaniards drove off the hostiles. But their camp was destroyed and their supplies looted. Unable to continue his mission, Vial returned to Santa Fe without Lewis or Clark.

As for those hardy explorers, they were heading toward the Rockies, unaware of the drama unfolding around them, unaware that Lewis was being stalked.

In the heart of the Upper Missouri, Lewis prevailed on the chiefs of the Osage Nation to send a deputation to Washington. This was a masterpiece of strategy as it put the government of the United States in possession of hostages for the safe return of the explorers.

In Washington, the Osage were an immediate sensation. Jefferson greeted them warmly, saying, "I set a Beloved Man, Captain Lewis, one of my own household to learn something of the people with whom we are now united, to let you know we were your friends. . . ."

Jefferson described the twelve Osages as the most gigantic he had ever seen. He was especially pleased that they "were innocent of the evils of liquor." Believing that the Osages were the most powerful nation south of the Missouri, he was anxious to secure their friendship and promised that "no harm ever be done [you] by this nation."

They were invited to the House of Representatives, where their clothes "jingled with little bells, such as we call hawks' bells," wrote the English visitor Charles William Janson.[8]

They were ornamented with a variety of foxes' tails and feathers, bones, ivory trinkets in different shapes, curiously carved shells, and pieces of hard polished wood. From the nose was suspended a small piece of silver; some wore this in the shape of a heart, and others round, and the size of a six-pence; and from each ear hung a fish bone, a piece of ivory, or some other fanciful ornament. The face of the first chief was painted all over the color of brick dust— that of the next in rank was half reddened; another a fourth part; others were half black, and the remainder of the natural color. A single lock of hair alone hung from the middle of the back of the head, to which was tied an enormous fox's tail, or a bunch of feathers of various colors; the whole forming a most grotesque, yet interesting group.

That night the Osages appeared on stage at a theater on Pennsylvania Avenue, where they were civilized enough to insist that the manager pay them half the net proceeds, plus a supply of rum. Either their innocence had been less than the president had supposed, or they had been quick to adapt to Potomac customs.

To entertain their audience, the Osages did a war dance consisting, said Janson, "of stamping in procession round the stage in indifferent figures, and screaming in horrid discord . . . the taking off the scalp of the supposed victim was executed with such adroitness that the deception was not to be perceived. Before the conclusion of the entertainment, the greatest part of them were intoxicated."

The next morning the chief was found dead of drink in his bed and a grand funeral was held, attended by several members of Congress. Jefferson's presence was not reported.

On May 26, 1805, while in eastern Montana,[9] Meriwether got his first glimpse of the fabled Rockies, the source of the Missouri. The dimly limned line of mountains ahead of him was "partially covered with snow. And behind these mountains—at a great distance—a second and more lofty range stretching across the horizon, their snowy tops lost in the sky . . ."

He climbed to a more elevated point of land for a better view: "I thought myself repaid for my labor, as from this point I beheld the Rocky Mountains for the first time. . . . The mountains were covered with snow and the sun shown on it in such a manner as to give me the most plain and satisfactory view. . . . While I viewed these mountains,

I felt a secret pleasure in finding myself so near the head of the heretofore conceived boundless Missouri. . . .''

The party had crossed the plains and were now entering the forested valleys and peaks, meeting and recording the great tribes—Mandan, Cree, Crow, Shoshone, Flathead, Nez Percé, Cheyenne, Arapaho, Kiowa, and Sioux. Lewis wrote Jefferson that he wanted no part of the latter:

> These are the vilest miscreants of the savage race and must ever remain the pirates of the Missouri until such measures are pursued by our Government as will make them feel a dependence on its will for their supply of merchandise. Unless these people are reduced to order, by coercive measures, I am ready to pronounce that the citizens of the United States can never enjoy but partially the advantages which the Missouri presents. . . . They [the Sioux] view with contempt the merchants of the Missouri, whom they never fail to plunder when in their power. Persuasion or advice with them is viewed as supplication and only tends to inspire them with contempt for those who offer either.

Lewis knew that there was but one sure way to find the source of the Missouri—to locate the legendary Great Falls which were so constant in Indian legend. Indians had told Finiels and other French explorers in St. Louis that a range of high snowcapped mountains to the west were the source of the great Missouri River, pouring forth from waterfalls bigger than Niagara and entering the Mississippi at St. Louis. As Finiels reported:

> . . . Indians agree [the Falls are] its source, which has been explored by no European. . . . This river has a fearsome reputation where its waters strain against the flanks of the mountains and are compelled to struggle constantly against the rocks that cross their course. The falls by which it descends onto the plain are not, it is said, any less wondrous; their dizzy height stuns your gaze; their swiftness is a kind of impetuous fury, with the waters leaping out onto the plain as if they are indignant with the constraints just overcome; the thunder in the air, the echoes reverberating through

the flanks of the mountains, provide a spectacle that makes the famous Niagara Falls pale in comparison, if you believe the astonishment and surprise that sweeps across Indian faces when you question them about the sources of the Missouri.

The Falls of the Missouri, near present-day Great Falls, Montana, are not as huge as Niagara, but they are indeed spectacular in their own right.[10]

By mid-June, the party was ascending through the middle of Montana, traveling through buffalo country, breaking their way through the unexplored vastness of a continent. On June 13, they left camp at sunrise, the men wearing dressed skins and moccasins for the rugged snowcapped mountains ahead. Lewis himself was weak with dysentery. The party was split into small sections, looking along several streams flowing into a prairie canyon as they sought some sign of the Falls. Appropriately, it was Lewis himself who was the first to find them while traveling with Silas Goodrich, the Corps's most expert fisherman.

Lewis heard the great waters before he saw them, a thunderous rush. Toward this point he directed his steps; the noise increased as he approached and soon became too tremendous to be mistaken for anything but the Great Falls of the Missouri: "My ears were saluted with the agreeable sound of a fall of water and, advancing a little further, I saw the spray arise above the plain like a column of smoke, which would frequently disappear again in an instant. . . . I hurried down the hill to gaze on this sublimely grand spectacle . . . the grandest sight I ever beheld."

At the point where he broke onto the cascade, the river was three hundred yards wide, boiling over a perpendicular cliff, the water falling in one smooth, even sheet over a precipice of at least eighty feet.[11]

It was as if the whole of the Missouri had been suddenly stopped by one huge shelf of rock, without a single niche, "and with an edge as straight and regular as if formed by art."

Beyond the Great Falls, Lewis observed another, similar cascade, just slightly smaller. About three miles farther on, he came to another.

As the rest of the party came up, it was discerned that they had encountered not one single great falls, but a series of majestic cascades, five falls encompassing ten miles of the mighty river. "It was," said Lewis, "one continued scene of rapids and cascades which I readily perceived could not be encountered with our canoes."

In the middle of the cascades, they found a little island in the middle of the river, "well covered with timber." Lewis noted in his journal that at the center of the island was an eagle's nest which had been earlier described by the Mandans:

> *Here on a cottonwood tree an eagle had fixed her nest, and seemed the undisputed mistress of a spot, to contest whose domination neither man nor beast would venture across the gulfs that surround it, and which is further secured by the mist rising from the falls. This solitary bird could not escape the observation of the Indians, who made the eagle's nest a part of their description of the falls, which now proves to be correct in almost every particular, except that they did not do justice to the height.*

The water was foaming over high masses of rocks, throwing up so much spray that the sun formed a rainbow above it. That night, Lewis and the party feasted on buffalo hump, buffalo tongue, marrow bones, trout, and something extra, as Lewis recorded:

> *Our work being at an end this evening, we gave the men a drink of spirits, it being the last of our stock, and some of them appeared a little sensible of its effects. The fiddle was played and they danced very merrily until nine in the evening when a heavy shower of rain put an end to that part of the amusement, though they continued their mirth with songs and festive jokes and were extremely merry until late at night. We had a very comfortable dinner of bacon, beans, suet dumplings, and buffalo bear, etc. In short we had no just cause to covet the sumptuous feasts of our countrymen this day [July 4]. One elk and a beaver were all that was killed by the hunters today, the buffalo seem to have withdrawn themselves from this neighborhood, [but] the men inform us that they are still abundant about the fells.*

It was at the Falls that Lewis had his closest encounter yet with a grizzly, an almost fatal adventure.

Although they were familiar with brown bears and black bears in the East, neither Lewis nor Clark had even heard of grizzlies until they wintered with the Mandans. The Indians had many stories to tell, to which the explorers had listened with great astonishment. The Mandans said they were occasionally able to kill grizzlies, but more often grizzlies killed them. It took six to ten warriors to kill a single bear and even then the risk was so great that the same ceremony used to launch a war party was used to launch a grizzly hunt.

Lewis was skeptical. Indians with bows and arrows and a few bad rifles might have problems with grizzlies. With his men, all expert with the rifle, it would be a different story.

It was into the spring, not long after they left the Mandans, that they saw the first grizzly tracks. They were enormous. Half again as long and three times as wide as the tracks of a large man. No one had ever seen anything like them. But they did not see bears. This frustrated Lewis, who doubted the Mandan accounts of their ferocity and expected they were timid. These "fierce" bears must be extremely wary and shy, Lewis thought.

A few days later, Lewis and one of his men encountered their first grizzly. Two of them, feeding together. Without hesitation, they shot at both bears and wounded them. They thus violated what would become their first law of grizzly hunting: never be around one with an unloaded rifle. They had emptied both guns at the same time.

One bear fled. But the other took after Lewis and chased him nearly one hundred yards before his partner could reload and kill it.

When all the excitement was done, the terror turned out to be nothing but a three-hundred-pound cub. *That* gave the men something to think about.

On another day, Clark and a French guide killed another grizzly, but only after pumping ten bullets into it. "Its measurements were six hundred pounds in weight and nine feet in length," Clark recorded. When it stood on its hind feet, it was three feet taller than Lewis, who was the tallest man in the party. This size, plus the bear's amazing capacity to absorb bullets, gave the expedition even more to think about.

At the Falls of the Missouri, Lewis was out buffalo hunting. While he was skinning the animal, he looked up to see a grizzly, twenty feet away, wanting a meal and advancing on Lewis with deadly purpose. Lewis took up his gun to shoot, but in a single instance of shock realized that his gun was empty. He had violated Rule Number One; he had not reloaded after killing the buffalo.

The grizzly stepped up its pace toward Lewis. The explorer looked around. He was on an open plain with not a bush or a tree within less than half a mile. Nearby, however, some one hundred yards away, was the Missouri River.

Lewis figured to retreat to the river in a brisk walk until he could jump in. The idea was to get into the water at such a depth that he could stand but the bear would be obliged to swim. In such a situation, Lewis could defend himself with his espontoon, a short spear he carried with him at all times.

The bear, however, had different ideas. As soon as Lewis turned for his brisk walk to the river, the bear pitched after him, jaws slavering, and at full gallop.

Lewis took off at a dead run and hit the water with a leap. The bear never did oblige him by coming into the river.

Neck deep, Lewis stayed in the water until dark, when he crawled out and headed for camp. Not two hundred yards from the river, he stumbled upon a mountain lion, which promptly chased him away. Less than a quarter of a mile later, the winded explorer came upon a buffalo herd and was charged by three bulls. He again took to his heels.

That night, finally arrived safe in camp, he wrote in his journal: "It seemed that all the beasts of the neighborhood had made a league to destroy me . . . or to amuse themselves at my expense. These bears being so hard to die rather intimidates us all. I must confess that I do not like the gentlemen and had rather fight two Indians than one bear."

In August, the Corps reached the headwaters of the Missouri, a confluence of three streams on a vast, flat plateau some hundred and twenty miles due south of the Great Falls. As good Democrats, Lewis and Clark named the streams the Jefferson, the Madison, and the Gallatin. They chose to continue upstream on the Jefferson, the most westerly of the three little rivers, so small it could be easily waded.

On August 13, the expedition topped the Continental Divide. They were in country never before seen by white men. With incredibly skillful woodsmanship, after examination of a hundred streams and the interrogation of many Indians, they located the source of the Columbia.

"Here," wrote Lewis, "I first tasted the waters of the great Columbia River." The link with the Pacific was about to be completed.

And here, in a remarkable coincidence at the apex of the continent, they met Shoshones. But they were not just Shoshones, they were the very clan of Sacajawea's people, led by her brother, Chief Cameahwait.

The Shoshone woman had been with the Corps since they left the Mandans four months earlier with Sacajawea carrying her infant son, Baptiste, in a cradleboard on her back. She had proved invaluable on the trip, having among other feats saved Clark's life during a severe illness. He returned the favor a few days later after leaving the Great Falls.

In that adventure, most of the men were busy with a portage around the falls while Clark, Charbonneau, and Sacajawea walked the banks of the Missouri, with Baptiste slung on his mother's cradleboard. Shortly after they started, an enormous black storm struck the river with heavy winds and "a torrent of rain and hail" more violent than Clark had ever seen.

Before he got out of the bottom of the ravine, the water was up to his waist. Then a wall of water came plunging down upon the small party, "tearing everything before it," including large rocks and much mud. Sacajawea just had time to grasp her baby in her arms before the cradle was ripped from her back by the swift current. Putting his gun and shot pouch in his left hand and occasionally pushing Sacajawea before him, Clark scrambled up the steep, mud-slick hillside using only his right hand. Charbonneau was of little help, his fear immobilizing him. Sacajawea and Baptiste would have been lost had it not been for Clark.

Now, as if repaying him and the Corps, she identified the country they were entering as her own. She said that where the three rivers came together was where her relatives lived part of the year. Without regret, she told of her capture there by the Minnetarees.

Lewis wrote that she showed "no sorrow in recollecting the events or of joy in being again restored to her native country; if she had enough to eat and a few trinkets to wear I believe she would be content anywhere."

Clark would also record in the journals that while Charbonneau "has been very serviceable to us, his wife [has been] particularly useful among the Shoshones. Indeed, she has borne with a patience truly admirable the fatigues of so long a route, encumbered with the charge of an infant. . . ."

The first Shoshones encountered were three squaws. Surprised by Lewis's scouts, they had no chance to run. Instead, the women fell to their knees, bowing their heads and awaiting death. Lewis laid down his gun. "I took the elderly woman by the hand and raised her up, repeated the word *Ta-ba-bone*," which Sacajawea had told him meant "white man" in Shoshone. "I stripped up my shirt sleeve to show her my skin to prove to her the truth of the assertion that I was a white man, for my face and hands, which had been constantly exposed to the sun, were quite as dark as their own. They appeared instantly reconciled and, the men coming up, I gave these women some beads and a few moccasins, awls, some pewter looking-glasses and a little paint."

As the women guided Lewis and his scouts to the Shoshone camp, some sixty warriors galloped up, all armed with bows and arrows, some with a few muzzle-loading muskets.

They received the white men with friendship, and after a powwow the chief agreed to accompany Lewis back to the main party. Then came the incredible coincidence of Sacajawea meeting her brother, as recorded by Lewis:

The chief (Cameahwait) was conducted to a sort of circular tent or shade of willows. . . . The moccasins of the whole party were then taken off, and after much ceremony the smoking began. After this the conference was to be opened. Glad of an opportunity of being able to converse more intelligibly, Sacajawea was sent for;

she came into the tent, sat down, and was beginning to interpret, when, in the person of Cameahwait, she recognized her brother. She instantly jumped up, and ran and embraced him throwing over him her blanket, and weeping profusely. The chief was himself moved, though not in the same degree. After some conversation between them she resumed her seat and attempted to interpret for us; but her new situation seemed to overpower her, and she frequently interrupted by her tears. After the council was finished, the unfortunate woman learned that all her family were dead except two brothers, one of whom was absent, and a son of her eldest sister, a small boy, who was immediately adopted by her.

With the Shoshones' invaluable help, Lewis and Clark obtained horses and continued their search for the Pacific.

August 18 was Lewis's thirty-first birthday. They had conquered the Rockies and found the source of the Missouri. Now, at the Continental Divide, in the midst of his greatest adventure, Lewis had self-doubts, writing of his reflections:

This day I completed my thirty first year, and conceived that I had in all human probability now existed about half the period which I am to remain in this world. I reflected that I had as yet done but little, very little indeed, to further the happiness of the human race or to advance the information of the succeeding generation. I viewed with regret the many hours I have spent in indolence, and now sorely feel that want of information which those hours would have given me had they been judiciously expended. But since they are past and cannot be recalled, I dash from me the gloomy thought, and resolved in future, to redouble my exertions and at least endeavor to promote these two primary objects of human existence, by giving them the aid of that portion of talents which nature and fortune have bestowed on me; or in the future, to live for mankind as I have heretofore lived for myself.

Not long afterward, the party reached the Clearwater River and descended it to the Snake, which they followed to the Columbia.

Finally they reached "the Great Pacific Ocean which we have been so long anxious to see," wrote Lewis.

"There is great joy in camp. We are in view of the ocean . . . and the roaring or noise made by the waves breaking on the rocky shores may be heard distinctly."

They wintered on a high bluff overlooking the crashing surf of the Pacific. For four and a half months they waited there to sight a trading ship and take passage home. In March, disappointed at the lack of contact, they headed back across the Rockies.

It was on the return that the expedition had its most severe encounter with hostiles.

On July 3, 1806, the party recrossed the Continental Divide at Traveler's Rest Creek, near today's Missoula, Montana. There the party separated, Clark retracing to the source of the Missouri and later crossing to the Yellowstone. Lewis spent some time exploring in the Marias River section of Montana. There he met a party of Blackfoot Indians[12] who attempted to steal some horses and supplies. In the ensuing skirmish, one was killed by Lewis and another wounded. This was the only Indian killed during the expedition. To avoid vengeance, Lewis headed quickly downstream.

On August 11 while hunting, Lewis was wounded, though not seriously, by one of his party. The next day he met Clark and that party and the recombined expedition headed down the Missouri. At Fort Mandan Charbonneau was paid off and left the party with his wife, Sacajawea, and their son, Baptiste. One of the expedition members, John Colter, also received permission to leave the party at that point because he wanted to explore more of the country. (Colter is credited with being the first to map and describe what is now Yellowstone National Park.)[13]

On September 23, 1806, the expedition entered St. Louis. The adventure was ended and Lewis immediately wrote Jefferson:

It is a pleasure that I announce to you the safe arrival of myself and party at twelve o'clock today at this place with our papers and baggage. In obedience to your orders we have penetrated the continent of North America to the Pacific Ocean and sufficiently

explored the interior of the country to affirm with confidence that
we have discovered the most practicable route which does exist
across the continent by means of the navigable branches of the
Missouri and Columbia rivers.

Lewis signed off with a warmer, more personal note, "I am very
anxious to learn the state of my friends in Albemarle and particularly
whether my mother is yet living. . . . The whole of the party who
accompanied me from the Mandans have returned in good health,
which is not, I assure you, to me one of the least pleasant considerations
of the voyage."

Governor-General Wilkinson was not on hand to greet the explorers.
He had been ordered south by President Jefferson to counter a Spanish
military incursion into western Louisiana. On the day Lewis arrived in
St. Louis, Wilkinson and a handful of troops had just made camp on
Bayou Pierre and opened negotiations with the invaders.

In St. Louis, the day following their arrival, the two captains dined
with Wilkinson's friend August Chouteau, then after dinner went shopping for clothes for the triumphal return to the East.

In Washington, Jefferson received the news with glee, making it part
of his message to Congress. With pleasure, he wrote Lewis that "the
unknown scenes in which you were engaged and the length of time
without hearing from you had begun to be felt awfully. I assure you
of the joy with which all your friends here will receive you."

Twenty-seven men had made the entire journey. They had traced the
Missouri to its source, crossed the Rockies, and found their way down
the Columbia to the Pacific. Going and coming, they had explored six
thousand miles of the then unknown West, yet even in moments of
need and peril they had kept accurate observations on latitude and
longitude; on birds, plants, animals, and Indian life; on topographical
features; and on trade possibilities. Maps made by Clark remained the
only accurate maps of the region for decades.

Every day of the journey was recorded in one or more of the journals
kept by Lewis, Clark, and four other members of the expedition. The
first to be published (1807) was a highly fictionalized version of Sergeant Patrick Gass's diary. A condensation of Lewis and Clark's dia-

ries, with annotations by George Shannon, were used for the Nicholas Biddle edition. Recognized as the earliest authentic account of the expedition, the Biddle was published in 1814.[14]

The Lewis and Clark Expedition had been a stunning success. But back east, storm clouds were brewing. Rumors were rife that Aaron Burr was gathering an army to seize the western territories and create his own nation. His accomplice was said to be James Wilkinson.

The Conspirators

· · · · · · · · · ·

A_ARON_ B_URR_ _HAD BEEN_ out of a job since March 4, 1805.
What to do? At age forty-nine, he shied away from the laborious
reconstruction of a law practice. National politics was out, at least
temporarily. And Burr was ruined in his former political power bases
of New York and New England. But opportunity might lie in the West,
in the valley of the Mississippi and the new lands of Louisiana. He
was popular out there, possibly even more so since he had killed
Hamilton, who had been regarded as an enemy of the region.

West it would be, but first he would visit the British ambassador, Sir
Anthony Merry, with whom Burr had been in more or less regular
contact since the duel.

In the spring of 1805, the former vice president came calling on
Merry to tell the minister that the inhabitants of Louisiana intended to
exclude themselves from the United States. Although Burr made no
explicit mention of his role in such plans, Merry forwarded a report of
the meeting to his government in London in a dispatch marked "Most
Secret":

> *Mr. Burr . . . has mentioned to me that the inhabitants of Louisi-*
> *ana seem determined to render themselves independent of the*

*United States, and that the execution of their design is only delayed
by the difficulty of obtaining previously an assurance of protection
and assistance from some foreign power, and of concerting and
connecting their independence with that of the inhabitants of the
western parts of the United States, who must always have a command over them by the rivers which communicate with the Mississippi. It is clear that Mr. Burr (although he has not as yet confided
to me the exact nature and extent of his plan) means to endeavor
to be the instrument of effecting such a connection.*

Burr did ask for aid, saying the separation could be accomplished
only if the British put a fleet at the mouth of the Mississippi and loaned
him half a million dollars for expenses. The support of the English
fleet made sense to Merry because Spain was now protected by France
and France was at war with England. Burr did not view this as treason.
Everyone from Jefferson to the Creoles at New Orleans not only wanted
but expected war with Spain so that the United States would acquire
the Floridas, fix the western border of the Louisiana Purchase, and
open up Texas and Mexico for immigration and trade.

Burr saw himself as the liberator of Spanish America, a role Jefferson
hoped to reserve for himself.

After taking a few weeks to put his affairs in order, Burr left Washington for a tour of the West. For the first leg of the trip, Burr traveled
with two distinguished companions. One was John Smith, a senator
from Ohio who had lost favor with the administration because he had
voted for the acquittal of Justice Chase. The other was Jonathan Dayton, former Speaker of the House, Federalist ex-senator from New
Jersey, and a speculator in western lands who would give his name to
Dayton, Ohio.

He dropped Dayton and Smith at Cincinnati, but only after the three
had formed a company to (1) dig a canal around the Falls of the Ohio
at Louisville; (2) operate a bank with a paper capital of a million
dollars; and (3) speculate in land.

At Pittsburgh, Burr purchased a houseboat which he described to his
daughter Theodosia as "sort of a Noah's Ark." It was a square-ended
barge about sixty feet long and fifteen feet wide with a superstructure

containing a living room with fireplace, two bedrooms, and a well-furnished kitchen with a fireplace. The New Yorker marveled that such a pleasant accommodation could be built for two hundred dollars.

There were no sails or oar, just a tiller, and Burr's ark simply glided down the rivers, an odyssey that left him astonished at the many houses of brick and other signs of civilization he saw along the river.

Continuing on alone to Fort Massac on the Ohio, Burr met with Wilkinson in a tête à tête. They were together for four days of secret meetings, details of which are to this day unrecorded. Wilkinson then loaned Burr the use of a government barge and a company of soldiers to accompany the "ark" on the trip down to New Orleans.

Burr made numerous stops. His longest before New Orleans was at Natchez, Mississippi Territory—"a town of three or four hundred houses," Burr informed Theodosia. "The inhabitants, traders and mechanics, [are] surrounded by wealthy planters, among whom I have been entertained with great hospitality and taste." Burr found the planters living in remarkable wealth, comparable to that of the Alstons in South Carolina—not unlikely because Natchez had begun as an English settlement, then had an easy endurance under the Spanish flag until the Americans took control in 1795.

Natchez had many attractions, including climate and English-speaking inhabitants, and was favored over New Orleans as a base by Wilkinson and Burr.[1]

In estimating Natchez at three or four hundred houses, Burr apparently was speaking only of the main part of the town, literally the upper half. In 1806, Natchez had some six thousand population, being a major trading center boosted by the opening of the Natchez Trace. Then as now, Natchez was two towns, one being the original settlement on a shelf of riverfront land, which was known as "Under-the-Hill," and where in proper season two hundred boats might be lying at the landing.

Under-the-Hill was "full of boatmen, mulattoes, whorehouses of the most wretched sort, in short, the refuse of the world," wrote an early visitor. "For the size of it there is not, perhaps, in the world a more profligate place," wrote John Bradbury in 1810. Not long afterward, the actor Tyrone Power[2] spoke of establishments "more obscene in their appointments than the lowest of the itinerant hells found at our races." Virtually all of the vice dens were confined to the riverfront.

The town proper, in both senses of the word, was seated on a two-hundred-foot-high bluff overlooking the landing. With broad streets and handsome public buildings, it was the principal market and shipping center in the region for cotton and other farm products. Its land artery was the Trace, a federal road that ran from the river port north some five hundred miles to Lexington, Kentucky, passing through Nashville, Tennessee, on its way.

Originally a buffalo path, the Trace had begun as an Indian trail leading from village to village and was a thoroughfare for war parties. In 1699, South Carolinians began using the Trace to trade with the Chickasaw Nation. Soon afterward, French traders set up business at French Lick, site of Nashville, and they, too, began using the road south to the Indian nations.[3] In time, the constant travel of traders, Indians, explorers, settlers, sailors, and missionaries through the path of ancient trees wore down the trail twenty feet and more below the surrounding ground.

European and American travelers began using the path regularly after 1765 when the region passed into British hands. After the opening of the Mississippi by treaties with the Spanish in 1795, the road became one of the main traveled highways of the western country.

As a federal road, the Trace dated from 1800, the year the Adams administration ordered a network of game trails and Indian paths combined into a "post road" for the mails. Not long after Jefferson took office in 1801, use of the Trace was increased by flatboat crews who brought the exports of the back country west of the Alleghenies down to market in New Orleans. Rather than fight the current going back upriver, the boatmen, known as "half alligator and half horse," sold their flatboats, keelboats, and barges for wood in New Orleans and returned by foot or pony up the well-worn trails to their homes.

The Trace's most recent improvement had been "cut by order of General Wilkinson," Burr wrote Theodosia, "but actually [is] nothing but bayou and swamp, underbrush and forest, venomous snakes and swarming insects."[4]

Upon taking office, Jefferson had assigned Wilkinson to be Indian commissioner for the region. The job appears to have been offered as a boon to supplement Wilkinson's meager $225 a month army pay, but it entailed real labors and duties. The extra post gave the general the dual tasks of managing the army and overseeing the federal government's relations with the many tribes of the southern United States—Creeks, Choctaws, and Chickasaws. According to his expense accounts, the general traveled some sixteen thousand miles through forests and inland waters on public business from 1800 to 1803. Wilkinson was instructed to improve the old Indian trails and post road and make them into a military "highway," and in 1801 the Choctaws and Chickasaws gave permission to build the highway across their lands.

From the beginning the Trace was a robber's paradise—a road for the hunted and the hunters. Along the path meandered pioneers, soldiers, post riders, preachers, merchants, and boatmen. The Trace had several names including "The Devil's Backbone," "The Old Chickasaw Trail," and "the Path of the Choctaws."

In 1805, the year before Burr's visit, the Choctaws and Chickasaws had agreed to assist travelers by allowing hostelries or inns along their share of the Trace, provided the establishments were operated by men of their nations. The Chickasaws also ceded claim to a forty-mile-wide strip of land running along the north bank of the Tennessee River.

It was into this strip of former Chickasaw Territory that a man named Robert Griner would come in 1808 to set up a "stand," or inn, which were the regional terms for a tavern.[5] Griner's Inn has come down through history as "Grinder's Stand."

On June 25, Burr arrived in New Orleans, some one hundred and fifty miles downriver from Natchez. Burr's visit was advertised well in advance. Beginning at Baton Rouge,[6] and for some ninety miles above the city, people were lined up along the man-made levees on both sides of the twisting Mississippi to see Burr riding in an elegant barge fitted out with gaudy sails and colors, ten oars, and an escort of soldiers.

The river was often a mile wide in this region and the levees ran continuously along both banks, plantation after plantation, each touching the next, making a continuous hundred-mile-long community of plantations, farms, and fields, connected not by roads but by the river.

As Burr got nearer to New Orleans, he came upon "massive sugar-houses, neat summer houses, and numerous negro villages succeeding each other in such a way, that the whole distance has the appearance of one continued village. The houses are airy and neat, some of them splendid, and in the midst of orange groves and pretty gardens, in which are the delicious cape jasmine. . . ."[7]

One hundred miles above the mouth of the Mississippi, Burr came around a great crescent in the river and onto New Orleans itself, the Mississippi Valley's great commercial capital, situated on the American east bank.

Burr, the Man in the Iron Mask, as he would become known, was received like royalty. Journeying leisurely before admiring crowds, he passed bayou villas built and decorated in the Italian style, stuccoed in white and yellow paint, with iron columns supporting the galleries and avenues lined with orange trees. As he entered the city proper, the houses were of brick, some several stories high. The streets were dirt or mud but bordered by sidewalks, called *banquettes*, which were made of planks fastened flat in the mud.

At the center of the city were the Cabildo, the Cathedral, and the "French Market," which stretched for half a mile, with "negroes, mulattoes, French, Spanish, Germans, all crying their several articles in their several tongues."

It was August and New Orleans was steamy hot. Men and women both were dressed in cotton. Silk was worn at night, but only for balls or other decorative occasions. The men were less sensibly dressed than women, their heads sunk in high collars, arms and hands buried in long sleeves, and legs encased in high boots. The French women were rather plain, matronly in dress and manner, and being upstaged of late by refugees from Christophe's Haiti—light-skinned whites and mulattoes who were tall and lithe as palmettos.

One of the Haitians had just married Edward Livingston, a friend of Burr's and a former congressman and mayor of New York City, who had migrated to New Orleans to seek his fortune.

It was a city given to sensuous pleasures, full of music and passion. Here was "roulette," the wheel of fortune; horseraces and card games; every facility for gambling with tables piled high with golden dollars and doubloons; a vice to tempt every eye and inflame any blood.

Burr was honored with a series of balls and the ladies walked to them barefoot, preceded by slaves who carried lanterns and their satin slippers.

During his stay in New Orleans, Burr spent considerable time with members of the Mexican Society, sometimes known as the Mexican Association, an organization of some three hundred men who shared a desire to free Mexico from Spain, particularly if the secession benefited their property holdings. A leading member of the society was Daniel Clark, the Irish-born American consul in New Orleans who would become a central figure in the "Burr Conspiracy."

The existence of the society was one of the causes of strained relations between the United States and Spain. Another was Jefferson's ardent and ill-concealed desire to possess the Floridas. By midsummer of 1805, the president seemed to have brought himself to the point of fighting for them.

Wilkinson had supplied Burr with a letter of introduction to the Spanish boundary commissioner, Casa Calvo, who was still in the city. But Burr's visits to the Mexican Society made it impossible for the Spaniard to receive him. The marquis was worried. In case of war, did Burr intend to lead an expedition against Mexico? Casa Calvo wrote Wilkinson complaining that the friend commended to him had become altogether too intimate with members of the "Mexican Association."

Another worried observer was the Louisiana governor, W.C.C. Claiborne, who kept a close watch on Burr, reporting to Secretary of State James Madison that Burr had been in conference with Juan Ventura Morales, a onetime chief Spanish civil officer of Louisiana. Morales, said Claiborne, "has more information but less principle than any Spanish officer I ever met with; his wealth enables him to make many friends among them, I am sorry to inform you, and . . . during Colonel Burr's continuance in this city he was marked in his attention to Morales, and [also] in habits of intimacy with Livingston, [Daniel] Clark" and others with Spanish connections.

At the end of his three weeks' sojourn, Burr returned north—up the river to Natchez and then overland on the rough and dangerous Natchez Trace.

On August 1, Burr was in Nashville as the guest of Andrew Jackson.

During this entire trip, Burr had discussed his plans, or maybe his dreams, of invading Mexico with thousands of people. But he had done nothing that even his most devoted enemy could construe as contrary to the laws of the United States. He had recruited no men, armed no soldiers. He had only talked and talked.

On August 2, 1805, with Burr in Nashville and Wilkinson in St. Louis, a suggestion of treason was hung around his neck by the *Gazette of the United States*, a Philadelphia newspaper, the largest Federalist publication in the nation, and a bastion of Hamilton sentiment.

Under the heading QUERIES, the *Gazette* asked:

> *How long will it be before we shall hear of Colonel Burr being at the head of a revolutionary party on the western waters?*
>
> *Is it a fact that Colonel Burr has formed a plan to engage adventurous and enterprising young men from the Atlantic states to Louisiana?*
>
> *Is it one of the inducements that an immediate convention will be called from the states bordering the Ohio and Mississippi to form a separate government?*
>
> *Is it another that all the public lands are to be seized and partitioned among the states, except what is reserved for the warlike friends of Burr in the revolution?*
>
> *How soon will the forts and magazines and all the military posts at New Orleans and on the Mississippi be in the hands of Colonel Burr's revolutionary party?*
>
> *How soon will Colonel Burr engage in the reduction of Mexico . . . aided by British ships and forces?*
>
> *What difficulty can there be in completing a revolution in one summer, among the western states, when they will gain the Congress lands, will throw off the public debt, will seize their own revenues and enjoy the plunder of Spain?*

The queries contained the germs of all treason charges later to be made against Burr. Other newspapers quickly picked up the *Gazette* story, reprinting it with comment for or against, depending on the politics of the editors. Whence came the story? It appears to have been a preemptive strike by the Spanish, probably planted by the shrewd Spanish ambassador, the Don Carlos Martínez de Yrujo, who was in Philadelphia at the time.

Certainly the Spanish government was aware that Burr was talking up an invasion plan. From New Orleans, the onetime consul Daniel Clark wrote to Wilkinson that "the Spanish government is much alarmed by the rumor of a projected invasion of their provinces, under Colonel Burr . . . of Aaron the First on the throne of the Montezumas, ruling over a realm stretching from the Alleghanies to Darien with My Lord Wilkinson, in gorgeous apparel, on the highest step of the dais, second to Burr only."

The letter was not one written by a dark conspirator caught in treachery against his country. Instead, Clark seemed entertained that his name was linked with Burr's and Wilkinson's, writing the general tongue-in-cheek, "I am now supposed to be of consequence enough to combine with Generals and Vice Presidents. . . . The tale is a horrid one, if well told. Kentucky, Tennessee, the state of Ohio, and part of Georgia and Carolina, are to be bribed with the plunder of Spanish lands to the west of us, to separate from the Union."

Clark asked Wilkinson to "amuse Mr. Burr with an account of it." But the letter arrived one day after Burr had left St. Louis to return east.

When Burr did hear about the Clark letter, he was undisturbed, writing Clark. "Pray do not disturb yourself with such nonsense." Not only was Burr undisturbed, but Jefferson, too, seemed calm, making no response to the accusations in the *Gazette*.

All this was happening as Meriwether Lewis and William Clark were struggling toward the headwaters of the Missouri.

On Burr's return to the East, he met in St. Louis with Wilkinson, then in Louisville paid $5,000 down plus an agreement to assume $30,000 in debt to buy from Charles Lynch of Kentucky a claim on some 350,000 acres of rich farmland on the Oachita River, in what is now northeastern Louisiana. This purchase, too, would figure in the charges of treason.

Back in St. Louis, Wilkinson and his Indian agent, Pierre Chouteau, had sealed a new trade treaty with the Osages. In a letter to Secretary of War Henry Dearborn, Wilkinson outlined a plan to send an American army to Santa Fe, enclosing a map with instructions on how to do it. Wilkinson said the distance was not over nine hundred miles and there was only one mountain range to cross. Close enough. The distance is slightly more than nine hundred air miles, but there are two mountain ranges to cross, both of them difficult—the Ozarks and a tip of the Rockies.

But the letter had more interesting aspects than mere geography. For it seemed to lay the groundwork for the so-called Burr scheme. Wilkinson advised Dearborn that he should begin building a network of arsenals and magazines along the route so that *if* war with Spain should occur, he could march immediately on Santa Fe with a force of two thousand men.

By November, Burr had returned to Washington, where he learned from Merry that the British government had made no response to his requests for money.

Not long afterward, Burr was invited by Jefferson to another tête à tête followed by a dinner at the White House, the details of both conferences going unreported. It seems apparent, however, that the president wanted the Spanish to believe they were discussing incursions into Spanish territories.

The conferences took place on November 30, a day when Jefferson was preparing a "war message" against Spain for Congress, saying he was looking for any means to force Spain out of the Floridas. But this was for show, a public bluff. Jefferson was secretly informing Congress at the same time that the United States could not afford to go to war with Spain.

This information was certainly known to Burr, who in early January wrote Wilkinson: "You will know, long before this can reach you, that we are to have no Spanish war, except in ink and words." This was a reflection of Jefferson's mood, not the Spanish, because even as Wilkinson received the letter, Spanish troops were gathering their forces on the Texas-Louisiana border, and troops from Havana were arriving in Pensacola.

By the time of the November White House meeting, the newspapers had been full of Burr's alleged plot to sever the nation, or to make unilateral war on Spain. The Spanish ambassador, Yrujo, was amazed that Jefferson would not only fail to denounce the rumors, but actually invite Burr to supper. Was it all part of the bluff?

"I know," Yrujo informed Madrid on December 5, 1805, "that the

President, although penetrating and detesting as well as fearing [Burr]
. . . not only invites him to his table, but about five days ago had a
secret conference with him which lasted more than two hours, and in
which I am confident there was as little good faith on one side as there
was on the other.''

Just a few days after the Burr dinner, Jefferson received an unsigned
letter with a Philadelphia postmark warning that Burr was a new "Cati-
line," a conspirator. But the anonymous, anti-Burr writer may have
been Yrujo, who was extremely well informed on American political
matters and had a penchant for mischief. Whoever the penman was,
he described himself as a patriot, but disguised himself by printing his
message in block letters—indicating that the writer feared Jefferson
would recognize the handwriting. He reported that Burr was not only
plotting the demise of the Jefferson administration but also the over-
throw of the American Constitution. The writer was uncommonly well
informed about Burr's talks with Ambassador Merry, warning that the
Britisher and Burr were working together toward a separation of the
western states.

As far as is known, Jefferson paid no more attention to the letter
than he had to the newspaper articles.

By now, Wilkinson had settled in at Governor's House in St.
Louis. He was initially received with great favor by the population,
according to his territorial secretary, Joseph Browne. "The citizens
are well satisfied with the administration of Governor Wilkinson,"
Browne reported to Secretary of State Madison. Browne warned,
however, that it would take a stern and fair hand to keep the citizens
in line:

> *The great mass of the American settlers are in general a very*
> *illiterate set of men, who had been driven by their debts or their*
> *crimes from the American states and took refuge under the Spanish*
> *monarchy. . . . They lead a semi-savage life, dependent on the*
> *chase and a miserable Agriculture. They are excellent woodsmen*
> *and in case of Indian hostilities would be useful soldiers, if they*
> *could be subjected to military control, but their erratic habits have*
> *extremely weakened, if not destroyed, every thing like patriotism.*[8]

St. Louis's honeymoon with Wilkinson proved to be brief. Because of the national transfer of flags, land disputes were common and the governor systematically sided with his friends, and benefactors, against all others. In reaction, officers of an entire army battalion north of St. Louis resigned their commissions in protest against their governor-general's favoritism toward certain landowners. Furthermore, Rufus Easton, one of three territorial judges appointed by the president, complained in a letter to Jefferson that Wilkinson had committed "innumerable alterations and forgeries" in order to illegally seize lands for himself and friends:

> *The French inhabitants are convinced that the government of this Territory is not the government of the United States, but the government of General Wilkinson. . . . The open acts of violence, the midnight riots, and above all the contempt of the judicial authority, as manifested and committed during the command of Wilkinson have convinced all classes of citizens that he is not only a bad man, but that a military administration of civil government is ill suited to the Constitution, and that this form cannot long exist in a Republican government—a government of Laws and not of men.*[9]

The high chief of all the Osages complained to William Clark that Wilkinson had taken away seven horses and refused to pay for them. Another of the territorial judges, John Lucas, complained that "under the spurious regulations of Governor Wilkinson" land fraud had become "vigorous and endemic."

Wilkinson's most severe attacks, however, came from the Congress, where Jefferson's House majority leader, John Randolph, split with the president on the matter of Wilkinson's appointment. Already unhappy with Jefferson over his handling of foreign policy, Randolph objected to Wilkinson's combination of civil and military authority and introduced resolutions to ban the holding of plural offices. News of Randolph's resolutions was promptly sent to Wilkinson by his and Jefferson's friend, Senator Samuel Smith, the same General Smith who had given Delaware congressman, now senator, Bayard the guarantees that cinched the "deal" for the presidency in 1801. Wilkinson informed the president that his resignation as governor-general would be a defeat not only for him but for Jefferson, too. The new governor wanted a chance to prove himself and his loyalty to Jefferson—to whom he himself was "prepared to give his last breath and last drop of blood." Wilkinson heaped invective on Randolph, whose "mad career" threatened to "spread the poison of disaffection everywhere."

Jefferson dismissed all the complaints, writing his friend Samuel Smith, with copies to Wilkinson, "Not a single fact has appeared which occasions me to doubt that I could have made a fitter appointment than General Wilkinson."

Shortly afterward, in January 1806, Jefferson began receiving the first of a series of conspiracy warnings, saying there was a plot afoot against the government and the chief conspirators were James Wilkinson and Aaron Burr. The warnings came from Joseph Hamilton Daveiss, the U.S. attorney for Kentucky, and an ardent Federalist and Hamiltonian. Daveiss was also first cousin to Justice John Marshall, and Jefferson had good cause to be wary of him. Thoroughly convinced that Wilkinson was in Spanish pay, Daveiss referred Jefferson to Andrew Ellicott's earlier report to the Adams administration in which Don Manuel Gayoso, the governor of Spanish Louisiana, described Wilkinson's payments.

After reading the Daveiss letters, Secretary of the Treasury Albert Gallatin told Jefferson that, unbelievable as the accusation seemed, Wilkinson should be watched:

Of the General I have no very exalted opinion; he is extravagant and needy, and would not, I think, feel much delicacy in speculation on public money or public land. In both these respects he must be closely watched; and he has now united himself with every man in Louisiana who had received or claims large grants under the Spanish government . . . [but] of betraying his interest to a foreign country I believe him to be altogether incapable. Yet Ellicott's information, together with this hint, may induce caution. . . .

Jefferson now asked Daveiss to forward all information he had about the alleged plot. Because of communications difficulties, it was nearly two months before Daveiss replied to the president. He submitted a long list of conspirators, and all of them were Jeffersonian Democrats—Wilkinson, Burr, Jefferson's Attorney General, John Breckinridge, the young lawyer Henry Clay, two judges, two senators, and Governor William Henry Harrison of Indiana Territory. Daveiss's fantastical list seemed to have been drawn from every prominent Democrat visited by Wilkinson and Burr in the previous six months.

Like later historians, Jefferson found it a bit too much to believe. He would not acknowledge the list until September, when he was formally pressed by Daveiss. However, immediately after receiving the list, Jefferson invited his former running mate, Burr, to another White House dinner, the second in four months. It seems possible, even likely, that Jefferson may have used the occasion to discreetly question Burr about the list. But all we have in the way of record is Jefferson's memoir, written a month later, saying that—at a dinner initiated by Jefferson—Burr asked for some federal employment and was rejected. It seems incredible that a president of the United States would invite a man accused of murder and treason to dinner and not ask him about such subjects. If that wasn't the purpose of the dinner, then what was?

By now, Jefferson had seen a series of newspaper reports, an anonymous letter from Philadelphia, and three very explicit communications from his federal prosecutor in Kentucky, all alleging a Wilkinson-Spanish conspiracy.

In his memoir, Jefferson painted a picture of Burr as having a chip on his shoulder while at the same time being a supplicant, a picture that is inconsistent with any other we have of the proud New Yorker. Nevertheless, Jefferson's version is the only version we have of the meeting.

Burr insisted, Jefferson recorded, "that he had supported the administration, and that he could do me much harm; he wished, however, to be on different ground . . . if I should have anything to propose to him." But Jefferson told Burr that the lack of outcry over Burr's stepping down from the vice presidency a year earlier was proof that "the public had withdrawn their confidence from him . . . that as to any harm he could do me . . . I feared no injury which man could do me."

Burr would claim unto his deathbed that in the plot to invade Mexico he was doing Jefferson's work, that Jefferson wanted him, Burr, to intimidate the Spanish. Was this what the dinner was truly about? Did Jefferson ask Burr to call off the invasion of Mexico so that the nation could pursue the matter of boundary disputes through more peaceful means?

And what was the harm that Burr, down and out, could do to a sitting president? In Jefferson's mind, the answer may have come a month later when, at Burr's instigation, affidavits were taken from two key congressional figures—James Bayard and Samuel Smith. These were the affidavits that argued that Jefferson had made a deal with then-congressman James Bayard of Delaware for the presidency in 1801. Although the affidavits were never made public in either Burr's or Jefferson's lifetimes, Jefferson recorded in his diary that Burr had them. Some historians believe that from that date on, Jefferson was determined to ruin Aaron Burr.[10]

Burr left no record and Jefferson's version is suspiciously incomplete. There was one last visit between the two, on April 12, 1806, when Burr went to say good-bye prior to his second departure for the West.

The Lewis and Clark expedition had returned to St. Louis in the late summer of 1806 with a proud public acclaiming them as national heroes. Lewis's return to Washington took months as he was feted in virtually every village along the way. By September he was still in Illinois. By mid-November, he was no farther east than Frankfort, Kentucky. He did not reach the nation's capital and the welcoming hand of Jefferson until late November.

Meanwhile, Burr had rejoined his friend Dayton in Ohio. Both were now sadly in want of funds. Their hopes received another setback with news of the death of Prime Minister William Pitt in England and the sudden recall of Ambassador Merry. It was now certain that there would be no British ships or British money for an attack on Mexico.

In his trip the previous summer, Burr had become friendly with the eccentric Harman Blennerhassett, a young Irish aristocrat who had eloped from the Isle of Man with his niece, Margaret Agnew. To escape ostracism they had come to Marietta, Ohio, where society was delighted to receive them. There they built a mansion on an island in the Ohio River, converting a wilderness into an English garden.

To build his western Eden, Blennerhassett had spent much of his fortune and now, in the summer of 1806, he was looking for ways to replenish his coffers. Burr proposed that they become partners in the Bastrop land grant, a proposition so attractive to Blennerhassett that he invested several thousands. It was this money that Burr used to close his deal on the Louisiana land, a fact that goes far to confirm that whatever Burr's intentions prior to the March dinner with Jefferson, he was now more interested in peaceful real estate dealings than in war. Burr could always attack Mexico with the Bastrop lands as his base, should Jefferson or a succeeding government change their minds.

Burr began to build boats and recruit young men for the Bastrop, Louisiana, colony. While his small flotilla was being assembled, Burr left Blennerhassett's Island and journeyed to Tennessee for another meeting with Andrew Jackson.

Even as Burr was having supper with Jefferson, Spanish troops had appeared in Texas and made their way across the Sabine River east into American territory that was clearly marked as part of the Louisiana Purchase.

About the same time, relations with England had worsened because of a series of maritime disputes. Flexing their muscles, the English reinforced garrisons in Canada and landed an army in the Bahamas, prepared to go to war at the first excuse.

On March 14, some six months before Lewis and Clark returned from their Pacific journey, an alarmed Jefferson ordered Wilkinson to delegate his gubernatorial chores in St. Louis and head south as fast as he could to repel the Spaniards and drive them out of Nacogdoches and back across the Sabine. Wilkinson, however, was in no hurry to fight his Spanish paymasters and managed to ignore these orders for the next five months. Not only was he heavily engaged in his private St. Louis business, including land speculation, but he was organizing a fur-trading company with the Chouteaus. Perhaps even more important to him, a war with Spain now would be premature to the scheme he was arranging with Aaron Burr.

During the summer, details of what was perceived as that scheme were printed in the newly established newspaper, *The Western World*, published in Kentucky by U.S. Attorney John Daveiss, who dished up anew the tales of Wilkinson's old Spanish plot. Daveiss then asked why a man accused of taking Spanish bribes was still retained as head of the army, a question that, despite its bite, was ignored by Jefferson.

It wasn't until August 16 that Wilkinson, accompanied by his ailing wife, left St. Louis on barges headed downriver. Ann Biddle Wilkinson was ill with tuberculosis, a disease her husband was helpless to cure although her frailty does not seem to have been the cause for his delay. They stopped at Natchez to set up headquarters at the house of Wilkinson's friend Stephen Minor, also known as Don Estevan Minor, a Spanish subject and former commandant of the region for Spain. Minor had been a principal citizen of the town for twenty years and he volunteered to keep the general's ailing wife at his plantation. Wilkinson was certainly in no hurry to confront the Spanish and it is likely that through Minor he sent messengers to the Spanish on how to avoid conflict.[11]

Leaving his wife in Natchez, Wilkinson went west to Natchitoches, reaching the "war front" by October 3—seven months after his orders to proceed at "all speed." His military zeal may have been dragging anchor but his customary bluster was at full sail. He wrote the secretary of war, "If means and men are furnished, I will soon plant our standards on the left bank of the Grand River," meaning the Rio Grande, some six hundred miles away on the Texas-Mexico border.

At that same time, Wilkinson was writing to congressional friends, "I shall be obliged to fight and flog them. . . . I shall as surely push them over the Sabine and out of Nacogdoches as that you are alive, although they outnumber me three to one."

In fact, it was Wilkinson's troops who outnumbered the Spanish three to one. Nevertheless, by the time he got to the actual battleground, he had put aside whatever lust for war he might have had.

In a parley with his opposite number, a Colonel Simón de Herrera, Wilkinson negotiated an agreement whereby the Spanish would retire west of the Sabine, then and now the dividing line between Louisiana and Texas, and the Americans some distance to the east. The land in between would be neutral. This unilateral accommodation to Spain reversed longstanding American claims to parts of western Louisiana and Texas. It was a clear loss for the Americans, but Wilkinson claimed a major victory, and Jefferson, who wanted no war with

Spain, endorsed the pact when he received the news. Elsewhere in the country, the truce was seen as an embarrassing retreat from Spanish aggression.

By now Burr was back in Nashville, being hosted at a dinner by Andrew Jackson. With an eye on Mexico, Jackson raised his glass to Burr, and sneered at Wilkinson's Sabine treaty. A week later, the still simmering Jackson put the Tennessee militia on alert, saying that the Spanish already had taken up an "unjustifiable and insulting position on the river Sabine, in the territory of Orleans."

In his reluctance to face up to the Spanish, by negotiating the Neutral Ground Treaty, Wilkinson had in fact betrayed the filibustering scheme he had arranged with Burr. James Wilkinson had signed his own name to the Neutral Ground Treaty and if he violated it, he could be sure the Spanish would retaliate—most likely by revealing his role as a paid spy.

What to do?

The answer came on October 8, when Burr's young and ardent confederate, Samuel Swartwout, arrived at Natchitoches to hand Wilkinson a coded letter accompanied by a note from Jonathan Dayton, which was also in code. The first message had been written by Burr in July while he was in Philadelphia, where he and Dayton were trying to raise funds.

Strangely, the letter handed to Wilkinson was written in the third-person. It told Wilkinson that on November 15, Burr and his recruits would descend the Mississippi in small boats to New Orleans which would be used as a staging area for the invasion at Vera Cruz. The letter gave Burr's assurance that Wilkinson would be second in command and that further instructions would be sent via Swartwout.

Because of the peculiar phrasing, it was and is not clear who wrote the letter. But several historians believe that Burr wrote an original that was altered by Dayton when he translated it into code.

Dayton, who was unsure of Wilkinson's steadiness in the Spanish scheme, took the original and converted it into a complicated cipher, making a number of translation mistakes and adding bombastic exaggerations designed to appeal to Wilkinson. The most fantastical of these was an inflation of the number of recruits ("500 or 1,000") and the promise that a British fleet led by a "Commodore Truxton" had agreed to support the Mexico invasion. Neither in Burr's original, later recovered, nor in Dayton's translation, however, was there mention of fomenting a rebellion of American states. It stated only the intention of attacking Mexico.[12]

In a code masked by hieroglyphics, the altered Burr-Dayton letter said:

Your letter postmarked 13th May is received. I have at length obtained funds, and have actually commenced. The Eastern detachments, from different points and under different pretense, will rendezvous on Ohio on 1 November.

Everything internal and external favor our view. Naval protection of England is secured. Truxton is going to Jamaica to arrange with the admiral there and will meet us at Mississippi. England, a navy of the United States ready to join and final orders are given to my friends and followers. It will be a host of choice spirits. Wilkinson shall be second to Burr only and Wilkinson shall dictate the rank and promotion of his officers.

Burr will proceed westward 1 August—never to return. With him go his daughter and grandson. The husband will follow in October with a corps of worthys . . . Send a list of all persons known to Wilkinson westward of the mountains who could be useful, with a note delineating their character. . . .

Burr's plan of operation is to move down rapidly from the Falls [Louisville] on fifteenth November, with the first 500 or 1000 men in light boats now constructing for that purpose; to be at Natchez between the 5 and 15 December, there to meet you; then to determine whether it will be expedient in the first instance to seize on or to pass Baton Rouge. . . .

The people of the country to which we are going are prepared to receive us—their agents, now with me, say that if we will protect their religion and will not subject them to a foreign power, that in three weeks all will be settled.[13]

The accompanying note from Dayton warned Wilkinson that he was about to be dismissed but encouraged the general to stand fast, insisting that there was a way out:

It is now well ascertained that you are to be displaced in the next session [of Congress]. Jefferson will affect to yield reluctantly to the public sentiment, but yield he will. Prepare yourself therefore for it; you know the rest. . . . You are not a man to despair or even despond, especially when such prospects offer in another quarter. Are you ready? Are your numerous associates ready? Wealth and glory, Louisiana and Mexico.

The warning shook Wilkinson. The Sabine confrontation with the Spanish had left him unsure of how to proceed. Should he abandon his Spanish paymasters and deal with Burr? Or should he disengage from the conspiracy and salvage what profits and securities he could manage? Wilkinson was more afraid of Jefferson than of Burr, more frightened of losing the rank he had than of forfeiting the place he hoped to gain. Furthermore, if he moved against the Spanish, there stood the matter of their revenge.

Wilkinson decided to save himself. He would give Burr up. As always when backed into a corner, the general proved resourceful. He would put this awkwardly worded, barely decipherable communication to his own use. The newspapers had been full of "Burr conspiracy" stories and Wilkinson knew that despite much posturing, the president wanted no fight with Spain. But right now the situation was a tinderbox, ready to burst aflame at the least spark. Surely, not only Jefferson but the Spanish as well would be grateful to whoever put out the fire.

By special courier, the general sent a top-secret message to Jefferson, saying that he had learned of

a numerous and powerful association, extending from New York to Louisiana, in which active, influential characters have been engaged for six or eight months . . . to levy and rendezvous eight or ten thousand men in New Orleans for a descent on Mexico; it is expected that the van will reach New Orleans in December . . . and it is purposed that the expedition shall sail for Vera Cruz about the first of February.

Wilkinson avoided mentioning the source of his information except to say it rested on "broad and explicit grounds." He did not name

Burr, saying he didn't know "under what authority the enterprise is projected, from where its funds are derived, or what might be the intention of the leaders in relation to the Territory of Orleans."

To cover his tracks, Wilkinson added a personal memo to the president, saying he had been invited to join the assault on Mexico under the excuse that the president had endorsed it. However, if the president hadn't endorsed it, then he should be advised that there would be a revolt in American territory as "an auxiliary step to the main design of attacking Mexico." Wilkinson said he was uninformed of the conspiracy and "ignorant of the foundation on which it rests, of the means by which it is supported, and whether any immediate or collateral protection, internal or external, is expected."

Wilkinson said he would be moving his small force to New Orleans "to be ready to defend that capital against usurpation [and] violence."

On October 21, now back in Natchez and en route south to New Orleans, Wilkinson again wrote to the president, this time defending against the accusations made in *The Western World*: "I have at times been fearful your confidence might be shaken by the boldness of the vile calumnies leveled at me," but, said Wilkinson, Jefferson should be reassured by the endorsement of his two predecessors: "I have not only enjoyed but merited the confidence of General Washington . . . and that honest but wrong-headed President Adams approved my conduct."

As chance would have it, on that very day twelve hundred miles away in Washington, Jefferson was indeed having doubts, writing in his journal that he had "suspicions of infidelity in" General James Wilkinson.

Jefferson received the original letter of warning on November 17. A week later the president received a second dispatch from Wilkinson, reporting that it was Burr who was leading the expedition down the Mississippi to disrupt the Union.

By now, the president had been listening to this and similar reports of a western plot for nearly two years. Just three weeks earlier, the Cabinet had deliberated on the actions and purposes of Burr, although the former vice president was only an item at the meeting, not the purpose of it.

To Jefferson, it seemed that Wilkinson's position, and therefore the nation's, was full of peril. In front of the general was a Spanish force capable of giving him a good deal of trouble; behind him was New Orleans, full of disaffected Spaniards and Frenchmen; descending the Mississippi was Burr, allegedly with an armed force more numerous than Wilkinson's own.

It is at this juncture that Jefferson seems to have finally decided to act as if the Burr rumors were true. But adding to Jefferson's dilemma was a lack of legal counsel. He had no attorney general to consult with because John Breckinridge was ill in Kentucky (where he would die in December). When Jefferson raised the possibility of arresting Burr to prevent the attack on Mexico, Secretary of State Madison advised him that he could not use regular troops because of constitutional considerations.

While still at Natchez, Wilkinson also wrote to his friend Vicente Folch, the Spanish governor of West Florida, suggesting that Spain secure Baton Rouge against a projected Burr attack. Wilkinson even proposed that the Spaniard should combine forces with him against their common foe. He maintained that his measures were designed to protect not only the American territory and the Floridas, but the "Mexican dominions" as well. He invited Folch to meet him at New Orleans and Folch accepted.

By now, Wilkinson was quite pleased with himself. By the simple expedient of throwing Burr to the sharks, he had reestablished himself both with the President *and* with the Spanish.

Wilkinson next wrote the viceroy of Mexico, José de Iturrigaray, asking for $111,000 in compensation for stopping the Burr expedition. The letter was datelined Natchez and posted on November 17, a bare three weeks after Wilkinson's second communication to Jefferson. The message was personally couriered by Wilkinson's aide-de-camp, Captain Walter Burling.

Wilkinson told the viceroy that he had learned of a plot that threatened "destruction to the realm of Mexico. This infernal combination is composed of backwoodsmen from Kentucky and the settlements along the Ohio. It is led by able and experienced men and officers distinguished in the American Revolution, who have been secretly promised the cooperation of a British naval force.

"New Orleans is to be the first victim of their rapacity. Afterward they are to attack Vera Cruz, and then will follow the conquest of the city in which your Excellency resides. . . ."

Wilkinson advised the viceroy to "place Vera Cruz in a condition to beat back a force of 129 men," which was the number of persons Wilkinson actually believed to be in the Burr party.

Wilkinson said that by warning the viceroy he was "risking my life, my good name, and my property by the change I have made in the military arrangements without the knowledge of my government," which was a reference to his Sabine River treaty. He asked that after his letter had been translated, it "be placed in cipher in the archives" and the original destroyed, so that "you will see that my name is not divulged to the British, French, and American governments."

Wilkinson then got to the gist of it:

I have arranged to expend the sum of 85,000 pesos in shattering the plans and destroying the union and harmony among the bandits now being enrolled along the Ohio, and 26,000 pesos in the discretionary dispatch of supplies and counter-revolutionists, which sums I trust will be reimbursed to the bearer [Captain Burling] for whose safe return I ask your Excellency to furnish a suitable escort as far as the immediate neighborhood of Natchitoches.[14]

The viceroy forwarded the letter to his government, attaching a note of sarcastic commentary: "He finally comes to what I had anticipated, the question of payment for his services. He asks for $85,000 in one sum, and $26,000 in another."

Lieutenant Burling returned to Wilkinson empty-handed save for a letter from the viceroy wishing the general "happiness in pursuit of his righteous intentions."

Wilkinson was not to come out of the deal penniless, however. Using Burling's diary, he composed a passable monograph of the topographical route to Mexico City and forwarded it to Washington along with an expense account for $1,750 to cover expenses of the topographer. It was paid on order of the president.

Meanwhile, oblivious to the storm around him, Burr was sailing peacefully down the Mississippi with his nine boats of young farmers who were armed only with tools and a few hatchets and hunting rifles. Rumors concerning their mission, however, were given to great exaggerations. In Pittsburgh, young Frederick Bates was an admirative witness, writing his brother:

> *All Pittsburgh is in commotion. Colonel Burr's enterprise appears to be matured for execution, and large stores of provisions are daily loading on board the boats for the supply of his troops in the lower countries. Natchez will be the rendezvous, but their object and destination are unknown, except to those in whom the leaders have thought proper to confide. The most intelligent with whom I have conversed appear to imagine that the army will be composed of about ten thousand chosen men, who will remain in the neighborhood of the Spanish settlements, until a declaration of war, or other political events shall authorize our government to justify the preparations, and avow them as their own. Most of the young men in this vicinity, respectable by birth, education and property, are descending the river.*

In Kentucky on November 4, 1806, U.S. Attorney Daveiss transferred his attack from his *Western World* newspaper to the federal court at Frankfort by filing his own affidavit moving "that Aaron Burr should be arrested and compelled to find security for his appearance; and that a writ should be issued . . ." Daveiss added that he "was in possession of the most satisfactory evidence, that Aaron Burr, Esquire, had formed an association for making war against Spain, invading Mexico, and forming a distant empire in the western country; and that he was raising forces, and purchasing the necessary provisions and stores for that purpose."

When Burr received the news, he dropped all other business and turned back to Frankfort to clear his name as fast as he could. On November 25, Daveiss appeared in the Frankfort court to present all the evidence he had. The grand jury came back quickly, presenting "no true bill" and pointedly noting that Daveiss lacked evidence that in "the smallest degree" indicated any guilt. To emphasize Burr's exoneration, the town gave a ball in the colonel's honor.

Burr, restive and ambitious, of vivid imagination, with every-thing to gain and everything to lose, continued downriver with his farmers.

Despite the acquittal, Jefferson chose to view the expedition as a great danger. Spurred by his longtime animosity toward Burr, an ani-mus further fueled by the Bayard election-fix affidavits, the president now turned the weight of his office with ferocity against his onetime running mate. He pursued Burr with a vindictiveness that came as no surprise to Federalists and other old foes.

Although the Virginian has come down to his current historical place as sort of a demigod, a part-human, part-divine incarnation of virtues, he was not unanimously regarded as such in his own time. Alexander Hamilton described him as "a man as fond of place and power, and as great a hypocrite as ever lived."

Jefferson recorded that on November 25 he convened the Cabinet:

Present at first the four heads of department . . . Dispatches from General Wilkinson to myself of October 21, by a confidential officer (Lieutenant Smith) show that overtures have been made to him which decide that the present object of the combination is an expedition by sea against Vera Cruz . . . we are satisfied that Swartwout has been the agent through whom overtures have been made to Wilkinson. We came to the following determinations— that a proclamation be issued (see it), and that orders go . . . to stop armed vessels suspected on good grounds to be proceeding on this enterprise. . . . General Wilkinson [is] to direct the station of the armed vessels; and if the arrangements with the Spaniards will permit him to withdraw, let him dispose of his force as he thinks best to prevent any such expedition or any attempt on New Orleans, or any of the posts or military stores of the United States. (He is also to arrest persons coming to his camp and proposing a concurrence in any such enterprise, and suspected of being in camp with a view to propagate such propositions. . . .)

Even as the Cabinet was meeting, Wilkinson had arrived in New Orleans, where on November 25 he met pleasantly in a private dining room with his chief artillery officer, Lieutenant Colonel Comstock Freeman.

Heretofore, Wilkinson had confined his accusations to a Burr plot against Mexico which, while contrary to national policy, was not necessarily treasonable. Now, with Freeman, Wilkinson was emboldened to audition a wider conspiracy—the treason of severing the United States.

After swearing Freeman to secrecy, Wilkinson confided that while in Natchitoches he had been invited to join a Mexican invasion. According to Freeman's later affidavit, the general said that "Colonel Burr had formed a vast conspiracy or plot against the United States, that the object was to separate the western from the Atlantic states; to assemble a force in the western country, descend the Mississippi, seize upon New Orleans and the shipping there, and then by the way of Vera Cruz invade the Mexican provinces."[15]

Wilkinson told Freeman that Burr had promised him "second place" in the government of the new empire and "since Colonel Burr had no heirs," the general's two sons would succeed to the throne of Mexico. Wilkinson then asked Freeman if he would like "to be a brigadier and have fifty thousand dollars." Freeman replied he would like it very much, if "I could have it honorably."

In the next several days in New Orleans, Wilkinson talked with at least four other men "in confidence" about the alleged Burr "treason" plot. They all found it believable. Satisfied with what amounted to his dress rehearsals, Wilkinson next made it official by going to Governor Claiborne and giving him the story about Burr, the capture of New Orleans, the severance of states, and Mexico. Wilkinson suggested that to stop the enterprise Claiborne should proclaim martial law, thus giving Wilkinson absolute power.

While promising support, the governor refused to proclaim martial law, grouching to subordinates that the general's advice sounded more like an order than a request. It did not deter Wilkinson, who now proceeded on his own unofficial authority to impose a dictatorship which silenced any rumors or information against him.

On December 14, 1806, the militia was called out. Seamen were impressed and fortifications repaired. Panic spread throughout the city as Wilkinson's critics were either thrown in jail for treason or sent into exile. No one was safe from being jailed on charges of "machinations against the state."

America would not see the like of such a totalitarian reign of terror until the Civil War, when the Union Army's "corps of marshals" made similar raids on newspapers and arrests of suspected foes in northern cities.

In New Orleans, Burr's friends within reach were arrested and shipped off to Washington without a chance to be heard in court. When an editor criticized the denial of hearings under habeas corpus writs, he was jailed. A lawyer who sought the writs was jailed. Additionally, Wilkinson placed an embargo on all shipping and set the whole city to work at building defenses. He spurred their efforts by spreading tales that Burr's invasion would lead to "Negro insurrection."

It became apparent that Wilkinson's military crackdown was directed against Wilkinson's critics rather than against Burr and his descending hordes. A nervous Claiborne asked Wilkinson to yield to the civil authorities. The general refused.

Among the first to be arrested was Burr's emissary, Samuel Swartwout, who was taken in shackles across the Mississippi, kept "in a poor inhospitable shed and deprived of the necessities of life," according to his later affidavit. When the guard came to take him away, Swartwout tore himself free and ran toward the river shouting, "I had as well die here as in the woods," and plunged into the turbulent black Mississippi. The men were ordered to shoot, an officer later testified, "but owing to the great rain, three of the guns flashed in the pan, and the others would not take fire. The men pursued and took him. But for the wetness of the powder, he would have been murdered." On Wilkinson's orders, Swartwout was put in chains and placed aboard a ship and taken back east for trial.

Also snatched up without warrant or cause was John Adair, Burr's friend and a former senator from Kentucky, who had the bad luck to arrive in New Orleans at the "time of the terror," as Orleanians called it. Adair was dragged from the dinner table and paraded through the streets by a company of soldiers. He was then moved twenty-five miles downstream to a tent in a swamp where he was held incommunicado during a week of torrential rains. Denied clothing and medicine, he was ultimately shipped to Baltimore, where he won his release due to lack of evidence. Returning to New Orleans, he denounced Wilkinson as "a pensioner of Spain and a traitor to his country" and filed a lawsuit charging Wilkinson with conspiracy and unlawful arrest.

Jefferson, sponsor of the Bill of Rights, was indifferent to the purification of one of the nation's largest cities. He was four-square behind his general, not only approving but even endorsing Wilkinson's illegal arrests, saying in a later communication that Wilkinson's ends justified illegal means:

> The laws of necessity, of self-preservation, of saving our country when in danger, are of higher obligation. To lose our country by a scrupulous adherence to written law, would be to lose the law itself with life, liberty, property & all those who are enjoying them with us; thus absurdly sacrificing the end to the means.[16]

With such extraordinary rationalization, the author of the Declaration of Independence said he approved of the "defensive operations for New Orleans." After hearing of the expanded treason plot, first from Claiborne and then from Wilkinson, Jefferson now seemed committed to the idea that not only was Burr a traitor but that Wilkinson became Burr's confidant only to learn more about the plot. As for the pogrom against civil rights, the president excused Wilkinson by telling Governor Claiborne: "On great occasions every good officer must be ready to risk himself in going beyond the strict line of law, when the public preservation requires it." In Jefferson's eyes, all these men were "notorious conspirators" who had forfeited their constitutional protections.

Proclaiming the existence on "the western waters . . . of criminal enterprises," Jefferson was more than glad to try Burr for treason and on November 27, 1806, sent out orders for Burr's arrest.

Following his triumphant acquittal in the federal court at Frankfort, Burr had resumed his journey downriver to Chickasaw Bluffs, present-day Memphis, where the fort commander not only declined to stop Burr but undertook to raise a company of men for him and send it on after him.

Proceeding farther downstream, Burr's flotilla duly arrived at Natchez on January 10. There Burr learned of yet a new federal warrant. Once again, he surrendered. A hearing was held on the evidence and Burr's flotilla was inspected by a Mississippi grand jury, which found there was no cause for Burr's arrest. Nevertheless, a hard-line Jeffersonian judge blatantly overrode the grand jury's findings and had Burr arrested. By now Burr had been halted three times, freed by law twice, but was still in custody.

He was freed on bail posted by friends in Mississippi, but required to appear daily in court.

About this time, the president told Congress that Burr was engaged in a treasonable attempt to sever the Union:

> It appeared that he contemplated two distinct objects, which might be carried on either jointly or separately, and either one or the other first, as circumstances should direct. One of these was the severance of the union of these states by the Allegheny mountains, the other an attack on Mexico. A third object was provided, merely ostensible, to wit the settlement of a pretended purchase of a tract of country on the Washita [Ouachita], claimed by a Baron Bastrop. This was to serve as the pretext for all his preparations, an allurement for such followers as really wished to acquire settlements in that country, and a cover under which to retreat in the event of a final discomfiture of both branches of his real design.

In the meantime, word had filtered upriver concerning Wilkinson's reign of terror in New Orleans. Further news came reporting that the general had dispatched men to seize Burr, to kidnap him if necessary. Not only was the report accurate, but Wilkinson's hounds were already in the field.

At Natchez, Burr's files—containing papers which, he said, could prove Wilkinson's perfidy—were broken into, their contents "tumbled and abused." It would later be proved that Wilkinson had put a personal bounty on Burr's head and had commissioned men, including army officers, to do him injury if they couldn't capture or kill him. Among these bounty hunters was a federal officer, the Chickasaw Indian agent, Silas Dinsmore, who would swear that Wilkinson had promised him five thousand dollars if he "cut off" Burr at the river. Dinsmore thought the whole thing so outrageous that he wrote a friend:

We are in a flurry here hourly expecting Colonel Burr & all Kentucky & half of Tennessee at his [back] to punish General Wilkinson, set the negroes free, robe the banks and take Mexico. Come and help me laugh at the fun."

Another bounty hunter was Dr. John Carmichael, visiting in New Orleans. He was pressed into service by Wilkinson, who sent the doctor back to his home in Mississippi to grab Burr. Two army officers would later testify that they, too, under orders from Wilkinson, had gone to Natchez with a party of five men "dressed in citizens' clothing" and "armed with dirks and pistols" to seize Burr and kidnap him from the Mississippi authorities if necessary.

In Washington, congressional leader John Randolph was outraged at reports that Wilkinson was arranging Burr's assassination. We hear of the assassination schemes from New Hampshire senator William Plumer, who wrote in his diary:

John Randolph says within a few days he has seen a letter from General Wilkinson written to a friend in this city [Washington] that contains this idea. That although Aaron Burr's treasonable plans are suppressed—he will soon revive them. To prevent which, its best to take him off—and that he has provided two or three men who are well qualified to effect that laudable service for their country. The plain English of which is that Wilkinson has men in pay to assassinate Burr.[17]

On January 16, 1807, John Randolph demanded that the president clarify for Congress his proclamation that described a conspiracy to set on foot "a military expedition of enterprise against the dominions of Spain; that for this purpose they are fitting out and arming vessels in the western waters of the United States. . . ."

Randolph asked Congress to force Jefferson to name these conspirators and asked, to what end did they conspire?

Jefferson replied to Congress and Randolph on January 22, saying that "Burr" was "the principal actor, whose guilt is placed beyond question."

And there it was. The president of the United States had publicly announced that the man awaiting trial was guilty "beyond question." Furthermore, although Jefferson mentioned various letters he had received testifying to Burr's guilt, he neglected to say they had been written by Wilkinson. His references to the general were only to praise his actions in New Orleans, where the commandant of the army had acted "with the honor of a soldier and the fidelity of a good citizen."

It was not only Randolph who was appalled. John Adams emphasized a principle of American justice: "Even if Burr's guilt is as clear as the noonday sun, the first Magistrate ought not to have pronounced so before a Jury had tried him."

Although Burr probably was unaware of Wilkinson's murderous efforts, he knew the general as well as any man and it would not have been hard to see the handwriting on the wall. Burr was now in Wilkinson's district. He would be pursued and harried until he was brought before Jefferson in chains, or worse. There was no man in the world that Wilkinson wanted dead more than Burr. With Burr dead, Wilkinson was a hero. Burr alive was a monstrous threat.

For Burr, there seemed to be no escape backward or forward, no sanctuary in his own country. Desperate now, fleeing Wilkinson even more than Jefferson, he secretly visited his farmers and urged them to go on across the river to the Bastrop lands and settle there, as many of them did, becoming the early pioneers of the region.

As for Burr himself, although tried and released twice—by Kentucky and Mississippi grand juries—he remained a fugitive under bond to a vindictive Jeffersonian judge. Disguising himself, he now disappeared into the wilderness, headed for refuge in Spanish West Florida, where he hoped to catch a ship; to where is unknown. It is likely that he didn't know.

As Burr set out in flight, the president was writing an old friend, former Democratic senator from New Hampshire John Langdon, of his fear that Burr might escape the hangman's noose:

Our Cataline is at the head of an armed body (we know not its strength), and his object is to seize New Orleans, from thence attack Mexico, place himself on the throne of Montezuma, add

Louisiana to his empire, and the Western States from the Allegheny
if he can. I do not believe he will attain the crown; but neither am
I certain that the halter will get its due.

While Jefferson was justifying his actions to Langdon, he was telling a dinner guest, diarist Senator Plumer, that the conspiracy would
be put down without much trouble despite its extensive nature. The
president told Plumer the countryside was loyal to the Union, and to
him. He also wrote Wilkinson expressing confidence that the "fugi-
tives from justice" would be apprehended long before they reached
New Orleans. The president boasted that the "enterprise" was already crushed, but warned the general not to relax his defense of the
city.

Three weeks later Burr was recognized and arrested in Alabama,
then taken under guard to Fort Stoddert at the head of Mobile Bay, a
scant fifty miles from the border of Spanish West Florida. Burr wrote
to his friend Charles Biddle in Philadelphia: "I was arrested a few days
since by a party of the United States troops. . . . This proceeding is
the more extraordinary as the grand jury . . . acquitted me in the
completest manner of all unlawful practices or designs. The report of
this grand jury also censured the conduct of the government . . . and
for this reason I am told that the printers have not thought it discreet
to publish that report entire. . . . What I write must be inspected by
an officer of the guard."

With Burr's arrest, Wilkinson felt confident enough to return to the
Minor plantation in Natchez, where his wife remained ill of tuberculosis. She would die there on February 23, 1807.[18]

Ten days later in Alabama, the fifty-one-year-old former vice president was taken by horseback north to Richmond, a trip during which
he remained docile and depressed except for one pathetic attempt to
escape. As the party was passing through Chester in South Carolina,
the prisoner jumped from his horse, crying to a group of bystanders
that he was Aaron Burr, and claiming the protection of civil authorities.
But a gigantic guard grabbed tiny Burr, seized him in his arms and put
him back in the saddle. It was said that there were tears in the little
colonel's eyes.

On March 26, 1807, Burr arrived at Golden Eagle Tavern in Richmond, where he was locked up in a second-floor bedroom to await trial on a charge of treason. If convicted, the penalty was death.

What had Burr done? If the *worst* could be believed, he had talked to individuals about severing western states from the East—a common topic in those times, and as we have seen, one often engaged in by Jefferson himself. Burr also *may* have discussed an attack on Mexico, another popular topic among tens of thousands of Americans, including the president. But there had been no army of men and boats to further a "severance of the union of these states," as Jefferson had told Congress. Burr had outfitted only a small colony of farmers and taken them down the Ohio and Mississippi rivers to Natchez, where they were to homestead the Bastrop lands.

John Randolph remained outraged at the manner of the various arrests, saying that "whenever government comes into court demanding justice to be done upon an individual, it should come with clean hands. . . ."

The grand jury hearings and the trials that followed in the spring and summer of 1807 were among the best and worst episodes of jurisprudence in American history. John Marshall would preside not as Chief Justice but as federal district judge because the alleged act of war necessary to the charge of treason had occurred in his Virginia circuit.[19]

While it is difficult to think of Jefferson as a tyrant, he behaved as a tyrant in these proceedings. Nevertheless, Marshall did not wither. In the face of bald threats of impeachment from Jefferson and his prosecutor, Marshall stood courageously for the Constitution and zealously protect the rights of the accused against the might of the government. At the same time, Marshall, who despised Jefferson and was despised in return, would sign subpoenas ordering the president of the United States to appear in court and place himself at the mercy of attorneys defending Burr. Marshall also would appoint as foreman of the jury John Randolph of Roanoke, Jefferson's kinsman and onetime protégé, who had fallen out with the president and was well known to now loathe him. Jefferson, on his side, would lose control of himself for a season. Not only did the president set up a public mood against Burr that amounted to persecution, but Jefferson would order the jailing of Burr's defense counsel, calling him, "an unprincipled and impudent" traitor who should be tried for treason.

Trial and Error

● ● ● ● ● ● ● ● ●

THE TRIAL WAS the grandest thing to happen in Richmond since 1779 when the small town was made the capital of Virginia because, perched on seven hills that overlooked the rock-strewn James River, Richmond was considered safer from British attack than the original capital at Williamsburg.[1] This assumption proved too optimistic when, two years later, the state government was forced to flee Richmond in advance of British dragoons.

Grand jury hearings on Aaron Burr and the trial proper would run from March into September. Not a planter from the Shenandoah to the Tidewater was missing. The people filled the streets, patronized the taverns, and gathered at corners to hear orators denounce the traitor Burr or the tyrant Jefferson, depending on their persuasions. Present were hunters in deerskins, small farmers from the low country, barefoot boys, women in gingham, gentry in velvet.

For reasons that remain obscure to this day, Jefferson was betting his popularity on convicting Burr. Either Burr must fall or the president must emerge, at best, as ridiculous for failing to convict a traitor, or at worst, as a cruel despot for persecuting an innocent man.

"Everything depends on James Wilkinson," said the prestigious Edmund Randolph, Burr's senior counsel and attorney general and secretary of state under George Washington. "Wilkinson is in reality the alpha and omega of the present prosecution. He is, in short, to support the singsong and the ballads of treason and conspiracy which we have heard delivered from one extremity of the continent to the other.''

But Wilkinson was not there, still busy terrorizing New Orleans and brooding in Natchez, where he was heavily occupied with protecting his flanks from the charges of Spanish bribes.

Without Wilkinson's testimony and evidence, cool heads figured there was grave doubt about the government's case.

On March 2, the new British ambassador, David Erskine, reported to his government that the administration was ''generally believed to have created a greater alarm'' than Burr's actions could justify. He wrote that Wilkinson's horrors in New Orleans were being widely condemned.

Part of Jefferson's problem was a perceived hypocritical stance on the charges against Burr. It was well known that in 1799 Jefferson had proposed secession by individual states as a remedy to the Alien and Sedition Acts. Now, a bare eight years later, he wanted Burr hanged for allegedly plotting the same thing.

As the trial got under way, Jefferson pretended to stay aloof, remaining away from the White House and staying at his home at Monticello that spring and summer, asserting that his sole source of information about the happenings came from newspapers. In fact, his protégé Meriwether Lewis was sending almost daily reports, as was prosecutor George Hay. To Hay, Jefferson expressed his outrage at Chief Justice Marshall's conduct. ''Burr's trial goes on to the astonishment of all, as to the manner of conducting it.''

On March 30, four days after Burr's arrival, grand jury hearings began with John Marshall settling in beside U.S. District Judge Cyrus Griffin, who was to assist Marshall.[2] The first day of hearings were held in a private room of the downtown Eagle Tavern, which proved too small. The next day the proceedings were moved to the state capitol, which had been designed by Jefferson when he was minister to France, a magnificent, columned building high on a hill overlooking the town.

U.S. Attorney Hay moved that Burr be committed on two counts: (1) the felony of treason against the United States, because he had plotted severance of states; and (2) a misdemeanor in that he had prepared an expedition against Mexico. In the matter of treason, Hay said that on December 10, 1806, at Blennerhassett's Island, Burr had "with traitorous compassings, imaginations and intentions falsely and traitorously" joined and assembled "with a great multitude of persons . . . to the number of thirty . . . and upwards, armed and arrayed in a warlike manner . . . prepared and levied war against the United States."

Despite his intense pressure to prosecute Burr, Jefferson was well aware that the colonel had committed no overt act of treason against the United States, and if he had ever harbored an idea of separating the western states, those ideas had been abandoned. Proof of that could be found in a letter of April 2, 1807, when the president wrote James Bowdoin, his minister in Madrid, saying that no treason existed, but that the quickness of the Burr trial gave superb proof of the good faith of the United States toward Spain. "In suppressing the enterprise meditated lately by Burr against Mexico, although at first he proposed a separation of the western country . . . yet he very early saw that the fidelity of the western country was not to be shaken and turned himself wholly toward Mexico."

From the letter, one can infer that Jefferson had a hidden agenda, namely, that he was prosecuting Burr, the would-be invader of Mexico, to placate Spain and gain ownership of Spanish Florida. It will be recalled that Jefferson was so anxious at this time to appease Spain that he had endorsed Wilkinson's shameful Sabine River treaty, at some political cost to his reputation.

Had the April 2 letter been produced in court, it is doubtful a trial would have taken place, because it showed there had been no crime, that Jefferson only wanted a "show" trial to impress Spain.

But trial there was, and to protect himself Burr assembled an illustrious cast of defense attorneys. The colonel himself presented an opening argument on the conjectural nature of the government's accusation and the "astounding irregularity" of its recent actions against him. An even more explicit defense was laid out by another of Burr's defense counsel, John Wickham, who said Wilkinson had drawn Burr into a scheme against Spain just in order to betray it and win Spanish favor and Spanish gold:

> *Our ground of defence is, that Colonel Burr's expedition was in concurrence with General Wilkinson against the dominions of the King of Spain, in case of war. If we prove, that, at the time Wilkinson was pretending to favor Burr's expedition, and secretly determined to defeat it, he was receiving a Spanish pension, this will explain his conduct. He defeated the enterprise of Burr by hatching a charge of treason against the United States, on purpose to serve the King, whose money he was receiving.*

In this arraignment hearing, Chief Justice Marshall listened closely to both sides as they outlined their cases and on April 1 delivered the first of his opinions. It was a stunner.

After reviewing the government's case and the evidence it hoped to present, Marshall said, "There is nothing in the testimony which can in the most remote degree affect Colonel Burr." Under the Constitution, said Marshall, treason required an overt act of levying war or giving aid and comfort to the enemies of the United States. By the government's own evidence, Burr had been two hundred miles away when the only thing occurred which could be twisted into an overt act of war—the gathering of some thirty men on Blennerhassett's Island. A man could not commit an overt act unless he was actually there, and even though Burr's might be the brain that hatched the plot, if there was a plot, and Burr might have provided muskets with which war might have been levied, if he was not present, then he was not guilty of treason.

The felony charge of high treason was dismissed. No death penalty. Now there remained only the charge of high misdemeanor—in that Burr may have plotted an attack on Mexico. That case was bound over for May 22, when a grand jury would hear further evidence on whether to indict Burr for high misdemeanor.

Jefferson was furious. He had been deprived of a righteous hanging. He had been handed an enormous embarrassment which he blamed on *ing out a wild project against Mexico. Wilkinson is entirely devoted to us. He enjoys a considerable pension from the King. With his natural capacity and his local and military knowledge, he anticipated with moral certainty the failure of an expedition of this nature. Doubtless he foresaw from the first that the improbability of success in case of making the attempt would leave him like the dog in the fable with the piece of meat in his mouth; that is, that he would lose the honorable employment he holds and the generous pension he enjoys from the King.*

These considerations, secret in their nature, he could not explain to Burr; and when the latter persisted in an idea so fatal to Wilkinson's interests, nothing remained but to take the course adopted. By this means he assures his pension; and will allege his conduct on this occasion as an extraordinary service, either for getting it increased or for some generous compensation. On the other hand, this proceeding secures his distinguished rank in the military service of the United States and covers him with a popularity which may perhaps result in pecuniary advantages, and in any case will flatter his vanity. In such an alternative, he has acted as was to be expected; that is, he has sacrificed Burr in order to obtain, on the ruins of Burr's reputation, the advantages I have pointed out.[3]

The perceptive Yrujo knew his general well. By the time of Yrujo's report, Wilkinson had already sent his special envoy to the viceroy of Mexico seeking a bonus of $116,000.

In response, by mid-April 1807, West Florida's Governor Folch had led a battalion of three hundred Spanish troops to Spanish Baton Rouge in anticipation of Burr's attack, having, as Folch said, been "perfectly informed of the state of things of Burr's intentions" by Wilkinson.

Visiting New Orleans on April 23, Folch was received by Wilkinson and his entourage as a conquering hero. Folch wrote: "I can only say that if the President himself had come to New Orleans they could not have given him a better reception than the one I experienced."

In a series of private meetings, Wilkinson, the general who had sworn to drive the Spanish to the Rio Grande, pleaded with Folch to give him help in refuting Burr's attorney's accusations of Spanish bribes. Wilkinson basically wanted Folch to perjure himself. When the

the Chief Justice, who was immune from po
Burr could not be hanged, then perhaps there c
Constitution to remove the judge who freed hi
judge both [Burr] and the judges for themselves,'' t
''If a member of the executive or the legislature doe
is never far distant when the people will remove him.
nation had seen the arrogance of Marshall, Jefferson fe
be pressure to change the laws so that justices could mo
impeached. The people and Congress ''will see then and a
error in our constitution which makes any branch independei
nation.'' The president even saw a silver lining in these dark c
''If [the court's] protection of Burr produces this amendment, it
do more good than his condemnation . . . and if his punishment c
be commuted now for a useful amendment of the Constitution, I sha
rejoice in it.''

Back in New Orleans, even as his president awaited his presence in Richmond, Wilkinson was meeting with Vicente Folch, governor of the Spanish Floridas.

The Spanish had received full reports from Wilkinson on the so-called Burr plot and felt that through twenty years of bribing Wilkinson they had played a key role in saving Mexico from invasion and the United States from severance. As early as January 28, 1807, Spanish Ambassador Yrujo reported to Madrid that Wilkinson's loyalty to Spain, coupled with his military knowledge, showed him that Burr's plot could never succeed. In addition, Burr's plot endangered Wilkinson's own pension from the king of Spain. By sacrificing Burr, Wilkinson not only removed the threat, but added to his value in the eyes of both the Spanish king and the president of the United States.

The Yrujo letter:

According to appearances, Spain has saved the United States from the separation of the Union which menaced them. This would have taken place if Wilkinson had entered cordially into the views of Burr—which was to be expected, because Wilkinson detests this [U.S.] government, and the separation of the western states has been his favorite plan. The evil has come from the foolish and pertinacious perseverance with which Burr has persisted in car-

Spanish nobleman showed reluctance, Wilkinson pressed his case by offering copies of coded reports he had sent to various Spanish officials, including Folch, on the movements of Burr and matters connected to the Sabine River agreement. Ultimately, Folch was "fully persuaded that he [Wilkinson] had acted conformably as suited the true interests of Spain." Folch agreed to give a carefully worded letter saying that he *had not seen any record* stating that Wilkinson was an agent in the employ of Spain.

After Folch returned to Spanish territory, he followed up his promise of aid by sending Wilkinson a coded message acknowledging that all evidence of Agent Thirteen's services to Spain had been concealed:

> *I have sent to the archives of Havana all that pertains to the ancient History, persuaded that before the United States are in a situation to conquer that capital you and I, Jefferson, Madison, with all the secretaries of the different departments, and even the Prophet Daniel himself will have made many days' journey into the other world.*"[4]

In a memorandum attached to his Spanish archives copy, Folch said that by "ancient History" he meant the charges made in *The Western World*. The "Prophet Daniel" was Daniel Clark.

Although his flanks now seemed secure, Wilkinson still hesitated in making the trip to Richmond. Despite Jefferson's urgent entreaties, the general was not anxious to face the rigorous cross-examination that awaited him as the government's chief witness.

In Richmond on May 22, the grand jury convened on the misdemeanor matters with John Randolph being named jury foreman.

For Jefferson, who was receiving reports from his prosecutor, Hay, and his observer, Meriwether Lewis, the characters were all familiar ones—a list of players drawn from the Samuel Chase debacle. Burr, who had presided at the Chase impeachment, was of course the defendant in this matter; John Marshall, who had appeared at the Chase trial as a witness, was now the presiding judge; Luther Martin, the bibulous barrister who had defended Chase so ably, was now a leading counsel in Burr's defense. But there were more: George Hay, who had been a principal witness against Chase, was now prosecutor; the precocious

William Wirt, another participant in the Chase trial, was now Hay's chief assistant. The House manager in the Chase prosecution, John Randolph, was jury foreman in the Burr case. Among visiting celebrities common to both dramas were Andrew Jackson and Washington Irving, the former a passionate spectator and the latter a working newspaperman. Jackson was so incensed by Wilkinson's role that he later deliberately bumped the general on the street, then challenged him to a duel. Certain where the true villainy lay, the outspoken Tennessean called Wilkinson "a double traitor. . . . Pity the sword that dangles from his felon's belt, for it is doubtless of honest steel." Wilkinson declined to duel the fierce Tennessean.

In a modern review of the Burr case, Chief Justice William H. Rehnquist has concluded that "from the beginning of the proceedings, Thomas Jefferson took an inordinate interest in obtaining the conviction of Burr, and alternately importuned Hay and badgered him with suggestions. It was thus particularly important to Burr that the judge who tried him not be overawed by the chief executive's zeal for conviction."[5]

Marshall was not overawed. Despite a barrage of threats from Jefferson and Hay, the Chief Justice remained firm on protecting the defendant's rights and he was fair to both sides in his conduct of the trial.

Nevertheless, the prosecutor was dismayed at Marshall's rulings and surprised at the amount of legal and popular support for Burr: "There is among mankind," Hay wrote Jefferson, "a sympathy for villainy which sometimes shows itself in defiance of every principle of patriotism and truth."

As foreman, Randolph held no brief for Burr or Jefferson and was utterly disdainful of Wilkinson. That star witness was still delayed in his coming and for three weeks the grand jury was able to do nothing.

While waiting for Wilkinson, Burr contrived the idea of going on the offensive and unleashed his legal bulldog, Luther Martin, to ask the court to *force* the president to produce all documents pertaining to the government's case of treason.

This was a momentous test of the Constitution. Could a court *order* a president to do anything? Was the chief executive subject to the same laws as the common citizen?

The audacious Luther Martin thought so. Rising slowly from the defense table, pausing to sip from a stone jug of whiskey he kept at his side, Martin told Justice Marshall that in pronouncing Burr's guilt, "the President has assumed to himself the knowledge of the Supreme Being . . . he has let slip the dogs of war, the hell-hounds of persecution. Would this President of the United States, who has raised all this absurd clamor, attempt to keep back the papers which are wanted for this trial when a life itself is at stake?"

Martin asked that a subpoena duces tecum be issued, requiring the president to produce the papers in court. The issue now before the court was simple: Could a president be summoned by subpoena?

The debate that followed was furious and went on for several days. Jefferson's own answer was regal: It was the unique right of the president "to decide, independently of all other authority, what papers coming to him as President the public's interest permit to be communicated."

Marshall did not shrink from the challenge, declaring that there was nothing in the Constitution that forbade such summoning, nor in any common-law precedent save "in the case of the king." But a president, Marshall noted with some pleasure, was not a king. "The king can do no wrong, that no blame can be imputed to him, that he cannot be named in debate. Since a President can do wrong and since he can be named in debate, he is not an anointed king, and so like any man is answerable to the law."

John Marshall then summoned Thomas Jefferson to Richmond.

Immediately, the historic subpoena was sped to Washington by special messenger. Marshall, of course, was like Joseph Stalin's pope: He had no army divisions. So to avoid an unenforceable confrontation, he followed his ruling with the observation that Jefferson would not need to personally appear in court, that the court would be satisfied if the original letter of General Wilkinson and related documents were dispatched.

The president complied, albeit in a red rage. Some say he became deranged by the order. Undone by his fury, Jefferson insisted to Hay that all of Burr's attorneys were accomplices in treason, and he instructed Hay to arrest and indict the chief irritant, Luther Martin, on that charge:

. . . fix upon him misprision of treason at least [to] put down this unprincipled and impudent federal bulldog and add another proof that the most clamorous defenders of Burr are his accomplices.

Hay, however, was able to argue Jefferson out of that position and neither Martin nor any of the other attorneys was arrested.

Finally, on a Saturday, June 13, Wilkinson arrived by stage from Norfolk, where he had disembarked after taking a ship from New Orleans. The following Monday, he appeared in court, boastfully writing the president:

I little dreamed of the importance attached to my presence here. . . . I saluted the bench and in spite of myself my eyes darted a flash of indignation at the little traitor . . . The lion-hearted, eagle-eyed Hero, jerking under the weight of conscious guilt, with haggard eyes in an effort to meet the salutation of outraged honor; but . . . his audacity failed him. He averted his face, grew pale, and affected passion to conceal his perturbation. . . .

That description of the general's staring down of Burr is at odds with that of other witnesses. Washington Irving reported that Wilkinson came into court "strutting and swelling like a turkey cock," discharging "a wondrous cargo of a mighty mass of words." According to Irving, there was no stare-down, save that Burr gave the general "one look of withering scorn."

In four days of testimony, Wilkinson introduced letters and coded documents and otherwise did his damnedest to sink his old friend. In addition, the grand jury listened complacently to almost equally damning testimony, mostly fanciful, from four dozen government witnesses claiming Burr had told them of a plan to separate the states.

During the testimony, Samuel Swartwout got his revenge. After emulating Andrew Jackson by deliberately bumping Wilkinson off a Richmond sidewalk, Swartwout publicly posted the general in the newspapers as "a traitor, a forger, a perjurer, a coward and a poltroon" for refusing Swartwout's challenge.

It was not a happy visit for the general because at this time Burr's defense made a motion to charge Wilkinson with contempt of court on grounds he had "used unlawful and oppressive means . . . in abuse of the process of this court" to bring witnesses illegally from New Orleans.

The grand jury, led by Randolph, got Wilkinson to admit that he had altered parts of the famous cipher letter in order "to incriminate" Burr.

Appalled at Wilkinson's bland confession of forgery, Randolph insisted that Burr be released and that Wilkinson be charged with perjury. "Never such a countenance did I behold," said Randolph to a friend, adding that Wilkinson was wholly guilty but wholly protected by the president:

> *There was scarcely a variance of opinion amongst us as to [Wilkinson's] guilt. Yet, this miscreant is hugged to the bosom of the government. . . . W. is the most finished scoundrel that ever lived; a ream of paper would not contain all the proofs; but what of that? He is the man whom the King delighteth to honor.*

Then came to testify the New Orleans merchant and onetime Spanish consul Daniel Clark, former close friend of Burr *and* Wilkinson. Seeing Clark, the general was utterly dismayed, telling Hay that Clark could ruin him. Wilkinson was "terrified beyond description," Hay would tell Jefferson.

In the witness chair, Wilkinson was asked by defense counsel Wickham if the general had explored the possibilities of kidnapping and murdering Burr when the defendant was in Mississippi. "Did you send officers in disguise to take Colonel Burr?" Wickham asked.

"I sent three."

"What were their names?"

Prosecutor Hay was on his feet pleading the Fifth Amendment, saying that the answer would put Wilkinson in jeopardy if he had acted without orders, which he had. Wickham did not press the issue, but asked instead, "Did you direct them to go without uniforms?"

Wilkinson said he "believed" he did.

"Were they directed to conceal the object of their mission?"

"I think," hedged Wilkinson, "I did mention the propriety of going in the attire of private citizens to elude the vigilance of Burr's spies. . . . They were sent privately and success depended on it."

Despite Wilkinson's admissions, which included forgeries of Burr's cipher letter, in the face of Clark's testimony and Randolph's efforts, the political makeup of the grand jury was so heavily Jeffersonian that indictments for treason and misdemeanor were nevertheless brought against Burr and Blennerhassett. The grand jury was empowered to indict on both charges even though the Chief Justice had earlier discounted the charge of treason. Two days later the jury indicted Jonathan Dayton, Senator John Smith, and three lesser names.[6]

As for Wilkinson, he narrowly escaped indictment by a close vote of nine to seven, which was the exact makeup of Jeffersonian loyalists to the others.

Randolph was not happy. "The mammoth of iniquity escaped," he complained in reference to Wilkinson. "Not that any man pretended to think innocent, but" Wilkinson is "the only man that I ever saw who was from the bark to the very core a villain. The proof is unquestionable . . . suffice it to say that I have seen it, and that it is not susceptible of misconstruction." The soured Virginian had never seen "human nature in so degraded a situation as in the person of Wilkinson before the Grand Jury; and yet this man stands on the very summit and pinnacle of executive favor."

Meanwhile, defense counsel Luther Martin was blistering the president's gullibility, saying Wilkinson "instilled as much poison into the ear of the President as Satan himself breathed into the ear of Eve."

Among "proofs" given Jefferson of Wilkinson's treasons were statements of Ohio senator John Smith. Unaware that he had been indicted, still viewing himself as a friend of the administration, Smith had written Jefferson from New Orleans:

> *Although I am the friend of General Wilkinson, I think it my duty to inform you, that it has been confidently asserted to me by one of your friends and mine, since I arrived in this city and only two days ago, that General Wilkinson has been in Spanish pay for many years and that the most unequivocal proofs of it are in the hands of a few designing Federalists, who are waiting with anxious hope for the time when you may have committed your reputation with the General's and then publish the evidence of his guilt.*

The well-informed Smith added that a collusion between Wilkinson and Spanish Governor Folch had been or would be attempted.

The president filed the letter, as he had so many other complaints against Wilkinson. Indeed, in that same month of July, after warnings from Daveiss, Smith, and Randolph, after Wilkinson's own admission that he had lied and altered the cipher letter, Jefferson was still insisting on Burr's guilt, and was regretting that "the bias of the Constitution" would probably turn Burr free.

The president wrote his friend Du Pont de Nemours:

> *Burr's conspiracy has been one of the most flagitious of which history will ever furnish an example. . . . Yet, altho' there is not a man in the U.S. who is not satisfied of the depth of his guilt, such are the jealous provisions of our laws in favor of the accused, and against the accuser, that I question if he can be convicted.*

As the process entered its crucial days in early August, Burr's daughter Theodosia arrived from South Carolina with her husband, Joseph Alston. The glamorous couple moved into Luther Martin's quarters and there Theodosia became the queen of Richmond society. Despite her natural anxieties, she presided at the Eagle with such charm that Martin told her father, "I must marry her, Colonel. I shall kill her unworthy husband, and then she will be mine, by right of conquest."

"You have my blessing," replied the amused Burr, who in fact might not have minded the replacement of Alston, whom he despised as a weakling.

After a six-week recess because of summer heat and government-requested postponements, the trial proper began August 17, ending two weeks later.

When all testimony was done, it appeared clearly that the "Burr Conspiracy" was not in Kentucky and with Burr, but in Washington and New Orleans and with Jefferson and Wilkinson. It was realized that Burr, for his part, had betrayed no oath. He entered no conspiracy. He gave no allegiance or information to a foreign government. He took no foreign money. In short, he committed no crime. And on September 1, so the jury found after a very brief deliberation.

The president was beside himself. The trial, he recorded, was what it had been intended by Justice Marshall from the beginning—to clear Burr and keep the evidence hidden from the world. Jefferson instructed Hay to collect all the evidence and preserve it most carefully. "These whole proceedings will be laid before Congress." With luck, there would be an impeachment of the Chief Justice.

There was still the charge of "misdemeanor," the Mexican invasion, to face. That, too, was short, although some fifty witnesses testified against Burr, including most particularly Wilkinson who, according to Washington Irving, acted like "a sergeant under court-martial." There was no evidence, however, to show that Burr had planned anything hostile to Spain except in the event of war with the United States. Hay moved to nolle prosequi, or dismiss, the charge, thus hoping for a dismissal without a verdict. But Marshall sent the case to the jury on September 15 and half an hour later the jury reported, "Not guilty."

But, incredibly, Burr still was not freed.

It was a repeat of the Mississippi grand jury disgrace. Burr had been brought before the court; evidence had been heard; the jury had acquitted him; and yet, thanks to Jefferson, he remained a prisoner.

Now, under Jefferson's direct orders, Hay successfully moved to have Burr held for trial in the district of Ohio, on a charge of preparing an expedition against Spain, the specific charge of which Burr had already been acquitted. Ohio being in another judicial district, however, Marshall let the charge stand, and it remains standing to this day, neither withdrawn nor tried.

Newspapers now turned on Jefferson like snarling tigers, deriding the trial as "King Tom's puppet show" and "Much ado about nothing."

Even more telling was Prosecutor George Hay's confidential communication to Jefferson. Hay had entered the Richmond proceedings with full confidence in Wilkinson and his story, the man and the tale being backed and endorsed by the president. Now Hay was compelled to tell Jefferson:

General Wilkinson said to me the other day that as soon as he got to Washington, he should solicit an inquiry before a court martial into his conduct. I hope he will do so, and whether he does or not, I hope the inquiry will be instituted. The declaration which I made in court in his favor some time ago was precipitate and tho' I have not retracted it, everybody sees that I have not attempted the task which I, in fact, promised to perform. My confidence in him is shaken, if not destroyed. I am sorry for it, on his own account and because you have expressed opinions in his favor. But you did not know then what you will soon know, and what I did not learn until after, long after my declaration above mentioned.

Hay was referring to the continuing reports—from U.S. Attorney Daveiss, who again informed the president that Wilkinson had taken the pay of the Spanish; from Senator Smith, who repeated his accusations against Wilkinson, saying the general's intrigues with the Spanish were more than he could stomach; and from Daniel Clark, who had copies of Spanish documents showing Wilkinson's collusion. There was no lack of information as to Wilkinson's guilt.

The president continued to turn a deaf ear, although the evidence was heavily before him that his commander of the army had been and was then in the pay of Spain.

But Thomas Jefferson was above all a practical man and he still had uses for Wilkinson. He had had need of him at the time of the trial, not only to pursue the hated Burr but as a link to Spain. The president saw the Spanish empire crumbling before Napoleon's armies, and Jefferson wanted to protect American interests by securing Spanish Florida. Traitor though Wilkinson might be, Jefferson would not turn on him because, as Randolph observed, the president had put his reputation in the same bottom.

In the trial itself, Jefferson in effect had pardoned the general in return for his turning state's evidence against Burr. Once that was done, he chose to approve of Wilkinson wholly, even though the president exposed himself to such political assaults as John Randolph's gibe that Wilkinson was "the most finished scoundrel that ever lived" but was nevertheless "the man whom the king delighteth to honor."

Historians such as Dumas Malone have excused Jefferson's protection of Wilkinson on grounds of national expediency, the ends justifying the means:

There is no sufficient reason to doubt that, throughout this affair, his primary concern was for domestic security against present and future danger. The persistence of the Union was far from assured during his presidency and he was determined to preserve it. At times—as in his condonation of Wilkinson's conduct in New Orleans—the vision of individual liberty by which his steps had so long been guided may have been partially obscured by the vision of Union. One is reminded of Abraham Lincoln. At times he may have appeared to shift his priorities—as indeed, any responsible statesman must sometimes do.

Following the trial, an outraged John Randolph continued to gather evidence for a congressional investigation. Hearing of this and hoping to head it off, Wilkinson publicly challenged Randolph to a duel. Randolph, no physical coward, easily recognized the ploy and declined the challenge, saying to Wilkinson, ''I cannot descend to your level.''

Four months later, Randolph presented the same evidence that the grand jury had seen concerning Wilkinson's Spanish bribes and the forged Burr cipher letter. The evidence seemed clearly to reveal Wilkinson's complicity. Randolph moved that the president be requested to institute a public inquiry into the conduct of the general with relation to his having ''corruptly received money from the Government of Spain or its agents'' while in the service of the United States.

After two weeks during which the House concerned itself with little else than the Wilkinson debate, the resolution was adopted by a substantial majority. Feeling was so strong on the subject that a second resolution was unanimously passed. It called on Jefferson to provide Congress with *all* information bearing on conspiracies between foreign agents and American citizens, or tending to show that any officer of the United States had corruptly received money from a foreign government. The resolution was introduced by Jefferson's son-in-law, John Eppes, and strongly supported by Jefferson's former personal secretary, William Burwell.

But Jefferson would not move. Although he had created the crisis by prosecuting Burr, he could not afford a trial of Wilkinson. The nation faced an almost impossible dilemma. England was threatening to blockade the ports. British troops were massed in Canada and the

Caribbean, threatening in the north and in the south. Western Americans wanted war with Spain. Half the New Englanders wanted to secede from the Union. The other half wanted to restore British rule. A trial of the army's commandant, favored by the president, would absorb all the energies of the government and tear the thin threads that bound the nation. The westerners would pursue their goals unchecked. The New Englanders, seeing the central government absorbed, would make alliance with the English. So, in Jefferson's eyes, protecting Wilkinson became tantamount to protecting the nation.

Jefferson adroitly pulled the rug out from under the House investigation by informing Congress that a court of inquiry had already been set up by the secretary of war at Wilkinson's request and had commenced its proceedings. A frustrated Randolph objected that the board was a bogus court, consisting of three military officers, all of lower rank than the commanding general, and advised by a judge advocate appointed by Jefferson.

Even the friendly Dumas Malone has written that Jefferson's defense of Wilkinson would have "been described in our day as a whitewash."

As for Aaron Burr, Jefferson had broken him. Marked as a traitor and threatened by angry mobs in Baltimore, Burr borrowed money from friends and left for Europe, where he would spend the next four years, not returning to the United States until May 1812. Soon thereafter he suffered the deaths of his grandson and his beloved daughter, Theodosia. After resuming a small law practice in New York, he married a wealthy widow at the age of seventy-six. She soon sued for divorce, claiming he was dissipating her large fortune. The divorce was granted on September 14, 1836, the day Burr died.

Louisiana, 2

• • • • • • • • •

As THE NATION PREPARED for the Burr trial, President Jefferson was sounding out James Monroe to be governor of Upper Louisiana, asking him to replace General Wilkinson, whose term had more than a year to run. Monroe, who was then in England trying to negotiate a maritime treaty, declined. Jefferson came back with a second offer, saying that the governorship wasn't without monetary reward. It offers, said the president, "the finest field in the United States for acquiring property." When Monroe again politely declined, Jefferson turned to Meriwether Lewis. On February 26, 1807, a month before the trial, Lewis was officially appointed.

Appointing a loyal Virginian to replace Wilkinson was Jefferson's first step in clearing the "second office" in government of Burrites. Next to go was Wilkinson's secretary (and Burr's brother-in-law), Joseph Browne, who was replaced by another Virginian, Frederick Bates. And yet a third Virginian—Lewis's partner, William Clark— was sent out to take over from Indian agent Pierre Chouteau, a close ally of Wilkinson's.

The above-named men took their offices immediately, but Lewis himself dallied in Virginia until at least the third of November, 1807. On that date he wrote to a friend, Mahlon Dickerson of Philadelphia, concerning his departure to St. Louis. In closing the letter, the apparently lonely Lewis turned his attention to bachelorhood, and his dogged, and inexplicably futile, search for a wife:

> . . . *am now on the eve of my departure for St. Louis. So much for business, now for the* girls.
>
> *My little affair with Miss A-n R-h has had neither beginning nor end on her part; on my own it has had both* . . . am now a perfect widower with respect to love. *Thus floating on the surface of occasion, I feel all that restlessness, that inquietude, that certain indescribable something common to old bachelors, which I cannot avoid thinking, my dear fellow, proceeds from that void in our hearts, which might, or ought to be better filled. Whence it comes I know not but certain it is that I never felt less like a hero than at the present moment. What may be my next adventure god knows, but on this I am determined,* to get a wife.

In another part of the letter, Lewis referred to his regard for a "Miss E- B-y," whose memory he considered "provokingly *important.*" Continuing in a schoolboy tone, the thirty-three-year-old bachelor asked Dickerson to write often "about the *girls.*" What comes across clearly in the letter is that Lewis, a national hero, is achingly alone. Furthermore, he is returning to the wilderness, where his only intimate friends seem to be William Clark and Meriwether's brother, Reuben Lewis, who was accompanying him to St. Louis.

Soon after the Dickerson letter, the Lewis brothers left their Albemarle home and we next hear of them in Fincastle, Virginia, where they are visiting the home of George Hancock, William Clark's father-in-law. Here, the bachelor explorer set his eyes on one Letitia Breckenridge, whom Reuben Lewis described as "one of the most beautiful women I had seen . . . but unfortunately for his Excellency [Meriwether] she left the neighborhood two days after our arrival."

Meriwether's whereabouts for the next three months haven't been discovered by biographers. The remainder of November and all of December and January are blanks. What was he doing? He wasn't working on his journals. Not a page had been written since he arrived in St. Louis in September 1806. His intensity on courting a wife suggests he may have been pursuing that goal, but we are not advised of details.

Still a bachelor, Lewis arrived in St. Louis on March 3, 1808, nearly thirteen months after his appointment. He was once again on the Mississippi, the river that seemed to be a metaphor of his life.

Lewis's life before the governorship was as deep and clear as the upper river. But from the time he took his seat in St. Louis, the journey was one of unrelieved turbulence.

The unhappy times began immediately. In local matters, Lewis would be repeatedly betrayed by his jealous underling, Territorial Secretary Bates, who had run the governor's office in Lewis's absence.

Bates was an ambitious young Virginian who was seeking his fortune on the frontier. He was of flexible politics, having been a Jeffersonian Democrat, then a Federalist, and now back to Democrat again. In 1797, he had served in Detroit under General Wilkinson and was quite close to the general at the height of the Burr "conspiracy."

When Bates reached St. Louis, he was still on friendly terms with Wilkinson. After the disgrace of the Burr trial, however, Bates seems to have cooled in his regard for the general—although it is unknown how much of that was convenient pretense and how much was genuine distaste. What is clear is Bates's enmity toward Meriwether Lewis.

Bates's condescension is evident in letters to his brother:

> *How unfortunate for this man that he resigned his commission in the army. His habits are altogether military and he never can, I think, succeed in any other profession.*

The new governor had trouble on the national level, too, with rumors beginning to circulate in Washington that Lewis was somehow allied with Burr in a new conspiracy, using St. Louis as a base.

Lewis was indeed engaged in a St. Louis adventure, but it was with General Wilkinson and it was under Jefferson's orders. Lewis, as civilian governor, and General Wilkinson had organized a scouting expedition into areas then claimed by Spain and Great Britain, intrusions that provoked both governments.

Lewis also may have been lured by Wilkinson into some questionable private enterprises. For example, by December 1808, Lewis had bought more than five thousand acres of vacant land for which he paid, or obligated himself to pay, two to three times his salary as governor. Where was Lewis to get the money? Not from Jefferson, who was perennially broke. Not from book royalties. He hadn't touched the journals for more than a year. Wilkinson, however, seems a likely source.

Except for its isolation, St. Louis was not a hardship post. The town had an easygoing democracy and food was varied and plentiful. People at all levels ate well, with meals featuring vegetables, cereals, fruits, and meats, supplemented by dairy products and fish. The Spanish-African foods of New Orleans had crept north in the form of gumbos, spicy dishes of chicken, crawfish, okra, tomatoes, and beans. American cider and local beer were in abundance, and for the wealthier classes, Madeira, claret, and brandies were sent in from the East or down from Canada. Merchants sold a variety of other goods including silks, linens, and lace; flatware for the table and ornaments for the ladies; tools for tradesmen and wagons for travelers. In bad weather, all classes wore the capote, or hooded cloth coat, which was available in various fabrics.

Visiting shortly after Lewis arrived, Washington Irving thus described the frontier city:

> *Here were to be seen about the river banks, the hectoring, extravagant, bragging boatmen of the Mississippi with the gay, grimacing, singing, good-humored Canadian voyageurs. Vagrant Indians, of various tribes, loitered about the streets. Now and then, a stark Kentucky hunter, in Leathern hunting-dress, with rifle on shoulder and knife in belt, strode along. Here and there were new brick houses and shops, just set up by bustling, driving, and eager men of traffic from the Atlantic states, while on the other hand, the old French mansions, with open casements, still retained the easy indolent air of the original colonists.*

Under Governor Lewis's encouragement, newspapers were established, with the *Missouri Gazette and Louisiana Advertiser* on July 12,

1808, being the first paper ever published west of the Mississippi. A year's subscription to the weekly was three dollars cash or four dollars in barter, called "country produce."

The *Gazette* was supplemented by newspapers imported from the East, usually arriving four or five weeks after publication. Lewis also opened the original post office in St. Louis and made arrangements for the first book publisher.

Lewis was a Mason, the earliest of that order to locate west of the Mississippi. As governor, many of his key appointments were Masons, including Joseph Charles, publisher of the *Gazette*.

Another part of Lewis's job had to do with Indian relations and trading. It had been at his strong suggestion that Jefferson replaced Wilkinson's business partner, Pierre Chouteau, with William Clark.

All these accomplishments were done against the wishes of Frederick Bates, Wilkinson's friend who had become Lewis's bitter and influential enemy. Bates was now bragging to his brother that he was bearing "in silence the supercilious air of the Governor," even to the point of snubbing him in public:

> . . . *There was a ball in St. Louis. I attended early, and was seated in conversation with some gentlemen when the Governor entered. He drew his chair close to mine. There was a pause in the conversation. I availed myself of it. Arose and walked to the opposite side of the room. The dances were now commencing. He also rose, evidently in passion, retired to an adjoining room and sent a servant for General Clark. . . . He complained to the general that I had treated him with contempt and insult in the ballroom and that he could not suffer it to pass.*

Bates closed with the smug observation that Lewis deserved the rebuff: "He knew my resolutions not to speak to him except on business and he ought not to have thrust himself in my way."

Whatever policy Lewis proposed, Bates opposed. To Bates, Lewis "has fallen from the public esteem and almost into the public contempt. He is well aware of my increasing popularity, for one scale sinks as the other rises, without an increase of gravity. . . . [He] has for some

time feared that I was at the head of a party whose object it would be
to denounce him to the president and procure his" dismissal.

In public meetings, Bates took to openly challenging the governor's
authority. Finally, Lewis had enough. He cornered Bates in his office.
The secretary wrote an account of it to his brother:

> "Well," said he, "do not suffer yourself to be separated from
> me in the public opinion; when we meet in public let us, at least,
> address each other with cordiality." My very humanity yielded a
> prompt assent to this request, and for this I am resolved to take
> every opportunity of convincing the people that however I may
> have disapproved and continue to disapprove the measures of the
> Governor that, as a man, I entertain good opinions of him. He
> used me badly, but as Pope says 'Twas when i Knew no better.

Another problem for Meriwether was that Wilkinson's interference
in the land-claims process had polarized the settlers. These were the
frauds that territorial judge John Lucas had described as "vigorous
and endemic." There was a strong suspicion among settlers that the
general-governor sided with whoever put bribes in his pockets and that
Bates had been brought in to hide and whitewash the Wilkinson
schemes. It was among Lewis's most important tasks to smooth those
feelings and correct injustices that had come about during Wilkinson's
brief tenure. In the opinion of some historians, such as Jonathan Daniels, Bates was an ally of Wilkinson's in these matters.[1] Bates not only
had confrontations with Lewis and Clark but also with other officials
including Wilkinson's critic, Judge Lucas of the land board.

The source of Bates's unremitting hatred of Lewis has never been
pinned down. Daniels suggests that Bates was compromised by his
obligations to Wilkinson and his duties to Lewis:

> Bates may have been fearful of Wilkinson, with whom he had
> been once "on very intimate terms," about something that the
> general required him to keep hidden. . . . [Bates's] hatred of
> Lewis, as he expressed it himself, is certain. Yet ambition and
> jealousy do not quite account for the dimensions of his violent

antipathy which seems almost to have approximated personal fear. . . . At a time when Jefferson was listening to Wilkinson's lies, Wilkinson helped put the politically shifting Bates in office to cover up his corruption in St. Louis. Bates tried and failed due to the unco-operativeness of his colleagues on the land board. From them or other sources, Lewis learned too much. . . .

Another historian, Donald Jackson, traces Bates's rancor back to Lewis's 1801 appointment as secretary to the president. Jackson cites a note written in May 1801, in which Bates's father says the appointment should have gone to one of his sons, either Frederick or his brother, Tarleton.[2]

Despite Wilkinson's land manipulations and Bates's obstructions, Lewis managed to restore order and harmony to the territory. Jefferson would later note in Lewis's obituary that the young governor "determined at once to take no sides with either party, but to use every endeavor to conciliate and harmonize them. The even-handed justice he administered to all soon established a respect for his person and authority and perseverance and time wore down animosities and re-united the citizens again into one family."

Lewis's peacemaking skills embraced not only the settlers but Indian relations, which had greatly deteriorated under the combined administrations of his predecessors. Because of his friendship with the Indians Lewis was able to hold a council with representatives of the Sac, Fox, and Iowa tribes in St. Louis in August 1808. A tract of country was ceded to them as a result. Shortly thereafter he established the first fortification (Fort Madison) in that region. At the same time, William Clark, now Indian agent, concluded an important treaty with the Osages and established Fort Osage.

In 1808, Lewis organized the militia of the Louisiana Territory, naming the elder Auguste Chouteau as colonel of the St. Louis Regiment. It was in that year that Lewis established the first post office, obtaining the appointment of postmaster for his friend and fellow Mason, Rufus Easton. (It was Easton who had complained, unsuccessfully, to President Jefferson that Wilkinson had committed "innumerable alterations and forgeries" in order to illegally seize lands for himself and friends.)[3]

The governor's personal affairs, however, were in disarray. Jefferson was impatient to see the journal manuscript, writing often to obtain some idea of progress, if any.

Jefferson had scolded him in July 1808, writing:

> *Since I parted with you in Albemarle in September last, I have never had a line from you, nor I believe has the Secretary of War with whom you have much connection through the Indian department. . . . The constant persuasion that something from you must be on its way to us has as constantly prevented our writing to you. . . . The present letter, however, is written to put an end at length to this mutual silence. . . . We have no tidings yet of the forwardness of your printer. I hope the first part will not be delayed much longer. Wishing you every blessing of life and health, I salute you with constant affection and respect.*

Because of personal debt, Lewis feared he might have to declare bankruptcy. He had planned to bring his mother to St. Louis and provide her with a home, but those plans were temporarily shelved because of lack of funds.

As for a wife, St. Louis was a desert. There were simply few, if any, young women of his class. There were no Theodosia Burrs. And for a governor and representative of the president, something like a Theodosia was considered a prerequisite to marriage. But in St. Louis, such a match was unlikely because the population was small and the unmarried women were few and uneducated.

Compounding Lewis's worries were the lack of work on his journals and his loss of favor with the president.

Jefferson was worried about Lewis's failure to keep him informed. He pounded Lewis with further messages from Monticello, commenting on Indian affairs and other business. No answer. When Jefferson heard that Lewis had written Governor Harrison of Indiana that summer, the president groused to others like a sulking parent: "It is astonishing we get no word from him."

Throughout 1808 and deep into the summer of 1809, Jefferson, who left office in the spring of 1809, was still looking for words from Lewis, asking about the still unpublished history of the expedition to the Pacific:

I am very often applied to know when our work will begin to appear, and I have so long promised copies to my literary correspondents in France, that I am almost bankrupt in their eyes. I shall be very happy to receive from yourself information of your expectations on this subject.

That letter was never read by Lewis. By the time of its arrival, he had departed St. Louis on a mysterious errand to the east.

Jefferson left office in March 1809, being succeeded by James Madison. Of nearly equal importance to Lewis was the loss of Jefferson's secretary of war, Henry Dearborn, with whom Lewis was on good terms. Dearborn was succeeded by William Eustis, and from then on, the attitude in Washington was changed. Lewis was no longer the gifted prodigy, the president's protégé. He was now just another political appointee in the field.

The first evidence of change hit St. Louis in July 1809, when Secretary Eustis refused to honor a draft of nineteen dollars—*nineteen dollars!*—submitted by the governor. Dearborn would have honored it without question. But Eustis refused, forcing Lewis to make it up from his own pocket. Officiously, Eustis reminded Lewis that remonstrances to the Executive Mansion would do no good. "The [new] President has been consulted and the observations herein contained have his approval."

There were other exchanges with the War Department over official expense reimbursements. To keep the peace among the Indian tribes along the Missouri, Lewis had purchased several hundred dollars' worth of tobacco and trade goods. Those expenses, too, were challenged.

Eustis next wrote Lewis questioning his authorization of a "commercial expedition" west of St. Louis which had been led by a Wilkinson ally, Pierre Chouteau. The expedition, in fact, honored a long-standing promise by President Jefferson to return a Mandan chief to his village. Tribal animosities had prevented the chief's return, however, until after Jefferson left office. Nevertheless, Eustis felt the expedition should have been resubmitted for approval by him or the president, and scolded

Lewis accordingly: "As the object & destination of this Force is unknown," huffed Eustis, "it is thought the Government might, without injury to the public interests, have been consulted . . . it cannot be considered as having the sanction of the Government of the United States. . . ."

On receipt of the letter, Lewis exploded. He felt he was being falsely accused of treason and responded hotly:

Yours of the 15th July is now before me, the feelings it excites are truly painful. . . . I have been informed representations have been made against me. All I wish is a full and fair investigation. I anxiously wish that this may reach you in time to prevent any decision relative to me.

I shall leave the Territory in the most perfect state of Tranquility which, I believe, it has ever experienced. I find it impossible at this moment, to explain by letter, and to do away by written explanations, the impressions which I fear, from the tenor of your letter, the Government entertain with respect to me, and shall therefore go on by the way of New Orleans to the City of Washington with all dispatch. Thursday next I have appointed for my departure from Saint Louis. I shall take with me my papers which I trust when examined will prove my firm and steady attachment to my Country, as well as the exertions I have made to support and further its interests in this quarter.

I do most solemnly aver that the expedition sent up the Missouri under the command of Pierre Chouteau, as a military command, has no other object than that of conveying the Mandan Chief and his family to their village—and in a commercial point of view, that they intend only to hunt and trade on the waters of the Missouri and Columbia Rivers within the Rocky Mountains and the plains bordering those mountains on the east side—and that they have no intention with which I am acquainted to enter the [Spanish] Dominions, or do injury to any foreign power.

Be assured Sir, that my Country can never make "A Burr" of me. She may reduce me to poverty; but she can never sever my attachment from her.[4]

Only two years earlier, Lewis had been Jefferson's liaison at the trial of Aaron Burr. Now, it seems he feared that he might be the man in the dock. Or, another interpretation, that he was being set up on false charges, as Burr had been.

He was not about to let the matter rest with the letter to Eustis, and on September 4, 1809, accompanied only by a servant or valet named Pernier, Lewis boarded a flatboat and headed downriver to New Orleans. The *Gazette* would note that he "set off in good health for New Orleans on his way to the Federal City."

Lewis's motives for the trip were several. First and most obvious were the expense accounts. We know he also intended to deliver his nearly completed journals for publication in Philadelphia and to visit with President Madison in Washington. Although it is not certain, it is highly likely that he also planned to see his retired benefactor Jefferson in Monticello.

But there may have been more to the trip than finances, manuscript, and personal calls. His strong reaction to the "Burr" threat suggests something much stronger. Lewis may have had further intelligence concerning land frauds by James Wilkinson which he wished to discuss privately with either Madison or Jefferson.

That Lewis knew of such land frauds is incontestable. He had been informed of Wilkinson's swindles as early as January 1804, when Lewis was waiting at Cahokia on the east bank of the Mississippi across from St. Louis. There Lewis had become friendly with John Rice Jones, then a forty-five-year-old lawyer at Kaskaskia. Buried in today's files of the War Department in the National Archives is a letter from Jones saying that a scheme of fake "Spanish land grants west of the Mississippi is known to "Captain Lewis and he has informed the President."[5]

Jones, who would later become a Missouri Supreme Court judge, was not only a friend of Lewis's, and of Indiana Governor Benjamin Harrison's, but also a partner of Judge Rufus Easton, who would later be appointed postmaster by Lewis. (It was Easton who had complained to President Jefferson that Wilkinson had committed "innumerable alterations and forgeries" in order to illegally seize lands for himself and friends.)

Jones and Easton were among the earliest and closest friends in the Missouri Territory to their Masonic brother, Meriwether Lewis. Those two men also were the first, and the loudest, to publicly complain of Wilkinson's land grabs and, as Jones specifically stated, Lewis was aware of it as early as 1804. What more would he have learned as governor? It seems Lewis had informed Jefferson of the land frauds, apparently to no avail, in 1804. Did he have more to tell Madison in 1809? Or, more to the point, did James Wilkinson *think* Lewis had something else to tell?

Down in New Orleans, the general had plenty to occupy his suspicions.

Despite the publicity and denunciations at the Burr trial, Wilkinson remained traitorously involved with the Spaniards. Even the merest suspicion of Lewis's knowledge of this would have had Wilkinson shivering in his boots. The accusations of political enemies like Clark or Randolph were one thing. But the words of a nationally honored Jeffersonian favorite were something quite different.

Wilkinson, now in New Orleans, was certainly aware of Lewis's trip. It had been in the newspapers, and as early as July, Territorial Secretary Bates was writing friends that the trip was planned. It would have been impossible for Lewis to enter or leave New Orleans without Wilkinson's knowledge because on July 19 of that summer the general had put himself in charge of all ship traffic passing through the port.

Wilkinson also may have planted the seeds in Secretary Eustis's mind that falsely tied Lewis to a Burr-like plot. It will be seen that prior to the Eustis letter to Lewis, Wilkinson was informing the secretary of just such a "conspiracy to seize New Orleans involving an American officer and others."

A replay of the 1806 Burr "plot" seemed to be under way. General Wilkinson already was in trouble down in New Orleans because of an unraveling army-stores scandal which was killing hundreds of his soldiers. As with the Burr "plot," Wilkinson hoped to escape blame by inventing a "conspiracy" for him to expose. He began writing of a plot to seize American territory.

Was there such a conspiracy? Details are unclear because the documents were long ago mysteriously removed from the National Archives, but at the time, Secretary Eustis was sufficiently alarmed to authorize martial law in New Orleans.

Wilkinson's actions in the summer of 1809 bear striking parallels to his conduct three years earlier, as follows:

One, the general was in jeopardy. In 1806, news had leaked concerning Wilkinson's Mexican invasion scheme with Aaron Burr. In 1809, a scandal was breaking concerning Wilkinson's abuse of troops at a Louisiana encampment known as Terre aux Boeufs.

Two, to divert blame, the general invented a mammoth conspiracy to sever the nation. In 1806, the general's finger pointed at Aaron Burr. In 1809, it seems to have been aimed in the direction of Meriwether Lewis.

Three, Wilkinson used forged letters to support his accusations.

Four, martial law was declared, giving the general full control of his immediate base, New Orleans, and the ability to silence critics and squelch evidence there.

Five, the escalation of the above events led to dire consequences for both of Wilkinson's victims—Aaron Burr in 1807 and Meriwether Lewis in 1809.

The Burr trial ended in the fall of 1807 with Wilkinson still under public scrutiny because of his alleged collaboration with Spanish authorities. To bypass John Randolph and the House inquiry, however, President Jefferson arranged a court of inquiry to investigate the accusations. The military court convened on January 2, 1808, and publicly exonerated Wilkinson on July 4 of that year. The verdict was approved by Jefferson shortly afterward.

Jefferson's involvement in Wilkinson's exoneration was the fruit of their mutual manipulations. The president and the general had a symbiotic relationship, using each other to further their individual schemes. But ultimately, Jefferson became so involved with Wilkinson that he risked sacrificing his reputation in order to save it.

One fruit of the Jefferson-Wilkinson collaboration was the Vicente Folch letter. It will be recalled that a pivotal point in Wilkinson's successful defense was the letter the general solicited from Folch, governor of Spanish West Florida. The published letter was aimed at disproving any connection between the general and the so-called Spanish conspiracy. With skillful evasion, Folch conveyed the impression that Wilkinson's relations with Spain had been of a commercial business nature and in no way detrimental to the United States. Folch repeated his earlier statement, saying carefully that there was *in the archives under his control* no document whatever to show that Wilkinson ever received a salary or pension from Spain.

Folch certainly did not go to the general's aid out of friendship, because he had low regard for Wilkinson. For example, in December 1808, the governor had written to the captain-general of Cuba that although he had defended their agent, he did so "to protect a person who is persecuted for having revealed secrets" to the Crown, but "my friendship does not and cannot exceed these limits for the person of whom I speak lacks all qualities which might recommend him to my friendship, if considered as a private individual."

Folch's word as a Spanish gentleman was accepted by the military court, but not by John Randolph nor by the chief witness against Wilkinson, the New Orleans merchant and former U.S. consul Daniel Clark.

Their suspicions were well grounded. As we have seen, Folch in fact had sent all the incriminating documents to Havana. Folch's cover-up of Wilkinson was not only out of duty—acting, as Folch wrote Wilkinson in a coded personal letter, "as befitting a faithful servant of the noble Spanish Monarchy"—but because the governor also expected a favor in return.

At the time, Jefferson was using a carrot-and-stick approach to persuade the Spanish to give the United States control of Spanish Florida, which stretched from Baton Rouge through Mobile Bay and Pensacola and thence to the peninsula. Jefferson's "stick" was an embargo which prevented American goods being shipped into that territory. The "carrot" was Wilkinson.

Jefferson felt strongly that the Emperor Napoleon's conquest of Barcelona and Madrid would lead inevitably to the loss of Spain's American colonies. The president wanted Wilkinson to sound out the Spanish authorities in Havana on the subject of their impending independence;

further, to suggest to them the possibility of an alliance to which Spanish America, Brazil, and the United States would be parties.[6]

As for the second mission, Jefferson agreed to let Wilkinson approach Folch with an offer to secretly bypass the president's own embargo. Jefferson wanted Folch's good services on the Havana mission and Folch needed to feed his deprived population. Wilkinson was going to help both men in their designs.

The basis of Folch's bargain was that in return for the false exoneration, Wilkinson would use his authority to ease past the embargo and transport fifteen hundred barrels of desperately needed flour to Pensacola, the capital of West Florida.

In a separate maneuver to protect the Floridas against British intrusion, Jefferson obtained congressional authority to expand the regular army and to activate various militias to gather in New Orleans. The president then empowered New Orleans governor Claiborne to explain to Folch that the action was against the British and no aggression was intended against the Spanish. Claiborne dutifully passed on this message to Folch at Baton Rouge and to the Spanish consul Vidal in New Orleans, adding the president's message that the United States wanted simply to prevent any other nation from occupying territory to which the United States had claim. This was in fact not only a veiled warning to Great Britain but also to Spain against an aggressive presence along the Atlantic and Gulf coasts of America.

Wilkinson, still at Washington in December 1808, was now ordered to leave on his three-pronged mission: first to Havana; then to Pensacola; and finally to New Orleans, where he would take command of the army being assembled against Great Britain.

For Wilkinson, the mission was a godsend. Not only could he serve his president, but he could use the trip to fulfil his bargain with Folch. As for Jefferson, with his usual cynical finesse, he knew his commandant was peculiarly suited to the task because of Wilkinson's many personal Spanish connections, legal and, to Jefferson's mind, perhaps illegal. But the president had no way of knowing, as we know now from the Spanish correspondence, that by 1808 the Iberians looked upon Wilkinson as a discredited agent, his cover "blown" by the Burr trial. Simply put, the Spaniards no longer trusted Number Thirteen.

Either way, it cost Jefferson nothing to open this back-door communication. The chance was worth the effort, and for Wilkinson it offered a means to redeem himself in the eyes of both Washington and Madrid.

As it turned out, however, the mission proved futile. The general reached Havana while the inhabitants, contrary to a move toward independence, were in passionate support of Spain because of French occupation of the motherland. So hostile was the feeling against *all* foreigners that Wilkinson was prevented from even meeting with Captain-General Someruelos. Not that it made much difference. Folch's warnings against Wilkinson to that same officer had already ensured a snub.

After his rebuff at Havana, Wilkinson stopped at Pensacola with his cargo of grain and flour, but Folch was not there, having gone on to Baton Rouge. The general was unable to do more than unload his cargo of illegal goods.

When he reached New Orleans, things got worse.

By the spring of 1809, the city had recovered from Wilkinson's earlier depredations. Coming down the Mississippi from the north were iron and manufactured goods from Pennsylvania and Ohio; whiskey from Kentucky; grain from Illinois; cotton from Tennessee and Arkansas; and furs from St. Louis—virtually all of it passed on to ships bound for South America, for Europe, and for the Atlantic coast.

The masts of the sailing ships made the sky a forest and from the Place d'Armes at the center of the city boatmen could walk for a mile from ship to ship without ever touching the dock or land. The water was covered with life. There were gold and silver bullion, olives, dates, ocelot, cougar, beaver, and buffalo, alive and in skins; snapping turtles, sugar, water moccasins, molasses, flour, whiskey, tobacco, corn, beef, hogs, pork, turkeys, Kentucky rifles, lumber, apples, butter, cheese, onions, and wild alligators and bears in wooden cages. There were white men with black wives and black men with white wives. There were black men, free and prosperous, dressed up like lords in purple and fine linen; and there were white men in rags and chains.

The favored meeting place of judges, generals, soldiers, merchants, and planters was Maspero's Exchange, a bar and coffeehouse where handbills such as these were posted:

NINETY NEGROES FOR SALE.

I have about 90 negroes, just arrived from Richmond, Va., consisting of field hands, metif and meamelouc house servants, carriage driver, two seamstresses, several very fine female cooks (all quarterons), one blacksmith, one carpenter and some excellent wagons and harness, and one very fine riding horse, all of which I will sell at the most reasonable prices.

You could buy nurses, field hands, hairdressers, mechanics, seamstresses, house servants, wagoners, plowmen, carpenters, clerks, books, bakers, and butlers. You could buy them for cash, on credit, or win them in a lottery:

Fifty lottery tickets. $20 apiece. Prize is my slave girl Amelia, 13 years of age. Trade, pure and simple.

The downstairs of Maspero's was a large room with many tables and chairs. There was a long oak bar, forty feet in length, topped with marble where the drinks were made and served. Behind the bar was the largest mirror in the country. At each end of the bar was an auction block. These were for the sale of slaves. Most southern cities, like Richmond and Natchez, had special markets where the slaves were sold and could be sold nowhere else. In New Orleans there was no official place. Slaves were sold everywhere and anywhere one could get up a crowd.

After unloading his cargo at Pensacola, Wilkinson continued to the Mississippi, meeting with Folch in Baton Rouge and with Consul José Vidal in New Orleans. To the general's dismay, both insisted that any discussion of alliance with the United States must include England because she was helping Spain in the war against Napoleon. Neither Vidal nor Folch believed that Napoleon would ultimately conquer Spain, as proved to be true. In further reproach, Folch pointedly told

Wilkinson that it was not fitting to divide the possessions of a parent
[Spain] before her demise.[7]

Enraged, frustrated, and insulted, Wilkinson now wrote Secretary
Eustis saying that because of Spanish attitudes and the menace of Great
Britain he wanted permission to seize West Florida with his new army.
He simultaneously wrote his influential friend General Samuel Smith
of Baltimore suggesting that the United States authorize him to buy
West Florida for $500,000. He hinted that Mexico also could be won
for the United States and volunteered to lead troops there, too.

Finally arriving at his military assignment in New Orleans, Wilkinson
found the city more crowded than ever. Tent camps had been set up
along the levee to house two thousand troops sent downriver to prepare
for the British invasion. News had gone around town that General
Wilkinson had arrived to take command and, strange as it might seem,
this was happily received by the citizens. American soldiers, having
spent their pay long ago, had outdone themselves in inventing new
varieties of begging and thieving and the citizens wanted some order
restored. It was felt that Wilkinson, whatever his faults, would restore
discipline and order.

Wilkinson found his command composed almost entirely of "undis-
ciplined recruits, men and officers alike, with few exceptions, sunk in
indolence and dissipation, without subordination, discipline or police,
and nearly a third sick . . . without paymasters; men deserting in
squads; the military agent without a cent in his chest, his bills protested
. . . medicines and hospital supplies scarcely sufficient for a private
practitioner."

To house his "army," Wilkinson chose a rise of land downriver
from the city which was called Terre aux Boeufs ("Land of Cattle").
It was not a coincidence that the twelve-hundred-acre site was owned
by a Wilkinson business associate, Spanish surveyor Carlos Trudeau,
the father of a lady whom the general had been courting since his
wife's death less than two years earlier. In return for a substantial
bonus paid back to himself, Wilkinson leased Terre aux Boeufs sight
unseen at an exorbitant price from his future father-in-law.[8]

From afar, Terre aux Boeufs looked miserable and uncomfortable.
Up close, it was worse—a death camp. The flat pasture of tough
palmetto scrub with little shade was about eight miles below New

Orleans on the east bank of the Mississippi, and there, beginning in May 1809, the general ordered his troops assembled. By June, they were entirely moved. Three weeks later they started dying.

Wilkinson's only consideration had been the kickback, a payment he received from Trudeau in exchange for leasing the land. Originally, the general had no idea Terre aux Boeufs was such a hellhole. Its name had given him visions of rolling pastureland. Instead, it was a pestilential pit fit only for mosquitoes, alligators, and moccasins, all of which it had in ample population.

The new army camp stretched for miles, a forbidding swampland broken only occasionally by ridges and "islands" of higher land. Shade was scarce and one could not imagine a worse place for an army bivouac. Part of the land was covered with heavy grasses, and here and there in the prairies of grass there stood a gnarled live oak, giving shade with its twisted and far-flung, moss-grown branches. The remainder of Terre aux Boeufs was but a steamy swamp of willows, cypress, palmettoes, marsh grass, alligators, mosquitoes, and snakes.

In this swamp beside and below the natural levees of the river, the general concentrated his two thousand suffering troops—virtually all of them unacclimated northerners drained from garrisons on the Atlantic seaboard, the Ohio, and the upper reaches of the Mississippi.

Upon Wilkinson's arrival, an advance party of soldiers cleared for his headquarters about thirty acres at a rise of land protected by a natural levee of the river. Tents were laid out in parallel lines to form streets several hundred yards long. If it had been Wilkinson's design to weaken his own troops, he had picked the perfect spot to do it.

The troops dug pitiful drainage ditches and latrines which were virtually useless because the camp was some three feet below the ordinary level of the river. When the rains came, which was often, the ditches and latrines overflowed into the tents. Flies were everywhere, moving fiercely from drainage ditches and latrines to kitchens and the bodies of the men, nesting in the filthy straw of their bedding. Nets which had been paid for were not provided and the clouds of mosquitoes made the men frantic, forcing the bedridden to weep in their misery. The heat rose from the ground in steaming waves and whenever the wind blew from the direction of the camp, the whole city of New Orleans could smell the stink.

Nevertheless, Wilkinson wrote the secretary of war that the only disadvantage to the site was its nearness to New Orleans, where, said Wilkinson, his nemesis Daniel Clark, the former American consul, could "corrupt and seduce men and officers from their duty." Terre aux Boeufs's advantages, the general said, were military location, the site making it easy to defend against British ships coming upriver, and health considerations, including "the best fresh water in the country," nearness to medicine markets, and the availability of doctors.

Not content with profiteering from the site, Wilkinson also made kickback arrangements with New Orleans merchant James Morrison to provide stores. When the stores arrived, the flour was moldy and full of worms and bugs. Only the whiskey was adequate. The pork had a strange rust color and the men avoided it. The beef was absolutely unfit to eat. His soldiers already were poaching on the oxen and he had forbidden his officers to interfere. Soon dozens more men were dying each day.[9] An epidemic of disease and bowel complaints raged unchecked. Every day, five to ten men were carelessly buried by the weak survivors beneath a few scant inches of loam.

By the first of August, 1809, Terre aux Boeufs was a plague spot. Sixty percent of the men were on the sick list; 963 were down with "chills and fever" brought on by malaria, dysentery, and scurvy. The few doctors were handicapped by the lack of medicine and hospital supplies. Those of the 600 troops not on the sick list were too weak to police the camp.

The role of mosquitoes in spreading malaria was not then known, nor the source of dysentery. But the cure for scurvy was common knowledge—a good diet of fresh fruit and vegetables to supplement the regulation ration of bread, salt beef and pork, and dried beans and peas. But the paymaster had fled in fear of disease and there was no money for fresh food. Many of the young officers exercised their option to resign; a few others deserted, as did some men from the ranks.

In Washington, Secretary Eustis was receiving reports of death and sickness. Eustis may have been a misfit in his military Cabinet post, but in the matter of health conditions he had expertise, for he was a licensed physician, having been an army surgeon during the Revolution. The conditions—which the general blamed on fate and his subordinates—became a scandal. After questions were raised in the

Congress, Eustis ordered the army from New Orleans to the high ground behind Fort Adams. The fort had been established as an outpost below Natchez to guard the confluence of the Red River and the Mississippi, a semi-settled region of pine woods and swamp-rimmed prairie, plantations of sugar cane, rice, and perique tobacco.

When Wilkinson did not move immediately, Secretary Eustis sent a second order.

Wilkinson again resisted the move, claiming he had not received the original order until late in May and the second in mid-June. This was not believed in Washington because there was a well-established mail route between Washington City and New Orleans in 1809. The mail went once a week, and the time of transit was nineteen days.[10] "No one believed him," Henry Adams would write. "Wilkinson's reputation warranted the belief that he suppressed the order in the belief that he knew best. This was no new thing on his part."

Although the sick and dying did not seem to noticeably disturb the commandant, he was furious with Eustis for what Wilkinson perceived as an usurpation of authority, protesting to the secretary that he was being asked to "abandon the country I was commanded to protect." How the city was to be defended by a disabled army which was 60 percent *hors de combat* was not addressed.

The general denounced the order to move the troops as "peremptory" and "certainly a reproach either to my judgement or motives." Wilkinson argued that his new site of Terre aux Boeufs was well chosen, but—because of their weakened condition when he arrived—the troops were too feeble to move. None of this was his fault.

Meanwhile, the "army" was crumbling. Not only were the troops about to revolt, but news of their plight had reached the city, where deserted soldiers were begging for food on the streets. Covering up with his usual bluster, Wilkinson wrote the secretary that he must further delay the move to Fort Adams until September because of sickness and delay in obtaining boats.

Wilkinson complained that Eustis was relying too much "on the opinion of others," a reference to Captain David Porter, a twenty-nine-year-old naval attaché who had complained that Wilkinson and Claiborne looked "upon the country as a big orange which they have a good right to squeeze."[11]

Eustis was not amused, correctly seeing in Wilkinson's lengthy dissemblings a disobedience to orders and a challenge to himself and the new president. The secretary had already set Governor Meriwether Lewis straight on that score and he was determined to put this other Jefferson protégé in his place, too.

But in these bureaucratic wars, Wilkinson was a tougher nut to crack than Lewis. The general sat firm, despite a third order, which arrived on the nineteenth of July. But accompanying the latest instruction was a concession to the general—authority for Wilkinson to seize command of all ships in the port of New Orleans for use in moving his troops upriver.

Wilkinson's troubles were compounded in Philadelphia that September when Daniel Clark published his book, *Proofs of the Corruption of General James Wilkinson*, about the arrangement between Wilkinson and the Spanish. The work was also published serially in many northern newspapers, several of which used the occasion to denounce the general as "a traitor" and "an executive favorite" to whom "the people's money" was given.

Unlike the earlier bribe accusations, Clark's new charges were too precise to be ignored. Secretary Eustis again contacted Wilkinson, insisting he wanted answers, not only to the scandal at Terre aux Boeufs but also to the Spanish conspiracy. To Wilkinson's further alarm, he was now ordered to surrender his command and return to Washington immediately.

Despite the fact that his army was even weaker because of disease and malnutrition, Wilkinson finally agreed to move upriver. He began loading his barges and sailing ships, spurred, it seems, not only by Eustis but by even more barbs from Daniel Clark and John Randolph.

The general would write with self-pity in his *Memoirs*:

> *Whilst laboring in the public service on the Mississippi and encountering every ill that could afflict a man, my enemies had been active to accomplish my ruin. In Philadelphia, Clark had published his* Proofs, *an artful and scandalous libel, and Randolph, in Virginia, was intriguing with idle, dissipated and unprincipled malcontents, who . . . had shrunk from duty at New Orleans. The excitements . . . produced clamors which appalled*

the cold selfish, timid heart of President Madison. . . . I was
accordingly recalled from my command to conciliate the traitors I
had baffled. But why complain?

The move upriver proved as deadly as staying in Terre aux Boeufs.
The weather was insufferable; the sick were worsened by the stress
and steamy heat of bucking the Mississippi currents; the boats were
overcrowded. It took forty-seven days to reach Fort Adams. Of 935
men embarked on the boats, 240 died. Of the 1,953 regulars sent to
New Orleans that spring, 795 died and 166 deserted—a total force loss
of 49 percent.[12] By comparison, fighting on that same ground near
Terre aux Boeufs a few years later, Andrew Jackson would lose but
13 dead while destroying a British army of 7,000 troops.

The Terre aux Boeufs affair became a national scandal and at Natchez
Wilkinson found orders awaiting him to turn over his command to
General Wade Hampton and proceed immediately to Washington City
for inquiries.

Still, he didn't go, claiming ill health. But in fact he was healthy
enough to once again report a plot of "treason" against the United
States. Like the Burr case, it appears to have been a Wilkinson effort
to deflect blame and ingratiate himself with the administration.

On September 3, 1809, Wilkinson sent an emergency dispatch by
special courier to Secretary Eustis reporting a "Spanish plot" to seize
New Orleans. The general said he had learned of the plot just "a few
days ago" from the mayor of New Orleans. Wilkinson said Daniel
Clark had enlisted the services of one of Wilkinson's junior officers,
a Lieutenant Newman, to foment insurrection:

I have known for some time that a club of Frenchmen, Spaniards
and others, at the bottom of which I have considered my friend
Clark, have been endeavoring to excite jealousies in the Spanish
provinces against the government of the United States, the most
distinguished and enthusiastic Spaniards in this quarter, and my-
self personally. But I had no conception of the industry of these
agents, or of the complications of the plan. I have reasons to
believe [Lieutenant Francis] Newman is a principal."

The similarities to the Burr frame of three years earlier were striking. Enclosed with the communication to Eustis were letters allegedly written by Newman to a Spanish confederate, but which Wilkinson conceded were "probably forged." Wilkinson then named some other army officers he believed to be involved in the "plot" and said he was "watching" them. Wilkinson also referred to a "Captain Hughes" whom he had sent to Chihuahua but declined to give Eustis a copy of his orders to Hughes, saying it would not be "proper in these wild times to transmit you the transcript of my orders and agency in that affair—knowing how much I had been made a victim of suspicion in all my dealings with Spaniards." He did feel free to inform Eustis that Hughes's mission was one of "intelligence" gathering. Then, as he had in his 1807 justifications to Jefferson, the general dropped in as many names as he could muster in a self-testimonial:

> *From the period of General Washington's administration through the times of his successors I have been taught to believe it was my duty to acquire every information on topographical and political matters which might [several words indecipherable] to our country. My labors have not been totally unproductive, and for my little services in this way, I have received the acknowledgements of Washington, Adams, and Jefferson. But as I once said to Hamilton, "If it is only appreciated that I am to confine myself to strict, professional reports, you shall find me dumb on every other topic."*

The effort is so clumsily close to the Burr plot that it defies belief. There is a "conspiracy" to seize New Orleans. There is a forged letter; and there is the involvement of trusted confederates. Also as in the Burr case of three years earlier, Wilkinson was not content with a single communication, sending Eustis another frantic warning two weeks later.

And once again the gullible Governor Claiborne came under Wilkinson's seemingly hypnotic suggestions and bought completely into the allegations. On the same day of Wilkinson's communication, the governor sent to Eustis his confirmation that such a scheme existed.

That a conspiracy did not exist is suggested by the fact that nothing more ever came of it except the exchange of several letters.[13] The whole matter seems to have vanished after Wilkinson reached Washington City seven months later to face the questions raised by Clark and Randolph.

In the meantime, Eustis had received the dispatches in mid-October but did not dignify the alarm with a direct reply. The response instead came not from him but from Secretary of State Robert Smith, who sent his communication to Governor Claiborne, pointedly ignoring Wilkinson. Smith said the Newman plot "as described" seemed to be a "revival of Burr's plan under different circumstances." But the secretary was not convinced:

> The letters signed "Francis Newman" are not altogether intelligible. They speak of a Plot—the object of which is Independence—but whether this is to be extended both to Mexico, and what was formerly Louisiana, or confined to one or the other of these countries, is not distinctly stated. If our territories are the object, it is treasonable; if those of Spain, it is contrary to law. In either case, it is your duty to use every effort in your power to defeat it.

Shoving the commandant further out of the picture, Smith ordered Claiborne to arrest all involved and to act with General Hampton, "who supersedes General Wilkinson."

Modern archivists have been unable to determine Wilkinson's whereabouts during October of 1809 when all this "plot" was coming to a head. Although Wilkinson claimed he was too ill to travel to Washington City, he seems to have engaged in a myriad of activities from September 20, 1809, his last official communication from New Orleans, until March 5, 1810, when he married Celestine Trudeau in that city.[14]

Wilkinson's final letter to Eustis concerning the "plot" is dated September 20, at which time the general was headed upriver to Natchez. On that same date, Meriwether Lewis was at Fort Pickering, some four hundred miles to the north. For the next three weeks of Lewis's life, he and the general would never be less than seven days' ride from one another, and often closer.

As for Francis Newman, he seems to have survived his brief moment in history's spotlight without injury. War Department records show he was promoted to captain on October 1, 1809, which was before Wilkinson's accusations would have been received in Washington. However, Newman was honorably discharged six years later with the same rank of captain and there is no indication of a court-martial.

The Killing, 2
• • • • • • • • •

DURING ALL THIS ACTIVITY, Meriwether Lewis was in St. Louis, undecided as to whether he should journey to Washington City. His territorial secretary, Frederick Bates, was impatient, writing that Lewis "has talked for these twelve months of leaving the country. Everybody thinks now that he will positively go in a few weeks."

Finally, on August 30, 1809, Lewis met with the governor's council and made arrangements for his absence. Three days later Lewis and his valet, John Pernier, took passage on a barge, loading aboard two trunks which contained all his papers relative to his Pacific expedition; two saddles and bridles; three rifles, plus pistols, tomahawks, and knives. In a saddlebag, which he kept constantly at his side, he carried what he called "state papers," the contents of which are unknown.

Bates gleefully bade Lewis bon voyage on September 4, 1809, mistakenly writing to a friend that the governor was being recalled in disgrace by Washington: "He has been too unfortunate to expect a second nomination" as governor.

At New Madrid, some two hundred miles below St. Louis, Pernier was forced to take Lewis ashore to see a doctor. They stayed in a hotel three days, where in a burst of caution Lewis made out his last will and testament, a common practice for travelers at the beginning of a long journey. He bequeathed all his estate to his mother, Lucy Marks, "after my private debts are paid, of which a statement will be found in a small minute book deposited with Pernia [Pernier], my servant." A succession of earth tremors then hit the region, proving so alarming that Pernier had Lewis placed on a litter and carried aboard another boat. The *Gazette* reported:

> . . . *his Excellency Governor Lewis was much indisposed at New Madrid, we were informed yesterday by a person direct from that place, that he seen him set off in good health for New Orleans, and on his way to the Federal City.*[1]

Lewis's trip was common knowledge, having been announced in the newspapers, probably to the alarm of General Wilkinson, who must have wondered if a new disaster was about to descend upon his guilty neck. As far as we know, Wilkinson knew nothing about the expense-account flap between Lewis and Eustis. But the general was in very hot water concerning Terre aux Boeufs and the Spanish bribe, as we have seen.

Now, at the very time of Wilkinson's concerns, came this mystery trip by his successor in St. Louis. Was Lewis about to provide further proof of scandalous dealings?

The general's anxieties were increased by the likelihood that should Lewis arrive in New Orleans, protocol would require the general to greet him before Lewis moved on to Washington. Would it be a confrontation? The general wasn't sure. But he didn't like the prospects.

But unknown to Wilkinson, Lewis had fallen ill, probably from malaria, while on the river above Chickasaw Bluffs. The governor and Pernier next came ashore at the Bluffs' Fort Pickering, where Meriwether was for a second time carried ashore.

The forty-foot-high Chickasaw Bluffs at Memphis are a commanding presence over the broad Mississippi. The Chickasaws, fierce and war-like first cousins to the Choctaws, were there when the first whites— de Soto and his party—arrived in 1541.[2] For the next hundred and fifty years, control of the Bluffs seesawed among the French, English, and

Spanish, being finally resolved in 1795 when U.S. army troops took control and built Fort Pickering.

When Lewis arrived in 1809, the commandant was Major Gilbert Russell. He made two rooms in the fort available for the governor and Pernier.[3]

Russell will be an important witness to certain events and personalities surrounding Wilkinson's death, but we know little of the man other than that he was a protégé of Wilkinson and that he sometimes took a hard line on his officer candidates marrying campside whores. Witness this War Department note made in Russell's service record, dated April 4, 1811:

> *[Captain Russell] stated that some time ago he joined in recommending Sarg. Major Mullen for a commission and now withdraws his name from said recommendation, because said Mullen married a common prostitute and has prevaricated on oath.*

Although Lewis had been stationed at Fort Pickering in 1797, he and Russell were apparently unacquainted. Russell had shuttled in and out of the army, first enlisting in 1803, then resigning in 1807. On the recommendation of General Wilkinson, Russell returned a year later to the relatively lofty rank of captain, was quickly promoted to major, and given command of the fort just four months prior to Lewis's arrival. His reentry into the army, his rapid promotion, and his command of the fort had been greatly assisted by Wilkinson, according to War Department documents.

At the time of Lewis's arrival, Russell was making numerous requests to Wilkinson seeking leave to visit Washington and argue his case against "malicious charges" that Russell felt were being made against him—a feeling of unspecified persecution that seemed to be sweeping through government in the wake of the Burr scandal and the new Madison administration. Wilkinson ignored the furlough requests, possibly because he wanted Russell to keep an eye on Lewis.[4]

Russell certainly seemed to associate his duties with keeping Lewis under surveillance. After Lewis arrived, Russell wrote Wilkinson that if he could be granted immediate leave he would personally escort

Lewis to Washington by land. Wilkinson, however, again denied the furlough.

While Russell fretted, Lewis recovered, and after a short rest at the fort he and Pernier boarded another downriver vessel headed for New Orleans. But before Lewis and Pernier left the landing, Russell persuaded or forced the governor to be removed from the vessel and returned to the fort for further recuperation.

Russell would later report that Lewis had arrived on September 15 and then immediately "set off intending to go to Washington by way of New Orleans. His [word blurred] rendered it necessary that he should be stopped until he would recover, which I done and in a short time by proper attention a change was perceptible. . . ."

Based on that slim, surviving clue from Russell, it would seem that Lewis did not intend to stop long at Fort Pickering but at Russell's insistence had been removed from his boat. At any rate, medicine was obtained and Lewis was again put to bed.

During his second recuperation, this one lasting eight days, Lewis canceled the New Orleans segment of his trip, but gave different reasons for doing so.

In some communications, Lewis said he chose to abandon the river and go overland because it would be less physically taxing. In other references, he said he feared he might be captured by the British. Neither reason contradicts the other, but neither is fully convincing.

Traveling by ship would have been far cooler, more comfortable, and easier on his mind and body than walking or riding a horse through steamy Mississippi delta land in late September and early October. A ship or barge also would have allowed him to take all his luggage and trunks, which land travel did not. As for the menace of the British navy, newspapers of the nation, including the St. Louis *Gazette*, were full of news about impending war with Great Britain and certainly that news was available to Meriwether Lewis. But the threat of war was no more, or no less, real in late September at Fort Pickering than it had been in early September when Lewis chose to leave St. Louis by boat and descend to New Orleans and thence via sailing ship to Washington.

Nevertheless, on September 16 Meriwether wrote President Madison that he was heading inland via Mississippi and Tennessee because he feared "the original papers relative to my voyage to the Pacific falling into the hands of the British."

Lewis's letter to Madison was rough, containing a number of erasures and bearing evidence of Lewis's fatigue, and possibly malaria, but it was lucid—showing no signs of a confused or depressed man who intended to kill himself:

> *I arrived here yesterday about 2 o'clock p.m. very much exhausted from the heat of the climate, but having taken medicine feel much better this morning. My apprehension from the heat of the lower country and my fear of the original papers relative to my voyage to the Pacific Ocean falling into the hands of the British has induced me to change my route and proceed by land through the state of Tennessee to the city of Washington. I bring with me duplicates of my vouchers for public expenditures which when fully explained or rather the general view of the circumstances under which they were made I flatter myself they will receive both sanction and approbation. Provided my health permits, no time shall be lost in reaching Washington. My anxiety to pursue and fulfill the duties incident to the internal arrangements incident to the government of Louisiana has prevented my writing to you more frequently.*

Six days later, Lewis gave a somewhat different reason for his change of course. The second letter was written to his old friend Amos Stoddard, the former commandant at St. Louis, whom Lewis believed to be some three hundred miles farther downriver, at Fort Adams near Natchez.[5] Lewis says in the Stoddard letter that he had intended to visit the fort, but that trip, too, is now canceled—not because of the British, but because of "indisposition":

> *I am now on my way to the City of Washington and had contemplated taking Fort Adams and Orleans in my route, but my indisposition has induced me to change my route and shall now pass through Tennessee and Virginia. The protest of some bills which I have lately drawn on public account form the principal induce-*

ment for my going forward to this moment. An explanation is all that is necessary I am sensible to put all matters right.

Fort Adams, of course, is the precise location where General Wilkinson had been ordered to bring himself and his troops. Indeed, Wilkinson may already have been personally at Fort Adams by the time Lewis wrote the letter on September 22. It appears that it may have been Wilkinson, not the British, that Lewis wanted to avoid.

Lewis asked Stoddard to send him two hundred dollars which Stoddard was holding for him. The letter exhibited the sureness of a man who now intended to reach Washington alive and well: ''You will direct [the $200 draft] to me at the City of Washington until the last of December after which I expect I shall be on my return to St. Louis.''

We can see from Lewis's own words that at this juncture he seemed in fair health, had good mental resources, and planned to finish his business in the East as soon as possible, then return to St. Louis. However, it was just as his health had returned that men elsewhere began to circulate rumors of suicidal madness. Perhaps the earliest documented example of the sort was a curious letter written by a Lewis acquaintance, Captain James House, to House's friend Secretary Bates.[6] On September 28, at the time of the letter, House was in Nashville and Lewis was still at Fort Pickering. House wrote to Bates that the governor was *said* to be deranged:

I arrived here [Nashville] two days ago on my way to Maryland. Yesterday Major Stoddart [sic] of the Army arrived here from Fort Adams, and informs me that in his passage through the Indian nation, in the vicinity of Chickasaw Bluffs, he saw a person, immediately from the Bluffs who informed him that Governor Lewis had arrived there (some time previous to his leaving it) in a state of mental derangement, that he had made several attempts to put an end to his own existence, which this person had prevented, and that Captain Russell, the commanding officer at the Bluffs had taken him into his own quarters where he was obliged to keep a strict watch over him to prevent his committing violence on himself and had caused his boat to be unloaded that the key be secured to his stores.

*I am in hopes this account will prove exaggerated though I fear
there is too much truth in it. [But] as the post leaves this tomorrow
I have thought it would not be improper to communicate these
circumstances as I have heard them, to you.*

It is hard to know what to make of this letter. Does it have any basis
of truth? Does it refer to the illness at New Madrid, or some new
problem at the Bluffs?

The writer appears to be the same Captain James House who prior
to his own departure from St. Louis had asked Lewis to carry a heavy
trunk of his by sea to Baltimore. House presumably then set out overland straight to Nashville, where he encountered ''Major Stoddart,''
who of course is Lewis's above-mentioned close friend Amos Stoddard, who Lewis mistakenly thought was still at Fort Adams.[7]

And who is the stranger telling Stoddard, and presumably others, of
Lewis's ''mental derangement'' and suicide attempts, *plural*? This is
the only mention of derangement known to have been made during
Lewis's lifetime although after Lewis died several people would claim
they knew him in moments of insanity, including Thomas Jefferson
and Major Russell. The strongest of these statements would come
from Russell and was discovered only in the 1990s. Was Russell the
instigator or promoter of the rumors, possibly to justify his seizure of
Lewis and his effects? Are the suicide attempts real, or fabrications to
justify Russell's boarding of the governor's vessel? Why did Russell
fail to make such claims while Lewis was alive?

Russell not only told Jefferson of Lewis's ''derangement'' but also
gave similar information to Meriwether's closest friend, his expedition
co-captain William Clark. In a letter written by Clark to his brother
Jonathan about six weeks after Lewis's death, Clark has Russell describing Lewis as deranged, possibly from illness, and suicidal. Therefore, while we are uncertain that Russell was the source for the House
information, he was definitely the source who told Jefferson and Clark
that Lewis was insane. Russell also was most likely the source of
information coming out of Fort Pickering concerning alleged attempts
at suicide. Was Lewis suicidal, as Russell was telling some of the most
important men in the nation? Or was the commandant making it up?

Perhaps the best test of Lewis's true condition at the fort will come from examination of what is undisputed concerning both Lewis's and Russell's activities there.

Lewis was not so ill, or deranged, that it prevented him from writing lucid letters to President Madison and to Amos Stoddard. But it is clear that Lewis experienced some sort of physical disorder at New Madrid, then at Fort Pickering as he descended the Mississippi in hot, steamy weather.

A modern medical investigator has suggested that Lewis was a victim of malaria, symptoms of which were seen as early as 1803 when he pulled his boat ashore on the Ohio River prior to meeting with William Clark for the Pacific expedition. Wrote Lewis at the time:

> *I was seized with a violent ague which continued about four hours and as usual was succeeded by fever which, fortunately, abated in some measure by sunrise the next morning . . . and was entirely clear of fever the next morning . . . felt much better but extremely weak.*

Lewis apparently kept medicine for such attacks for he wrote Clark from Washington City on March 11, 1807:

> *My dear Friend, I took some pills last evening after your departure from which I found considerable relief, and have no doubt of recovering my health perfectly in the course of a few days.*

The medical investigator, the late Dr. E. G. Chuinard, says, "The records show clearly that both Lewis and Jefferson had malaria and that this malady probably explained the abnormal actions of both. . . . Lewis was sick with malaria, accounting for his fevers, general illness and deliriums on his fatal journey . . ."[8]

Malarial symptoms include chills, high fever, and delirium, which take five to seven days to break. But malaria was common on the frontier at the time and it is unlikely that Russell would have mistaken the symptoms for madness—unless he *chose* to pretend the malaria was insanity.

The illness, whatever its nature, affected the governor's trip significantly, causing him to put ashore at New Madrid, then Fort Pickering, and gave a basis for Russell's rumors that he had tried to kill himself. That the suicide attempts are rumors, not fact, is suggested by the absence of any details from Russell or anyone else. Russell, however, does describe Lewis's illness and, as we will see, goes into considerable description about Lewis's "drinking habits." But nowhere will we see detailed accounts of the far more serious and dramatic matter of suicide attempts.

The extent of Lewis's illness is also brought into question by his choice of an overland trip, a journey that was not necessarily shorter and was certainly much harder on a sick man than a voyage by sea. Only a man in good health would contemplate such a trip because it would be fraught with hardship and even danger. About this same time, in 1805, another famous American, twenty-two-year-old ornithologist James Audubon, barely survived a murderous innkeeper in a strange preview to Lewis's fate.

As for Russell's real belief in Lewis's insanity, it is contradicted by the fact that Russell was convinced enough of Lewis's mental and physical reliability to lend him a small fortune.

At the very time Russell insists that Lewis was insane, Russell himself was offering to accompany him to Nashville and presumably all the way to Washington. In addition, the commandant actually loaned the governor, a stranger, the equivalent of four months of his army pay. This loan was in the form of $100 in cash, and two horses and a saddle, for a total of $379.58, which was secured by a promissory note signed by Lewis on September 27, 1809:[9]

> *I promise to pay to Capt Gilbert C. Russell on order or before the 1st day of January next, the sum of three hundred and seventy nine dollars and fifty eight cents for value received.*

The note has been verified by experts as signed by both Lewis and Russell. There is a postscript in Russell's hand referring to a saddle which Russell also had loaned to the governor.

It is the last document known to be written by Lewis—just two days before he left Fort Pickering and fourteen days before his death.

The most reasonable conclusion from the provable conduct of the two men, therefore, is that Lewis wasn't insane and that Russell made him significant loans in full expectation of being repaid within a few months.

It remains unclear why Russell told stories of insanity and suicide.

As for Lewis's decision to go overland rather than by sea, it would seem ill-advised from the standpoint of health. So why did he do it? The British were nowhere near New Orleans in 1809, but General Wilkinson was, and he had just assumed control of all shipping in and out of the port.[10] News of that action would likely have reached Lewis as he was coming downriver, certainly by the time he landed at Fort Pickering and Chickasaw Bluffs.

We now come to a most mysterious figure in Lewis's final days—the federal agent to the Chickasaws, James Neelly.

When Lewis arrived at Chickasaw Bluffs, Neelly was at the Chickasaw Agency, approximately one hundred and fifty miles to the southeast in the middle of present-day Mississippi. Neelly was newly appointed to his job, having been sworn in as agent on August 9 of that year—less than six weeks before Lewis first put in at the Bluffs.

We know from his appointment papers that Neelly was a nominee of General James Wilkinson. Where they met is unknown, but Wilkinson had been closely involved with the Chickasaw country since the 1790s. Furthermore, given the odd spelling of the surname, this may be the same James Neelly of the Indiana Territory who petitioned President Jefferson in 1808 to remove from office one of Wilkinson's sworn enemies—Judge John Rice Jones, the friend of Lewis's who had complained of Wilkinson's land frauds.[11]

Neelly looms large in the final days of Meriwether Lewis. It is from Neelly, directly and indirectly, that Thomas Jefferson will hear the suicide version of Lewis's death. Neelly was also the senior, indeed the *only*, federal officer in Lewis's vicinity at the time of death. But the agent's story is full of holes and contradictions. The agent himself, a brief blip on the screen of history, is too much a mystery to be believed without corroboration. And there is none.

What we know most starkly about James Neelly is this: He was poor; he was indebted to General Wilkinson for his job; he made inexplicably strong efforts to meet and then accompany Meriwether Lewis on his last journey; and he was in the vicinity at the moment of death.

War Department records show that shortly after Neelly's appointment he was pleading for a government loan to move down to Mississippi from

Nashville. On August 27, 1809, he wrote Secretary of War Eustis that at the Chickasaw headquarters he had found the "old agency house untenable" and wanted money to build a new one "to put my family in."

That agency was in central Mississippi, about one hundred miles south of the Tennessee line. It was adjacent to the Chickasaw headquarters called Big Town, the principal village of that tribe. Big Town had been chosen as a site for the Chickasaw Indian Agency by Silas Dinsmore, one of the men Wilkinson tried to recruit in 1807 to kidnap or assassinate Aaron Burr. By 1809, however, Dinsmore was still in the region but had relinquished his role as agent, being eventually succeeded by Neelly.

Big Town was situated in a large open valley. It consisted of about three hundred wooden houses and huts of the slave-owning Chickasaws.[12] Extensive cornfields surrounded Big Town, as well as tobacco fields and orchards of apples and peaches. The main village was flanked by smaller settlements of Chickasaws, each containing three or four huts and often with fields of tobacco and corn along a creek.

Neelly had just settled in as the American representative in Big Town when, in early September, he took into custody a prisoner named George Lanehart who had robbed some saddlebags of money near the agency. It was among Neelly's particular duties as agent to transport the American citizen Lanehart from Big Town to Nashville, one hundred and eighty miles due north.

This must have been an important assignment for Neelly because Lanehart had robbed the home of James Colbert, an Englishman who was the wealthiest and most politically powerful plantation owner in the Mississippi Territory. That there was particular community interest in seeing Lanehart transported to Nashville for trial is corroborated by a petition for his arrest signed not only by Colbert but by eight other of the territory's most influential white residents, including the legendary trader Samuel Mitchell.[13]

But faced with his first assignment, which was to transport a politically sensitive prisoner, Agent Neelly subcontracted the job to a man named Jeremiah Love. According to War Department records, Neelly paid Love ninety dollars—slightly more than Neelly's monthly pay of eighty-three dollars—to make the five-day trip to Nashville.[14]

After making his arrangement concerning the prisoner, Neelly himself then set out straight as an arrow in a different direction—going one hundred miles northwest to Chickasaw Bluffs, where, for the first time, he met Meriwether Lewis. A few days later, Lewis accepted Neelly's offer to guide him to Nashville.

Was the meeting a coincidence? Apparently not. Major Russell seemed surprised by the agent's arrival and would say that Agent Neelly "seemed happy to have it in his power to serve the governor."

What an extraordinary development. An impoverished federal agent, new to the job, makes a major arrest, but instead of proudly delivering his prisoner to Nashville, he instead pays someone else a month's salary to do the job for him while the agent rides off in a different direction to intercept Meriwether Lewis.

It may be conjectured that Neelly was ordered to do so. And the man who most likely issued those orders was Neelly's patron and benefactor, General James Wilkinson.

Neelly's detour to Fort Pickering came at the exact time when Wilkinson was rejecting requests from Major Russell to accompany Lewis to Nashville.

In a later letter to Jefferson, Russell expressed annoyance that Neelly, and not he, had been chosen to accompany Lewis:

> I had made application to the General [Wilkinson] and expected leave of absence every day to go to Washington on the same business with Governor Lewis. In consequence of which he [Lewis] waited six or eight days expecting that I would go on with him but in this we were disappointed and he set off with a Major Neely [sic] who was going to Nashville.

Russell found it peculiar that his legitimate mission was spurned while Neelly almost magically appeared at the Bluffs ready to guide Lewis across two hundred and fifty miles of wilderness to Nashville.

Neelly offered to guide Lewis across Chickasaw lands, which reached from Fort Pickering eastward and north to the Tennessee River. From there, he and Lewis would go up the Natchez Trace to Nashville.

Once they left Fort Pickering, the group would be deep in Wilkinson country. It was Wilkinson who made the treaties with the Choctaws and the Chickasaws who inhabited the Natchez Trace area of Mississippi, Alabama, and Tennessee. It was Wilkinson who obtained the appointment to the army of Fort Pickering Commandant Russell. Wilkinson who sponsored Neelly. And it was Wilkinson who, under Jefferson's orders, had converted a winding series of old Indian and buffalo trails into a federal road running from Natchez, Mississippi, to Nashville, known as the Natchez Trace. Wilkinson knew the Trace like the back of his hand.

Leading a small remuda of horses, the party departed on September 29, 1809. The group consisted of Lewis and his man Pernier, and Neelly and his servant, identified only as a black man. Lewis left two trunks at the fort, but carried with him the trunks of expedition manuscripts, a handsome brace of pistols, a "tommyhawk," a dirk, a gold watch, some of his financial papers and about $220, the latter consisting of a "Treasurer's Check" for $99.58 he had borrowed from Major Russell and another $120 in cash he is estimated to have had remaining from St. Louis.[15]

The packhorses carried a stock of provisions—biscuit, flour, bacon, dried beef, rice, coffee, and sugar. Hobbles were taken to prevent the horses from straying at night. It was felt there would be no danger from Indians because of Neelly's presence. Their path into the interior of Mississippi was across open country along the high ground between the Coldwater and the Tallahatchie rivers. Briars and thorny bushes grew close to high ridges on both sides here, often making it necessary for the party to travel single file.

Other than that general information, we have no precise description of the early part of their journey. The participants are silent. We know from a traveler who later passed through Big Town that Lewis and his party stopped there for two days to rest and the governor sent word back to the Bluffs for Russell to hold his trunks rather than send them east by boat. We are told by Neelly that Lewis experienced some delirium at the agency, but recovered sufficiently by the time they left on October 6. They made fifty miles a day for the next two days.

The party crossed the Tennessee River on the afternoon of October 8 or the morning of October 9. Although there is no documentary proof, it is highly likely they used Colbert's Ferry. The Tennessee River, then as now, was a wide, deep stream with a very rapid current which made it impossible to ford. The only way across it in that region was to use the ferry—unless a man brought his own boat.

They would have paid their toll to George Colbert, another link in the Wilkinson chain. George Colbert had been a prominent member of the Wilkinson organization that built the military highway. George was one of five Colbert brothers, the sons of the famed, or infamous, James Colbert, an Englishman who had moved in with the Chickasaws in 1767 and led them as allies with the English in the Revolutionary War. The family, described as "pirates" by some of their contemporaries, were shrewd, strong traders who had married Chickasaw brides and had thus provided for nearly half a century the main link between the world of the white men and the Chickasaws.

George Colbert, the son, was a striking-looking man with the pale skin of his Scottish forebears but with Indian features. "Tall and slender," Governor Claiborne described him, with "straight black hair which came well down to his shoulders."

According to another acquaintance, Colbert was:

> An artful designing man more for his own interest than that of his [Chickasaw] nation . . . very shrewd, talented man and withal very wicked. He had two wives. . . . He and his brother had a large farm and about forty Negroes working. We bought some corn, pumpkins, and corn-blades, for which he charged us a very high price.

After building the road in 1801–1802, General Wilkinson granted George Colbert a license to operate a ferry and build "a suitable house for stand purposes."

By the time Lewis arrived in 1809, George Colbert had been running his ferry across the Tennessee for seven years. During that time, he had built a plantation house and was cultivating a farm of about four hundred acres planted with cotton, vegetables, and grains.

After crossing the Tennessee, the Lewis party traveled throughout the day of October 9, making camp at the head of the Green River. According to Neelly, when they woke up on the morning of the tenth, Lewis saw that two of the packhorses had wandered away during the night. Neelly volunteered to stay and round them up while the governor and the two servants went ahead. There was a white man's house some fifty miles farther north, Grinder's Stand, which Neelly knew, and he would catch up there.

As Neelly would tell it, the loss of two horses caused the party to split up near Little Swan Creek in south-central Tennessee. Lewis turned his horse onto the slightly depressed trail of the Trace and rode north. Trailing behind him a quarter of a mile or more were Pernier and the other servant.

After a long day's ride and some fifty-five miles north of the ferry, Lewis broke out of the woods and into a clearing that held two log cabins and a stable. Above this small meadow of civilization, there rose a haze of chimney smoke, for in October the days might be warm but the evenings always brought a chill.

The size of the establishment and the presence of two separate houses suggested that it was a public hostelry, and when Lewis inquired he was so advised. He was given one of the cabins for his night's lodgings. The family occupied the second cabin, which was separated from the first by a twelve-foot-wide breezeway. They have been reconstructed by the National Park Service, so we know that both cabins had fireplaces and each cabin had a door facing the Trace, which was about twenty yards distant. When Lewis's servants arrived, they were put up in a third building, the stable, which was about one hundred yards from the joined cabins.

It is generally agreed by those involved that Priscilla Griner's husband and their sons were away, probably helping with the harvest at their Duck River farm some twenty miles to the north.

Everything that follows is in dispute. The nearest we get to documented evidence comes from four basic sources: (1) a Nashville weekly newspaper which may have relied on a coroner's jury report; (2) a letter from the agent Neelly to Thomas Jefferson; (3) a similar letter from a Nashville army officer to Jefferson; and (4) a series of interviews with Mrs. Priscilla Griner, the landlady and operator of the inn who seems to have been nearby when Lewis died but may not have been an eyewitness to the death.

When Lewis rode into Grinder's Stand he had actually bypassed the Trace, which turned off to the east a few miles south of the inn.[16] The

fact that travelers and post men were using the new Trace while Griner
had deliberately located his tavern on a bypassed section suggests the
innkeeper may have been more interested in the bootleg sale of whiskey
to Indians than in accommodating occasional riders like Meriwether
Lewis.[17]

We have already seen in Chapter One Professor Alexander Wilson's
account of the murder. We can now turn to an earlier version, a
newspaper account that was the nation's first information on Lewis's
death.

The news was broken by the Nashville weekly, the *Democratic
Clarion*, ten days after the death.[18] In sum, the report said Lewis and
his servants had supper and drink, then retired to separate quarters
where the governor slept alone. Mrs. Griner heard shots, the servants
wouldn't respond to her cries until dawn, and then the servants claimed
to have heard Lewis confessing he had inflicted the fatal wounds on
himself. He had fallen under the influence of a "deranging" malady
for about six weeks. And he died possessing papers of "great value"
to the government.

The *Clarion*'s account appeared in a black-bordered obituary on page
3, saying that Lewis had arrived at the inn alone on horseback, followed
a short time later by two servants. Significantly, there is no mention
of Neelly:

    . . . *Meriwether Lewis, governor general of Upper Louisiana on
his way to Washington city came to the house of Mr. Grinder near
the Indian line in this state—called for his supper and some spirits
of which he partook and gave some to his servants.*

    *Mr. Grinder not being at home, Mrs. Grinder retired to the
kitchen with her children; and the servants—after the governor
went to bed which he did in good order—went to a stable about
300 yards distant to sleep. No one was in the house with the
governor—and some time before midnight Mrs. Grinder was
alarmed by the firing of two pistols in the house—she called to the
servants without effect—and at the appearance of daylight the
servants came to the house when the governor said he had done
for himself. They asked what, and he said he had shot himself and
would die, and requested them to bring him water, he then laying*

on the floor where he expired about seven o'clock in the morning of the 11th—he had shot a ball that grazed the top of his head and another through his intestines and cut his neck, arm and throat with a razor. When in his best senses he spoke about a trunk of papers that he said would be of great value to our government. He had been under the influence of a deranging malady for about six weeks—the cause of which is unknown. . . .

The writer paid respects to Lewis's services as governor, saying that he had repaired rifts caused by his predecessor, the much-disliked Wilkinson:

The territory of Upper Louisiana had been torn to pieces by party feuds. No person could be more proper to calm than he appeared and all was quiet. The limits assigned this notice do not admit of a particular details of his executive attributes—suffice it to say that the parties created by local circumstance and Wilkinson soon were united—the Indians were treated [fairly,] the laws were amended, and judicious ones adopted.[19]

The news spread around the country fairly rapidly, reaching Washington, Philadelphia, New York, and other centers where it was reprinted in other newspapers during the ensuing two to three weeks.

For example, Mahlon Dickerson, a close friend of Lewis's, had read of the death by October 22, the day he recorded the news in his diary.

Articles on Lewis's death appeared in Jefferson's Virginia by October 27 when the Staunton *Republican Farmer* gave details similar to those in the *Clarion.* Two days later Lewis's exploration partner, William Clark, reported hearing about it while traveling through Kentucky. In Washington, the November 15 issue of the widely read *National Intelligencer* described the death by gun and knife and raised doubts about suicide: "We can hardly suppose however, that an incident of this kind alone could have produced such deplorable consequences."

Lewis was one of the four or five top federal officers in the land, ranking just below the presidential Cabinet. Jefferson had told Madison, in fact, that the governorship was the second-highest-ranking office in the nation. But beyond rank, Lewis was also an international celebrity and the well-known protégé of Jefferson. Nevertheless, despite the astonishing circumstances of his death, there was no government inquiry. No official, federal or local, is known to have inspected the scene other than an unconfirmed visit by Neelly.

The second direct source concerning Lewis's death comes from that alleged visit by Neelly. It is a report written by the agent and sent to Jefferson at Monticello. The letter was penned by Neelly in Nashville two days prior to publication of the *Clarion* article. While not identical, the accounts are similar enough that a mutual influence is certain, but the nature of this influence is unclear. Did the newspaper interview Neelly? Or did Neelly and the newspaper both receive information from a common third source?

There are two significant dates attached to Neelly's letter—the day it was written and the day it was received by Jefferson.

Neelly wrote his letter on October 18, ten days after Lewis's death. On that same day Neelly was interviewed in Nashville by the region's ranking army officer, a Captain John Brahan. On the same busy day, Neelly also wrote and placed two ads, unrelated to the Lewis death, in the *Clarion* and wrote his expense accounts for the War Department. There is no evidence of Neelly's presence in Nashville prior to that date and the flurry of activity suggests he arrived either on October 18 or the night before.

That raises the question of his whereabouts for the seven or eight days following Lewis's death. Nashville was a mere sixty miles from Grinder's Stand. Where was Neelly in the meantime?

Neelly's letter didn't reach Monticello until November 21, six weeks after the death. By that time Jefferson had almost certainly heard the news from newspapers or other sources.

The Neelly letter has been the suicide proponents' prime evidence, Jefferson Exhibit Number One, as it were. It is quoted here in full:

Sir, Nashville Tennessee 18th Octr. 1809
It is with extreme pain that I have to inform you of the death of His Excellency Meriwether Lewis, Governor of Upper Louisiana who died on the morning of the 11th Instant and I am sorry to say by Suicide.
I arrived at the Chickasaw Bluffs on or about the 18th of Septem-

ber, where I found the Governor (who had reached there two days before me from St. Louis) in very bad health. It appears that his first intention was to go around by water to the city of Washington; but his thinking a war with England probable, & that his valuable papers might be in danger of falling into the hands of the British, he was thereby induced to change his route, and to come through the Chickasaw nation by land. I furnished him with a horse to pack his trunks &c. on, and a man to attend to them. Having recovered his health in some degree at the Chickasaw Bluffs, we set out together. And on our arrival at that Chickasaw nation I discovered that he appeared at times deranged in mind. We rested there two days & came on. One days Journey after crossing [the] Tennessee River & and where we encamped we lost two of our horses. I remained behind to hunt them & the Governor proceeded on, with a promise to wait for me at the first houses he came to that was inhabited by white people. He reached the house of a Mr. Grinder about sun set, the man of the house being from home, and no person there but a woman who discovering the governor to be deranged, gave him up the house & slept herself in one near it. His servant and mine slept in the stable loft some distance from the other houses. The woman reports that about three o'clock she heard two pistols fire off in the Governor's Room. The servants being awakened by her, came in but too late to save him. He had shot himself in the head with one pistol & a little below the Breast with the other. When his servant came in he says, I have done the business my good Servant give me some water. He gave him water, he survived but a short time. I came up some time after, & had him as decently Buried as I could in that place. If there is any thing wished by his friends to be done to his grave I will attend to their Instructions.

I have got in my possession his two trunks of papers (amongst which is said to be his travels to the Pacific Ocean) and probably some vouchers for expenditures of Public Money for a Bill which he said had been protested by the Secy. of war; and of which act to his death, he repeatedly complained. I have also in my care his rifle, Silver watch, Brace of Pistols, dirk & tomahawk; one of the Governors horses was lost in the wilderness which I will endeavour

*to regain, the other I have sent on by his servant who expressed a
desire to go to the governors Mothers & to Monticello: I have
furnished him with fifteen Dollars to Defray his expenses to Charlottesville; Some days previous to the Governor's death he requested of me in case any accident happened to him, to send his
trunks with the papers therein to the President, but I think it very
probable he meant to you. I wish to be informed what arrangements
may be considered best in sending on his trunks &c. I have the
honor to be with Great respect Yr. ob. Sert.*

*James Neelly
U.S. agent to the Chickasaw Nation
The Governor left two of his trunks at the Chickasaw Bluffs in
the care of Capt. Gilbert C. Russell, Commanding officer, & was
to write to him from Nashville what to do with them.*

Neelly kept Lewis's pistol, tomahawk, and knives but sent other
effects on to Jefferson including the trunks, journals, private papers,
and a single shilling, which Neelly said was all the cash he found on
Lewis.

In sum, his version says Lewis rode in alone and no one was at the
inn but Priscilla Griner. The servants slept in the stables and about
3:00 A.M. the woman heard two pistol shots. The servants finally
investigated and found Lewis wounded, saying that he had shot himself. Lewis died just before dawn.

In his report, Neelly made no mention of knife or razor wounds and
claimed, contrary to the newspaper, that Mrs. Griner was alone at the
inn. But Neelly and the newspaper did agree that the servants discovered the wounds. And they agreed it was the servants who heard
Lewis's confession of suicide and witnessed his death. Neelly said he
"came up some time after" the death and "had him as decently Buried
as I could in that place."

As noted above, there was a gap of seven or eight days between the
time Neelly left Lewis's body at Grinder's Stand and the time he
penned the Jefferson letter. It is unclear where he spent the time. The
ride from the inn to Nashville in that era was done by post men in less
than a day. For example, John Swaney, post rider on the trace from
1800 to 1807, would regularly cover the distance in less than sixteen

hours, rain or shine.[20] But Neelly vanished for more than a week before
hitting Nashville with his storm of activity on the eighteenth of October.

Thus we see that Governor Lewis's reputation was tied so closely to
Jefferson that the two ranking federal officers in the region, Neelly and
Brahan, both wrote to the retired ex-president at his isolated plantation
of Monticello, not to their commander in Washington, President James
Madison.

Despite Brahan's personal connection to Lewis, the normally courteous Jefferson did not answer his letter or that of Neelly.

Captain Brahan, who also wrote to Secretary Eustis and Amos Stoddard, made no statement as to whether he thought Lewis capable of
suicide or if he believed Neelly's telling of it. He was very careful to
make attributions: "Major Neeley [sic] informs me that he discovered
some days previous to the death of Governor strong proofs of a derangement in his mind." Presumably, Brahan accepted the tale. As far as
is known he took no further action.

Neelly, in turn, had claimed his source was Mrs. Griner.

Although the mail between Nashville and Washington was supposed
to take but eight days, Neelly's letter didn't reach Monticello until
November 22, possibly because it wasn't carried by the regular mails
but by the servant Pernier.[21]

Four days after receipt of the letter, Jefferson used Pernier to take
Lewis's effects to President Madison, asking that they be properly
distributed with the personal papers going to Lewis's family. Jefferson
endorsed Pernier, telling Madison that Pernier had his "assurances and
constant & affectionate esteem." We know little more about Pernier.
He has been variously described as a French Creole, a Spaniard, a
mulatto, and a former servant of Jefferson's who had accompanied
Lewis to St. Louis.[22]

Jefferson made no mention of suicide to Madison nor did Jefferson
say that Pernier gave any details about Lewis's death. Jefferson and
Madison both undoubtedly knew of that death before Pernier and the
Neelly letter arrived at Monticello. Newspapers had spread the story
relatively quickly. As noted above, the Nashville Clarion first ran
the story on October 20 and it was soon picked up by neighboring
communities. Lewis's partner, William Clark, was in Kentucky and

reported hearing about it on October 29. The report appeared in Virginia on October 27 in the Staunton *Republican Farmer* with details similar to those in the Nashville *Clarion*.[23] The news began to reach Philadelphia about mid-November when a law firm advised client Pierre Chouteau, Wilkinson's friend, that although Lewis's "death has not yet been publicly announced," it would be wise for Chouteau to begin attaching Lewis's property in St. Louis.[24]

All of those reports described severe knife wounds—a detail unmentioned by Neelly. Most mentioned Grinder children and servants being present. The contradictions suggest that either Neelly gave the papers one version and Jefferson another, or that there was another source of information. It has long been suggested that this second source was a local coroner's jury assembled at the death scene.

It was nearly three months after Lewis's death that Jefferson received any information at all from Major Russell. The Fort Pickering commandant told Jefferson that Lewis had arrived ill, recuperated in six days so that he "was perfectly restored in every respect," and then set off with Neelly carrying two trunks, papers "of both a personal and private nature," and about $120 in cash. In this initial communication, Russell referred to the death as "untimely" but made no mention of suicide, drunkenness, or depression.[25]

However, less than four weeks later, Russell wrote a second, angrier letter to Jefferson, saying Lewis's

> . . . *death may be attributed solely to the free use he made of liquor which he acknowledged very candidly to me after his recovery and expressed a firm determination never to drink any more spirits or use snuff again both of which I deprived him of for several days and confined him to claret and a little white wine.*

Then, in an incredible passage, Russell claimed that Lewis had been led to his death by Neelly, an agent with a terrible penchant for drink. Russell implicated Pernier as a companion to the "murder":

> *After Leaving this place by some means or other [Lewis's] resolution left him and this Agt being extremely fond of liquor, instead of preventing the Govr from drinking or putting him under restraint*

advised him to it & from every thing I can learn gave the man every chance to seek an opportunity to destroy himself. And from the statement of Grinder's wife where he killed himself I can not help believing that Purney was rather aiding & abetting in the murder than otherwise.

Russell said flatly that Lewis would have been alive if Neelly hadn't been his guide. Furthermore, Neelly not only kept Lewis drunk but was making false claims against the government for money owed:

He [Neelly] seemed happy to have it in his power to serve the Govr—but for his making the offer which was accepted I should have employed the man who packed the trunks to the Nation to have taken them to Nashville accompanied the Govr. Unfortunately for him, this arrangement did not take place or I hesitate not to say he would this day be living. . . . This Neelly also says he lent the Govr money which cannot be so for he had none himself & the Govr had more than $100 in notes and specia besides a check I let him have. . . .[26]

Nevertheless, despite Russell's accusations and in the absence of any official investigation, on April 18, 1810, Jefferson endorsed Neelly's suicide theory. This came after reading newspaper accounts, talking with Pernier, and receiving letters from Captains Neelly, Brahan, and Russell. As far as is known, Jefferson had no other source for his conclusions. But, in a letter to Russell, Jefferson for the first time declared Lewis not only to have been a suicide but to have been mentally unbalanced:

He was much afflicted & habitually so with hypochondria. This was probably increased by the habit into which he had fallen & the painful reflections that would necessarily produce in a mind like his.[27]

Jefferson may have thought his verdict effectively closed the case. But that was not to be.

Postmortem

•••••••••

THOSE WHO HAD known the governor in St. Louis were surprised at the report of suicide and madness. On October 31, John Burke Treat wrote to Secretary Bates from Washington that he heard the news from the secretary of war, who "mentioned to me his having by this day's mail received an account of the extraordinary death of Governor Lewis; for which no one here undertakes to account for—and certainly the short acquaintance I had with him at St. Louis in June [1809] wholly precludes any reason" for suicide, "an act so very extraordinary and unexpected."

The story had been quickly circulated. William Clark was in Kentucky and reported hearing about it October 29: "Met Mr. Fitshugh who told me of Gov. Lewis death." (Suicide proponents have made much about an alleged letter from William Clark to Jonathan Clark dated a day earlier in which Clark says he first learned of the death through a newspaper and adds, "O! I fear the weight of his mind has overcome him," a statement that has been often cited to confirm that Lewis had a depressed personality. The letter, however, is of questionable authenticity.)[1] By mid-November the news had also reached Philadelphia, where a law firm advised client Pierre Chouteau to begin attaching the governor's property.[2]

The prefatory note in the *National Intelligencer* said the Washington paper had received a letter ''from a gentleman in Russellville, [Kentucky,] to his friend at present in Lexington dated Russellville, October 20, 1809.'' The name of neither gentleman was mentioned, but the Russellville man wrote:

> *A gentleman from Nashville informs me that he conversed with a person who had seen governor Meriwether Lewis buried on the 12th inst. about 40 miles beyond Nashville on the Natchez road— The accounts are that Governor Lewis arrived at a house very weak, from a recent illness at Natchez, and showed signs of mental derangement. After a stay of a few hours at the above house, he took his pistols and shot himself twice, and then cut his throat.*[3]

The person ''who had seen governor Meriwether Lewis'' was probably James Neelly, who was also the source for the following story, which appeared at Russellville, Kentucky, in *The Farmer's Friend*, datelined Nashville, October 20, 1809:

> *It is with extreme regret we have to record the melancholy death of his excellency MERRIWETHER LEWIS, Governor of Upper Louisiana, on his way to the city of Washington. The following particulars are given us by a gentleman who travelled with him from the Chickasaw Bluffs:*
> *The governor had been in a bad state of health, but having recovered in some degree, set out from the Chickasaw Bluffs and in traveling from that to the Chickasaw nation, our informant says, he discovered that the governor appeared at times considerably deranged, and on their arrival in the nation, having lost two horses, the governor proceeded on, and the gentleman detained with a view of hunting the horses. The governor went on to a Mr. Grinder's, on the road, found no person at home but a woman; she observing something wild in his appearance, became frightened and left the house to sleep in another near it, and the*

two servants that was with him went to sleep in the stable. About three o'clock the woman says she heard the report of two pistols in the room where he lay, and immediately awaked the servants who rushed into the house, but too late he had shot himself in the head and just below the breast, and was in the act of cutting himself with a knife, The only words he uttered was "It is done. My good servant give me some water," and expired in a few moments after.

It is impossible to form any correct conjecture what ever could have produced so horrid a determination in the mind of a man whose respectability and talents were as permanent as those of the deceased, his mind had been accustomed to the greatest industry and enterprise, his expedition up the Missouri, and travels to the Pacific ocean, will be productive of the most beneficial results to our country, and will at once show the greatness of the man. Our informant has taken charge of his two trunks of papers which is supposed to contain the manuscripts of his travels to the Pacific ocean. He gave directions some days previous to his committing the act, that if any accident should happen to him, his trunks should be sent on to the President of the United States, from which circumstance we concluded that from some unknown cause, he had been induced to commit the rash deed. He had been often heard to speak of drafts which had been protested by the Secretary of War, and it is supposed this circumstance may have occasioned his uneasiness of mind.

He was as decently interred as the place would admit.

We now have several newspapers, published far apart and shortly after Lewis's death, all saying he died with his throat cut. Furthermore, the *Intelligencer*, despite its obvious error of placing Lewis at Natchez, gives us a date of burial—October 12—by a man who claims to have been a witness to it.

The one exception to the throat-cutting account is Neelly's letter to Jefferson. It differs from Neelly's Russellville version in two significant ways, as follows:

	Neelly to Jefferson 10/18/1809	Neelly to *Farmer's Friend* 10/20/1809
Deathbed statement:	"I have done the business my good Servant give me some water."	The only words he uttered was "It is done. My good servant give me some water," and expired in a few moments after.
Nature of wounds:	He had shot himself in the head with one pistol & a little below the Breast with the other.	. . . he had shot himself in the head and just below the breast, and was in the act of cutting himself with a knife.

Neelly is also the probable source for the throat-cutting report in the *Intelligencer*. The differences are significant. In the letter to Jefferson, Neelly builds a strong case for suicide. There are two bullet wounds and an explicit statement. In the newspaper report, or reports, however, the wounds go beyond the normal suicide pattern and the statement is ambiguous: *"It is done."*

In all other matters, Neelly's two known versions agree: No one was home but the woman; Lewis was agitated; the servants slept in the stables; two pistol shots were heard about three in the morning; the woman promptly awakened the servants, who rushed in and found him dying; and he died immediately afterward, before dawn.

It is apparent that Neelly gave Jefferson one version and the papers another. Since he rode upon the scene after Lewis's death, he attributes his information to Mrs. Griner. And here we find even more contradictions with her version as given to ornithologist Wilson some eighteen months later. There is no mention of cuts or a suicide statement except that Lewis asks his servants to finish him off *after* he is found wounded. And Mrs. Griner refers to at least two of her children being present.

Furthermore, she says Lewis died several hours after his initial wounds, "just as the sun rose above the trees."

	Neelly Version	Priscilla Griner to Wilson
Deathbed statement:	"I have done the business my good Servant give me some water."	No suicide mention but says it is "so hard to die."
When and how died:	Predawn and survived but a short time.	Sun above the trees, and lived in agony for hours.
Who was there?	Nobody but the woman.	Herself and at least two children.
Nature of wounds:	. . . he had shot himself in the head and just below the breast, and was in the act of cutting himself with a knife.	Head and side, no cuts mentioned.

We now have three versions from two people and all differ in important ways: (1) who was there; (2) when Lewis died; (3) what he said; and (4) the nature of the wounds.

Contradictions can be expected in any eyewitness account, but here we have basically a single witness—Priscilla Griner—who is allegedly telling her tale to Neelly and then to Wilson. Her version differs from Neelly's and Neelly's two versions differ from each other. We know, at minimum, that Neelly misrepresented some of his story because of the differences between the Jefferson letter and the *Farmer* interview.

Furthermore, the *Clarion* account differs from both. It will be recalled that the *Clarion*'s unnamed source agreed that children were there, but said the shots came "some time before midnight"; that servants found him around 7:00 A.M.—which is to say, more than seven hours later—wounded with bullets in the head and intestines;

that his "neck, arm and throat [were cut] with a razor"; and that the servants reported he had killed himself. It does not mention Mrs. Griner's hearing any deathbed statement, nor does it mention Neelly at all.

Priscilla Griner's account was in agreement with the *Clarion* in reporting that her children were present. Significantly, she made no claim of having personally heard a confession of suicide, but seemed to relate only what the servants said.

More information was added to the tale some three months after Lewis's death when Jefferson received some skimpy information from Major Russell, the Fort Pickering commandant.

Russell reported that Lewis had arrived ill, recuperated in six days so that he "was perfectly restored in every respect." Russell referred to the death as "untimely" but made no mention of suicide, drunkenness, or depression.[4]

Less than four weeks later, however, Russell wrote the angry letter to Jefferson accusing Neelly of indirect murder. Putting the blame squarely on James Neelly, Russell said that if the agent hadn't shown up at Fort Pickering and intervened with his offer to be a guide, Russell would have employed his own guide, even himself, to take Lewis to Nashville. Neelly's presence was a fatal mistake, said the commandant.

That Lewis was habitually "afflicted" is a curious and unsolicited denunciation from Jefferson. That accusation had never appeared before in any writings about the young frontiersman. His "habit" may be a reference to drink and, as we have seen, Lewis had at least a soldier's normal enthusiasm for alcohol. It also may be a reference to opium for Lewis and the Corps of Discovery had that medicine in their inventory on the trip to the Pacific.

But why did Jefferson, who knew Lewis probably as well as any man save William Clark, suddenly decide there was a strain of insanity existing in the Lewis lineage—a strain no historian before or since has ever turned up? Indeed, there were more indications of insanity in the Jefferson-Randolph line, including Jefferson's own alleged beating of slaves and his conduct at the Burr trial. Further, we have seen in the Hemings affair that drunken carousing and much odder habits were no strangers at Monticello or elsewhere in the Jefferson clan.[5]

Why did Jefferson dwell morbidly on Lewis's "habit"? If Lewis had been a "confirmed alcoholic," Jefferson would surely have known of it, and being aware of it, would he have asked Lewis to serve as his personal secretary? Nor does it seem likely that after two years of White House association, the president would have selected Lewis to lead the crucial Pacific expedition.[6]

There was no "habit" mentioned by Clark or any of the other members of the expedition; no "habit" mentioned by anyone anywhere else in Lewis's lifetime. We hear of it only in Jefferson's POSTMORTEM assessment, coming from a man who seems determined to pass off the death as a suicide.

Why?

One strong possibility was to prevent further investigation. Jefferson didn't want to call it murder because then someone would have looked for the murderer.

Lewis's private papers were sent to Jefferson at Monticello by Madison's presidential secretary, Isaac Coles, who had received them in Washington. Coles informed Jefferson on January 5, 1810, that he and William Clark had opened the trunks and were returning the private papers for Jefferson to keep until they could be claimed by the Lewis family's representative, William Meriwether. The "public papers" went to their respective responsibilities—expedition documents to Clark, military and gubernatorial papers to the War Department. Other private letters were sent to William Meriwether in Richmond.[7]

Jefferson stayed uninvolved throughout those matters. He made no arrangements for burial, and as far as is known, made no further inquiries about the circumstances of death. There were no letters of condolence to the family, no record of his conversation with Pernier, no eulogy in the newspapers. However, what the Sage of Monticello did do, quickly, was to file a claim against Lewis's estate for one hundred dollars, which apparently Jefferson had loaned to his protégé some six years earlier.

Other than a few passing minor references in letters to Madison, Monroe, and others, the suicide verdict given to Russell was Jefferson's last comment on the matter until a biographical sketch written August 18, 1813, in response to a request from Paul Allen, editor of the Lewis and Clark journals, which were finally nearing publication. After several thousand laudatory words concerning Meriwether's background, his skills, and his journey to the Pacific, Jefferson made these observations concerning the death:

Governor Lewis had from early life been subject to hypochondriac affections. It was a constitutional disposition in all the nearer branch of the family of his name, and was more immediately inherited by him from his father. They had not however been so strong as to give uneasiness to his family. While he lived with me in Washington, I observed at times sensible depression of mind, but knowing their constitutional source, I estimated their course by what I had seen in the family. During his Western expedition the constant exertion which that required of all the faculties of body and mind, suspended these distressing affections; but after his establishment at St. Louis in sedentary occupations they returned upon him with redoubled vigor, and began seriously to alarm his friends. He was in a paroxysm of one of these when his affairs rendered it necessary for him to go to Washington. He proceeded to the Chickasaw Bluffs where he arrived on the 16th of September, 1809, with a view of continuing his journey thence by water. Mister Neely [sic], agent of the U.S. with the Chickasaw Indians, arriving there two days after, found him extremely indisposed, and betraying at times some symptoms of a derangement of mind. The rumors of a war with England, and apprehensions that he might lose the papers he was bringing on, among which were the vouchers of his public accounts, and the journals and papers of his Western expedition, induced him here to change his mind and to take his course by land through the Chickasaw country. Although he appeared somewhat relieved, Mr. Neely kindly determined to accompany and watch over him. Unfortunately, at their encampment after having passed the Tennessee one day's journey, they lost two horses, which obliging Mr. Neely to halt for their recovery, the Governor proceeded under a promise to wait for him at the house of the first white inhabitant on his road. He stopped at the house of a Mr. Grinder, who not being at home, his wife alarmed at the symptoms of derangement she discovered, gave him up the house, and retired to rest herself in an outhouse; the

*governor's and Neely's servants lodging in another. About 3
o'clock in the night he did the deed which plunged his friends
into affliction and deprived his country of one of her most valued
citizens. . . .*

*To this melancholy close of the life of one whom posterity will
declare not to have lived in vain I have only to add that all facts
I have stated are either known to myself, or communicated by his
family or others for whose truth I have no hesitation to make
responsible. . . .*

As Jefferson saw it, stress on the expedition had soothed Lewis's
"affliction," while the sedentary nature of residence in St. Louis
stimulated it to the point that he killed himself at Grinder's Stand. It
is a medical theory probably unique to the master of Monticello.

Jefferson's eminence was such that his suicide verdict wasn't seriously challenged until 1893 when Elliott Coues published his edition
of the Lewis and Clark Expedition journals. Coues cited strong local
legend in Tennessee that argued that Lewis had been murdered.

As Coues points out, the nature of the wounds weighs against the
suicide view. It is hard to believe that a man who had spent his life as
a frontiersman and soldier would so botch a suicide as to shoot himself
two or three times and slash and stab himself severely and repeatedly
and still not be dead.

According to newspapers, Lewis was shot in the chest with the ball
passing through the intestines and exiting in the lower back. Dr. E. G.
Chuinard, the late-twentieth-century surgeon and historian who studied
the Lewis case for years, has written that "this second shot would be
expected to have killed Lewis instantly, or have disabled him so that
he could not have gone through all the perambulations described by
Mrs. Griner."

Chuinard says the wound indicates a kneeling position and theorizes
that Lewis may have rolled off his buffalo robes to surprise someone
burglarizing his trunks.[8]

To further muddy the waters, in Tennessee there is an oral tradition
that says Lewis was shot from behind.

By this tale, which first surfaced in the early 1800s, a mail rider named Robert Smith said he was making his route the morning of the eleventh when he found a dead man lying beside the trail near Grinder's Stand. Dismounting, he examined the body to see that a bullet had penetrated from behind the head to the lower trunk. A few hundred yards farther on, Smith encountered a crowd in the yard of the inn discussing the death. This may have been a coroner's jury, which local tradition and common sense say met at the site.[9]

Unfortunately, Smith made no written report, but the oral history received some corroboration in 1848 when the Tennessee legislature decided to honor Lewis with a monument at his grave. There were several graves in the area, and to determine which might be that of Lewis the committee interviewed descendants of Robert M. Cooper (a member of the coroner's jury and friend of post rider Smith), who gave them enough information to identify the corpse.

It was exhumed, said the legislative report, and "the upper part of the skeleton was examined." According to the oral tradition, a hole was found in the back of the skull as Smith had reported. The legislative report didn't mention if the skull contained a hole or not, but after viewing the skeleton the committee officially declared in favor of murder: "The impression has long prevailed that under the influence of disease of body and mind . . . Gov. Lewis perished by his own hand. It seems to be more probable that he died by the hands of an assassin."[10]

Although there is dispute over whether or not there was a coroner's inquest, those who hold that there was such an inquiry have been unable to produce any records. They infer that the records of the 1809 coroner's inquest were mysteriously removed or destroyed. However, a check of the Tennessee state archives shows they are intact for the period. Numbers are in sequence and no pages are missing. There is an entry for Friday, September 22, 1809, and the next entry is December 19, 1809—representing the last entry for the third quarter and the first entry for the fourth.

Perhaps the best source for local records of that period is historian and genealogist Jill Garrett of Columbia, Tennessee, who believes that there was an inquest but the report was never filed. She suspects it may be in someone's attic. Jury foremen didn't begin forwarding reports to the county courthouse until about 1814, she says.

"Inquests were conducted by local justices of the peace, in this case Mr. Samuel Whiteside, who lived about two miles from Grinder's inn. The docket would have been his personal property to have been passed down through the family. There was a Whiteside descendant in this town [Columbia] who told me about twenty years ago she had it but the book has vanished somewhere in the family. I doubt that it shows much anyway, other than how much it cost to bury him."[11]

The closest we have to any eyewitness to Lewis's final hours is Priscilla Griner, from whom we have already heard two different stories—the versions quoted by Neelly and then by Alexander Wilson.[12] In 1838, Priscilla gave a third version of what happened, and that version may be the most truthful.

Most of what is known about Priscilla and the Griner family comes from the files of genealogist Garrett, whose research is based on tombstones, court records, and family papers. It was Garrett who found that Robert Evans Griner, son of Joshua Griner of Stokes County, North Carolina, married Priscilla Knight of the same county and moved to Tennessee in 1807. Mrs. Garrett also has established the following: In 1809 Robert Griner was about forty-two years old; Priscilla was five to ten years younger; she had given birth in June to a son, Robert F. Griner; and at the time of Lewis's visit there were seven other children, including five sons and two daughters. The eldest daughter was named Eliza, age unknown, and the other was Bethenia, about ten at the time. Ms. Garrett has established further that Priscilla's husband, Robert Evans Griner, lived until 1827 as a prosperous farmer and Priscilla herself died in the late 1840s. Their son Robert F., who was nursing at Priscilla's breasts when Lewis called, died December 28, 1876.

According to other records, the Griners' first domicile in the region seems to have been near the community of Shipp's Bend in Hickman County, about thirty miles due north of where Lewis died. Sometime in 1808, they purchased the land at the inn site and built their small tavern. That it was a tavern, more than a place of lodging, is suggested by the fact that in that same year of purchase the Trace route was shifted to the east, bypassing Grinder's Stand. That they remained in business suggests strongly that Griner was selling illegal bootleg liquor to the Indians.

Since all sources agree that the "husband was not at home," it is likely that he and the sons were up north tending to harvest at their Shipp's Bend farm. We may surmise further that Priscilla, who "sent two of her children to the barn," was at home with the two daughters and undoubtedly the baby, who would have been nursing at the time and obviously too young to be sent to any barn.

Thus, the likely setup when Meriwether Lewis rode in on the night of October 10 was that Priscilla was at home with the two young girls and her infant son. She was rattled by Lewis's appearance, her place now being off the Trace. And from that point on, we will let her tell the story as she did to a schoolteacher in 1838.

In this final version, she adds the startling information that three men rode up and quarreled with Lewis, who responded by drawing a brace of pistols to frighten the intruders away. Some hours afterward, Priscilla heard *three* pistol shots, not two, and the wounded Lewis fell out of her view somewhere in the trees. Adding another curious detail, she says that when she saw Lewis again, he and Pernier had changed clothes. Pernier also was wearing Lewis's gold watch. She sent to neighbors and to Neelly for help but Lewis died before they got there. This final version, given some ten years before Priscilla died, also fits more closely to the oral tradition and the tale of mail rider Robert Smith.

The version of Priscilla's final printed interview comes from an unnamed Arkansas schoolteacher, who said he had become friendly with the aged Mrs. Griner while he was stationed for several months in her region of Tennessee. The unnamed teacher later gave his narrative to an Arkansas newspaper and it was widely reprinted throughout the country. Mrs. Griner took the teacher to the site of the old inn, where, the teacher says:

> when I visited the grave in 1838 I could scarcely distinguish it from the common ground; it being grown over with shrubbery of different kinds, and no stone, no palings, no monument to tell whose grave it was. Grinder's old stand had long been collapsed to ashes. The field was grown up with bristles and briars, and it was lately a dreary, solitary looking place. . . .
> She said that Mr. Lewis was on his way to the city of Washington,

*accompanied by a Mr. Pyrna and a servant belonging to Major
Neely.*

*One evening, a little before sundown, Mr. Lewis called at her
house and asked for lodgings. Mr. Grinder not being at home, she
hesitated to take him in. Mr. Lewis informed her that two other
men would be along presently, who also wished to spend the night
at her house and as they were all civil men, he did not think there
would be any impropriety in her giving them accommodations for
the night. Accordingly she consented to let them stay. Mr. Lewis
dismounted, fastened his horse, took a seat by the side of the house
and appeared quite sociable. In a few minutes Mr. Pyrna and the
servant rode up, and seeing Mr. Lewis, they also dismounted and
put up their horses. About dark two or three other men rode up
and called for lodging. Mr. Lewis immediately drew a brace of
pistols, stepped towards them and challenged them to a duel. They
not liking this situation, rode on to the next house, five miles.
This alarmed Mrs. Grinder. Supper, however, was ready in a few
minutes. Mr. Lewis ate but little. He would stop eating and sit as
if in a deep study, and several times exclaimed, "If they do prove
anything on me, they will have to do it by letter." Supper being
over, and Mrs. Grinder seeing that Lewis was mentally deranged,
requested Mr. Pyrna to get his pistols from him. Mr. P. replied,
"He has no ammunition, and if he does any mischief it will be
done to himself, and not to you, or any body else." In a short time
all retired to bed; the travellers in one room, as Mrs. G. thought,
and she and her children in another. Two or three hours before
day, Mrs. G. was alarmed by the report of a pistol, and quickly
after two other reports in the room where the travellers were. At
the report of the third, she heard some one fall and exclaim, "O
Lord! Congress relieve me!" In a few minutes she heard some
person at the door of the room where she lay. She inquired, "Who
is there?" Mr. Lewis spoke, and said, "Dear Madam, be so good
as to give me a little water." Being afraid to open the door, she
did not give him any. Presently she heard him fall, and soon after,
looking through a crack in the wall, she saw him scrambling across
the road on his hands and knees.*

After daylight, Mr. Pyrna and the servant made their appear-
ance, and it appeared they had not slept in the house, but in the
stable. Mr. P. had on the clothes Mr. L. wore when they came to
Mrs. Grinder's in the evening before, and Mr. L.'s gold watch in
his pocket. Mrs. G. asked him what he was doing with Mr. L.'s
clothes on. Mr. P. replied, "He gave them to me." Mr. P. and
the servant then searched for Mr. L., found him and brought him
to the house and though he had on a full suit of clothes, they
were old and tattered, but not the same he had on the evening
before; and though Mr. P. had said that Lewis had no ammuni-
tion, Mrs. G. found several balls, and a considerable quantity of
powder scattered over the floor of the room occupied by Lewis;
also, a canister with several rounds in it. When Mr. Lewis was
brought to the house, he opened his shirt bosom, and said to
Mrs. G., "Dear Madam, look at my wounds." She asked what
made him do so? He replied, "If I had not done it, somebody
else would." He frequently asked for water, which was given to
him. He was asked if he would have a doctor sent for; he an-
swered no. A messenger, however, went for one, but did not get
him. He attempted to cut his throat, but was prevented. Some of
the neighbors were called in. He frequently cried out, "O how
hard it is to die. I am so strong!" He, however, soon expired.
Major Neely was sent for, and he and Mr. P. buried him and
took possession of his effects. Mrs. G. heard that P. went to Mr.
L.'s mother and that she accused him of murdering her son,
that he finally cut his own throat, and thus put an end to his
existence.[13]

Should the story be believed? Can the fantastical elements such as
the changing of clothes be explained? It seems they can. The very
peculiarity of it helps confirm it. Even a small part of her story,
the rumor about Pernier, is corroborated by none other than Thomas
Jefferson, who wrote Captain W. D. Meriwether on August 21, 1810:
"You probably know the fate of poor Pierney [Pernier] his servant
who lately followed his master's example," referring to reports that
Pernier had killed himself in Washington, D.C.

There is no documented confirmation of Pernier's actual suicide, but that does not detract from the fact that both Thomas Jefferson, at the nexus of events, and Priscilla Griner, isolated in the wilderness, both heard the rumor. Did Pernier do it? Not likely, for reasons we shall see.

It Was Murder

•••••••••

MURDER OR SUICIDE? The only historical evidence we have for suicide is Neelly's word endorsed by Thomas Jefferson. We have no statements from an eyewitness to the actual death. There was no note. Not even a clear statement from the deceased. We are left with Neelly's word, which in fact seems based on what he was told by Priscilla Griner. She, however, makes no direct claim of suicide but alludes to what the servants said. The *Clarion*, too, attributes the suicide claim to the servants, but we do not hear from the servants. This is thin stuff, indeed—no direct statements or any other kind of evidence is known to us or history. The balance is tipped further against suicide by what *is* attested to by several witnesses—multiple bullet and knife wounds.

Given the type of wounds, the personality of Meriwether Lewis, and a series of contradictory facts, it is difficult to support a suicide verdict. If suicide is ruled out, it leaves us with accidental death by his own hand or homicide. But we can safely rule out the first category because accidental multiple wounds with single-shot pistols also seem impossible. A man can't very well trip over a stool and shoot himself twice and then cut his own throat by accident.

Which leaves us with what is possible and likely: Death by another's hand, either by accident or deliberation.

In short, murder. If so, what scenario of murder can answer these contradictions:

(1) Lewis's initial intention to journey by sea, then his change to the Trace; (2) Neelly's strange arrival at Chickasaw Bluffs; (3) Pernier's silence (was he drunk and saw nothing?); (4) Jefferson and Neelly's promotion of a suicide theory; and (5) the absence of any investigative report, a report stymied by Jefferson, who apparently didn't want one, and possibly quashed by a coroner's jury that feared to make a judgment.

We can find some important answers in the more bizarre aspects of Priscilla Griner's 1838 story, a narrative which on close examination amplifies rather than contradicts her 1811 version given to Alexander Wilson. The 1838 story, which apparently was unknown to journals editor Elliott Coues, answers some questions Coues raised after reading the Wilson interview. Coues did not believe what Mrs. Griner told Wilson:

> . . . the narrative of Mrs. Griner is . . . not to be believed under oath. The story is wildly improbable upon its face; it does not hang together; there is every sign that it is a concoction on the part of an accomplice in crime, either before or after the event. . . . Mrs. Griner was privy to a plot to murder Governor Lewis, and therefore had her own part to play in the tragedy, even if that part were a passive one.[1]

In Coues's view, Mrs. Griner may have stumbled onto the murder after the fact and "she told a story to shield the actual criminal or criminals. [Only] on either of these theories could we understand Mrs. Grinder; otherwise her story is simply incredible."

Both the 1811 and the 1838 accounts begin with Lewis's disheveled arrival at the inn or country tavern. Both accounts, and that of the *Clarion*, say Priscilla's children and family servants were on the premises. The presence of females and a baby is supported not only by the logic of Mrs. Griner having borne an infant less than five months earlier but by a newspaper account in 1891 that unintentionally verifies the presence of a teenaged white cook and "females of the family" who were washing dishes when the fatal shots were heard in Lewis's room.[2]

Other factors common to both stories are the absence of Robert Griner and the sons of the family, the shots heard late at night, and the failure to immediately investigate what was happening next door to her.

What the 1838 story *adds* to the mix is the startling note that after Lewis arrived, two or three men rode up and quarreled with him. Lewis, she said, "immediately drew a brace of pistols, stepped forward and challenged them to a duel." Intimidated, the men rode off. Were they there looking for whiskey? Or were they following the governor?

Alarmed at Lewis's belligerence, Priscilla Griner asked Pernier to disarm the governor. But Pernier waved aside her anxieties, saying, "*He has no ammunition.*" Whether he had ammunition or not, Lewis had only two single-shot pistols. Now Mrs. Griner adds the curious statement by Lewis: "If they do prove anything on me, they will have to do it by letter."

Much later, Lewis, Pernier, and the black servant all retire, to the same room, she thinks. Late at night, "two or three hours before day," she hears a shot followed a second later by two more. As in her earlier story, she peeks through a crack to see the governor at her door begging for help. He wanders from there across the road—presumably the Trace, which is the only ancient road archaeologists have found at the site.

Now comes daylight and the very strange section where the servants appear—not from the cabin where she thought them to be, but from the stable. Furthermore, Pernier is wearing Lewis's fine clothes and Lewis's gold watch. She is amazed, probably suspicious, and when she asks where he got them, Pernier replies matter-of-factly: "He gave them to me."

Now the servants—whether hers or Lewis's, she doesn't say—retrieve Lewis from the road. And this part of the story seems to dovetail with the post rider Robert Smith's tale. Smith said he rode up on the Trace and found Lewis's body beside it. Dead, Smith thought. But maybe not. Because Mrs. Griner says, in 1838, that he was carried back to the cabin and a doctor was sent for, though none was obtained.

Priscilla is surprised by the way Lewis is dressed—in tattered clothes, not the ones he wore the night before. Those are worn by Pernier. What is going on? No one else seems to notice because Lewis is tearing off his shirt to show his wounds.

Now he attempts to cut his throat, but is stopped. He cries out, "How hard it is to die." But then he dies in front of neighbors, another matchup with the Smith story, which also described neighbors.

In this version, unlike her 1811 tale, she mentions Neelly. He is "sent for." Where was he? Perhaps Neelly had tried to kill Lewis on the trail *before* he got to Griner's, which would explain his absence and peculiar failure to investigate. Where was he? She doesn't say. Neelly takes charge of all of Lewis's effects, but apparently makes no comment about Pernier's wearing Lewis's clothes. She later hears that Pernier killed himself, the same rumor heard by Thomas Jefferson.

Now all of the contemporary accounts, with the possible exception of the *Clarion* but including Neelly's and by extension Brahan's, were based on what Priscilla Griner said. Her 1838 tale is by far the most detailed, and the most sensational: A confrontation; *three* shots; and Pernier wearing the governor's clothes.

Is there any reason to believe this more fantastical story than her earlier ones? There is. It is more believable because of one salient change in Priscilla's life: Her husband, Robert Evans Griner, had died in 1827.

Priscilla's initial version, as filtered through James Neelly, was sparse indeed. Only bare facts. And when interviewed directly by ornithologist Wilson in 1811, apparently in the presence of her husband, she added details but still left gaping questions. Was she under restraint from her husband?

Probably.

Griner was selling liquor illegally to the Indians, and possibly guns. There was no other reason for him to build and operate an inn that was off the Trace. Engaged in such illegal pursuits, Griner would have wanted as little attention as possible and would have told his wife to say the minimum. Which she did, until long after he was dead.

There is only one thing that seems to impeach her 1838 story and that is the bizarre change of clothes. What a curious element. At first, it is so outlandish that it seems to invalidate the entire tale. But what if Lewis was indeed in a panic—as evidenced not only by his frantic behavior upon arrival and his strange statement about proving things against him but also by his uncharacteristic pugnacity in confronting the strangers. Meriwether Lewis was no frontier "alligator" roughneck playing the bully. He was one of the highest and most prominent public officials in the United States, a man known for his affability.

Lewis must have been under a strain indeed to have flared as he did—a man pursued who wanted to escape.

It seems not unlikely, therefore, that after the strangers left, Lewis decided to disguise himself and make a discreet flight into the night. He had ridden in alone; why not ride out alone? He instructs Pernier to change clothes with him, sweetening the deal by throwing in his watch. He then sends Pernier and Neelly's man off to the stables while he waits alone in the cabin; perhaps napping, perhaps drinking. But waiting for first light so that he can get his horse and continue up the Trace to safety in Nashville.

Then, as he waits in the dark with perhaps only the embers from the fireplace lighting the room, there comes an intruder. Perhaps it was one of the men Mrs. Griner saw him confront earlier. Or maybe it was an assassin, or someone intending to rob or probe Lewis's saddlebags and trunks.

At any rate, there is a confrontation. Shots. First one, followed by two more, quick ones. Lewis staggers out of the cabin into the yard. The intruder vanishes.

It is actually the only scenario that answers all the questions, except one: Who was the intruder?

Maury County locals have long suspected it was Robert Griner. According to Cooper Frierson, a descendant of an alleged member of the coroner's jury, all six jurors believed Lewis was murdered by Griner but were afraid to say so because of Griner's murderous reputation and Griner's friendship with the Chickasaws, who presumably would be out of sorts if their favorite bootlegger was hanged.

According to Frierson, descendants of the jurors said that the jurors:

> *Had all the proof they needed to convict him [Griner] but were afraid to do it, for they said the murderer was one-half Indian and would kill them. . . . The jury was satisfied that it was not suicide.*[3]

But if Griner did it, how does one account for the silence of Neelly and Pernier? Neelly might have been intimidated because he had to work and live in the region. But Pernier was in no jeopardy. Also, there is no evidence of Griner's guilt, and although it is irrelevant whether he was "one-half Indian" or not, there is no evidence of that, either.

Why was Lewis murdered? For money? Lewis had only about one hundred dollars cash. Even though people have been murdered for less, it was probably not for money. Moreover, Lewis's gold watch, customized pistols, and other valuables were not taken. Neelly never accused the servants or the Griners of such a deed. Nor would he have jeopardized his own career for such a paltry amount. This is the same Neelly who had just paid a similar amount for his substitute to transport an important prisoner.

We do not hear anything more from Neelly concerning Lewis or the Griners although Neelly's duties would have carried him past the inn numerous times during the next twenty-seven months until June 1812, when Neelly was fired in disgrace for unknown reasons.[4] After that he vanishes.

According to Major Russell and other sources, Lewis was shot in the chest with the ball exiting in the lower back. Dr. Chuinard says that "this second shot would be expected to have killed Lewis instantly, or have disabled him so that he could not have gone through all the perambulations described by Mrs. Griner."[5] Dr. Chuinard says the wound indicates a kneeling position with Lewis rolling off his buffalo robes to surprise someone burglarizing his trunks.

Based on the preceding assumptions, the intruder was most likely Neelly.

As for motive, the agent would have been vulnerable to temptation because we now know he was in financial difficulty at the time of his appointment, living in Nashville and asking for government help to build a house for himself and his family at the Chickasaw Agency.[6] But his fortunes improved rapidly, because by January 1812 he had bought a farm "in Duck River country," the farm having been located by Lewis's half brother John Marks, who was attempting to recover a horse and other property improperly retained by Neelly.[7] Marks said he had ridden

*into Duck River country in search of Mr. Nealy [sic] to recover
the property of dear Meriwether which he had [and] in which I
failed in fact as Nealy himself was at the Agency house in the
Chickasaw Nation for although I got a part of the property, to wit
the horse and gun, Nealy himself lives at the agency house in the
Chicasaw nation and so I was informed carries the dirk and pistols
constantly with him. The horses and rifle were given up to me by
Mrs. Nealy, both of which I have brought with me to Albemarle.*[8]

We should also take into consideration not only those who were at
the scene, but those who were not.

How do we explain Jefferson's verdict? Why did Jefferson insist
there was a strain of insanity existing in the Lewis lineage—a strain
no historian before or since has turned up? Why did he dwell on
Lewis's "habit"? It is mentioned only by Jefferson, who seemed
determined to pass off the death as a suicide. Why? One strong possibility was to prevent further investigation. Had Jefferson called it murder,
someone would have looked for the murderer and attention would have
certainly focused on General James Wilkinson.

When Burr was a threat, James Wilkinson commissioned vigilantes
to comb the West and capture or kill him. We have no such proof that
Wilkinson contemplated similarly fatal designs for Meriwether Lewis,
but we know from the Burr case that Wilkinson was *capable* of doing
it. And in the summer and fall of 1809 the general was in a panic. The
news of Lewis's trip downriver to New Orleans must have shaken him
to the core. It is reasonable to assume that Wilkinson would set his
spies on the governor, as he had on Burr. The agents would have been
asked to find out what they could and send reports to the general in
New Orleans or Natchez.

Wilkinson had important and powerful friends and protégés all along
Lewis's path—Bates in St. Louis, Russell in Chickasaw Bluffs, and
the newly recruited Indian agent Neelly at Big Town. It is from these
Wilkinson men that the world first heard the reports of "derangement"
and "insanity" and "suicide" attempts. Only from them. Even the
strange information from Bates's friend Captain James House comes
from a man "immediately from the Bluffs. . . ."

About the time the rest of the nation was reading of Lewis's death "by reason of suicide and madness," General James Wilkinson was in Natchez preparing to turn over command of his army to General Wade Hampton.[9] The general also was under orders to report immediately to Washington to be interviewed by the administration concerning the Terre aux Boeufs scandal and the renewed accusations by Daniel Clark concerning Spanish bribes.

As usual, Wilkinson was in no hurry. He dallied in Natchez, turning over his command to Hampton on December 19—more than two months after Lewis's death. A month later, on January 22, 1810, Wilkinson was still in Natchez when John Randolph spurred resolutions through two House committees directing President Madison to reply to accusations about the fatal neglect at Terre aux Boeufs; to determine whether Wilkinson had corruptly received money from Spain; and to determine whether he had been feloniously connected with Aaron Burr.

Wilkinson was a lusty, boasting, often charming man but a drunkard with a murderous bent. He was astonishing. He made intrigue a trade and treason a profession. He was protégé and betrayer of George Washington and Jefferson's chief witness in the treason trial of Aaron Burr. He was a spy honored, promoted, and reconfirmed by three successive presidents while at the same time being the most highly placed traitor known to American history.

And he was viciously paranoid.

About the time of Lewis's death, Wilkinson was writing in his journal that his enemies were preparing "an artful and scandalous libel, and Randolph in Virginia is intriguing with idle, dissipated and unprincipled malcontents."[10]

Wilkinson is the unseen force here, the conductor hidden in the pit. When Lewis headed downriver, James Wilkinson was in New Orleans despite long-standing orders to move north. He did so only after Lewis landed at Chickasaw Bluffs. Was the general waiting for the governor? Moving north only when he received word that Lewis had changed his plans, or after Russell persuaded him to change plans?

At the Bluffs, Lewis was detained by Russell, Wilkinson's appointee.[11] As Wilkinson headed upriver, another of his appointees, James Neely, dropped all other business and scooted for the Bluffs, leaving behind an important prisoner, George Lanehart. Arriving at Chickasaw Bluffs, Neely had his seemingly accidental meeting with Lewis ("He seemed happy to have it in his power to serve the Govr.'') and offered to guide the governor back across some two hundred and fifty miles of wilderness. Why?

We know nothing of what happened on the trail except for what Neelly has told us. The angry accusation from Captain Russell, whose source is unknown, was that Neelly encouraged Lewis to drink. We don't know if the story about the missing horses is true. We don't know why Lewis arrived alone at the inn, although we can reasonably infer that he felt he was being pursued. We don't know his true relations with either Russell or Neelly. And we don't know the whereabouts of Neelly in the eight or nine days between Lewis's death and Neelly's appearance in Nashville. Where was he? Although the War Department records cited no specific reasons for firing Neelly other than general dissatisfaction, there is a suggestion that Neelly may have deserted his post.[12]

To move in closer to what actually happened the night of Lewis's death, let us return to Fort Pickering, where Lewis changed his route. In 1809 the British were nowhere near New Orleans. But General James Wilkinson was. And Wilkinson was in trouble. Conditions at Terre aux Boeufs had already resulted in his recall. John Randolph was breathing down his neck on the Spanish matters. These were scandals in the making. Wilkinson may well have feared that Lewis was about to spring another. It will be recalled that Lewis was well aware of the land bribes Wilkinson had taken while he was territorial governor.

Three years earlier Wilkinson had been in a similar jam when he suddenly "discovered" a plot by Burr. On the eve of Lewis's departure to New Orleans and Washington, Wilkinson announced a second traitorous scheme, namely the alleged "Spanish conspiracy to seize New Orleans" involving Lieutenant Newman and Daniel Clark.[13]

Whether the conspiracy was completely an invention by Wilkinson or whether he was exploiting existing rumors as he did in the Burr case is unclear. But Wilkinson succeeded in sufficiently alarming the administration to the point where it authorized Governor W.C.C. Claiborne to declare martial law.[14]

Five months after Lewis's death, Wilkinson finally appeared in Washington to face his accusers. To avoid the House hearings, the administration again implemented a court-martial, and again Wilkinson was acquitted. If Lewis had been alive, would the general have escaped? The testimony concerning land fraud would have weighed very heavily against the general.

In the meantime, the general's Natchez Trace partners did not fare so well.

Two years after Lewis's death, Major Russell was ordered arrested by his commanding officer and later discharged from the army. There are no surviving records to show why or what happened to bring down such a relatively high-ranking officer.

A year after Russell's arrest, the Madison administration abruptly discharged James Neelly, again without specific reasons being cited.

Another mystery figure in the drama was John Pernier, Lewis's trusted servant, who made a leisurely but seemingly direct path to Virginia immediately after leaving Neelly and Brahan at Nashville. Following his interview with Jefferson, Pernier next went to visit Lewis's family, presumably to claim some $240 Pernier said was owed by the governor in back wages. The family, however, seems to have sternly rebuffed him in the belief he was implicated in the murder. About seven months later, Jefferson reported that Pernier has died a suicide in Washington.

Wilkinson seems to be our man, a general endeavoring to cover up his crimes; a man who did not hesitate to use whatever men or measures were required to protect his interests. As we have seen, he regarded his agents and co-conspirators as expendable. He did not hesitate to seek the removal of anyone whom he saw as a danger. Wilkinson is the logical suspect, a man who could paint Meriwether Lewis as another "Burr" in more ways than one.[15]

Thomas Jefferson's complicity is a substantial one and includes his endorsement of the suicide theory, his suppression of an investigation, and his years-long protection of Wilkinson. Jefferson, as we have seen, justified that protection in two confidential letters he wrote shortly after Lewis's death. Jefferson told Governor Claiborne, "On great occasions every good officer must be ready to risk himself in going beyond the strict line of law when the public preservation requires it." Expanding on that philosophy, he told another correspondent that he had defended Wilkinson because the ends justified the means: "The laws of necessity, of self-preservation, of saving our country when in danger, are of higher obligation. To lose our country by a scrupulous adherence to written law, would be to lose the law itself . . . thus absurdly sacrificing the end to the means.''[16]

Jefferson went to great lengths in order to protect his reputation. In these matters, this goal became all-consuming to the point where he denied justice and betrayed his godson.

Jefferson didn't want an investigation. He accepted the stigma of suicide because he feared a greater scandal, which is why we hear no details of his conversation with Pernier. An investigation would surely have led to Wilkinson, who was already preparing for hearings before the Congress. As John Randolph had said, Jefferson had put his reputation in the same bottom, and if Wilkinson sank, so did the ex-president's reputation.

A few years earlier, Jefferson had made considerable effort to appease the blackmailing journalist Callender, a man who posed a far lesser threat than James Wilkinson. Jefferson then used Wilkinson in his grotesque attempt to frame Aaron Burr for treason. He used the general again in a futile effort to subvert the Spanish in Havana and yet again to bypass his own blockade of West Florida. Wilkinson carried many state secrets, and Jefferson could ignore him only at great peril.

Accidental accomplices to the Jefferson cover-up in the sacrifice of Meriwether Lewis were the coroner's jurors, who also did not want too close an investigation. Living unprotected in the wilderness, subject to barn burnings in the dark of night, or even worse from the killer or his friends, they took the easy way out.

To this day, Meriwether Lewis lies at Grinder's Stand, near the spot where he fell. His grave is the centerpiece of a ghostly monument in seldom-visited woods. As for the others:

During the lengthy congressional hearings in the spring of 1810, John Randolph scorched Wilkinson with hard evidence of Spanish bribes and the abuses at Terre aux Boeufs. In a desperate attempt to escape political embarrassment for the Democrats, Wilkinson persuaded President Madison to allow an army investigation of his conduct. The president refused until the congressional hearings ended in

political squabbling with no clear ruling on the general's guilt or innocence in either of the key matters. Finally, on June 1, 1811, Madison
ordered a court-martial to convene on September 2 in nearby Fred-
ricktown, Maryland.

The general faced eight specific charges: (1) that he requested and
received pay from the Spanish provisional government of Louisiana
with the intent of working against the interests of the United States;
(2) that he collaborated with Spanish officials in plans to dismember
the United States; (3) that he joined with others [Aaron Burr] who
planned treasonably to separate the lands west of the Allegheny Mountains from the United States; (4) that he failed to carry out his duty as
a commissioned officer to expose known conspiracies to commit treason; (5) that he helped plan military expeditions against Spanish territory at a time when Spain was at peace with the United States; (6) that
he refused to obey written instructions from the War Department to
remove troops from New Orleans to Fort Adams and Natchez; (7) that
he neglected his duty to see that his troops received good and wholesome provisions, and proper health treatment; and (8) that he misap-
plied government funds and property for his personal benefit and
knowingly paid for bad provisions.

On Christmas Day, 1811, the court acquitted the general on all
charges. Madison approved the findings on February 14, 1812.

So egregious was the verdict that although he made no public comment, Thomas Jefferson felt compelled to justify to friends why he had
maintained a relationship with the general, writing James Monroe:

> *I have ever and carefully restrained myself from any opinion
> respecting General Wilkinson, except in the case of Burr's conspir-
> acy, wherein, after he had got over his first agitations, we believed
> his decision firm and his conduct zealous . . . and although injudi-
> cious, yet meriting, from sound intentions, the support of the na-
> tion. As for the rest of his life, I have left it to his friends and his
> enemies to whom it furnishes matter enough for disputation. I
> classed myself with neither.*

As was often the case with Jefferson, his memory proved convenient
to his reputation. As president, Jefferson had gone far beyond accepting

Wilkinson's word in the Burr trial. This was the president who wrote his friend Samuel Smith, "Not a single fact has appeared which occasions me to doubt that I could have made a fitter appointment than General Wilkinson." It was Jefferson who assigned Wilkinson to explore the upper Mississippi; who instructed the general to develop a fifteen-day express mail service from Washington City to New Orleans; who had him design and build the Natchez Trace; who appointed the general head of the army and governor of Upper Louisiana; who protected him by deflecting a congressional investigation and arranging a special court-martial; and who sent him on the secret mission to Cuba. For many years before and after the Burr trial, Thomas Jefferson had put himself in the "same bottom" as his disgraced general.

Four months after Wilkinson's acquittal, the United States declared war on Great Britain, largely because of ongoing maritime disputes.[17] After a brief return to New Orleans, Wilkinson was ordered to direct operations against British forces in the area of Canada that is bounded by the St. Lawrence River and Lake Champlain. Because of various failures, including heavy casualties, Wilkinson was relieved of command and ordered to appear before yet another court-martial, the third in seven years. His trial opened in Utica, New York, on January 3, 1815, on charges of neglect of duty, unofficerlike conduct, drunkenness, and disobedience to a War Department order. He was acquitted three months later.

President Madison, saying he regarded Wilkinson as Jefferson's legacy, again signed the verdict reluctantly, noting there was "much in the conduct of both the general and the court not to my liking and needing explanation."[18]

Upon his retirement, Wilkinson wrote the self-serving *Memoirs of My Own Times* (1816), which had little success either in protecting his reputation or in commercial sales. In 1820, the aging general moved to Mexico where he died five years later, apparently a victim of opium poisoning. He was put to rest in an unmarked grave in the old church of San Miguel in Mexico City.

His protectors, Thomas Jefferson and John Adams, followed him a year later, both dying on July 4, 1826, suitably enough the fiftieth anniversary of the Declaration of Independence.

In a final bit of irony, or perhaps ultimate justice, the much-abused

Aaron Burr outlived them all. At age seventy-six, he married a wealthy New York widow, Eliza Jumel. She sued for divorce soon after, claiming he was committing matrimonial offenses "at divers times with divers females." Her divorce was granted on September 14, 1836, the day Burr died. In that final year of his life, Texas won its independence, prompting this comment from the onetime Texas intriguer:

There! You see? I was right! I was only thirty years too soon! What was treason in me thirty years ago, is patriotism now!

From the orbit of the planets to the agonies and ecstasies of life, it is all a matter of timing.

Notes

· · · · · · · · · ·

THE KILLING, 1

1. See *History of the Lewis and Clark Expedition*, edited by Elliott Coues (New York: Dover Publications, 1979), Vol. I, p. xlv. This Dover edition is an unabridged republication of the four-volume edition published by Francis P. Harper, 1893. Hereafter referred to as Coues.

2. Donald Jackson, *Letters of the Lewis and Clark Expedition with Related Documents, 1783–1854* (Chicago: University of Illinois Press, 1978), Vol. 2: Jefferson to James Madison, November 26, 1809, p. 475. Hereafter referred to as Jackson.

3. *Grinder* has been the accepted spelling of this name although the family used and uses *Griner* and this is the spelling on their tombstones in the Griner family cemetery in Shipp's Bend of Hickman County, Tennessee. We will use *Griner* in my narrative but *Grinder* when directly quoting from original documents.

4. Based on later archaeology, the two cabins she describes were actually side by side under a common roof and separated by a breeze-way some five feet wide.

5. Coues, Vol. I, p. xliv, reporting Wilson's letter. I have been

unable to locate the original, but the Coues version is widely accepted as authentic.

6.   Coues.

7.   Jackson, Vol. 2, Jefferson to Russell, April 18, 1810, p. 728.

8.   For further discussion on this matter, see Paul Russell Cutright, "Rest, Rest, Perturbed Spirit," *We Proceeded On*, March 1986.

9.   In 1848 the state of Tennessee took notice of the grave and erected the monument. In 1925 the area was proclaimed a National Monument and since 1933 has been under the administration of the National Park Service.

10.   Wilkinson was commandant of the U.S. Army from December 15, 1796 to July 13, 1798, and from June 15, 1800 to January 27, 1812. See *The Historical Register of the United States Army, 1789 to 1889*, ed. F. B. Heitman, War Department, Washington, D.C., 1890.

THE NATION, 1774–1789

1.   George Mason (1725–1792) was elected to the Virginia House of Burgesses in 1759. A strong defender of liberty and a constitutional philosopher, he wrote the Fairfax Resolves (1774), describing the colonial position in relation to the Crown, and the Virginia Bill of Rights (1776), which Jefferson used as a model for the preamble to the Declaration of Independence. Mason was a delegate to the 1787 Constitutional Convention, but objected to the centralization of powers concept and refused to sign the document.

2.   The most prominent Virginian at the first Congress was Peyton Randolph, whose family had settled in Virginia in the 1670s. Randolph was Speaker of the House of Burgesses and first president of the Continental Congress. Other Virginia delegates included Patrick Henry and George Washington, neither of whom had reached national preeminence at the time.

3.   The so-called French and Indian Wars were a series of battles in colonial North America fought as part of a larger conflict, the Seven

Years' War (1754–1763) between France and Great Britain. In North America, British regulars and colonial forces led by such as Washington met initial defeat but prevailed in battles at Louisburg, Quebec, and Montreal. The Treaty of Paris (1763) gave almost all of French Canada to Britain, ending French military and political power in North America.

4.   Lee's new resolution also asked that the Congress empower the making of foreign alliances. What he had in mind was a treaty with France, England's hereditary enemy.

5.   The Virginia capital would move to Richmond in the spring of 1780.

6.   Arnold was placed in command of Philadelphia after being wounded at the battle of Saratoga. In 1780, he was given command of West Point, a fort he proposed to deliver to the British for a sum of money. The plan failed, and Arnold fled. He was made a brigadier general by the British and led raids on New London, Conn., and Virginia. He died in London.

7.   Despite the crushing victory at Yorktown, King George III continued to refuse to recognize American independence until a war-weary political faction, the Rockingham Whigs led by Edmund Burke and Charles James Fox, coerced such recognition from the king in exchange for parliamentary cooperation on other, and to the British larger, matters such as India. The Treaty of Paris was signed in 1783 with the British recognizing U.S. independence. It was only then that the British evacuated New York City and the Continental Army was disbanded. Recognition of U.S. autonomy soon followed from Sweden, Denmark, Spain, and Russia.

8.   The House of Delegates was one of the two houses of the General Assembly that had been established at the outset of war by Virginia's new constitution.

9.   Caesar was a farm laborer at Monticello who was trapped under the porch at Monticello for the three days that the British stayed. Jefferson later characterized him as ''being notorious for his rogueries.''

10. The Hemings family tree is given in *The Jefferson Scandals*, by Virginius Dabney (New York: Dodd, Mead, 1981); The Wayles-Hemings connection is also discussed at length in *Jefferson and Monticello*, a first-rate biography of the house and its builder by Jack McLaughlin (New York: Henry Holt and Company, 1988), *Ordeal of Ambition*, by Jonathan Daniels (New York: Doubleday, 1970), and *Jefferson the President*, by Dumas Malone (Boston: Little, Brown, 1970).

11. The deathbed description comes from McLaughlin, op. cit.

12. For a fuller discussion, see Chapter Nine.

HAMILTON AND BURR

1. Albert Bushnell Hart, ed. *The American Nation* (New York: Harper and Brothers, 1907), Vol. II, p. 153. Hereafter referred to as *American Nation*.

2. For example, the official Senate history of the First Congress in 1789 did not list members by federalist or anti-federalist labels, but did list them by political position. The Senate had seventeen "pro-Administration" members and nine "opposition." The House had thirty-eight pro-Administration and twenty-six opposition. Three and a half years later, members of the Second Congress at Philadelphia in 1793 were listed as "Federalist" with a capital "F," and "Democratic-Republican," meaning members of the Democratic party.

What had happened in the meantime was the polarization around the differing philosophies and interests of President Washington's two leading Cabinet officers—Hamilton and Jefferson. The Jeffersonians preferred farmers, small businessmen, and artisans and demanded a strict interpretation of the Constitution with an emphasis on states' rights and a small central government. The Hamiltonians—whose vision would prevail historically—favored a loose interpretation of the Constitution, big business, big government, big banking, and big manufacturing. In foreign alliances, Jeffersonians endorsed the new French Republic while Hamiltonians leaned heavily toward aristocratic Great Britain.

3.   In 1776, the various states represented at the Continental Congress had promised land to officers and soldiers who engaged in military service and served until the end of the Revolutionary War, or until discharged, and to the survivors of those killed in the war. The amount of land varied with rank. Privates and noncommissioned officers received one hundred acres, ensigns one hundred and fifty, lieutenants two hundred, captains three hundred, and so on up to major generals who received eleven hundred free acres. The law provided that the veteran could transfer, i.e., sell, his warrant to another person. As most of this land was in the undeveloped western portion of the nation, eastern speculators found a ready market among owners who were more than willing to accept a small amount of paper money in return for wilderness they lacked the means to farm.

4.   Jefferson's biographer, Dumas Malone, has argued, however, that the deal with Hamilton wasn't a *betrayal*, that Jefferson regarded it as an unavoidable *compromise*, from which he had salvaged the most he could.

5.   Universal suffrage was a fact for all adult white males in the United States by the 1820s, well before the development of a working-class identity. Some commentators have theorized that this led to political alliances being formed along regional and ethnic lines rather than along class lines, as was the case in European and other cultures. The thesis, however, ignores the heavy role of feudalism in forming the class distinctions in European society—a delineation that was greatly muted in American society. For a fuller discussion, see *Protecting Soldiers and Mothers: The Political Origins of Social Policy in the United States*, by Theda Skocpol (Cambridge, Mass.: Harvard University Press, 1993).

6.   At the time, the party sometimes referred to itself as "Democrats" and sometimes as "Republicans." For the sake of consistency, it will be referred to in this book as the "Democratic party." The party began referring to itself under that title in 1828 and formally took that name during its third national convention in May 1840.

7.   Mary Wollstonecraft was the mother of Mary Wollstonecraft Shel-

ley, the nineteenth-century novelist who in 1818 published *Franken-stein*.

8. Theodosia Burr, aged thirty, died sometime after December 30, 1813, being lost at sea in a storm off Cape Hatteras. On receiving the news, her father wrote to her husband, Governor Joseph Alston of South Carolina, that he felt "severed from the human race." Aaron Burr also had an adopted daughter, Nathalie.

9. The longtime New York political organization known as Tammany Hall dates from 1786. Formed by Revolutionary War veterans, it was named after a Delaware Indian chief, Tamanend, more popularly called Tammany. The mythical Tammany was sort of an Indian Paul Bunyan who roamed from the St. Lawrence to the Mississippi and who fought and "conquered the Evil Spirit by turning the disasters of his enemy to his own advantage, and increasing his own strength while he impaired theirs," according to a playful history written by Samuel Latham Mitchill, a Tammany-backed congressman of the early 1800s.

10. Perhaps the earliest case history described as "multiple personality" was published in 1791 by the German psychologist Eberhardt Gmelin in a paper entitled *Umgetauschte Personlichkeit* ("Exchanged Personality").

11. Readers will be reminded of the U.S.S. *Pueblo*, seized by North Korea while in international waters in 1968. The *Pueblo* was also a navy ship that gave up without a fight but its commander was not punished.

12. The Naturalization Act was repealed in 1802. The others were allowed to expire.

MERIWETHER LEWIS

1. Also known as the South Fork of the James River.

2. Richard Dillon, *Meriwether Lewis* (New York: Coward-McCann, 1965), p. 12.

3. He was active enough over the next several years to be named to the "degree of a Royal Arch" on October 31, 1799.

JAMES WILKINSON

1. An avid reformer, Rush established the first U.S. free medical dispensary (1786), worked for the abolition of slavery and capital punishment, and advocated a modern prison system and education for women. He was the author of *Medical Inquiries and Observations upon the Diseases of the Mind* (1812), the first American treatise on mental illness. He was treasurer of the U.S. Mint (1797–1813).

2. Taking command of the southern army in 1780, Gates was ignominiously defeated at Camden, S.C., on August 16, by General Cornwallis. Retiring to his Virginia plantation, Gates returned to active duty in 1782 at Newburgh, N.Y. Leaving the army in 1783, he moved eventually to Manhattan Island, where he died on April 10, 1806.

KENTUCKY AND SPAIN

1. *The Journals of Benjamin Henry Latrobe* (New York: D. Appleton & Co., 1905), p. 76.

2. Natchez was the ceremonial center of an important tribe of Muskhogean-speaking North American Indians, once the largest and strongest tribe of the southern Mississippi region. The site was occupied by the French in 1716, surrendered to the English in 1763, captured by the Spanish in 1779, and turned over to the United States in 1798, when it became capital of the Mississippi Territory.

3. W. R. Shepherd, "Wilkinson and the Spanish Conspiracy," *American Historical Review*, Vol. 9, April 1904, p. 490. Hereafter referred to as Spanish Conspiracy.

4. When the Spanish gave up Havana to the United States in the war of 1898 they left behind four centuries of archives from the Americas. Many of these were removed to Washington, D.C., where a few years later they were reviewed by Dr. I. J. Cox, editor of the *Mississippi Valley Historical Review*. It was Cox who finally verified the Spanish

transactions with General Wilkinson. For a more accessible example of his work, found in most major city libraries, see I. J. Cox, "General Wilkinson and His Later Intrigues with the Spaniards," *American Historical Review*, Vol. 19, July 1914.

5.   The building visited by Wilkinson was erected in 1770 and destroyed by fire in 1788. The present-day Cabildo was built in 1795 at the same site. A short street that now lies between the Cabildo and the river is named Wilkinson Row after the general.

6.   See Spanish Conspiracy, p. 128.

LOUISIANA, 1

1.   Once the most important port in the American heartland, Natchitoches fell victim to technology, being bypassed when the Great Raft was broken up and the Red River cleared all the way to Shreveport. Natchitoches is now a picturesque, quiet community of about forty thousand population. It was originally called Saint-Jean-Baptiste, being renamed in the early 1700s for an Indian tribe of the Caddo family which had a village nearby.

2.   The site, established in 1699 and abandoned in 1702, is in present-day Ocean Springs, Mississippi, not to be confused with modern Biloxi.

3.   Spanish rule was interrupted for twelve years beginning in 1680 when the Pueblo Indians revolted and sacked all settlements in New Mexico, killing some four hundred Spaniards. The victorious Indians celebrated by burning the capital of Santa Fe and all its records, washing baptized Indians in the Santa Fe River to cleanse the stains of Christianity, and annulling Christian marriages. The few surviving colonists were able to fight their way down to present El Paso where they regrouped and ministered to their wounds. The Spanish were unable to restore control until 1692.

4.   An excellent compilation of these early maps and descriptions can be found in *The Atlas of North American Exploration*, by William Goetzmann and Glyndwr Williams (New York: Prentice Hall, 1992).

5.   For the full text of the commission, April 30, 1793, see Jackson, Vol. 1, pp. 669–672.

6.   Blount was impeached in absentia in December 1798, a year and a half after the initial charges. His counsel argued that he was not subject to Senate trial because he had already been expelled. Furthermore, his alleged treason had occurred in Tennessee and he could be tried only there (where, it was certain, a Tennessee jury would have acquitted him in minutes). The argument prevailed and the Senate dismissed charges for lack of jurisdiction. A relieved Vice President Jefferson ordered Blount freed from federal charges. Still a free man, Blount died there in March 1800, almost a year to the day before his protector was sworn in as president.

JEFFERSON

1.   The various capitals of the United States have been:

MEETINGS OF THE CONTINENTAL CONGRESS

Philadelphia	September 5, 1774 to December 12, 1776
Baltimore	December 20, 1776 to February 27, 1777
Philadelphia	March 4, 1777 to September 18, 1777
Lancaster, Pa.	September 27, 1777
York, Pa.	September 30, 1777 to June 27, 1778
Philadelphia	July 2, 1778 to June 21, 1783
Princeton, N.J.	June 26, 1783 to November 4, 1783
Annapolis, Md.	November 26, 1783 to June 4, 1784
Trenton, N.J.	November 1, 1784 to December 24, 1784
New York City	January 11, 1785 to March 2, 1789

MEETINGS OF THE U.S. CONGRESS

New York City	March 4, 1789 to August 12, 1790
Philadelphia	December 6, 1790 to May 14, 1800
Washington, D.C.	November 17, 1800 to present

2.   The Senate remained closed to the public until 1795 when an exception was made for newspaper editors, who were allowed to report

proceedings. It wasn't until 1802 that the doors were opened to the general public.

3.   The surprising poverty of Delaware farm families is reported in *The Stolen House*, by Bernard L. Herman (Charlottesville, Va.: University Press of Virginia, 1992).

4.   Information on the Jefferson inaugural comes from a variety of sources including the *National Intelligencer*, Dumas Malone, Edward Channing, and Henry Adams.

5.   As Chief Justice, Marshall raised the Supreme Court to great prestige as he established basic precepts for constitutional interpretation. Important cases he presided over were: *Marbury* v. *Madison* (1803), which set a doctrine of judicial review; *Fletcher* v. *Peck* (1810) and *Dartmouth College* v. *Woodward* (1819), establishing doctrines of sanctity of contracts; *McCulloch* v. *Maryland* (1819), which expanded congressional power through implied power; *Gibbons* v. *Ogden* (1824), which designated national power over commerce; and *Cohens* v. *Virginia* (1821), which established the supremacy of the Supreme Court over state legislatures.

6.   Jackson, Jefferson to Wilkinson, February 23, 1801, Vol. 1, p. 2.

7.   Jackson, Jefferson to Lewis, February 23, 1801, Vol. 1, p. 2.

8.   Jackson, Lewis to Ferdinand Claiborne, March 7, 1801, Vol. 2, p. 675.

9.   Donald Jackson theorizes that the letter indicates a jealousy which may have been the source of resentment between Frederick Bates and Lewis. See Jackson, p. 134.

10.   For more details on James Hemings, see *Jefferson and Monticello*, by Jack McLaughlin (New York: Henry Holt and Company, 1988), p. 222.

LEWIS AND CLARK

1.   The reference here is to the prosecution of ranking members of the Reagan White House on charges they misled or lied to Congress

on certain matters of foreign policy. The prosecutions were considered by many to be political and vindictive because there was substantial documentation of repeated lying to Congress on such matters by Democratic administrations, including those of Presidents Franklin Roosevelt, Harry Truman, John Kennedy, Lyndon Johnson, and Jimmy Carter.

2.   For a fuller discussion of the political passions concerning the expedition and purchase, see "The Spirit of Party," by Arlen J. Large, *We Proceeded On*, February 1980.

3.   Benjamin Rush (1745–1813) was a member of the Continental Congress (1776–1777) who signed the Declaration of Independence. An avid reformer, Rush established the first U.S. free medical dispensary (1786), worked for the abolition of slavery and capital punishment, and advocated a modern prison system and education for women. He was the author of *Medical Inquiries and Observations upon the Diseases of the Mind* (1812), the first American treatise on mental illness. He was treasurer of the U.S. Mint (1797–1813).

4.   *The Stranger in America, 1793–1806*, by Charles William Janson (New York: The Press of the Pioneers, Inc., 1935; originally published 1807).

5.   Philadelphia was at the cutting edge of steam technology. The pump described was apparently only one of two functioning steam engines in the United States at the time, the other being in use on a ferryboat. The steam boiler was invented several times, dating back at least to Hero of Alexandria. But the first practical use came after 1769 when James Watt had patented his engine in England, an act generally regarded as the birth of the Industrial Revolution. The steamboat seems to have been invented in 1789 by the American John Fitch, who spent the summer plying his steam ferryboat around Philadelphia harbor. In 1807, Robert Fulton launched the *Clermont*, whose voyage between New York City and Albany pioneered the use of the steamboat for carrying passengers and freight.

6.   Both fashion accounts are from *American Nation*, Vol. II, p. 158.

7.   Part of a series of earthen mounds found along more than a thou-

sand miles of the Ohio and Mississippi river valleys. The mounds at St. Louis were removed in stages between 1854 and 1869 to make way for housing developments.

8.   Casa Calvo was the boundary commissioner assigned by the court to negotiate the borders between American Louisiana and the Spanish provinces of Texas and New Mexico.

9.   Both buildings are still standing and in good repair.

10.   Louisiana was ceded to Spain in 1762 as a result of the French and Indian War, and Great Britain gained control of Florida, which extended to the east bank of the Mississippi.

11.   These transactions are detailed in I. J. Cox, "General Wilkinson and His Later Intrigues with the Spaniards," *American Historical Review*, Vol. 19, July 1914.

12.   *Before Lewis and Clark: Documents Illustrating the History of the Missouri, 1785–1804*, edited by A. P. Nasatir (Lincoln, Neb.: University of Nebraska Press, 1990), Vol. 2, p. 753.

13.   The first European settlement at present-day St. Louis was founded in 1700 by Jesuit missionaries who gathered Indians from the surrounding area. The mission was abandoned within five years. In early 1764, thirteen-year-old Auguste Chouteau led fur traders from New Orleans to the abandoned mission site, where they established a trading post, naming it St. Louis after Louis IX of France.

14.   The Mandans are a Siouan tribe of North American Indians inhabiting the upper Missouri River area between the Heart River and the Missouri River, in Western North Dakota. Their urban life-styles and their occasional Caucasian features inspired many theories of origin, including postulations that they were one of the lost tribes of Israel. However, by the time of the Lewis and Clark expedition, the Mandans had been exposed to at least occasional white European contact for more than a century. These contacts may have been the cause of disease epidemics which reduced an original Mandan population of about 5,000 to a mere 1,000 or so when visited by Lewis and Clark. Today, about 350 Mandans live on the Fort Berthold Reservation in North Dakota.

15.   Sacajawea is a Hidatsa Indian word meaning "Bird Woman," which seems to have been her name in Shoshone. It was translated into Hidatsa because neither her French husband, Toussaint Charbonneau, nor anyone in the Lewis and Clark expedition could speak Shoshone. Charbonneau explained her name in English to Lewis and Clark as "Bird Woman" and used the Hidatsa term *Sacajawea* in doing so. It was formalized a decade later by Nicholas Biddle in his edition of the Lewis and Clark journals.

16.   "Sacajawea May Get More Credit Than Deserved," by Bob Gilluly, *We Proceeded On*, November 1992. After the expedition returned to St. Louis, Charbonneau abandoned her and she dropped from sight. Historians believe she died in 1813 or 1814 along the lower Missouri River. William Clark helped raise and educate her son, Pomp. Various narrators indicate that Sacajawea was more closely attached to Clark than to Lewis. It was Clark who reprimanded Charbonneau for slapping her on one occasion. It was Clark who included her in his party to see the Pacific and who became the guardian of her children. However, both Lewis and Clark showed considerable concern for her during a severe illness while on the march.

17.   Originally called Fort Massiac after the French minister of marine, the Marquis de Massiac, the fort was established in 1757 and variously abandoned and occupied until the Americans took it over in 1794. Located near present-day Metropolis, Illinois, the fort was on a high bluff overlooking the Ohio. It was situated on a bend which made it possible to survey the approaches for several miles both up and down stream.

RIVERS ARE CROSSED

1.   Aristides was the nom de plume of William Van Ness, a socially prominent New York lawyer who would later become a federal judge.

2.   Especially *Marbury* v. *Madison* (1803), where Marshall established the supremacy of the Constitution over congressional legislation and the court's role as interpreter of the Constitution. It also established the court's power to overturn unconstitutional legislation.

3.   Van Ness was the socially prominent New York lawyer who as "Aristides" had denounced the scattered accusations that Burr had been willing to make a deal to steal the 1801 presidency and offered, instead, proof of the actual Delaware deal made to assure Jefferson's election.

4.   This little-known event is reported in *Aaron Burr*, by Samuel Wandell and Meade Minnigerode (New York: G.P. Putnam's Sons, 1925).

5.   Friends soon paid off the obligations.

6.   Clinton was an early patriot and delegate to the Second Continental Congress. He was briefly a brigadier general in the Revolution and then was elected governor of New York (1777). He served to 1795. He served nearly four years as Jefferson's vice president, dying in office in 1808.

7.   Charles Maurice de Talleyrand-Périgord (1754–1838) was the ultimate survivor. Although a member of the Second Estate (the Church), he successfully proposed confiscation of Church property by Revolutionary France. After the fall of Maximilien Robespierre (1794), Talleyrand was grudgingly admitted to the Directory. He supported Napoleon and was foreign minister (1797–1807), but the two fell out over Napoleon's grand European ambitions, and Talleyrand was prominent in the restoration of the Bourbons (1814). At the Congress of Vienna (1814–1815) he showed superb diplomatic skill, exploiting tensions among the victors to the benefit of France. His unerring political sense led him to support Louis-Philippe, whom he served as minister to Britain (1830–1834).

8.   *The Stranger in America, 1793–1806*, by Charles William Janson (New York: The Press of the Pioneers, Inc., 1935; originally published 1807).

9.   Near present-day Cow Creek, Montana.

10.   See *An Account of Upper Louisiana*, by Nicholas de Finiels (Columbia, Mo.: University of Missouri Press, 1989). The falls were far more spectacular in Finiels's time than ours. The river and falls

have been dammed to such an extent that while great parapets of rock exist, there is little water flowing over them.

11.   In Lewis's day, the Great Falls were second only to Niagara as a North American waterfall. Unfortunately for modern sightseers, the view of the Falls has been greatly impaired by a series of dams, which have also reduced the water flow to little more than a trickle.

12.   Some sources say Piegans.

13.   A few years later Colter returned from an exploring trip of his own with the stories that gave the name of ''Colter's Hell'' to the region now included in Yellowstone National Park. Colter is generally credited with being the first white man to travel in that region of the country.

14.   Journals or diaries were written by Lewis, Clark, Gass, Sergeant Charles Floyd, Private Joseph Whitehouse, and Sergeant John Ordway.

THE CONSPIRATORS

1.   The immediate Natchez region was long the ceremonial capital of numerous Indian civilizations, concluding with the Natchez Indians who were virtually destroyed by military action of the French, Choctaws, and Chickasaws in 1730–1731. Fort Rosalie was established there by the French in 1716, with the English taking control in 1763 at the close of the French and Indian Wars. Natchez functioned as an isolated fourteenth colony up to and through the early part of the American Revolution. The Spanish captured Natchez in 1779 and retained control until 1798, when it passed into American hands.

2.   A forebear of the popular 1930s and 1940s movie star of the same name.

3.   In those early years, the predominant Indians were the Natchez, the largest and strongest tribe of the southern Mississippi region. Cousins to the Choctaws, Chickasaws, and Creeks, the Natchez were noted for their strong religious-political centers in which the sun played a major role.

4.   The actual engineering of the road was supervised by Lieutenant Edmund Pendleton Gaines, USA, who rose to be a major general during the war of 1812–1815. It was the only public road in that region, cut to facilitate the movement of troops and the transportation of supplies to and from the newly acquired "Spanish country."

5.   See "Stands and Travel Accommodations on the Natchez Trace," by Dawson Phelps, *The Journal of Mississippi History*, January 1949, p. 1.

6.   Founded by the French in 1719, Baton Rouge was named for a red (cypress?) stick that once served as a boundary marker between Indian territories.

7.   For further contemporary description of the river road, see *Recollection of the Last Ten Years*, by Timothy Flint (Carbondale, Ill.: Southern Illinois University Press, 1968; reprint of a series of letters first published in 1826).

8.   Browne to Madison, August 25, 1806, Louisiana-Missouri Territorial Papers, National Archives.

9.   Easton to Jefferson, December 1, 1806, Louisiana-Missouri Territorial Papers, National Archives.

10.   Most notable among historians who infer the affidavits as motive is Isaac Jenkinson in his *Aaron Burr* (Richmond, Va., 1902). Also see *Jefferson the President*, by Dumas Malone (Boston: Little, Brown, 1970).

11.   Don Estevan Minor's residence, a stuccoed brick structure, was at the west end of Irvine Avenue. By the middle of the twentieth century, it was being used as a rooming house.

12.   Authorship of the letter is discussed persuasively by historian Milton Lomask in *Aaron Burr: The Conspiracy and Years of Exile, 1805–1836* (New York: Farrar, Straus & Giroux, 1982), pp. 115–122.

13.   The translation comes from Milton Lomask, op. cit.

14.   See Spanish Conspiracy, pp. 533–537.

15. Freeman was a witness for Wilkinson at the general's 1811 court-martial. The conversation is reported in Freeman's examination by the court on September 12, 1811; see "1811 and 1815 Court Martials of Major General James Wilkinson," National Archives.

16. Jefferson to J. B. Colvin, September 20, 1810, quoted in Malone, op. cit., pp. 277–278.

17. The emphasis is contained in Plumer's original. See *Ordeal of Ambition*, by Jonathan Daniels (New York: Doubleday & Company, 1970), p. 346.

18. Standard texts list Mrs. Wilkinson's death as November 24, 1806, but family records support the later date. Author's interview with Gloria Wilkinson of New Orleans, October 29, 1991.

19. At the time, Supreme Court justices did dual duty as federal district judges.

TRIAL AND ERROR

1. The town of Richmond was first settled in 1609 by Captain Francis West on land purchased from the Indian chief Powhatan.

2. Marshall lived in Richmond at the time, having built a house in 1789 at the north end of Third Street.

3. See *The Formative Years*, by Henry Adams (Boston: Houghton Mifflin Company, 1947), Vol. I, p. 392.

4. The New Orleans meeting with Wilkinson was detailed by Folch in a letter to the captain general of Cuba, the Marquis de Sameruelos; See Spanish Conspiracy, p. 837.

5. *Grand Inquests*, by William H. Rehnquist (New York: William Morrow and Company, 1992), p. 117.

6. Smith at that time was en route to New Orleans.

1. See *The Devil's Backbone: The Story of the Natchez Trace*, by Jonathan Daniels (New York: McGraw-Hill, 1962).

2. See Jackson, Vol. 1, p. 134.

3. Other Freemasons who figured prominently in Lewis's life included his co-explorer, William Clark, and Alexander Stuart and William C. Carr, two attorneys who along with Clark were named by Lewis as co-executors of his estate and collectively described by the governor as his "three most intimate friends." Lewis's foe, Frederick Bates, also was a Mason, as was the owner of the inn where Lewis died, Robert Griner. Lewis was accepted into the Albemarle County lodge in January 1797, along with Peter and Samuel Carr, nephews of Thomas Jefferson. Lewis was elevated to Royal Arch Mason in October 1799. It is believed by some historians that Thomas Jefferson also was a Mason, although this has not been certified.

4. The remainder of the letter deals with Lewis's detailed argument concerning his government expenses. The full text is found in the National Archives, filed under Louisiana-Missouri Territorial Papers, pp. 290–292. More conveniently, the letter is reprinted in Jackson, Vol. 2, pp. 456–461.

5. The letter is from John Rice Jones to Judge Davis, January 21, 1804. See National Archives, "Correspondence to and from the Secretary of War," and Louisiana-Missouri Territorial Papers, National Archives.

6. Although Jefferson, of course, was some ten years premature in his assessment, his was nevertheless an accurate perception. Napoleon made his elder brother, Joseph Bonaparte, king of Spain in 1808, where he reigned until 1813. After Napoleon's defeat at Waterloo in 1815, Joseph transferred to the United States, where he died in 1832. In the meantime, Spain's three-hundred-year-old grasp on its American colonies was shaken loose by the French invasion of the Iberian Peninsula—a circumstance that led to colonial revolts in present-day Argentina, Venezuela, Colombia, Chile, and Mexico. Independence was not

realized, however, for another ten years or more, with Chile becoming independent in 1818 and Peru in 1821. In the latter year, the Spanish vice royalties of New Spain and New Granada were transformed into Mexico and Gran Colombia. Of the La Plata regions, Paraguay became independent in 1813, Argentina in 1816, Bolivia in 1825, and Uruguay, after prolonged conflict with first Argentina and later Brazil, in 1828. Mexico quickly lost control of Guatemala, El Salvador, Costa Rica, Honduras, and Nicaragua, which banded together in the Central American Federation (1825–1838) and then became separate states. The Texas Revolution and the Mexican-American War resulted in Mexico's ceding Texas, California, Arizona, and New Mexico to the United States. Like greater Mexico, Gran Colombia also disintegrated with the secession (1830) of Venezuela and Ecuador. Panama became independent of Colombia in 1903 during a dispute concerning construction of the Panama Canal.

7. See I. J. Cox, "General Wilkinson and His Later Intrigues with the Spaniards," *American Historical Review*, Vol. 19, July 1914, pp. 808–812.

8. Wilkinson would marry Celestine Trudeau in New Orleans on March 5, 1810.

9. The conditions, and Wilkinson's responsibilities for them, are detailed in Charles Gayarre, *History of Louisiana* (New Orleans: Hansell & Bro., Ltd., 1903), Vol. 4.

10. See *The Great Mail*, by Leonard Huber and Clarence A. Wagner (State College, Pa.: American Philatelic Society, 1949).

11. The letter from Wilkinson to Eustis was dated July 31, 1809; see National Archives, "Correspondence to and from the Secretary of War." Captain Porter went on to become America's most illustrious naval hero in the War of 1812, sailing the famous raider *Essex* against the British in the Atlantic and Pacific.

12. The casualty count is given in Charles Gayarre, *History of Louisiana* (New Orleans: Hansell & Bro., Ltd., 1903), Vol. 4, pp. 221–222.

13. Wilkinson to Eustis, September 3 and September 20, 1809, re-

port the conspiracy but although the latter letter is listed and briefly described in the War Department index (microfilm cassette m-221, roll 4), the actual document is missing, as are many War Department documents involving General Wilkinson, who was given free access to the files in preparation for his several courts-martial. Other letters relating to the conspiracy are Wilkinson to Eustis, July 2, 1809, and December 2, 1809, National Archives, "Correspondence to and from the Secretary of War" (microfilm cassette m-221, roll 33). Also see National Archives, Orleans Territorial Papers, for the letter from Secretary Smith.

14.   The couple departed for the East shortly afterward, arriving in Baltimore on April 16, 1810.

THE KILLING, 2

1.   *Missouri Gazette*, October 4, 1809. My copy was obtained at the Tennessee State Archives in Nashville.

2.   Chickasaws are closely related to the Muskhogean-speaking Choctaw, and then occupied northern Mississippi-Tennessee lands from Memphis into neighboring Alabama. Following de Soto, the Bluffs are not known to have been again visited by whites until 1673 when Jolliet and Marquette stopped to trade. La Salle followed 1692 and built a fort. Chickasaws were far more important in history than their numbers, never more than about five thousand, indicate. Allied with the English, they were hostile to the French and Spanish but quite friendly with Americans. Being slaveholders, they and their Choctaw brothers joined the Confederacy during the Civil War, for which both were punished severely by the loss of their lands. About six thousand now live in Oklahoma.

3.   In contemporary references and in subsequent histories, Russell is referred to as "Captain Russell." However, his service career is summarized in the U.S. Military Register and he is listed as a major as of May 1809.

4.   Russell's furlough requests and the endorsement of Wilkinson for his reinstatement as an officer in the army are listed in the National

Archives index under "Letters Received by the Secretary of War." The index on Microfilm 221, roll 4, lists the Wilkinson letter dated 1808/04/22 as document #19 on roll 33, with the note: "letter recommending Gilbert Russell for an appointment in the army." The actual document of recommendation is missing, however—another example of the purge of Wilkinson files in the War Department. There is no record of Wilkinson's response to Russell's furlough requests.

5.   The letter was forwarded from Fort Adams to Washington, presumably because that is where Stoddard had gone. The letter is at the Missouri Historical Society in St. Louis. More conveniently, see Jackson, Vol. 2, p. 466.

6.   Most references list a "James Howe," but an examination of the signature, on file with the Missouri Historical Society in St. Louis, seems to say "James House." Vardis Fisher in *Suicide or Murder?* also opts for House.

7.   A memorandum from Lewis to Russell referring to House's trunk is attached to Russell's letter of January 4, 1810, sent to Jefferson. A copy is in the library of the National Park Service at Tupelo, Mississippi. It would seem that Lewis had been entrusted with the trunk by House at St. Louis, figuring to carry it with him easily by sea to the East Coast. When Lewis changed his own plans, he asked Russell to see to it that the trunk was forwarded to a mercantile house in Baltimore. Lewis suggested that it be sent in the care of "Mr. Cabbeni," whom Lewis expected to be passing through Fort Pickering. This is probably a reference to the Cabannes, a prominent Creole family in St. Louis. The trunk instead was sent in the care of Benjamin Wilkinson, a St. Louis merchant who was a partner with Lewis and Clark in the Missouri Fur Company. The author has found no trace that Benjamin Wilkinson was related to General James Wilkinson.

8.   For the malaria diagnosis and discussion, see Dr. E. G. Chuinard, "How Did Meriwether Lewis Die?," *We Proceeded On: Official Publication of the Lewis and Clark Trail Heritage Foundation*, August 1991 and January 1992.

9.   The promissory note was first reported in *We Proceeded On*,

November 1987. The document is the property of Charles L. Hill, Jr., of Lotus, California.

10. Wilkinson had been given command of the shipping in mid-July. See National Archives, "Letters to and from the Secretary of War" (to James Wilkinson, July 19, 1809). Also see Royal Ornan Shreve, *The Finished Scoundrel* (Indianapolis: Bobbs-Merrill, 1933), p. 254.

11. The petition is in National Archives, "Correspondence to and from the Secretary of War." It complains that Jones is "tainted with foreign politics," a typical Wilkinson ploy in that it accuses others of his crimes.

12. Big Town was a few miles north of present-day Houston, Mississippi. The Chickasaws had been introduced to the custom of slavery by the English and kept their black slaves mostly for agricultural work.

13. The theft is described in an announcement by Neelly, the Colbert brothers, and others printed in the Nashville *Democratic Clarion*, October 20, 1809, Tennessee State Archives, Nashville.

14. Neelly's salary was $1,000 a year. On October 18, 1809, the same day he wrote Jefferson about Lewis's death, he wrote the War Department asking for reimbursement of his payment to Love. Reimbursement was denied "until a more proper explanation is forthcoming." None was. National Archives, Secretary of War's Office, letters received and sent, Indian Affairs Microfilm B-59.

15. In his letter to Jefferson dated January 4, 1810, Russell says, "He set off with two trunks which contains all his papers relative to his expedition to the Pacific Ocean, General Clark's land warrant, a portfolio, pocket book, memos and note book together with many other papers of both a public and private nature; two horses, two saddles, and bridles, a rifle gun, pistols, pipe, tommyhawk and dirk, all elegant and perhaps about $220 of which $99.58 was a Treasurer's Check on the U.S. branch Bank of Orleans endorsed by me. The horses, one saddle and this check I let him have. Where or what has become of his effects I do not know but presume they must be in the care of Major Neely [*sic*] near Nashville."

16.   The mail route had been changed in 1808 to accommodate a new post office at Columbia, Tennessee, which was northeast of Grinder's Stand. The new route ran from Nashville south some forty miles to Columbia, then hooked southwest another twenty-five miles to pick up the old Trace at Metal Ford at the Big Buffalo River. Grinder's Stand was about four miles north of that spot.

17.   In 1807, at age forty, Robert Evans Griner moved his family to Tennessee from North Carolina and opened a farm on the Duck River. In late 1808, he purchased the land at the inn site and opened his tavern. See "Stands and Travel Accommodations on the Natchez Trace," by Dawson Phelps, *The Journal of Mississippi History*, January 1949, and *A History of Hickman County*, by Jerome and David Spence (Nashville: Gospel Advocate Publishing Company, 1900).

18.   The *Clarion* is responsible for history's misspelling of the inn-keeper's name as "Grinder." Historians have faithfully repeated the mistake ever since, a testament either to the gullibility of historians or the enduring influence of newspapers. The family name is actually Griner, as reported in all their legal signings and on family tombstones. This has been established most authoritatively by Tennessee historian and genealogist Jill Garrett. An odd footnote to the family history is that Priscilla's great-great-grandson was Dan Griner, a St. Louis Cardinals pitcher who had the dubious honor of leading the National League with twenty-two losses in 1913.

19.   Nashville *Democratic Clarion*, October 20, 1809, Tennessee State Archives, Nashville.

20.   Swaney would leave downtown Nashville at 8:00 P.M. Saturday and arrive at Gordon's Ferry, some nine miles north of Grinder's, the following morning. See *The Great Mail: A Postal History of New Orleans*, by Leonard Huber and Clarence Wagner (State College, Pa.: American Philatelic Society, 1949), p. 19.

21.   By contract with the postal service, mail traveled at the rate of one hundred miles a day between Nashville and Washington, ibid., p. 17. Neelly's letter was logged in at Monticello on November 21, 1809, Jackson, p. 678.

22.   Jefferson to James Madison, November 26, 1809, Jackson, p. 475.

23.   Cited in Jackson, p. 746.

24.   Bryant and Schlatter to P. Chouteau, November 12, 1809, Missouri Historical Collection, St. Louis.

25.   Russell to Jefferson, January 4, 1810, Missouri Historical Society.

26.   Russell to Jefferson, January 31, 1810, Jackson, p. 748. A fuller text of the letter is quoted in Fisher, op. cit., pp. 115–116 and pp. 134–135.

27.   Jefferson to Russell, April 18, 1810, Jackson, p. 728.

POSTMORTEM

1.   See Jackson, Vol. 2, pp. 724–726. The letter is written in an ornate, operatic style not usually associated with Clark. No original is known to exist but a copy is on file in the Filson Club of Louisville, Kentucky. The Filson letter contradicts Clark's own handwritten journal concerning how and when he learned of the death. Furthermore, despite extensive searches, the Filson Club has been unable to locate an original. Its copy is a typed transcript donated in the early 1940s by Temple Bodley, a Clark descendant who, according to a Filson spokesman, "must have borrowed the original from someone else. We know no more about it." (Author's interview with Filson Club manuscript curator James Holmberg, November 18, 1991.)

2.   Bryant and Schlatter to P. Chouteau, Nov. 12, 1809, Missouri Historical Collection, St. Louis.

3.   *National Intelligencer*, November 15, 1809, Tennessee State Archives, Nashville.

4.   Russell to Jefferson, January 4, 1810, Missouri Historical Society.

5.   Jefferson's nephews, sons of his sister Lucy, were indicted for murder in Livingston County in western Kentucky, charged with the

1811 decapitation and dismemberment of one of their slaves for breaking a water pitcher. Despite their names, Lilburn and Isham Lewis
were in fact close kin to Jefferson and only distantly related to Meriwether Lewis. In December 1811, angered when a seventeen-year-old
slave named George broke one of their mother's pitchers, the drunken
brothers decided to make an example of George by hauling him into a
hog-killing house and tying him to the floor. They then summoned
their other slaves, locked the door, and proceeded to butcher George,
hacking off his head, arms, and legs. They threw his body into a
roaring fireplace. The slaves told neighbors, who told authorities, and
the brothers were indicted on March 18, 1812. Lilburn killed himself
prior to trial and Isham escaped. Tradition says he was killed at the
Battle of New Orleans. Jefferson rendered no verdict in this case.
See *Jefferson's Nephews*, by Boynton Merrill, Jr. (Princeton, N.J.:
Princeton University Press, 1977).

6.   Cutright, Paul Russell, "Rest, Rest, Perturbed Spirit," *We Proceeded On*, March 1986.

7.   Jackson, pp. 486–492.

8.   E. G. Chuinard, "How Did Meriwether Lewis Die?," *We Proceeded On*, November 1991, p. 8.

9.   Richard Dillon, *Meriwether Lewis* (New York: Coward-McCann,
1965), p. 208; and Jill Garrett Papers, Tennessee State Archives,
Nashville, and author's interview with Mrs. Garrett, Columbia, Tennessee, November 6, 1991. Mrs. Garrett is the retired Maury County
historian and a leading expert on the local documentation of Lewis's
death.

10.   Coues, Vol. 1, p. lviii. For details of the hole in the skull see
"Tragedy at Grinder's Stand: The Death of Meriwether Lewis," a
thesis to the graduate faculty of Middle Tennessee State University,
August 1978, by Martin Cooper Avery. A copy is in the public library
at Columbia, Tennessee.

11.   Author's interview with Jill Garrett, November 6, 1991.

12.   There have been several claimants to the role of eyewitness,

most noticeably an account given in the Nashville *Daily American* on September 16, 1891, by Christina Anthony. Ms. Anthony, who was born in 1814, said she was friendly with one Polly Spencer, who claimed to have been working for the Griners as a servant girl when Lewis visited. As related by Ms. Anthony, Polly Spencer's account adds little to what was already known but contends that Robert Griner was arrested for the murder, tried, and released. No one has found any evidence of such a trial.

13.   Philadelphia *American*, December 7, 1841, microfilm copy of which is in the archives of the National Park agency, Tupelo, Mississippi. The *American* explained that it was reprinting the story from the *North Arkansas*.

IT WAS MURDER

1.   Coues's objections were discussed in Chapter One.

2.   The Nashville *Daily American*, September 16, 1891, on file at the Tennessee State Archives, has a second-person interview with Polly Spencer, who says she was working at the Griners' as a teenage scullery maid in 1809 when Lewis visited. The Spencer account says she and other "females of the family" were washing dishes when they heard a shot in Lewis's room. They rushed in to find him dead in his bed. The only other detail she offers is the claim that Robert Griner was arrested, tried, and acquitted for the murder. There is, however, no evidence of such a trial or arrest.

3.   These remarks and many discussions about the coroner's jury are found in the Lewis Scrapbook of the Tennessee State Archives. Other documents in the collection state that the jurors found no powder burns on the front of Lewis's body or clothes and concluded he was shot from behind.

4.   National Archives, Secretary of War's Office, letters sent, Indian Affairs B-59.

5.   E. G. Chuinard, "How Did Meriwether Lewis Die?" *We Proceeded On*, November 1991, p. 8.

6.   National Archives, "Correspondence to and from the Secretary of War," microfilm cassette m-221, roll 27.

7.   John Marks to Reuben Lewis, January 22, 1812, letter copy from files of National Park agency in Tupelo, Mississippi.

8.   Ibid.

9.   Wilkinson to Secretary of War, July 31, 1809, National Archives, "Correspondence to and from the Secretary of War," microfilm cassette m-221, roll 33.

10.   Royal Ornan Shreve, *The Finished Scoundrel* (Indianapolis: Bobbs-Merrill, 1933), p. 252.

11.   According to the National Archives records of Wilkinson's communications with the War Department, he began moving his army upriver on September 1, 1809, and completed the operation "between the 20th and 30th of October." I've been unable to pinpoint the arrival date of Wilkinson himself at Natchez. His last communication to the War Department from New Orleans is dated September 15. In Wilkinson's 1810 court-martial Lieutenant Simeon Knight testifies that on September 15 he was summoned to Wilkinson's quarters at the time "when he was about leaving New Orleans himself and asked me if I was ready to ascend the river." It appears Wilkinson may have been in Natchez as early as September 20, 1809, but not before and not long afterward.

12.   The letter from Eustis begins, "Sir, from the present aspect of our affairs, and the hostile disposition manifested by several of the Indian tribes, it has been considered expedient that the government should avail itself of General James Robertson's services with the Chickasaws—he has in consequence, been appointed to succeed you. . . ." National Archives, Secretary of War's Office, letters sent, June 4, 1812, Indian Affairs B-59. Neelly may have deserted his post because the letter is addressed not to him at the Agency but to General Robertson "for delivery."

13.   Wilkinson to Dearborn, September 3, 1809, National Archives, "Correspondence to and from the Secretary of War," microfilm cassette m-221, roll 33.

14.   Dearborn to Claiborne, December 2, 1809, National Archives, "Correspondence to and from the Secretary of War," microfilm cassette m-221, roll 33.

15.   A similar conclusion is suggested by Jonathan Daniels in *The Devil's Backbone: The Story of the Natchez Trace* (New York: McGraw-Hill, 1962).

16.   Jefferson to J. B. Colvin, September 20, 1810, quoted in Malone pp. 277–278.

17.   While British depredations on U.S. merchant ships and impressment of U.S. sailors to serve on British warships were especially galling to the United States, war was not entirely contrary to American interests. Southern and western politicians looked upon war with Britain as offering a chance to expand U.S. territory into Canada and Spanish Florida, which was under the protection of Britain. War was also looked upon as a way of ending British support of western Indian tribes, who were a constant threat to the American settlements. New England, which was economically dependent on trade with Great Britain, was less enthusiastic about the war.

18.   Shreve, op. cit., p. 267.

Index

• • • • • • • • • •